EAGLES OF DUXFORD

THE 78TH FIGHTER GROUP IN WORLD WAR II

By

GARRY L. FRY

AIRCRAFT ILLUSTRATIONS BY BOB BOYD

PHALANX
Publishing Co., Ltd.
1051 Marie Avenue
St. Paul, MN 55118 U.S.A.
612/454-0607

ISBN: 0-9625860-2-1

Library of Congress Catalog Card No. 91-062776

Edited by John W. Lambert

Co-Published by:

PHALANX PUBLISHING CO., LTD.
1051 MARIE AVENUE
ST. PAUL, MN 55118 USA

IAN ALLAN
TERMINAL HOUSE STATION APPROACH
SHEPPERTON, TW17 8AS
UNITED KINGDOM

Printed in the United States of America

TABLE OF CONTENTS

FOREWARD by ROGER A. FREEMAN

Acknowledgements, Introduction, Dedication.

FORWARD

As a young onlooker during World War II my memories of the 78th Fighter Group are its aircraft in the sky above my home. Of many seen, the most memorable are the HL P-47s hurrying to put down on the airfield beside our farm on return from a successful day's fighting in late July 1943. Another is the first occasion the Group's P-51s passed over, clearly identified by the flicking effect of their half black, half white painted spinners. The achievements of one of the oldest and most accomplished fighter groups operating from the United Kingdom were only fully revealed in the years following the end of hostilities because of the requirements of wartime secrecy. Also officially secret was the location of the 78th at Duxford; but it was common knowledge to schoolboy enthusiasts for USAAF warplanes. This then sixteen year old learned from equally enthused friends that the "black and white checkers" also came from the "Duckpond" - and I am sure the Luftwaffe was also well aware of the 78th's base.

Garry Fry is of a later generation and did not know the checkerboard fighters in English skies, yet his enthusiasm for the 78th has led him to devote many years to studying and compiling the history of this distinguished organization. Moreover, his interest has led him to produce this comprehensive record of the Group from inception to inactivation. A near half century after the events, a not inconsiderable undertaking.

Most fighter units of World War II have, like old soldiers, faded away or taken new identities that leave only a lineal tie with the original entity. But the 78th is fortunate in that its old home, Duxford, has become a "living air museum" under Britain's Imperial War Museum. As any visitor will have seen, the 78th's tenure is permanently represented in the exhibits there.

In fact, this has come to advance the 78th as the representative of the USAAF fighter force in the European Theatre of Operation. With such prominence, there will be many people who will want to know more about the 78th Fighter Group. This book fills that requirement admirably.

Roger A. Freeman

ACKNOWLEDGMENTS

When I started tracking down the veterans of the 78th Fighter Group in 1976, I knew that unless they themselves were not wholeheartedly behind my efforts, I was doomed to fail. A work such as this is not my story, rather it is 100% their story. I could only be a score-keeper, collector and detective. But that is the thrill of it for me, so I must say to all of you whose names appear here, thank you for some memorable and wonderful times. I've truly enjoyed our walk together.

Most important are the me and their women of the wartime 78th who aided this effort. They are: James Aicardi, Kenneth Allstaedt, Arthur Arpin, Noel Assink, Richard Ballard, Harold Barnaby, Mason Barnard, Richard Baron, Roy Barron, Melvin Barth, Henry Bauer, Samuel Beckley, Robert Beeson, Thomas Bendorf, Lawrence Bernardy, John Bertrand, Warren Beuthling, Marvin Bigelow, Donald Bodenhamer, Erwin Boettcher, Fred Bolgert, Henry Bottoms, Herbert Boyle, Ira Brents, Edward Briski, Paul Busick, Walter Cannon, Tazewell Carrington, Eugene Carter, James Casey, Everett Chappell, Allen Clapp, Charles Clark, Lloyd Cogswell, John Colford, Francis Collar, Richard Conner, Alan Cowart, Mrs. Ginny Sidney Craig, Alvin Crocker, William Dacci, James Darrall, Harry Dayhuff, William Demme, Charles DeWitt, Francis Eaker, Robert Eby, Olin Gilbert, Clifford Glidewell, Mrs. Elsie Charles Gallagher, Mrs. Mildred Frederick Gray, Robin Gray(Davidson), Walter Haislip, Francis Harrington, Elmer Hartman, Roger Hearn, William Hegman, John Hemphill, Richard Hewitt, Hugh Holland, Richard Holly, Raymond Holt, John Holzhauer, Lynn Hosford, Thomas Hughes, Russell Hunter, Alexander Jadkowski, William Joachim, James T. Jones, Oliver K. Jones, Peter Keillor, Warren Kellerstedt, James Kinsolving, John Kirk, Peter Klassen, Robert Knapp, Mr./Mrs. Walter Knight, Dominic Kolinic, Glenn Koontz, Willard Korsmeyer, Frank Kulis, Huie Lamb, John Landers, Jesse Lee, Morris Lee, Milford LeMasters, Norbert Lentz, Charles London, Arthur Long, Frank Marcinko, Wilson Marks, Lloyd Marshall,

Amos May, William May, J. Patrick Maxwell, Junior McAdams, Maurice McCarthy, Melvin McNickle, Alden McVey, Jack L. Miller, Edward Misiur, Jesse Morrison, Carl Moschel, Jack Oberhansly, Frank Oiler, John Parbst, James Patton, Earl Payne, James S. Peterson, Richard Phaneuf, Peter Pompetti, Claude Pray, Julian Reems, Hayden Richards, Paul Saffold, Negley Sapper, John Saviks, Elmer Schelp, Bernard Schroeder, Percy Scott, Fred Sharp, Ralph Shoemaker, Montimore Shwayder, Donald Silveus, Roman Siudut, Harry Slater, Robert Spaulding, William Spengler, Boyd Sorenson, James Stallings, Earl Stier, Henry Strickland, Ernest Stroud, William Swalwell, Harry Teague, Harry Thompson, Robert Thuot, James Tudor, Estel Ulerick, Nicholas Vale, Noble Vining, Earl Walk, Albert and Carol Wendt, Delmar Wessel, Warren Wesson, John Wielinga, Donald Wilson, Robert Wise, Ernest Yerke, Arthur Yokom, Erlath Zuehl, and Harding Zumwalt. All these people provided the photographs, cassette tape interviews, letters, diaries, documents, records, accounts, and all the wherewithal that went into this book. The book's contents are credited to these great people with all my thanks. My contributions came from the official USAAF records held by the named agencies.

The photos in this book are the result of magnificent technical skill by the following photographers: Richard M. Hill (deceased), USN fighter pilot and dean of WWII carrier pilot history, Norman Taylor, premier U.S. aero photographer, and James Knutson and Joseph Miquelon, the two fine proprietors of Card-N-Camera Shop. My appreciation knows no bounds to these great fellows.

The gentlemen of the aviation historian brotherhood who assisted so ably with their input and data are: Richard Bagg, Mike Bailey (UK), Marvin Bradburn, Wayne Dodds, John Elam, Jeffrey Ethell, Roger Freeman (UK), Steve Gotts (UK) Andrew Height (UK), Tom Ivie, Ed Kueppers, John W. Lambert, George Letzter (deceased), Ernest McDowell, James McKinley, Wade Meyers, Tony North (UK), and my favorite AAF historian, Kenn Rust. Thanks a million, fellas.

The official government agencies that supplied assistance were: The Military Record Center, Washington National Records Center, GSA, Suitland, MD, courtesy of Archivist Richard Boylan and research assistant John Ritz; USAF Museum R/D, Wright-Patterson AFB, OH, courtesy of Director Charles Worman, Curator Ruth Hurt, and assistants Kathy Cassidy and Vivian White; the 8th AF Museum, Barksdale AFB, LA, courtesy of Director H.D. "Buck" Rigg; and a special thanks is given to the 8th AF Historical Society, courtesy of Editor, LtCol. John Woolnough (deceased).

I also wish to thank several aero buffs who always help my morale by their example and friendship: Jack Ilfrey, on of America's greatest fighter aces and editor of the best veteran newsletter I ever saw; and James Dietz, the best aviation artist in the world.

And a big acknowledgement to my co-pilot, Kathryn Ann Fry, for all the support and numerous chores tended to.

INTRODUCTION

This book is an attempt to provide the public with an honest window into the every day life of a World War II ETO fighter group - the Duxford 78th. The paths that led these men to ETO combat are also explored, so we will start early in the evolution of civilian to flyer/soldier, and not ignore this important transition. Therefore, the reader should be patient as the long road to combat is revealed. Also covered is the impression the young G.I. gained upon shipping overseas and how he learned to adapt to and love the English people and their country. Today these are very fond memories to the veterans.

This book is a view of every rank's war, not just the popular glamorized pilot's role. Pilots were a small minority of Eighth Air Force men, in a fighter group consisting of some 1,600 plus soldiers, mostly enlisted ranks. I have tried through first person stories and official records, to represent everyone's memories in our limited space. I wanted to tell the individual's reaction to this major lifetime experience, in his own words where we could obtain them.

Reference to military rank and middle initials is omitted as much as possible to avoid unnecessary repetition, impediments to space, and aid continuity. Ranks that are important may be found in the text, otherwise please consult the appendices. Today, forty eight years later, rank means little to the veterans, who are mainly happy to have shared the experience.

I have found it better to place many details in the appendices, rather than the main text, so I urge the reader to consult them to aid in fleshing out missions and events.

All dates are given as U.S. civil - month, day, year. The 78th radio callsigns and explanatory data are included in the Glossary terms. A total 78th victory list is not given, as this is readily available from sources quoted within. However, most of the major missions are included, along with each victory scored on that show. The day's losses are sometimes mentioned but all are covered in appendices.

My primary concern has been to include every scrap and tidbit of personal recall I could locate. The rest of the text is composed of fact, events, and data I consider important to the given record. I am to blame for any lack or error it may include.

Hopefully, the reader will credit to my account the enormous amount of time and records plowed through to get where we are today. Some items may seem trivial to some readers, but I've retained them as vital to the Big Picture and because past writers have ignored these interesting little colorings.

(Author's Note: I plan to privately publish a complete mission listing and aircraft roster of the 78th FG sometime in the future. Anyone wishing details on this may send a SASE to G.L. Fry, 174 Pauline Drive, Elgin, IL 60123 USA. When the list is ready you will be sent notice by your SASE.)

Garry L. Fry

DEDICATION

The time will come when thou shall lift thine eyes,
To long drawn battles in the skies,
While aged peasants, too amazed for words,
Stare at flying fleets of wondrous birds.

With these words which he attributed simply to an English poet named Gray writing in 1737, General William Kepner began the pre D-Day briefing for his group commanders.

This book is dedicated to the unnumbered veterans who went to war, one of whom was my father, Jesse Mason Fry, so we could enjoy the blessings of this great nation; those warriors who made the supreme sacrifice, who never returned to their loved ones for the blessing; those who contributed so much to this book, who have now gone on ahead to wait for us there. And my personal dedication is to my grandsons, Kevin and Kyle. May they never acquire a knowledge of war and its horrors.

Chapter 1

Genesis - Group Birth

The birth of the 78th Fighter Group was a small event in the larger picture of America at war. It was part of the frantic effort to organize and field an Air Force after Japan plunged America into the global conflict.

In order to set the scene of the times and explain events leading to the unit's formation in California during May 1942, it would be good to listen to some young pilots describe their routes to the 78th.

Morris K. Lee: "My flight training began at Major Mosely's Grand Central Air Terminal Flying School in Glendale, California in October, 1939. I received sixty-five hours of flying time, thirty-six hours solo, and twenty-nine hours dual with an instructor in a Stearman PT-13. The PT-13 was a well built stable biplane, with a 200hp Lycoming radial engine, that couldn't be beat for aerobatics. My instructor was a specialist in spins, notably the tailspin. He taught us (four-five students) precision spinning plus the standard maneuvers.

"While we were practicing in the San Fernando Valley and at Saugus, he took us to the valley's north end hills and engaged in sail planing. Cutting the engine, he showed us how convection current lift helped us maintain altitude while gliding. His instruction helped me overcome inadequate training later in the course.

"One happening haunts me from this time. I had been solo practicing lazy eights and chandelles. About time to return to the field, I decided a unique way to lose some altitude was to nose over forward into a dive, a method I'd never used before.

As I pushed forward sharply on the stick I raised up out of my seat. This scared me so much that I looked down to find my safety belt was unfastened. With a little more push, I might have been thrown out. Reflecting on what might have happened scared me even worse. I could have been dumped right out doing a slow roll. Hurriedly fastening the safety belt, I returned to the field, where it took me some time to recover from the incident. Several days later an instructor actually did dump out his student in a roll.

"We were in the Class of 1940-D. From Glendale we went to the 'West Point of the Air', Randolph Field, Texas, near San Antonio. February to May, 1940, we trained in BT-9s and BT-14s getting in seventy-nine hours flying time. Ground School got tougher as did the flying. School took one-half a day and flight training the other half. It was lights out at 10:00 P.M. and up at 5:00 A.M.

"Using BC-1s and AT-6s, our advanced flying was at Kelly Field, Texas. This was seventy-eight hours of formation, instrument, and cross-country flying. Included was a lot of night flying. The runway approach was right over our tent-city quarters. It seems nearly every student on final approach would 'gun' his engine with the prop in high RPM right above our sleeping tents. I found myself doing the same thing while I was night-flying.

"My first duty as a new Second Lieutenant Air Reserve, was in the 20th Pursuit Group at Moffett Field, California. By the time I had twenty-four hours in their P-36s, we got P-40s. The 20th and 35th Pursuit Groups split into four new groups and I

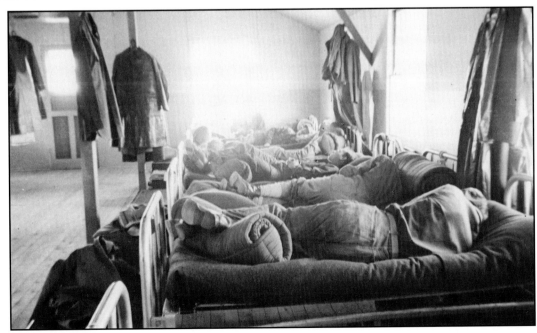

This scene of an AAF training barracks typifies the environment of Army life for the 78th trainee. Sleep was the most precious commodity for a new recruit. (Warren Kellerstedt)

When 78th mechanics arrived for training at Los Angeles Airport in 1942 they found it was being defended by an odd assortment of planes including this obsolete Republic P-43, Lancer, daddy to the P-47 Thunderbolt. (N. Sapper)

went to the new 14th Pursuit Group at March Field, California. This move in April, 1941, reflected part of the rapid expansion in the Air Corps. New personnel began to arrive faster than airplanes, and they became so scarce we had to use primary and basic training planes to keep up minimum flight time for our flight pay. Also at this time, ground officers from other branches came into the Air Corps to take over administrative duties from the pilots, who promptly nick-named these ground officers, 'Paddlefeet'.

"One night I was scheduled for a night flight in one of the P-40s, and I decided to fly to March Field from Hamilton Field about dusk. This would enable me to practice night-flying, radio navigation, and instrument-flying in one mission. It was fairly bright moonlight as I left Hamilton Field headed south. Tuning in on various radio ranges passing from Oakland, Modesto, and Bakersfield, I flew airways towards March Field. As I flew south of the Bakersfield beam over Tehatchapee Pass, I decided I'd had enough radio aids navigation. At about 9,000 feet altitude, sufficient to clear the mountains just south of Bakersfield with safety, I thought I'd tune in the Lancaster radio range, fly the north beam to the aural null directly over the station, and then switch off the radio range.

"Everything was going according to plan shortly south of Lancaster, when I decided to make my left turn. As I banked left, I looked down towards the ground over my left wing tip. There beneath me, way too close, were evergreen trees showing up in the moonlight! I was so scared I tightened my turn and headed back toward the Mojave Desert. When I thought it safe to straighten up my flight position, I looked off to my right rear where I saw an outline of the San Gabriel Mountains. They were about 10,000 feet high, and I was at 9,000 feet! A few seconds longer on that course and I'd have crashed head-on into a mountain top! From the Mojave into March Field, I made very sure I was in the middle of Cajon Pass with plenty of altitude. That lesson was never forgotten and I passed that way many

times later on giving the mountains their proper respect. A few months earlier, I'd been on an investigation team reporting on a classmate and his passenger in an AT-6, which had crashed fatally into the San Gabriel Mountains.

"It seems impossible that we crowded so many experiences into such a short time. Moves back and forth across California, up to Washington, ferrying fighters and bombers across the nation, visiting Lockheed Aircraft plant during the threatened worker's strike, training foreign pilots, testing and flying many types of aircraft."

Robert E. Eby: "My class was 41-H, which graduated October 31, 1941. As was typical, because pilots (students) could not be married, about half the class were married on their graduation day. I joined quite a few others that day on a trip to Reno, Nevada, where we found a Lutheran minister who married us in his home, rather than the usual Nevada three minute wedding. A lot of Mather Field graduates went into the 14th Pursuit Group, and later four of us ended up in the 78th Group.

"Some of our class and I were assigned to the 51st Pursuit Group at March Field, commanded by Major Tex Sanders. Ralph Himes and I were sent to the Group's 25th Squadron to fly P-40s.

"Pearl Harbor was really a mess on the West Coast, with most people expecting the Japanese to invade the mainland. We flew every plane to satellite fields each night for two -three days, and everyone was confined to the field. Eventually we could leave the base one night out of six."

Two days after Pearl Harbor, Hap Arnold had the Army Corps of Engineers building hard stands, dispersal taxiways, revetments, and sand bag devices on eighty-one West Coast airfields. California became a network of bases, satellite fields, and emergency flight strips, all part of the multi-service Western Defense Command. The AAF West Coast defense was vested in the 4th Air Force, headquartered at San Francisco, California with Major General George Kenny in command of approximately fifty-one sub-bases and auxiliary fields.

Robert E. Eby: "January 1, 1942 most of the 51st Pursuit Group shipped out for 'Code Plum', the Pacific Theatre. On the fifth, Ralph Himes and I transferred to the 14th Pursuit Group at March Field. Their Commanding Officer was Major Thayer Olds and we were assigned to the 49th Squadron led by First Lieutenant Arman Peterson. We had three days at Muroc Dry Lake for gunnery training in 51st Group P-40s, and, except for one hour transition in a P-36 for P-40s, that was the only fighter plane I had flown until joining the 14th Group.

"On January 7, 1942 our 49th Squadron moved over to Long Beach airport to check out in Lockheed P-38 Lightning fighters. One of the other Group Squadrons also checked out in the P-38 and the third squadron was flying P-66 Vanguards, a Vultee abortion we labeled the 'Vibrator'. After a month's checkout in the P-38, we flew to Mills Field, or what is now San Francisco airport. The 50th Squadron was at Oakland airport, California and the 48th Squadron was assigned to North Island Naval Air Station, San Diego, California.

"For the next three months the 14th Group trained new pilots and prepared for overseas duty. Twice a week the call came down from fighter command to ship a certain number of pilots overseas the next day. This was done by drawing names out of a hat. Our Group was one of two groups defending the entire Pacific coast. The other group was at Paine Field, Washington. We averaged more than one crash a week in the P-38s and pilot morale was low.

"The Air Force recognized this high fatality rate problem and sent Colonel Ben Kelsey around to the P-38 Groups to instill confidence and demonstrate proper reactions and techniques in flying the aircraft. I will never forget how he took off on only one engine, did slow rolls buzzing the field, and then landed, all with a single engine running. This showed the pilots that an engine loss did not need to be fatal. The P-38 had a reputation that you could not bail out without hitting the horizontal stabilizer. Eventually techniques were developed that, if it was under control, you could trim it up and dive over outside one of the booms."

A noteworthy incident illustrates the tempo of those times that Spring and Summer of 1942. A later famous Air Force personality, Richard Bong, was in the 48th Squadron at Oakland airport. One day he and his wingman, engaged in flight training in the Bay area. The Navy fighters out of Alameda Naval Air Station and Army P-38s were constantly engaged in mock combats, but the Navy had an edge in breaking off combat if they were losing. They could fly under either the Golden Gate or San Francisco Bay bridges, while the Army P-38s were forbidden to do so. This day Bong and his wingman were hot on the tails of two Navy planes who decided to escape by flying under the Golden Gate Bridge. As they flew under the bridge, Bong and his wingman stayed right on their tails. Unfortunately, the Hamilton Field Commander was crossing the bridge at the time. When he got to Hamilton he called operations and got the pilots' names. As punishment, Bong and his wingman had to appear before the 4th Fighter Command CO, General William Kepner.

Muroc Dry Lake AAF Base, CA, the cadre assembly center where the 78th was organized in full strength in May, 1942. The squadrons were assigned to their detached California bases from here. (USAF)

It was rumored that General Kepner sent them to the Pacific Theatre with the admonishment that they should buy plenty of Second Lieutenant's bars, because that's all they would be needing for a long time. The rest is history with Bong getting forty Japanese victories, winning the Medal of Honor and then being killed in a 1945 P-80 crash."

January 1942 : While the later 78th pilots were flying in the West Coast pursuit groups, the ground echelons of the prenatal 78th were being collected into cadres much further away to the East. Their 78th service started with a directive from 1st Air Force Headquarters, Mitchell Field, New York, arriving at Baer Field, Fort Wayne, Indiana. The order directed the constitution of the 78th Fighter Group composed of: Headquarters Squadron, 82nd, 83rd, and 84th Fighter Squadrons. (Note: They were actually Pursuit Squadrons at this time, but we will hereafter use the term Fighter Squadron for ease of continuity.) The date of this constitution was January 13, 1942.

Processing paperwork and checking tables of organization for details of proper personnel and equipment strength took until February 9, 1942, when the squadrons were officially activated by assigning a small cadre of men to each. The 82nd Squadron for example, was started with twenty-four enlisted men commanded by First Lieutenant George Nash. The organization was not exactly a crash program. By March 27th, the 82nd Fighter Squadron had ninety-two men and a Second Lieutenant CO. First Lieutenant Frank Wagner commanded the whole Group. Training progressed slowly as men filtered in from various specialty schools around the Eastern U.S. After packing hastily on April 25, 1942, the Group Squadrons climbed aboard a troop train at Fort Wayne, Indiana at 11:30 P.M. and rattled off across the Midwest towards the Western states.

An 82FS P-38 with red engine-cowl bands of the squadron near San Diego. Twin turbo-supercharged Allison engines carried the deadly firepower of a 20mm cannon and 4-50 Cal machine guns in the nose. Summer 1942 (Harry Dayhuff)

Chapter 2

California - Group Training

Noble Vining: "We left Baer Field with a train full of cadre assigned to the 78th. All the way west we congratulated one another as we would pass various army installations and air bases. As we passed an installation in the Mojave Desert at Muroc Dry Lake, California on April 30 1942, we could see in the distance, tents, and tar paper covered barracks. We all agreed that was the worst base we had passed yet, but as we passed it, the train began to slow down and a spur track appeared going in the direction of the camp which we could hardly see by then. You guessed it! We backed off into the spur and detrained at 10:30 A.M.

"We newcomers were generously given the tar-paper barracks by the permanent base personnel as they preferred the pyramidal tents to the barracks. We soon found out why when we went inside them. After chasing snakes, horned toads, and other varieties of wild life from the barracks, we tried to eliminate the dust and sand to bed down to the frigid nights and blistering days. This lasted about ten days or so and it was here that the squadrons were completed with personnel.

"Muroc Lake was a 4th Air Force gunnery training range. The base was established in 1933 when March Field began using its dry lake bed for bombing and gunnery exercises. They had a lot of Sergeant Pilots flying there and because of the desert environment, crashes were an everyday occurrence."

Robert Eby: "The 1942 AAF growth pattern for building new groups was to train a group, divide it, and add on to each complement, then build it up in experience until the parent unit went overseas and left behind a nucleus to retrain to combat readiness."

May 1942: May 7 found the 14th Fighter Group's Headquarters Squadron at Hamilton Field north of San Francisco at San Rafael on San Pablo Bay's western shore. Hamilton was built on a site donated to the War Department in 1930 as a bomber base for the defense of San Francisco. The bomber units left in March, 1941 and fighter units from old Moffett Field moved in for the West Coast defense. By July, 1942, the base was also serving as an aerial Port of Embarkation for the Pacific Theater.

The 14th Fighter Group was composed of the 48th Squadron at North Island NAS, San Diego, the 49th Squadron at Mills Field, South San Francisco, and the 50th Squadron at Oakland Airport. On this date the group was officially ordered split in half and the new half was designated the 78th Fighter Group.

Major Arman Peterson, who had been commanding the 49th Squadron, 14th Fighter Group, was assigned command of the new 78th Fighter Group. The new 82nd Squadron came out of the 48th Squadron with First Lieutenant Harry J. Dayhuff in charge. The 49th's splinter half became the 83rd Squadron led by First Lieutenant James J. Stone. Captain George M. McNeese took over the 84th Squadron which emerged from the 50th. The new 78th Headquarters Squadron set up shop with the 14th Headquarters Squadron at Hamilton Field. For the time being, each new 78th Squadron stayed at the same bases as their 14th parent unit.

The following day, May 8, 1942 the jigsaw shuffle began. First the ground echelons of the 82nd Squadron left Muroc Dry Lake and drove in truck convoy to their new home at North Island Naval Air Station, San Diego. While the 82nd was enroute, a mass of transfers began between all the various squadrons of the 14th and 78th Fighter Groups. A total of one hundred fifteen enlisted men from the 78th went to the 14th. A further five hundred sixty enlisted men were taken out of the 14th and assigned to the 78th. In the pilot and officer ranks, 59 officers and pilots left the 14th to join the 78th's various squadrons. The next day, May 9th, the remnants of the 49th and 50th Squadrons joined the 14th Fighter Group at Hamilton Field where they began to receive more men from AAF schools to train into readiness for their move overseas. The 48th Squadron stayed at North Island Naval Air Station until the 14th left for Europe. The 83rd Squadron left Muroc Dry Lake and settled at Mills Field on May 10th and the 84th Fighter Squadron moved to Oakland Municipal Airport the following day. There was a steady shuffling in and out until the 78th boarded the trains for the East enroute to England.

Headquarters Staff of the consummated 78th, now that pilots, ground officers, and enlisted men were finally wed together, was composed in its first form as follows: Major Arman Peterson, Group Commander; First Lieutenant Morris K. Lee, Executive and Operations Officer S-3; Captain George F. Nash,

Major Harry Dayhuff, first CO of 82FS in his P-38 at North Island NAS, CA. (Harry Dayhuff)

5

A sandbag gunpit erected by 84FS crewmen to defend Oakland Municipal Airport, CA. S/Sgt. Charles Clark, (foreground). October, 1942 (Charles Clark)

Adjutant S-1 Personnel; Second Lieutenant Robert E. Eby, Intelligence Officer S-2 and Assistant Operations Officer; and Major Charles T. Evans, Supply Officer S-4. The atmosphere of the new squadrons can be aptly described by these enlisted men.

Warren Kellerstedt's letter home: "Well, the 48th has finally split up and I am now in the 82nd Fighter Squadron. Most of the bunch I hang out with are here too, so I think I will like it OK. We have moved into the hangar next to the one we were in before, and the last couple of days new men have been coming in so that both outfits are up to full strength again. Right now we have only seven planes, P-38s, but we expect more pretty quick. When one of the other outfits ship out we will get their planes. We got sixteen new pilots today. They are just out of school and they have never flown one of these fast jobs before. They made them taxi the planes around for two hours this morning to get used to the feel and the controls. This afternoon they each went up for an hour. They could all walk away, so we figure that's pretty good. Two planes are out of commission though. One guy didn't get his wheels down all the way and the rear wheels collapsed after he landed. Down she came on two tail booms, it sure messed up the tail of that plane. The other guy was too busy landing to notice a Navy plane taking off and he plowed right into it. A wing was smashed up on each plane. Things will probably be pretty interesting until these guys learn to handle the planes adequately."

James Tudor "I was in a group that came from aircraft mechanic's school at Keesler Field, Mississippi. They pulled us out of class two months ahead of graduation in a sudden move. Some fellows on weekend pass in New Orleans were left behind. We were sent to Santa Monica, California and housed in the Edgewater Beach Hotel. Two shifts a day, five days a week we attended school at Lockheed Aircraft Company in Burbank. After studying the Hudson A-29 aircraft, we wound up in the 78th with P-38s. Other A&M mechanics trained at the Los Angeles Municipal Airport mechanic's school named 'California Flyers'.

"Living on North Island Naval Air Station wasn't too plush. Our bunks were set up in rows in one big hangar, and I learned to eat baked beans for breakfast in the Navy mess hall.

"Every morning we pre-flighted our P-38s before daylight. One morning as I was checking the magnetos on the left engine, the left wheel jumped over the chock and quickly circled the aircraft in a right turn. The left propeller tore into a mechanic's stand at the right wingtip. My buddy, Tommy Threlfall, was dozing there against the stand, and I thought for sure I'd killed him. In a few seconds I'd shut down the engines and I was out of the cockpit looking for him. Luckily he wasn't hurt. We did have to change the prop but the engine checked out okay. The P-38 brakes were tricky and you couldn't positively tell if they were locked.

"One night a young pilot brought his aircraft back after only a short time. We asked him what was wrong. He said he thought the plane was on fire. He had seen the two superchargers behind the engines glowing red hot in the dark sky. Another night one pilot landed very short, locked his brakes, and wore the tires down completely to the the rims enough to require new wheels. Fortunately he ran off into the sand at the end of the runway and no other damage was done to the plane. On another very sad occasion, one of our pilots came straight down at full power from 10,000 feet, hitting the ground on the Coronado Strand. The plane blew into a million pieces, and I was one of the detail to pick up the bits and pieces of the pilot and place them in a basket. We didn't recover more than five pounds of him altogether.

"Later several of us were sent to Mills Field, to support the P-38s used to train new pilots there. The P-38 was a lot of airplane for one man, and we lost many fine young fellows killed on takeoffs. One common mistake was a failure to switch gas tanks. The tank selector switch was manual and when one tank ran out, they'd forget to switch to one still containing gasoline, so down he went."

Harry Dayhuff: "At North Island, the bachelor officers were billeted at the famous resort Coronado Hotel, while the married officers rented on Coronado Island. One of our enlisted mens' main bitches was Navy chow, which meant beans for breakfast. I tried to set up our own field kitchen and ran into a hornet's nest of officialdom. It seems back in WWI, North Island was an Army base, and now the Navy was concerned that the Army was trying to take it back. My kitchen idea had to back off once it got up to the high brass. Otherwise we communicated fine with the Navy, and the only other minor problem was the traffic pattern at North Island. Our faster P-38s had to use caution not to overrun the slower Navy birds in the fancy system set up to land carrier type aircraft without radio control.

"The P-38 had had a number of unexplained fatal accidents and it had acquired a bad reputation. We had the first breakthrough of the problem at North Island. The clean P-38 easily reached the speed of sound and compressibility of which little was known. This pilot found himself in this situation, couldn't control the aircraft, and he couldn't bail out due to airstream turbulence. He released all the controls and said his prayers! The bird leveled off and he was able to land okay. The aircraft had wrinkled skin and damaged control surfaces. Lockheed sent down a team of engineers and carted the aircraft up to the plant for wind tunnel tests. Subsequently it was recommended the wheel should be pushed forward to pull out of a dive, because compressibility reversed the air flow over the control surface.

"We lost four pilots at North Island, Lieutenants Baugh, Hubbell, Sumner, and Seppich. Wendell Seppich was returning from Hamilton Field and he crashed into the sea off La Jolla, while trying to let down through a solid overcast. I had to break the news to his wife. We were all close friends."

June 1942: On June 23rd the 83rd Fighter Squadron left Mills Field and moved into Hamilton Field with the Group Headquarters Squadron. The 84th Fighter Squadron at Oakland Municipal Airport was joined by the Headquarters of 4th Fighter Command under Brigadier General William Kepner. By July 20th the 14th sister group had left for combat. Now the 78th's cycle of combat preparation turned with intensity.

Morris Lee: "We had a threefold mission to perform. First, to guard the West Coast against enemy attack. Secondly, to train

A 78FG P-38 in standard AAF day fighter colors. Colors are dark Olive Drab topside and Neutral Grey below. Yellow Flt. in squadron bands on engine cowls mark No. 70 as the 84FS CO's aircraft. Wheel covers may also be yellow. (Russell Hunter)

replacements for overseas combat units. Every six weeks or so we received a new class of flying school pilots to check out in P-38s and then we would allow them to participate in the scramble missions to investigate unidentified aircraft as ordered by the Information Centers at San Francisco and Los Angeles. Third, we were to prepare for combat by training in gunnery and readiness procedures. Our training was hit or miss until Major Peterson organized our group, unified our goals, and set it down in writing. The traditional Air Corps programs were crude and elementary. Everything was brought together in a logical sequence and then all members became qualified at it."

The 78th did not have any identifying insignia and after more pressing matters, the officers tried to come up with a suitable group badge and squadron insignias. After Washington turned down one design, Major Peterson decided to go with the 78th's ideas and it was not until September 26, 1942 that a shield design was approved by both parties. In heraldic terms it is described as: Shield - per pale indented azure and gules. Motto - "Above the Foe". An 84th Fighter Squadron design was approved on August 26, 1942 by General Headquarters. It is described as: On

a disc deep yellow, a black panther grasping two lightning bolts red, points extending over and through rim of disc in chief and base. The 82nd Fighter Squadron and 83rd Fighter Squadron did not have approved emblems until post World War II days in the USAF.

Hamilton Field was eighteen miles north of the Golden Gate Bridge. The Officer's Club was situated on a high hill overlooking the field. It had many modern conveniences, including a fine swimming pool, while the officer's quarters were artistically designed. The capable wives made things quite livable and created a fine air of hospitality. Many delightful evenings were spent in the Club and the homes of fellow officers, usually both, after Fred the bartender stopped serving drinks at 10:00 P.M. All of this was before gas rationing and the beautiful summer weather encouraged drives through the surrounding countryside. Many war brides would soon be left on the West Coast as a result of these pleasant living conditions and the storks were more numerous than sea gulls.

Robert Eby: "During this period all squadrons were constantly on alert with one flight of four pilots in readiness with

Oakland 84FS P-38G 42-12788 with night tarps coming off in early morning. Drying jacket and blanket denote Alert Duty crewchief slept with his aircraft. Fall, 1942 (Charles Clark)

the planes warmed up and ready to scramble on orders from Fighter Command. Many times a civilian would advise Fighter Command of a Japanese balloon off the Golden Gate and we would scramble a flight out. Invariably it turned out to be a cumulus cloud on a moonlight night. One night four of us were to fly a night formation. We were radioing and calling each other, whom we couldn't find in the blackout conditions. Suddenly 4th Fighter Command radioed that a Japanese submarine was reported several miles off the Golden Gate. We quickly found the trick to formations was to all head for the same point. After locating the supposed submarine, a call was sent back to 4th Fighter Command telling them a small fishing boat was heading into port."

September 1942: No sooner had the 14th Fighter Group left for combat, than rumors began to fly that the 78th would soon follow them overseas. In early September, Major Peterson called a staff meeting to inform everyone to prepare for a move, probably to England. Lists of shipment equipment were drawn up, plans for building field desks and other articles were carefully studied, and everyone in the group was busy making his will or executing power of attorney for his personal affairs prior to departure day.

Morris Lee: "I was charged with sending a few planes at a time to the main Lockheed plant at Burbank for modifications. When Lockheed called one morning and asked for four planes that day, I called 83rd Fighter Squadron where Lieutenant Cooper was assigned to lead the flight to Burbank. A few hours later he called from Squadron operations to inform me that they couldn't find the airfield at Lockheed. When I called the plant representative he said,'Oh, I forgot to tell you that the plant and field have been camouflaged.' Cooper flew back again, and later reported that the camouflage was so realistic, that they landed across streets with cars painted on them.

"Another duty I had as Group Operations Officer, was to develop a unified training program, which made it necessary to visit the scattered squadrons to conduct inspections. The squadrons were almost fully operational with twenty-five P-38s each. On one of my first tours of inspection I had a harrowing experience not easily forgotten. I borrowed Major Peterson's P-38 for a visit to 83rd Fighter Squadron at South San Francisco airport, parking it 100 feet in front of the maintenance hangar, which was a block south of the control tower. Then I had a short conversation in the ready room on the side of the hangar away from the field. As I was leaving through the main hangar with its big doors open, I looked up and saw a P-38 heading for the hangar on my left where the night crews were sleeping. Yelling for everyone to vacate the building away from the field, I ran around the crews' sleeping hangar to the field side, where the P-38 had crashed into the door frame post of the maintenance hangar. The pilot, a new trainee who had been shooting landings, raised up slightly from the cockpit and yelled,'Help me!' Before I or anyone else could do anything, he was completely engulfed in flames. The intense heat in a matter of seconds had boxes of ammunition exploding, forcing us to seek shelter behind sandbag revetments. Boxes of .30 and .50 caliber machine gun shells were stored nearby and began shooting in every direction. Meanwhile, we got the sleeping men out of the adjoining hangar. Several planes under repair in the hangar were soon aflame also. Fire units from nearby communities had to be called to help contain the major conflagration.

"As soon as things were under control I decided to return to report to the Group CO. As I was getting into Pete's aircraft, I discovered the nose section had been sheared off. We reconstructed what happened and decided the tower had advised the pilot to go around for another approach and his left engine failed, pulling him off course towards the hangars. Just before he got to the sleeping hangar he banked left and clipped the nose off of Pete's P-38 prior to crashing. I can still hear the pilot's

An old B-18 bomber, "JEANNIE THE MERMAID", used at Oakland by 84FS for tow-target flights, liaison flights, and spare parts chasing. Fall, 1942. (Charles Clark)

An Oakland airport 84FS P-38 with sandbags on the tail to raise it for nose-gear repairs. Army engineers erected revetments on many West Coast fields after Pearl Harbor as seen behind yellow cowl-banded No. 72. Fall, 1942 (Russell Hunter)

helpless cry as he slumped back into the seat behind a wall of flames.

"We were losing approximately a pilot a month to fatal crashes. One I had to investigate north of Hamilton Field had gone straight in from a vertical dive. The two engines required a backhoe to retrieve from ten feet in the ground. A jellied-like mass the size of two basketballs was all that was identifiable of the pilot.

"We had an A-20 twin-engine bomber at Hamilton, which I flew to get some LIFE magazine reporters airborne over the Bay area, to photograph some 84th Fighter Squadron P-38s in formation. Hans Groenhoff, their star aviation photographer was snapping shots from the A-20's waist. After an hour I buzzed Oakland Airport at about 450 mph - pretty fast for those days. I didn't realize until we landed at Hamilton that I nearly lost Groenhoff out of the belly hatch as I pulled up from the pass over Oakland. He had left his parachute on the seat to take photos, and he partially blacked out during the buzz and almost fell out the hatch on the pull-up. One of our pilots commenting on the November 16, 1942, Vol.13, No. 20 LIFE story said, 'It was a fair misrepresentation!'"

November 1942: When the movement alert order finally came through around the First of November, the 78th was up to full strength in both personnel and equipment, and anxious to go into action. The Group was led overseas by the following officers in command of their respective sections and sub-units. Group headquarters staff consisted of: Major Arman Peterson, commanding officer; Major Joseph L. Dickman, Executive Officer; Captain Erlath W. Zueh., Adjutant (S-1); Major John H. MacVeagh, Intelligence Officer (S-2); Captain Morris K. Lee, Operations Officer (S-3); and Major Charles T. Evans, Supply Officer (S-4). Captain Robert E. Eby was Assistant Operations Officer with a few sundry other duty titles. Captain Robert H. Holmberg was Medical Officer, Captain Ellis R. Veatch, Chaplain; Captain John R. Fry, Dental Officer; Captain Oliver K. Jones, Weather Officer; and First Lieutenant Hayden B. Kitchen was officer in charge of the Headquarters Squadron enlisted personnel.

Captain Harry J. Dayhuff led 82nd Fighter Squadron and his Flight Commanders were: A - Captain Robert Adamina, B - Captain Leonard Marshall, and C - Captain Herbert Ross. His staff was comprised of Lieutenant Delbert Southerland, S-1; First Lieutenant Firman Vorhees, S-2; First Lieutenant Jack Oberhansly, S-3; and Lieutenant Thomas Majors, S-4.

The 83rd Squadron was commanded by Captain James Stone, Jr. and the three Flight COs were: A-Captain James Cooper, B - Captain Charles London, and C - Captain Richard Decker. The staff consisted of Captain Gilman Ritter, Adjutant; Captain Jesse Davis, Operations Officer; Captain John Mackall,

Intelligence Officer; and Second Lieutenant Eugene Murphy, Supply Officer.

Captain Eugene Roberts was at the helm of 84th Fighter Squadron. The various Flight Commanders were A- Captain Harold Stump, B- Captain Clark, and C- Captain Jack Price. The staff was made up on Captain Vern Smith, S-1; First Lieutenant Jesse Morrison (Duke), S-2; Second Lieutenant Ray Routsala, S-3; and First Lieutenant Henry Trolope, S-4. At this time, the 78th had thirty pilots in each squadron and five pilots in the Headquarters Squadron.

It was generally understood that the Group was bound for England. Flying stopped and everyone readied for movement by train. Wives and sweethearts were kissed goodbye daily and nightly. At 11:15 A.M. on November 3, 1942 the "orphan" 82 Fighter Squadron climbed aboard Army trucks with all their gear and began their motor convoy to March Field at Riverside, just east of Los Angeles. They unloaded at 5:00 P.M. to begin a week's stay, preparing for rail movement to Camp Kilmer, New Jersey. The 84th Fighter Squadron left Oakland and joined the rest of the Group at Hamilton for the movement east.

Finally on Tuesday, November 10, 1942, all personnel were directed to their designated places to board the trains. Officers and men lined up in full field dress and equipment with the military bearing of an infantry regiment and marched to the trains. They traveled in Pullman coaches, the officers one in a berth and the enlisted men one in an upper and two in a lower berth. Train kitchens were set up and the men were served rations cafeteria style. Post exchanges were set up from which beer and Coca Cola could be purchased. The men spent their time playing cards, watching the scenery, wondering where they were going, and drinking beer. All in all, the trip was fairly comfortable with stops each day for exercises.

Noble Vining: "We were alerted to pack and paint boxes and crates with our own codes. Before leaving, I rummaged through a pile of books dumped on the day room floor by a charity society. I 'scalded' a copy of the 1923 Atlas of the World, and put my name and APO in it. During the trip across the continent, everyone from the CO on down borrowed it to look up something they came upon, but it always came back to me."

Morris Lee: "That was a sad day in November when the train pulled out headed east on a miserable ride. We stopped in Ogden, Utah for a few minutes, but not long enough for me to find out if my wife, baby and her mother had made it to Utah yet. We were not in cattle cars, but the old coaches they had pressed into service were anything but comfortable for sleeping. The baggage car used as a mess hall was cold and windy. I saw several guys step through the passage way only to find the plate empty upon entering the coach. Those strange air currents between the cars could take the sauerkraut and wieners right off the plate. Nobody complained much, saying it wouldn't have been any good anyway. The poker games lasted all night and all day throughout the several days' trip."

Camp Kilmer, an overseas staging area which covered many acres, was situated near New Brunswick, New Jersey. In the early morning of Sunday, November 15, 1942, the troop trains from March and Hamilton Fields pulled into camp. Each was met by Major Peterson and Captain Zuehl, who had flown on ahead to arrange for billeting and feeding the men. Regardless of how carefully advance orders are followed, staging areas invariably have different ideas. "That's not how we do it here." The 78th was no exception. On the West Coast all equipment and personnel baggage was labeled in various colors for each squadron. At Kilmer everything had be marked in white. The used stencils had been discarded at Hamilton Field, and to mark all the equipment by hand would have required days of work. No stencil paper was available at the camp and no passes or personnel were allowed out of the camp until the job was done. At this point, Second Lieutenant Sydney Craig, 82nd Fighter Squadron Assistant Intelligence Officer displayed some real initiative. He got on the phone to a nearby city and ordered some stencil paper. The store could not deliver it to camp but that didn't deter him. Craig's mother had come from Chicago to New Brunswick to see her son before he left for overseas. Sydney phoned her and she took a bus to Newark, took custody of the stencil paper and caught a bus to Camp Kilmer The stencils were soon cut and time was found to grant passes to visit relatives or tour New York City.

Camp Kilmer being spread out, the 78th was issued some trucks for transportation. A 78th officer entrusted with the duty of driving officers to the "O" Club and back to the barracks, inadvertently drove off from the club with a truck load of Army Nurses, leaving his comrades to find their way home as best they could. He became very embarrassed when his mistake was discovered, as he had unquestionably mistaken the gray blue uniform of nurses for that of the Air Corps.

An officer observed, "Colonel Peterson believed in advance planning, and prior to leaving Camp Kilmer, we salvaged two large crates used for film developing machines, which carried mess supplies from California. The pilots and crews all chipped in and bought enough American booze to fill up the crates. These were cleverly marked and shipped off with the other equipment overseas. Unfortunately, there must have been some breakage enroute, as only one crate was delivered eventually at Goxhill. There it was stored in a very conspicuous place with an armed guard on it every night. We voted not to open it until Christmas. What a momentous occasion!"

Earl Payne's Diary: " November 20, 1942, Camp Kilmer. Turned in sheets and pillowcases this AM. I have a sheet and pillowcase they don't know anything about and so I shall sleep well tonight. Ain't I lucky? About thirty fellas are going to Fort Dix to shoot their newly issued rifles. We got gypped on those we got, Springfield '03' models, instead of the Garands we all wanted. Officers and crew chiefs got pistols. Two others got machine guns. Had my last Typhus shot today, the worst of the series of three. The most painful! They gave the whole barracks a five minute physical today. It is a prerequisite for overseas shipment and they do all they can to NOT find anything wrong with a person. Two Ahhs, a cough, an operation not requiring mention taking several seconds, and a bend over forwards spreading the buttocks.

"November 21, 1942. We paid off the fellows on a partial payroll today and contentment reigns supreme. Just wait until morning and see the faces. They'll be broke and several fellows will have lost all their money through gambling debts and the rest penniless or to a close degree.

"November 23,1942. All our 'A' bags and small bags were packed this AM. We're to have a formation at 6:00 PM and march to the train. We are to be paid five dollars apiece after boarding the ship, government regulations, I suppose for incidentals. We are quite a sight now, flight jacket, leggings, BD, overcoat, rifle, full knapsack, canteen, first-aid kit, and the steel helmet, all on our person. Have been very busy filling out insurance forms and allotment blanks today. Got a money belt from my wife today."

LtCol Arman Peterson (L), inspects 84FS CO, Maj. Eugene Roberts soldiering for a field inspection at Oakland prior to moving to the East Coast. Kit includes pistol, gas mask, helmet, and leggings. (Robert Eby)

Chapter 3

Overseas - England Bound

Monday, November 23, 1942, the Trans Atlantic journey began.

Earl Payne"s Diary: "After standing out in cold driving rain in front of the barracks for an hour or so, we finally marched to the train. We arrived in New York at 10:15 PM and stood for another hour waiting to get on the ferry. The men were packed like sardines with the cold wind and rain blowing in their faces for the trip across the Hudson River. We finally pulled in where the Queen Elizabeth was docked next to the sunken Normandie, lying on its back like a huge beast. Going up two flights of stairs to our gangplank, a thing happened which made us all laugh in spite of our discomfiture. One little fellow about 5'3" had a long overcoat coming down to his ankles. Each time he stepped up he stepped on his coat and almost fell down under his heavy load. At the top he laughed with the rest of us about it.

"We got on the boat about 12:30 AM and I and three others are in a room 10'x5'. They are in a three decker bunk and I am on the floor. They say I'm the luckiest because I have a good thick mattress. There are about 13,000 on board including 3,089 officers and 300 nurses. There are U.S. soldiers, fliers, sailors, French fliers, British fliers, soldiers, sailors and many more nationalities."

Jack Miller: "How easy it is to leave the U.S. courtesy of the U.S. Army. A checker at the end of the gangplank calls your last name, you give your first name, and you're gone. Another man hands you tickets telling your room number and what time to eat chow. Stumbling and struggling I arrived on 'A' deck and looked for my room. Just imagine sharing a room with eleven other guys and all the baggage we were carrying. They had four sets of triple-deck bunks built in a little place hardly big enough for one human size bed.

"After much horseplay and wisecracking, we settled in our bunks of hard boards, straw-ticks, and blankets. Our slumber was ended about 5:00 A.M. the next morning by a clanging emergency bell. It was a lifeboat drill to acquaint us with our boats and stations. No sooner had we fought our way back to our cabin, when someone shouted we were moving, which proved all too correct. Hanging far out the porthole, I caught the last glimpse of the New York skyline and waved goodbye to the Statue of Liberty standing there proudly in the murky gray dawn with her torch held high.

"About 9:00 AM we went topside to look around and found we had picked up an escort of three destroyers. The wind was really blowing and the waves running high almost to the promenade deck we were standing on. The small destroyers were really having a time of it. They would go almost completely out of sight when a big wave hit them. Our course must have been south as it turned very warm, but the second day we swung north and made a three minute zig-zag course for England, while they passed out booklets titled, 'Guide to Great Britain'."

Army nurses caused ship officials some concern that proved justified. Hammocks were removed from the deck, one nurse was placed under guard, and other measures were taken. By the first few hours out, card games were in progress in every available space.

Noble Vining: "Sea-sickness was worse among those bunking at either end of the ship. As we zig-zagged, the bow rose ninety feet and dropped ninety feet. Sometimes it slipped off sideways in the middle of this motion, and you really held onto the bunk then.

"Thanksgiving Day we had boiled potatoes and Brussel Sprouts cooked with pretty strong mutton. Each table had one big dishpan. The routine was for two men from the table to fill the dishpan with food and return it to the table. When it was empty two men took it back filled with the leftovers and sometimes with what did not remain in their stomachs. They then washed it out and returned it full of water, which we were then to wash our mess gear in this cool greasy water. You can imagine how appetizing this procedure was. I tried to speak to the British officer in charge of the mess but he was so aloof that he wouldn't even speak to an enlisted man. I immediately reported the whole situation to the Group Flight Surgeon and he went into action. We soon had a serving line and the familiar GI cans with soapy hot water and two hot rinses."

Jack Miller: "The big disadvantage of being on a Limey ship was the chow. What a mess they served us for food. It would take hours to sweat out a chow line which wound its way down four flights to the mess deck. When the line got far enough that old familiar smell of mutton would drift upstairs, and I'd just return to the cabin. My main diet was Nestles bars and Pepsi-Cola from the PX in the bow. One of the cooks had quite a racket worked up. At night he would come around with a box full of ham sandwiches, just two slices of bread and a slab of ham. But I never tasted better sandwiches in my life. No one asked any questions about where he got the ham, they were so glad to get edible food. Another problem was washing with salt water, as it was impossible to lather. The salt clogged your pores and made your face and skin hard and dry.

"Day by day the tension aboard grew. The morning of the fifth day out someone raised the shout, 'Land Ho', and everyone rushed topside to see, and sure enough, lying off our port bow was the southern tip of Ireland. After that you could feel the pressure ease and everyone walked around with a big smile on his face."

Earl Payne's Diary: "November 28, 1942. We got our field rations today, six cans containing meat and beans, meat hash, stew, biscuits, sugar, candy and dried coffee, all to last us for two days.

"November 29, 1942-Sunday. After working our way up the Firth of Clyde, the ship dropped anchor at Gourock, near the town of Greenock, Scotland at 1715 GMT. I haven't had a bath for a week now and am pretty dirty. We left the ship this morning (November 30th) and loaded onto lighters at the waterline for the trip to shore, landing at Princess Pier. I saw several ships with their bows aiming at the sky out of the water. We lined up and marched to the train, just like the ones in the movies with doors open at the platform to each compartment and an aisle along the other side."

Queen Elizabeth, which carried millions of GIs across the Atlantic in WWII l also carried the 78th to England. (U S Army)

Jack Miller: "Our first big laugh at the difference between the new and the old world was their trains. Working on a grade opposite our train was the smallest engine and freight cars I'd ever seen. They looked almost like toys. Every station we came to, smiling ladies came along the cars passing out hot tea and crumpets, which tasted mighty good after living on chocolate bars and Coke for five days. The afternoon was a bright sunny one and we passed through some very beautiful country of rolling hills and woodland. Everyone started to think that this wasn't going to be half bad, but we learned later that when the sun shines over here, it is a rare occasion. Glasgow, Scotland was the first sizable town we stopped in and I felt that I had seen it somewhere before. It finally dawned on me that it looked just like old postcard pictures of American towns taken around 1900-1910."

Earl Payne's Diary: "The people all looked white and dirty from soot. They accepted all the cigarettes we offered in great haste and happiness, kids and all. I opened meat and beans as my ration and it sat cold and hard on my stomach. We stopped once in Edinburgh for a 'hot drink' and it turned out to be a very sickening sweet drink of chicory, which I threw away.

"We finally stopped at the little town of Goxhill in Lincolnshire, England on the East Coast at 0130 AM. It was really just a railroad stop with a few houses and as many pubs. You truly know what a blackout is when you see these towns. Not a light, beam or anything showing. It was dark! We walked two and one half miles to our encampment with full field gear and it was quite cold. We went right to the mess hall and ate a swell meal of Vienna sausage, sauerkraut, macaroni, and real good coffee and peanut butter. Imagine that!"

Jack Miller: "Being newly arrived in a country practically on the front line of fighting, we expected a Jerry plane to come diving down strafing the column during the three mile trudge to camp. I kept looking along the ditches for a nice spot, just in case."

Chapter 4

Goxhill - Combat Preparations

Earl Payne's Diary: "After our delightful repast, we went another mile or more to where we were to be quartered. I got stuck in a very cold 'tin can'. There are three wooden barracks and six tin cans in our squadron area billet. The latter are 50'x25' with a double thickness of corrugated iron in semicircle making the roof. Sixteen beds and one teeny-weeny coal stove are in it. The only heat is two feet from the stove and the rest is in complete cold. The beds do have springs and mattresses, so it could be worse. There are no latrines or water within a mile, and the mess hall just as far. For two days we had no electricity until I tapped into the officers' barracks lead-in with some phone wire and rigged a twenty-five watt bulb to read and write by. We are restricted here for three weeks and can't go over two hours walking distance away. We have ration cards for gum, candy, and cigarettes, however the amount is plenty for a week's consumption. The money gave me trouble at first, but am getting it mastered. Our laundry and dry-cleaning is free and this leaves little else to spend money for.

"The sun hardly ever shines and the days are short and dreary, it rains a lot and lately it's very cold and windy. Quite a bit of fog too. Got in a fight last night with a fellow refusing to quiet down after 10:00 PM., which I told him to do. Just a little flurry and he decided to go to bed without further ado. Got hearty commendations from the fellows this AM over it. None of them like him very much. Quite a few planes flying about last night, but as yet no air raids here.

"December 13, 1942. Got the rest of the baggage today and most of the others suffered great losses through thievery, but all my stuff remained intact. The adjutant hooked up his radio through a special transformer and we got Berlin and London broadcasts. About all war news, but in between was some some very good music. It sure seemed nice to listen to after having gone so long without it. The ground is very muddy since we arrived here. Some good old dust would be welcome!"

So the 78th settled into its first British station of WWII. Goxhill airfield was situated on flat land along the south bank of the Humber River Estuary opposite the City of Kingston-Upon-Hull. The official designation was VIII Air Force Station No. F-345, and the control tower radio call letters were GX. Unofficially the American units serving there referred to the base as "Goat Hill". The station had been built by the RAF in June, 1941. From August, 1942 a succession of new units from the U.S. received their theatre indoctrination training there.

Eighth Air Force was being used as a base of supply for the NW African Air Force at this time. The 78th arrived on December 1, 1942 and became part of the strategic reserve for "Operation Torch", the invasion of Western North Africa . The terminus of Goxhill was the hangar line, consisting of three large hangars with the control tower on the field side of these, and the station-group-squadron headquarters on the opposite side of the hangars among the various tech supply and service unit buildings. All these were over a mile from the mess halls and two miles from the living sites, a very well dispersed airfield built to RAF standards. The 78th's 333rd Air Service Group and some of its sub-units had preceded the group to England and readied the base prior to the 78th arrival.

Major Arman Peterson took over as Station Commander and set to work trying to make the base a more livable place. Billeting areas needed running water. The Officers' Club was a cold dingy place with two pool tables, a broken down ping-pong table, a reading room with no reading material, and a large room with a corner spot for a bar. The enlisted men had no recreational room on post and sent their spare time in barracks, at movies in the gym, and in nearby towns and pubs. Due to the mud, no one walked anywhere without galoshes.

Since no planes had arrived yet, the pilots and intelligence sections were all sent to operational RAF bases about a week after Goxhill arrival. These fields covered the Eastern and Southern coasts of England from Scotland to Land's End. The visits lasted from two weeks to a month, but by Christmas most had returned. Meanwhile, the various group operational and administrative officers plunged into the task of tuning Eighth Fighter Command operations standards

Oliver K. Jones: (Group weather officer) "Gad! It was miserable at Goxhill Airfield for this good ol' South Texas boy! There were absolutely no weather service facilities on base. I immediately set about getting a weather reporting teletype drop installed. This involved working through the Clerk of the Works (pronounced 'Clark' as in Clark Gable), who seemed to be overwhelmed by almost anything. Finally I got in touch with General Eaker's Staff Weather Officer at Pinetree (Eighth Air Force Headquarters), Colonel Mustin, who flew up to Goxhill Airfield in a Spitfire and heard my story. I soon had the GPO types swarming all over that old watchtower installing the British Creed Teleprinter and back-up. I had been Jeeping over to Kirton-on-Lindsey RAF station for my weather info and often the fog was so thick that even driving was out of the question. The carpentry shop built me specialized weather station furniture and we were in business as a forecasting station at long last. I also acted as sort of permanent airfield Officer-of-the-Day, ex-officio-without portfolio ."

Everett Chappell: "During the summer of '42 four of us armament section leaders were sent to Hollywood, California to learn how to develop movie film using a K.I.A. developing machine. After we got to Goxhill Airfield I first went with a bunch of fellows to pick up our Squadron vehicles from the depot. When I returned, I was assigned to the base photo lab. As I entered the building there was a KIA developing machine half out of the crate. Nobody there even know what it was for. When they discovered I knew a little bit about it, that then became my job for the war's duration."

With the field and various sites spread out in a ten-mile radius, travel on base was quite an effort. This was soon overcome by issuing bicycles from RAF stores to the required personnel. Shortly after, the hangar line looked like 42nd Street and Broadway with bicycle traffic instead of autos. December 15th was the day the happy pilots looked up to spot four sleek tailed P-38s whistling into the landing pattern and touching down on the runway. The planes were scattered among the sugar beets in the dispersal areas and flight operations began to

A south view from the tower at RAF Goxhill airfield. Three Westland Lysander Is in foreground with a Miles Master III fueling behind. In the foreground is a mobile floodlight beacon beside the ambulance and firetruck garages. (Russell Hunter)

ready the pilots for combat. Sunday night, December 20th events took a much more serious turn for the young rookie Americans.

Earl Payne's Diary: "I was playing poker about 9:00 PM when we heard two concussions, or rather felt them, in quick succession. The Charge of Quarters had just left, warning us that a 'Red' alert was on. They have three colors designating the extent of a raid. 'Red' means enemy aircraft are within fifteen miles, but continue what you are doing, 'black' means total blackout and run for shelter, and 'white', which means all clear.

So we immediately grabbed our helmets and gasmasks. I got my rifle and put five rounds of ammo in it. None of the others had been issued any ammo yet. I didn't want to be defenseless in case of paratroop landings, or low-flying strafing fighters. We headed for the shelter and found the place full of about two inches of water, so we just stood outside and watched. Nothing happened for a while, so we went back to our game in the barracks. One or two fellows staying outside, beckoned us out and then we saw quite a bit. They were over Hull, a large town eight miles distant, one of the most-bombed cities in England. It was a perfectly clear night and a full shining moon. No sooner were we out, than a plane zoomed across the skies dropping about a dozen flares over the town. The idea was that the bombers could dive down and bomb the lighted area, but anti-aircraft fire kept them up and nothing happened. After the flares began to fall, a lot of ack-ack started to fire and the tracers could be seen. The tracers appeared to be barely traveling, probably because we weren't close enough to see the actual firing. They followed a trajectory almost horizontal to the ground."

Jack Miller: "Sunday night, I was all alone on duty in the control tower. The only noise breaking the silence was the pacing back and forth of the machine gun crew on the roof. Suddenly the blackout curtains seemed to jump at me and the windows started a terrific rattling, then came the roar of an exploding bomb. I jumped about three foot up from that chair and hit the floor running. I was undecided at first whether to make for the nearest shelter or stay put, but I knew I didn't want to be alone, so I went up on the roof with the machine gun crew. It was almost like having a grandstand seat for the Fourth of July fireworks. Red tracer bullets streaking through the sky, the crack and flash of bursting flak high overhead, flares dropped by the planes trying to light up their target, and the red flash and roar of exploding bombs. I saw my first German plane crash flaming into the sea that night. It was very interesting and exciting to watch, but when one stopped to think that the people

on whom the bombs were falling were losing all their worldly goods and even some their lives, it quickly turned one's excitement to hate of war. After the surprise of the first raid we experienced on Hull, it came to be quite a common thing and no one paid much attention to it.

One night, the German broadcaster, Lord Haw-Haw, made the statement that the German Air Force would soon pay a visit to the new American fighter group at Goxhill. Although we waited in anticipation of that call, it never came in the four months we were there."

Negley Sapper: "The Germans would send their bombers over every Sunday night at 9:00 PM. This was their graduation exercises for their bombardiers. They could follow the river up the estuary and right where the river bends was the city of Hull. After a while I would never go to bed on Sunday when I was tired. I'd wait until they had bombed the Hell out of Hull, because I knew I'd be awakened by the bombing. This happened every week regular as clockwork. The first time I saw them bomb Hull I thought they were just down the road, because the ground rose between the base and the city."

The strange new experiences for the young GIs in a foreign country created a constant flow of impressions that lasted long into their later years.

Richard Ballard: "When we first came to Goxhill, they had this place on base called the 'NAFFI' which was run by a sort of Salvation Army. When you ordered one of these pints of their beer, that tasted about like tree stump water, the girl would say, 'That'll be six pence.' So I pulled out six American pennies and handed them to her. Heck, I didn't know six pence from six pounds at that time."

Allen Clapp: "About the first time Charlie Clark and I got passes, we decided we were going to go to Piccadilly in London. We got on the wrong train going in the opposite direction. After riding and riding, we discovered we were lost, so we got off at the next stop in Lincoln or somewhere. It was a couple hours wait for the next train and we wandered into a pub and bought a fifth of scotch whiskey, paying about $2.50 for that big bottle of Teachers Scotch. Man those people didn't even know who Americans were. We must have been the first they'd seen."

James Tudor: "It was at Goxhill that I learned to sleep between wool blankets without any sheets. I didn't think I could do it, but you learn. Later we were issued mattress covers, so I slit the side of it and slept inside the mattress cover. Our P-38 was parked on a hardstand carved out of a sugar beet field and they still were growing beets all around us. Sergeants had to pull guard duty on the aircraft at night and I got plenty of this chore. We had a wooden shack near the plane to get in out of the weather, with a coke fed stove for heat. On this we cooked some eggs and coffee from time to time. The eggs I got by trading Beech-Nut Chewing Tobacco to 'Charlie', the most popular British workman on the base. Fresh eggs were a premium. The mess hall gave us a steady diet of powdered eggs for breakfast, but they were no good however way you fixed them. In the little village close by, there was a small bakery and now and then we would con them out of a hot loaf of raisin bread. That was a treat for us.

"In our barracks we had a monkey named 'Jocko' and naturally he was teased a lot. We often gave him beer to drink and then he would really carry on. One night he grabbed some eggs I had in a paper bag and ran off. When I attempted to retrieve the bag, he nailed me right in the shoulder with his sharp teeth. Jocko died from an overdose of beer one night after we moved to Duxford."

A few days before Christmas Major Peterson, Group CO, was promoted to Lieutenant Colonel. The men gave up two weeks rations in advance, pooled it, and invited all of the English children from neighboring towns to come to GX for goodies and sweets. About 500 kids came and for many it was their first enjoyable Christmas. The war had scarred the lives of the simple folk of the Isles.

Many of the men were invited to British homes in a holiday exchange program. Each man who put in for an invitation took along some government rations to reimburse their host's larder. All reported having a pleasant visit with their English families. For those who stayed on base a sumptuous Christmas dinner was held in the Enlisted men's mess, with the officers serving it. Colonel Pete gave a brief speech after dinner saying, in effect, ' Like you all, I would rather be at home with my family, but failing that I am with those I'd next rather be with, the men of the 78th.' A program of jokes followed with Captain Marshall as host, music by Captain Monty Shwayder's improvised band, and community singing. At the finale everyone rose and joined in singing The Star Spangled Banner and God Save The King.

On Boxing Day a beautiful Ball was held in the Officer's Club. An array of lovely ladies were imported from the 30th General Hospital at Mansfield. Although there seem to have been some complications in getting them safely home, no casualties were reported and they returned again for a New

Year's Ball. They showed their appreciation by inviting the officers to a party in February. A large packing crate sent overseas as group equipment was opened for Christmas and those involved received their bottles of cheer. The mails had not caught up and gifts from home arrived after the holidays.

Morris Lee: "The American influence took effect and the mutton in our chow was replaced with Spam. Some got so they couldn't stand the sight of a slice of Spam. One group member got a late Christmas present from home. He opened his heavy package to find a ten pound can of Spam. They say he contemplated suicide, but was talked out of it. Insult was added to injury considering that his family and friends had to pool their ration coupons back home to buy it."

January 1943 : Again the GIs spent New Years with British families and sang songs while Big Ben struck twelve times over the wireless. The rain and mud continued through January as the men of the 78th were being sent all over England to various schools. Personnel and Finance Offices were busy cutting orders and paying out per diem to the travelers, who took the occasion to learn other lessons in their nightly maneuvers around Piccadilly Circus.

The entire camp took on a happier air as the pilots returned from Burtonwood and Scotland with the group's new P-38Gs. All went to work to become operational by late January.

James Tudor: " The crews had to hand-crank the P-38s to start them. We wound up an energizer and on the given signal, the pilot engaged the starter and kicked the engine off. With one engine running, the generator output would start the other engine unassisted With the pilots using the hand primer in this method we had lots of fires under the engines of the P-38s & 47s when they were overprimed. We really sweated out some pilots more than others. About the time you were ready to unleash the fire extinguisher, the engine would finally kick off and blow out the fire with propwash."

Robert Eby: "Colonel Pete was constantly thinking up needed projects. He put me to work bore-sighting the guns. I went to Eighth Fighter Command on 1-12-43 to obtain the ballistic data and it took me three days to get it. I had to go through the Eighth Fighter Command, Royal Air Force Fighter Command and the Air Ministry. Using my drafting instruments I brought overseas, I drew up alternate combinations of bore-sighting patterns in four color ink. Colonel Pete was anxious to sell these patterns to Eighth Fighter Command, which was

P-38G 42-12926 "MACKIE" is 82FS CO Major Harry Dayhuff's aircraft, named after his wife, Maxine. Markings include: white spinners, aircraft in-squadron No. 10, yellow bordered blue white star AAF insignia, two white squadron CO bands, and "MIKE" and "PAT" nicknames on the motor cowls. Aircraft slings two 165 gallon drop-tanks on wing pylons. Jan., 1943 (Harry Dayhuff)

setting the gunnery standards for the 4th, 56th, and 78th Fighter Groups. Colonel Pete was way ahead of the other groups and when they went to the Air Ministry, they were told the Yanks had been given the data once and that was enough. The Eighth Fighter Command Ordnance Officer ended up flying to Goxhill in order to get the ballistics data from myself for the other groups. I was very pleased when Colonel Pete returned from Eighth Fighter Command where he'd met with Colonels Chesley Peterson and Hubert Zemke. Our patterns were accepted and subsequently all P-47 groups in the ETO used this pattern until a few months before D-Day.

"Another project Colonel Pete gave me was to improve the gunsight. The American gunsight had a 60 mph ring that was inadequate for World War II speeds and Pete loved the beautiful 100 mph sight of the Spitfire. He tried to get Spitfire sights, but was turned down. I took a sight apart and found a small reticle which was a mirror on which was etched the circle and center dot. Playing around with my drafting dividers, I found I could scratch a 90 mph ring, but could not stretch it to 100 mph. I couldn't make a very clean ring with my tool, but Pete felt it was much better than 60 mph, so I went to a glass shop in Grimsby and had them cut reticles for our gunsights. The P-38s left for Africa before the 90 mph reticles were installed."

Warren Kellerstedt: "I was Major Dayhuff's armorer when he was squadron CO and recall the day we got our new P-38s and he got back into the air. He was buzzing the hell out of the Squadron orderly room, a wooden shack on the lane to the barracks area. Harry was coming closer and closer to the orderly room and he was just missing by inches a telephone pole that was standing up above the shack. All the guys watching were saying,'Boy, this guy can really fly!' When he finally landed and drove up to the shack, one of the pilots who had been watching him commented, 'Man, you were really coming close to that pole.' Harry looked up at the pole, got a weird look on his face, gulped once or twice, and said, 'Jeez! I never even saw that pole!' "

On January 12, 1943, Colonel Peterson announced to all the officers that the Group would be operational in February and that the P-38s would be up to full strength by January 15th. The Group was slated to furnish escort for General Eaker's bombers in hopes of cutting the losses over the French submarine pens. Twenty pilots were to go to a bomber field and help work out formations in practice missions with the B-17s.. The next day an air contingent and a motor convoy of crews went to the 305th Bomb Group at Chelveston, where they found the same mud and miserable living conditions. After eleven days of practice missions, a real mission was planned. The bombers were airborne and the Lightnings about to take off, when a teletype came through grounding the P-38s. This was the result of the Casablanca Conference in North Africa on January 14. General Hap Arnold had arrived to find that the Northwest African Air Force only had ninety P-38s to supply three whole groups, and he ordered the Eighth Air Force P-38 strategic reserves, the 78th's aircraft, to North Africa as soon as possible.

Colonel Peterson and his Squadron CO's had driven to London on January 24th, ostensibly to make arrangements for moving the group south to Duxford, Cambridgeshire. Upon their return to Goxhill next morning, they announced that all the group's planes must be ferried to North Africa as soon as they could be prepared. The Chelveston contingent returned to Goxhill and awaited the delivery of the Republic P-47 Thunderbolt, which was to replace the 78th's P-38s. Everyone was gloomy but hopeful about the change.

It was necessary to equip some of the P-38s with dust filters for African desert operations. The afternoon of the Chelveston return, several flights left for the Lockheed Lightning Modification Depot at Langford Lodge, Ireland, to receive the filters

.

Oliver K. Jones: "At this time I was probably the highest paid telephone operator in the British Isles. We had to have Lockheed's go-ahead from Langford Lodge before we could dispatch the aircraft. The only way to transmit their flight plans was by phone to Ireland. When the operations enlisted man got severely frustrated with trying to do the job, I volunteered to do it. The telephone routing was hinged on London, no East- West trunk lines. The first operator I contacted was at Lincoln, then London, Preston, and finally Belfast, with one or two more lost in between there somewhere. At the time, the British telephone operators were female and quite provincial and on a trunk call had one hell of a time communicating with one another in different parts of the country because of the markedly different accents. Being raised in Texas' lower Rio Grande valley, both Spanish and German were spoken at home and later I received a mixture of Texas accents at the University of Texas, so I had no trouble with the British and Irish accents. I got to where I told each one to make such and such a routing. These gals were real sketches with their 'dearies' and 'loves', and being new to the UK, I got a blast out of it."

Morris Lee: "After a day or two Jake Oberhansly sent us a wire from Langford Lodge. It introduced us to the new military code word, 'SNAFU'. When he returned we learned it meant, 'situation normal all fouled up'. The new code soon spread. The next flight relayed back, 'TARFU',' things are really fouled up'. The next bunch also had trouble getting work done on time, wiring back, 'FUBB' which decoded into 'fouled up beyond belief'."

Enroute to Langford Lodge on January 26th, the group suffered its first loss of pilots since reaching England. Over the Forest of Bowland southeast of Lancaster on the west coast, Lieutenants Henry Perry, 83rd Fighter Squadron, and Stephan White, 82nd Fighter Squadron collided in mid-air while flying in heavy cloud and both crashed to their deaths. The same day Lieutenant Donald Beals, 83rd Fighter Squadron was reported missing on a ferry flight to North Africa with a P-38. It was a saddened group of forty-three pilots who landed at Langford Lodge that evening with this latest misfortune to comprehend. Small wonder then, that when they had drowned their gloom in the pubs of Belfast, the MPs chased them out of the city with orders not to return with their carousing behavior.

When they sent the P-38s to Ireland to get them ready for North Africa, some of the 78th mechanics went along to work on them. One day they found a bunch of Lockheed's civilian mechanics trying to fix the landing gear on a B-17 they had jacked up on stands. The landing gear would not extend no matter what they tried. Group mechanics could hardly believe that these civilians couldn't find the problem. The 78th mechanics made a bet with the civilians that they could fix the aircraft. The civilians accepted and then one of the 78th crewmen climbed into the cockpit and hit the locking switch for the gear. The Lockheed people were shocked when the gear dropped down, because they didn't have a clue about the cockpit switch.

The first 78th P-47s arrived on January 29th, when four of the Republic Aviation aircraft were ferried in from the Air Depot.

Two ferry pilots were killed the next day while delivering the 78th's slowly growing P-47 inventory. These were the first P-47s the P-38 pilots had seen, and they caused quite a stir as everyone crowded around to examine the enormous strange new creature. After the usual study of technical orders and cockpit checks, pilots began their flight training in the new plane.

Charles London: "When I got back to Goxhill from detached service, I saw my first P-47. I remember thinking, 'Thank God we don't have to fly those things!' because the P-38 was much prettier. Well, the pilot was there to tell us that we were going to be equipped with P-47s. We didn't have any trouble transitioning back to single engines, because we'd all flown P-40s before. It was such a better airplane than the P-40, that we didn't have any problem learning it at all."

During January, 1943, the famous Polish "Warsaw-Kosciusco" 303 RAF Squadron was taking a rest from the 11 Group at Goxhill's satellite field, Kirton-In-Lindsey. The squadron sent over a pilot with his Spit-IX to explain RAF battle formations to the Americans, and then the whole squadron flew over to Goxhill to show their formations. The Poles and the 78th pilots became great friends and they continued to visit the 78th after the move to Duxford.

Oliver K. Jones: "When the Jugs arrived, they were accompanied by dire and sincere warnings NOT to put the machine in a vertical dive above 20-25,000 feet or so. Well, you know a young fighter pilot's reaction to this. Captain Herbert Ross, 82nd Fighter Squadron, had to lay one over at 35,000 feet. When he was finally able to talk sometime after his landing, he gave a graphic account of the dive's progress. Everything was okay at first, then all hell broke loose. At 27,500 feet or so the control surfaces started buffeting (localized Mach 1 resulting from Venturi [Bournilli] effects in the spaces between the control surfaces and structural members) with a resulting flailing around of the stick. That stick beat the hell out of ol' Ross. He last looked at the altimeter around 20,000 feet, but it was whirling around so fast, he wasn't sure. The airspeed indicator started on its second revolution and peaked at about 120 mph. I later extrapolated his speed at 820 mph, but he likely never got past Mach 1 at any time (760 mph MSL). He finally corralled the stick, but couldn't budge it to pull the nose up. He knew he'd had it, because the patchwork English farms were coming up at an alarming rate. Not knowing why, he thought of the elevator trim tab and cranked it in the nose-up direction. He was at about 10,000 feet when all the racket began to die down and the nose slowly came up. He leveled off at 5,000 feet and let down to a couple hundred feet. Flying past the tower, he asked the Airfield Officer of the Day, Lieutenant Abner Little, to advise him whether to try to

"Dawson County, Nebraska", a P-47 42-7963 was a gift aircraft paid for by civilian donations. It was lost on February 11, 1944 as HL-T with F/O Archie Daniels KIFA at Nuthampstead, UK. (William May)

land the damaged aircraft or go up and bail out. Abner had a marvelous central Texas drawl, in which he suavely replied, 'Hell, Ross, there ain't nothing wrong with that aircraft but a few holes in the control surfaces. Bring her on in and let's look at her.' I'll never forget Ross' voice on that radio. He could hardly speak, and understandably so.

"After landing OK he had to be helped from the aircraft and his little black moustache was even blacker against his deathly white face. He sat in a chair in Operations for thirty minutes or so before he could begin his statement. The P-47 was ruined - class 26ed. The air had beat the paint off the leading edges of all surfaces. The wing spars had been pulled back and the sheet metal failed at the wing roots. Vertical and horizontal stabilizers were pulled back with root failure, and most of the control surface fabric was stripped and hanging in tatters. It was the sickest looking lately new P-47 one can imagine and having only collided with air. We called Herb 'Rocket Ross' after that. He was one chastened jock.

"Captain 'Ajax' Adamina, 230 pound, 6'2" tall, ex-all American from College of the Pacific, always referred to himself in the third person, i.e. 'Ajax did this and so and so'. What did Ajax do? Well, nothing but (according to his account) go right up and repeat Ross' maneuver! His comment was, 'Didn't give ol' Ajax any trouble at all!' "

Erwin Boettcher: "On the night of February 6, 1943 I was duty Officer of the Watch. Approaching the 82nd Fighter Squadron hangar on my rounds, I smelled the very strong odor of gasoline fumes. I looked inside the hangar where the night crews were at work and discovered the P-47 Captain Ross had wrecked that day in a compressibility dive. The ruptured wing tanks were leaking copious puddles of aviation gas onto the

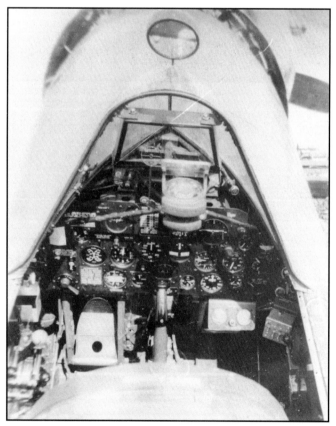

A P-47 cockpit. Note from the top: Large cowl flaps, Spitfire rearview mirror, armor glass screen, gunsight, instrument panel, control stick, rudder pedals, and lower left, throttle/mixture quadrant. (Charles Clark)

floor, filling the hangar with heavy fumes and creating the potentially deadly hazard of an explosion. Immediately, I ordered guards posted at the hangar entrances and got the crews working to clean up the gas spills, and had No Smoking posed around the hangar vicinity. It could have quickly become a tragic situation."

Colonel Peterson visited Eighth Fighter Command Headquarters on Sunday morning, February 7, 1943 and none of the 78th will ever forget his return. He sent word he would return from London that afternoon and all Group officers should assemble at 1500 hours in the Briefing Room. Speculation was running high, in view of the five B-25 Mitchell bombers that had landed earlier in the afternoon. When Colonel Peterson and his staff entered the room it was apparent the news was not good, for their facial expressions betrayed them. As Colonel Pete, only a lad of twenty-eight years started to speak, his voice trembled and his first words were filled with pathos, but he recovered himself and made the most difficult announcement of his career. All the pilots of the Group excepting Group Headquarters, Squadron COs and three Flight Leaders of each squadron were to be immediately transferred to North Africa to replace heavy combat losses and were to be ready to leave the next day, Colonel Pete expressed his deep regret, stating it was a military necessity, and as such shouldn't be questioned or criticized.

After this news, Captain James Stone decided this was the proper occasion to consume the remainder of the liquid refreshments smuggled into England by the Group, and announced that all officers should meet in the "O" Club after supper to carry out this decision. Under the directions of General John Barleycorn, who gradually took command in spite of efforts to overpower him, these officers really gave vent to their feelings. Berlin and Tokyo should have been as well bombarded as the club that evening. After the lights were put out by flying glasses and bottles, someone thought the place was on fire and the fire extinguishers were called into action. If Colonel Pete and his staff were shocked or disturbed, it was only because they were unsuccessful in hitting their targets and were required to return to their quarters in clothes soaked with extinguisher fluid.

Earl Payne's Diary: February 13, 1943. "Well, out of our three squadrons sixty-two or sixty three pilots left for Africa this morning. They have been waiting four or five days for the weather to clear to get off. I saw the cockpit of one of the P-38s. It had every available nook and cranny and space behind the pilot over the radio filled with the pilot's personal clothing. Engineering gave us a buzz at 10:30 AM that they would take off in ten minutes. We closed the office and went over to the field one hundred yards away. Soon, way across the field we saw planes taxiing onto the field. First a B-25 took off, then twenty two P-38s and then another B-25. The day was very sunny, but quite windy and cold, so I stayed for just that many and went back to the office. There were eleven planes in each flight headed by a B-25. They circled wide over the field getting into formation and then buzzed the field about twenty-five feet off the ground in a parting gesture to men left behind whom they had known for six or seven months. It was really a sight to see all the planes come across the field just off the ground. There was strict radio silence for security reasons. Most of the pilots were glad to get away and into action."

Charles London: "After they denuded our whole Group of planes and pilots, there we were with no airplanes to fly. They decided to send us off to different schools. I was sent to a British Commando school, which I definitely did not go for at all. Then I was sent to the big RAF base at Hornchurch, of Battle of Britain fame. Wing Commander Bentley was CO there and he wondered what we were supposed to do there. We said he was supposed to teach us to fight the war, so he quickly got us checked out in Spitfire Mark IXs. I got about three quarters of an hour in the aircraft. Then he says, 'Tomorrow we'll go on a Do' and we did.

"The next day we went over Calais to let the Germans shoot some flak at us, and to quote Bentley, 'Just to convince you that they really don't like you over there.' We were about to take off on another mission to see if we could goad the Hun into a reaction, when a teletype came in stating we were not supposed to fly. This was very embarrassing to us, because evidently he was just supposed to tell us war stories and not really let us get into it. Then I returned to Goxhill just before the move to Duxford, which was a beautiful country club compared to Goxhill."

On February 16, 1943 a new generation of 78th pilots were born in the form of forty-five replacements arriving from Eighth Air Force Combat Replacement Center #7 at Atcham, Shropshire. Previous pilots had been 100% USAAF-trained. This batch contained a number of RCAF/RAF-trained Americans. As representative of these foreign trained pilots, let us take a minute to trace an American RAF-fostered pilot's route to the 78th.

Harding Zumwalt: "The 83rd Fighter Squadron was a milestone in my military career, after I had completed Operational Training in Spitfires with the Royal Air Force and then transferred to the United States Army Air Forces in January 1943. I will always be grateful to the British for giving me the opportunity to fly fighter aircraft in spite of the corrective lenses which I had worn since childhood. I am confident that it was all made possible by many prayers - and being in the right place at the right time.

"I joined the Royal Air Force in late 1941, having heard of the United Kingdom Refresher Course from Canadian friends. They directed me to go to the Statler Hotel in St. Louis, MO where I received a physical; after which I was sent to Parks Air College in Illinois for a flight check, since previous flying experience was a requirement for acceptance into the United Kingdom Refresher Course. I had to return several times in order to pass the physical because of the glasses I wore.

"Our small group was sent to Spartan School of Aeronautics in Tulsa, Oklahoma where we received a whirlwind ground and flight training course. Our class came from all walks of life: a canning company executive from New Orleans, LA; a bootlegger and a rancher from Texas; an Oregon lumberman; movie people from Hollywood, California; a Frenchman (with a Brooklyn accent) from New York; and I, a musician by profession, had a taxidermist as my roommate. All of us had one thing in common. We were eager to fly for Her Majesty's Air Force.

"We began flying in the old Fairchilds, went to Stearmans, AT-6s, and finally took our cross-country training in a Spartan Executive. After graduation we went to Canada to receive our uniforms and then on to England, arriving in June 1942.

"We were stationed in Bournemouth on the southern coast while awaiting our assignments to one of the fighter Operational Training Units (OTU). While at Bournemouth we received excellent training in aircraft and ship recognition; also, we joined British troops training in the use of their weapons and in commando training.

"Finally we were assigned to Turnhill, a British airbase, and our flight training started in the Miles Master Mark I, an underpowered two-seater which could hardly get off of the ground under its own power. Next we flew the Miles Master III, a twin-row 850hp aircraft similar to the American AT-6. It was much faster and of laminated wood construction. We continued our flight training in this aircraft until we flew British fighters.

"On September 10, 1942, they shipped us to Calveley airdrome, where about a week later, I flew my first Hurricane. Those Hurricanes were not in the best of shape. The first two I got into, I refused to take off for various reasons - one of which was a dead magneto. The third aircraft had weak brakes, but after refusing two previous aircraft, I thought that I had better take this one, and anyway I was anxious to fly. The runway had an uphill grade, therefore, I planned to land slow enough to stop rolling before reaching the center of the field, taxi to the ramp slow enough so that little braking would be needed, and cut my engine before I arrived at the parking area. This was not in the best interest of safety, but it worked.

"The unusual method of landing gear retraction in the Hurricane was almost my undoing. You had to shift your left hand from the throttle to the stick, taking your right hand off of the stick to operate the gear control located on the right side of the cockpit. On my first takeoff I forgot to tighten the friction lock on the throttle, so when I let go of the throttle to raise the gear, the throttle started creeping to the rear reducing power, and I had

78th leaders flew an early first combat sortie over France in Spitfires under RAF direction. This low-altitude Spitfire VC DW-X of 610 County of Chester Squadron carries a 30 gal slipper style belly tank and sports two 20mm wing cannon. (Russell Hunter)

to make a mad scramble to regain takeoff power while my landing gear was retracting. And that was the story of my first flight in a British fighter! I had one more 'Hurri hop' that day and went back to the Master again.

"On September 21, 1942 we were shipped to Hawarden airdrome on the west coast where I had my first chance to fly Spitfires and it was love at first sight. Though quite old, with numerous coats of paint which were in the process of chipping off, the Spits were beautiful! They were Mark IIs that had seen many combat hours in the Battle of Britain, but once I got into the aircraft, I found that it flew like a dream. You wore it like a pair of pants. As you settled into the cockpit, closed the side door, and reached over your shoulder with one hand pulling the canopy closed, a feeling of euphoria enveloped you. I will never forget my first Spit ride; it was pure joy to fly.

"The engine was started by a shotgun starter; you pulled a ring to insert a cartridge within the chamber, pressed a button, and away she would go in a cloud of black smoke. The brakes were pneumatic and operated by air pressure from an air pump and an accumulator tank which was checked for full pressure before you taxied out for takeoff. The engine-driven pump could not provide adequate pressure at low taxiing RPMs so if you used excessive braking while taxiing to the far end of the field, you most likely would run out of air pressure and have to pull off to the side and wait for someone to service the brake system before takeoff.

"All systems operated very quickly. On command the gear popped right up into the wells, and on landing, full flaps were instantaneous, so that you had to pull back on the stick to compensate for the change in attitude. The climb rate was very impressive (3,000 fpm) and you felt that you could just about do an 'Immelman' from takeoff.

"The flying suits that they gave us were a beautiful sky blue with mouton fur collars and pockets. In cold weather we wore a silk inner liner which was very warm and comfortable. The gloves were long zippered gauntlets, and our boots were something else: fleece lined, loose fitting, and you couldn't run without losing them. (If you bailed out you would probably lose them from the opening shock.)

"All of our instructors and commanders had combat experience in the Battle of Britain and they passed this knowledge on to us, giving us an advantage which American-trained pilots did not have. They gave us low-level flying training where you flew to a map reference point at fifty feet altitude or less, returned in the same manner, and reported what you saw in order to confirm that you had followed your course. This training taught us to stay under the very effective German radar. If you could not fly low, you were in deep trouble.

"The Hawarden flight training area was fraught with numerous low level hazards with barrage balloons to the North and East, and mountains to the West, but with an open area to the South. I was up one day with a group of other Spits when bad weather moved in from the west coast. Operations recalled all aircraft, and it was a scramble to get the green pilots down on the ground. I was on final approach with two other Spits, all three of us racing to get in first before the weather moved in. Halfway down final, I decided that this was no way to stay alive very long, so I popped down underneath the scud, staying on the deck and headed South. Since in a Spit the compass was located under the instrument panel and almost impossible to read, you had to rely mostly on a map and visual reference to the ground for locating your position. So first I followed a railroad track, but gave up that idea because railroad tracks sometimes run through mountains. Then by staying under the cloud deck, which now was down to 500 feet and getting lower, I found an airdrome south of Hawarden and landed just before the rain hit. I phoned my squadron CO to inform him of where I was and that I was safe. He told me to stay there until he came down to get me the next day. Well, for some reason or other, the following morning,

after the weather had cleared, I took off and returned to Hawarden without waiting for my CO. Yes, I got into trouble for not following orders, but so much for the impatience of youth.

"The final flight before graduation was a formation flight with the Squadron CO. Once you had climbed to altitude, he would break away and try to lose you, while you would have to stay on his tail. If he lost you, you flunked the course. I remember it very well, as I did things I had never done before with an aircraft. After I passed the flight check and we were back on the ground, I asked the CO to show me what we had done. So he took me up again in a Masters, and we repeated the maneuvers.

"In gunnery training I was fortunate to come out above average. Although I did not stay in the RAF long enough to find out where they would have sent me, I heard that their policy for assigning pilots was that those with above average gunnery were sent to the Southeast coast to protect the facilities and airdromes around London. The remaining pilots were assigned to other areas of less activity such as Scotland for submarine patrol.

"We finished our Spitfire training at Eschott Airdrome in late December, 1942. During the process of transferring to the American forces, I went to London where we had the opportunity of joining either the USN or the USAAF. Some Americans failed to transfer for one reason or another. For instance, one of my friends had a prison record and the USAAF would not take him. The Navy wouldn't take me because my eyesight was not up to their standards, so I went across the street and joined the Air Force. I stayed in London for thirty days working out my transfer and purchasing uniforms.

"On February 11, 1943 I reported to Atcham Airdrome, where we continued proficiency flying in Spits until transferring to Goxhill and the 83rd Squadron. There I saw my first P-47, and it was quite impressive. The Jug weighed twice as much as the Spitfire and appeared large enough to house a couple of waist gunners in the rear. When I first taxied a P-47 it was just like driving a Cadillac, the way it would squat on its gear when you hit the break."

*March 1943 :*The motto, 'no pain, no gain', brought a cruel twist as the pilots sorted out the P-47.

Earl Payne's Diary: "Quite a tragedy befell this base today. Major Stone and his wingman were flying across the base. Above and behind them was another P-47 landing with a green light with its wheels down. Just as he flew over them, Stone's pair peeled off to land, and in doing so, his wingman's wing was sheared off by the wheels of the landing plane. The wingless aircraft spun earthward from about seven hundred feet. The pilot stayed with the plane to the ground and then was thrown about fifty feet from it, very much afire and dead. The other aircraft flew on for several more seconds, then the pilot bailed out suffering a broken leg, and the plane crashed to earth.

"About five minutes later I got on my bike and went over to where the wingman crashed in the communal site. It landed in the open parade area about one hundred feet from the messhall and the motor, torn from its holdings, landed fifteen feet from the theater. The plane was burning and the medics were hovering about the body, which was very badly mangled and about three quarters intact. His watch was still running, even after the crash, and into the day following. Fire-fighters extinguished the burning plane and then the "Meat Wagon" arrived with a stretcher, white sheet, and red rubber mat. The latter they placed over the stretcher and then placed the limp body on a portion of the sheet. This they accomplished only after cutting the still burning parachute from the body. Then the medics tore up the remaining sheet portion to equal sizes about the shape of a dish cloth and went over the vicinity picking up portions of the body. These sheets were very bloody in no time. When the body was moved onto the sheet, the head swung very freely and unnatural, rolling on the back and the arms protruded at a strange angle limply swinging. Looking at a body which just minutes previously, was capable of returning a salute, saying 'Hello', made me, and I am sure others present think,'Well, will it be this way with all of us?' "

This death exemplified a problem common to all soldiers.

Harding Zumwalt: "One of the pilots who came over from the states with me was killed in a training accident. He was my roommate, and his death affected me quite a bit. When one sees and experiences tragedy for the first time, it could have a lasting effect. This was a turning point for me; I had to make up my mind that I was going to steel myself against my personal feelings and continue to fly...which I did. And, in the future, I was able to continue on with my duties and keep my emotions under control. From then on, any accidents or deaths that occurred in the squadron had no effect on my flying."

There were also some close calls for GIs at Goxhill, some of whom may not have even been aware of how close to death they came, witness this story retold at postwar reunions: "One cold March night as we all huddled close to the little funnel stove in the Nissen Hut, the announcement came over the PA that German paratroopers had been dropped in the area. "Pop" scrambled up off his cot, put on all his battle gear, from helmet to leggings, grabbed his Thompson submachine gun, and ran out. Of course we followed and while standing there, a couple of fellows that had evidently been to the water spigot, came along the path rattling their canteens. We were all startled to hear Pop rack his gun and exclaim,"Here they come!" After some fast talking we managed to get the gun away from Pop. These two fellows, whoever they were will never know how close they came to being shot for Germans"

Robert Eby: "About March 20, 1943, Colonel Pete got some Spitfire gunsights for our P-47s and we only had a few days to install them. We looked everywhere for brass or non-metallic material to mount the sights, which sat right over the magnetic compass. We suspected steel would foul up the compass. Not finding these materials, we reasoned that since the metal would be directly below the compass, that it would not have an effect. So we made one gunmount and set up the plane on the compass rose to swing the compass, to determine its effect. Lo and behold the metal had no apparent effect on the compass, so we turned the Service Group loose to make mounts and install them in all the planes. They worked day and nights and we installed the Spitfire sights on March 29th. A couple days later Harry Dayhuff took off for Duxford and he became lost. Harry advised that his compass appeared to be twenty to thirty degrees off and, of course, the steel mounts were suspected. The metal didn't bother the compass when the plane was on the ground, but when it was flying, the metal was cutting the earth's magnetic field and thus affecting the compass.

"Now we were in a pickle, as we were only days away from going into combat, and we had useless compasses. Colonel Pete put pressure on our RAF supply liaison officer to get us some brass fast. After frantic calls all over England and to the Air Ministry, they found enough brass plate for us near Birmingham. I'll never forget the trip over there with this RAF officer. I was driving the Jeep and he was navigating from the shotgun side. Going through little villages, I would slow down and he would shout out questions for directions. It was a real exciting but hectic trip. We contacted the brass source and arranged for our truck to pick it up. Again the Service Group worked day and night to fabricate the mounts and install them in the planes. I'll have to take some of the blame for causing them to redo the job, and for a few days, I got an awful lot of dirty looks. They did a tremendous job working full time and installed the sights several days ahead of our first mission."

In January 1943. General Eaker requested of the British that his fighter groups be allowed to occupy some RAF fighter stations in the areas of his bomber groups, because of the shortage of bomber sized fields and the more elaborate communications facilities required for fighter operations. It was decided that the 78th would move temporarily to RAF Duxford for its operational debut, and then transfer to Halesworth in July, 1943 when that base was ready. The latter move never took place and the 78th remained at Duxford for the duration. On March 24, 1943 a small motor convoy of officers and enlisted men drove to Duxford as an advance party to prepare for the arrival of the entire group over the period of April 1-6, 1943.

Major Harry Dayhuff (L), his CC T/Sgt. Arthur Warnken, and unknown ACC on the wing of their P-47 showing the period markings on 78th Jugs. After 50 missions without an abort or aircraft failure, they went on the BBC Ben Lyon/Bebe Daniels radio show. (Harry Dayhuff)

A S/E aerial view of Duxford. Double hangars top are (L-R), 84FS, base theatre in single one, 82FS, and 83FS, with technical, engineering, and supply echelon shops around hangars beside the road. Base HQDRS is two story building between main gate and 82FS hangar, with MP Co. Hqdrs. facing it. (Russell Hunter)

Chapter 5

Duxford - Wartime Home

Earl Payne's Diary: " We left camp at 1:45 P.M. and only Major Zuehl knew where we were going. I can't figure out why I was his clerk for the trip. We are a preparation party to ready things for the rest of the group's arrival. We traveled all afternoon by combat car, Jeep, and weapon's carrier in which I rode, and arrived at 6:10 P.M. The RAF were relinquishing control of this old established airfield and there are a lot of WAAFs here. The facilities and accommodations are wonderful, the only kick being that the food is scant, but it will be better when our mess gets here. We can even have pies and biscuits.

"We are situated six miles from Cambridge and fifty miles north of London. The set up is practically a Shangri-La! The barracks are steam heated and of double brick. The hangar theater has an organ. The rest of the squadron will be here in about a week. In the meantime we are sure having the run of the place. Went to the theater this evening and saw a very good RAF show.

"April 6th: I have been to more dances in the past two weeks than ever before. I went twice to the Dorothy Cafe, three times to the REX Ballroom, and to the base theater with the WAAFs. Friday night is another one here with the Eighth Air Force Band comprising big names from bands in the States. The post officially opened yesterday and went on American rations. The RAFs and WAAFs here sure like the food. One said it was the first peaches he's had in twelve months."

Robert Eby: The officer's quarters are heaven after Goxhill. Now we eat and sleep in the same building. Three of us share a room, Himes, Lee, and myself. There is hot and cold running water in our room and a bath two doors down the hall."

Last year's waste paper was scattered everywhere, and the field was rough like a cow pasture meadow. The keen young Americans, who found it new and exciting after Lincolnshire, quickly remedied such minor items. With the new base and the prospect of imminent combat, spirits blossomed like sunflowers.

April 1943: RAF Duxford was to the British what Wright Field was to the AAF, the home of their air force research and development establishment between the wars. Built as a permanent station during World War I by German POWs, the Battle of Britain saw it function as the Headquarters Sector Station of RAF 12 Group, home of the famous "Bader Wing". Later the new Typhoon Wing was born there and the Air Fighting Development Unit also operated from there. Duxford was now Station Number 357-F of the fledgling Eighth Fighter Command of the Eighth Air Force. The station radio code letters were DX.

The grass flying field of 2,000 x 1,600 yards lay in a shallow valley southeast of the A-505 Royston to Newmarket Highway nine miles southwest of Cambridge. Rising ground to the northwest and southeast kept bad weather flyers very alert. The field eventually supported seventy-three hardstandings, of which twenty-six were tarmac and the rest pierced steel planking. There was no provision for night flying field equipment.

The field and technical site buildings were brick and wood. Along the highway on the north edge of the field, four hangars were situated in an ends-on row with the various engineering and quartermaster buildings between the hangars and the road. Running southwest to northeast, the squadron hangars were the 83rd and 82nd (the field side two story office annex housing Group Intelligence and Operations Sections), then "Ye Old Barn" base theater hangar, and 84th Fighter Squadron hangar. The three Squadron headquarters shacks were field side of their unit hangars. The 78th Group Headquarters was between the highway gate and 83rd Squadron hangar with MP Headquarters across the street.

Base living quarters were closely grouped on the north side of A505. Married Officer's Quarters were on the west side, the squadron barracks encircling the parade ground center, and the Officer's Club and Quarters were on the east side, with the ball and playing fields behind.

The small village of Duxford lay along the base boundaries to the East. Access to London was by railroad from Whittlesford Station to London's Liverpool Street Station via British L.N.E.R. line.

Fifty aircraft could take off from DX in a period of five minutes. Eight to ten would take off abreast, the leader flying straight ahead for two and one-half to three and one half minutes, turning, and coming back parallel to the field. The others, taking the inside route to catch up, would be formatted tight with him by the time they reached the field.

The changeover to American tenancy was smooth except for a running struggle between outgoing RAF Intelligence Officers and the incoming 78th RAF Liaison Officer, Flight Lieutenant John Harrison, to secure film projectors, Hunt aircraft identification trainers, and other pilot training aids. His RAF colleagues accused him of being anti British! By April 6, 1943 all of the 78th had moved to DX from Goxhill.

Of course there was the inevitable brickbat or two between the Allies. A member of the ground crew recalled, "I was an engine and supercharger mechanic with the 83rd Squadron hangar crew. When we first arrived at Duxford and found the hangars which our planes were to occupy in terrible condition. The RAF didn't measure up this time, as the floors of the hangars were thick with oil and sludge, which was left behind for us to clean. I shudder when I think of what might have happened during the cleaning operation. We used raw gasoline right out of the plane tanks and scrubbed the floors with it until the oil had disappeared and then used squeegees to scrape up the muck. One spark and we could have been cremated. God must have been with us as we did survive."

Sergeant James Aicardi: "In a humorous incident, the RAF inspector tried to put the entire hangar crew on charges for defacing the King's property. He became upset and agitated because we drilled holes in the hangar walls and installed an oil heating system for the little coal stoves. It worked fine and we no longer had to interrupt poker games to go out for coal."

The pilots and ground officers were soon comfortably established in their new club building.

Morris K. Lee: "The Officer's Club was on your right as you crossed the road from the hangars. It was an H shaped building with two-story ends. The main stem of the "H" contained a game room, vestibule, lounge, dining room, and bar. The wings were divided into rooms large enough for two or three officers per unit.

"All the officers contributed one pound each ($4.03) to start their Mess. From this investment the Mess Hall cooks and waiters, enlisted men, and the batmen (valets) British civilians were paid. This also stocked the bar and paid for the slot machines. Dividends from the slot machines and the bar soon returned our original investment, paid the help, and gave us additional dividend distributions."

Harding Zumwalt: "We would get up in the morning, have breakfast, and head down to the flight line to hang around the pilots' briefing room, catch up on aircraft recognition, and listen to a great collection of Glenn Miller records. Aircraft recognition was extremely important, because it really could be disastrous if you failed to identify an aircraft quickly and accurately. My RAF training was excellent. We received frequent exams in which aircraft silhouettes were flashed on a screen for 1/10 second intervals for identification. The passing grade was 100%.

"This training paid off for me later in my tour. While our squadron was flying over France one day, my flight dove on some aircraft which we spotted below and ahead of us. However, as I closed on them, I recognized that they were British Typhoons. I aborted the pass and alerted the others of my flight that the two bogies were friendly and to break off the pass. For some reason they didn't hear me, or believe me, and fired on the two Typhoons. There was quite an uproar about the incident when we returned and the pilots involved were transferred out of the squadron. This is a good example of how important speedy and accurate aircraft identification was.

"Most pilots had other responsibilities assigned to them when they were not flying such as: squadron personal equipment officer, maintenance officer, or squadron gunnery officer, etc. Always there was a lot of exercise, much of it in the form of volleyball. I assume that they felt that the exercise was a way of removing nitrogen from our systems before we flew at high altitude, thus reducing the effects of aeroembolism (the bends). For a similar reason we also were instructed not to drink "colas" before flying.

"As for high altitude, at 30,000 feet (plus) in the unpressurized cockpits, I had no real adverse effects other than tingling in my legs once in a while. The oxygen system in the Jug was a "demand" system. This was an improvement over the Spitfire oxygen system where we had to monitor and control the amount of oxygen that we received. I believe that German pilots had a "pressure-demand" system; and, as I experienced in later years in other aircraft, it is very difficult to breath against a system like that at high altitude in an unpressurized cockpit. It even makes speaking difficult. Our "demand" system was easily tolerated and far more comfortable."

Each member of the 78th contributed to the Group entity in different roles.

Staff Sergeant James Aicardi: "The majority of the hangar crew were specialists, e.g. instrument, armorer, electrical, hydraulic, radio, etc. Generally the specialists were also aircraft and engine mechanics, the same as the flightline crew chiefs and their assistants.

"The system went as follows. After a series of tests on entry into the Air Corps, men were selected for various schools. Those who qualified for actual work on the aircraft were sent to Aircraft and Engine school. After completion of school, some were assigned as Flight Engineers for the bombers, some were assigned to squadrons as crew chiefs, and others were sent to Specialist school for advanced training.

"It was the Specialist who pulled the major inspections at one hundred to two hundred hours. They were also responsible for maintaining the operational efficiency of their specialty, as well as trouble-shooting and correcting any malfunction reported by the pilot or crewchief. As they were also A&E men, they assisted major maintenance of aircraft when required.

"The 78th had excellent crews. I remember one 82nd Fighter Squadron armorer received the Legion of Merit for an incredible number of rounds fired in combat without a malfunction or misfire. This was a high award, as usually the Bronze Star was given for such work.

"We believed the pilots' lives were in our hands and it was a responsibility we did not take lightly. You could best understand this deep feeling if you stood beside a crew chief as he just kept staring at the skies long after the other ships had returned and there was no hope that his pilot would ever be back."

James Tudor: "Being a crew chief was a grave responsibility. When your plane took off on a mission, you pondered over every detail as to its mechanical fitness. Had you forgotten to do something such as replacing fuel and oil tank caps, safetying some part you may have replaced or a million other things. That pilot had placed his life in your hands, you cared what happened to him - he was your friend, believe me! It was a long wait and an anxious one until his return. Those that failed to return bore on your mind very heavily. The only slight relief would come when you found out their death was not the result of faulty maintenance.

"The 82nd flight line was located across the landing strip opposite hangar row on the south edge of the field. Some aircraft were parked in concrete revetments and the remainder on the grassy area with metal mats. Two line shacks were utilized by the crews. One long building was used by armorers in one end and the parachute fabric shop on the other end. The other shack was a small one used by ground crews while aircraft were on a mission or awaiting pilots to report for flight

"Wake-up time was normally 4:00 AM and the crews went immediately to the aircraft for pre-flighting. This involved, visual inspection of the aircraft, draining of fuel sumps, checking tires and shock struts, checking for brake leakage, engine run up for magneto check, oil and fuel pressure check, idle cutoff and other mixture control settings, prop controls, and on later aircraft, water injection was also checked. Refueling was performed after the last flight of the day and the tanks were topped off after the pre-flight.

"Much routine maintenance was accomplished on the flight line, such as spark plug changes, oil screen cleaning, magneto and generator changes, and much time was spent mounting and

Group officers relax in the "O" Club dining room with a venison steak dinner, a gift to the unit by a British landowner. (Robert Eby)

checking drop tanks. Inspections were done at night after the missions were completed, on 25-50-75-100 recorded flying hours, with each requiring greater depth as the hours increased. Major inspections were performed in the hangar by specialists and unless unusual problems were found, the aircraft was ready for action the following morning.

"The ground crews lived together so long, we became 'Family', sharing everything, the good, bad and in between. Working long hard hours, we still had lots of fun together. Each flight was put in the same general area in the barracks. The barracks walls were well decorated with pin-up girls such as Betty Grable, Rita Hayworth, Lana Turner, Alexis Smith and Vargas calender girls. Popular dance bands heard on Armed Forces Radio helped relaxing after the day.

"Free time for the troops was available once your plane was secured for the day. We had permanent passes to use when we were off. They just required you to sign out in the orderly room before leaving. A big 6x6 GI truck left the base at 6:00 PM for Cambridge and picked up between 11:00 and 12:00 PM for return to the base. Favorite GI haunts on base were The Sergeant Club, Duffy's Tavern, NAAFI-Red Cross Aero Club, Church Army, and Betty and Bunty's Cafe. Just adjacent to the base were The Plough and John Barleycorn pubs in Duxford village, The Brewery and the Waggon and Horses pubs at Whittlesford Station, and the Flower Pot in Little Abington. Towns farther afield were Hinxton, Sawston, Harston, Shelford, Thriplow, Fowlmere, Great Chesterford, Foxton, Melbourne, and Ickleton. Establishments the GIs were fond of in Cambridge proper included the Red Lion pub on Thrumpington Road, Bull Hotel (Red Cross Club), Dorothy Cafe, American Bar, the Criterion, and the Rex Ballroom.

"There we congregated with many of the bomber crews and hashed out the missions of the day, drank Mild & Bitter, threw darts, and sang. The bars closed at 10:00 PM and after singing 'God Save the King', many of us queued up for fish and chips wrapped in newspapers at places that sold them. It was the best fish and chips I have ever eaten.

"Three day passes were available every two or three months and most went to London on these occasions, where it was popular to stay at the various Red Cross Clubs at Rainbow Corner, Hans Cresent, and the Mostyn.

"A few humorous incidents involved the time our whole flight was quarantined in our barracks for three or four days with measles or something. We couldn't go to town or Duffy's Tavern, so some of our buddies filled up the bathtub with beer so we could enjoy our restriction. Another time, a British truck loaded with kegs of beer had a flat tire close to the flight line. While the driver was gone to get help, some "C" Flight characters stole a keg of his beer, took up the floor in the flight shack, and stashed the keg under the floor. The M.P.s looked everywhere and questioned many people after the driver reported his keg missing, but it was never found. We enjoyed it for many days."

Before the P-47 aircraft entered combat with the 78th, a great deal of maintenance, modification, equipment and supply requirements had to be satisfied. To service a sixteen aircraft fighter squadron combat mission, the following was necessary: Armament Section: eight armorers to load guns, two armament repairmen, a cameraman to load cameras, an ordnance man to load bombs, flares etc.; and supplies which included 25,600 rounds of cal.50 ammunition, sixteen magazines of movie film, two armament tool kits, two spare Browning machine gun kits, and one three-quarter ton weapons carrier.

The Engineering Section required: sixteen crew chiefs, one Flight Chief, two drivers of gas and oil trucks, one electrical specialist, and supplies amounting to 5600 gallons of aviation gasoline, ninety gallons of lubricating oil, five fire extinguishers, five gallons hydraulic fluid, two pounds grease, two gallons supercharger oil, sixteen sets of wheel chocks, two each crew chief stands, 1600 pounds oxygen, one tail wheel tire/tube, two

One of the 78th's favored Pubs, the Waggon and Horses, at Whittlesford station, where the men caught the north south LNER rail line to London or Edinburgh. (Charles Clark)

batteries, one booster pump, one hydraulic jack, two buckets, sixteen spare parts kits, six sets of spark plugs, three battery carts, one air compressor, one oxygen cart/fittings, and one jeep.

Communications Section needs were: ten radio repairmen and supplies of 50% replacement of SCR-522A radio sets complete, and two 24 volt battery carts

.

No praise could be too high for the P-47's engine. The Pratt & Whitney R-2800 Double WASP radial often achieved 1,000 hours of combat time. Perhaps the record for the 78th was held by S/Sgt. Stanley Crawford, 83rd Fighter Squadron, whose aircraft, "Percy", performed one hundred twenty-two missions and three hundred twenty combat hours without an abort or technical fault, which earned him the Legion of Merit.

During March, 1943, after the first European Theater of Operations P-47 missions were flown, a problem with the radios had to be solved. In the 78th, these difficulties were remedied in tests conducted with Major Robert's 84th Fighter Squadron aircraft P-47 WZ-Z. The paint on the bottoms of the engine magnetos were causing ungrounded electrical static in the radios. A first solution of placing mesh wire grounds under the magneto only partly worked. Scrapping the paint completely off the magneto bottom solved the problem.

Major Roberts came up with another finesse to improve the P-47 to which all his crew chiefs adhered. Beeswax was softened with gasoline and all the aircraft were polished to improve their airspeed.

One sergeant recalled "...the great aircraft waxing craze. It was great fun to forget about the wax, and slip and fall off a wing with a full tool box or try to take off the big heavy section of bottom cowl and have it slip and come crashing down on your foot. I believe the wax gave a whole two-five mph increase to the ship."

Robert Eby: "One of the poor things about the P-47 was the gun camera. The crew could set the lens opening before take off, but there was no way of changing it in flight. If we guessed on an overcast day and it turned out to be real bright, the film was overexposed and vice versa. It was very disappointing to the pilots to come back with a destroyed and get no confirmation from Fighter Command because of faulty exposure. The RAF Spitfires had a cockpit switch that gave the pilot two camera settings. We also bent the fiduciary marks back on our cameras because they blocked out a good area of the film."

Pilots returning from a mission sometimes forgot to disarm their gun switch and when they hauled back on the stick in the landing pattern to peel off, they would accidentally fire their guns into the sky. No one was ever hurt, but they got chewed out none the less.

The entrance to "Duffy's Tavern" EM's beer hall, was adorned with this humorous sign. Hall was on east end of Aero Club and served specially brewed beer for the club. Base athletic officer, Captain W.L. "Duffy" Owen was host and chief bullshooter. (Charles Clark)

Harding Zumwalt: "One undesirable thing about the P-47 was the location of the oxygen regulator under the engine primer in the cockpit. Occasionally the primer was subject to causing gas fumes to enter the regulator fresh air intake. As a safety measure I always remained on 100% oxygen before takeoff and after landing. The aircraft was smooth, forgiving, with good braking, and had a comfortable cockpit. It really was a pleasure to fly. You could count on the reliable engine getting you back, regardless of the abuse or damage it had sustained. Before being assigned to me, aircraft #8524 had been flown through the trees at the end of the runway by somebody test-flying it. The abuse seemed to have had no adverse effect on its aerodynamic stability whatsoever. My crew chief, S/Sgt J.D. McAdams, was an excellent mechanic, and I can never recall having to abort a mission for mechanical reasons. My aircraft was always ready to go when needed."

One of the first orders of business upon arrival at Duxford was to paint the new operational code letters of the squadrons on the P-47s. These codes had been used earlier on the 31st Group's Spitfires at Merston, UK before they moved to North Africa. The new codes were: MX for the 82nd, HL for the 83rd, and WZ for the 84th. The new codes went into battle on the first combat mission by the 78th Fighter Group on April 8th when Lieutenant Colonel Peterson and three of 84th Squadron's leaders flew to Debden and joined a fighter sweep by the 4th Fighter Group, along with members of the 56th Fighter Group also making their combat debut. It was an abortive effort recalled at the French coast due to 10/10ths cloud cover after a mere fifteen minutes of sortie time, a big disappointment to the 78th pilots.

A typical Duxford barracks was similar to this 84 FS room. The young GI's interests were hot airplanes and beautiful women as the adorned walls show. (Charles Clark)

Chapter 6

Combat - First Missions

April 13, 1943 marked the auspicious first regular unit combat mission of the 78th when 83rd Fighter Squadron went on a mission with the 4th Fighter Group in the early afternoon and the 82nd Fighter Squadron did a show with the 4th in the early evening. Both were high altitude sweeps dipping into France on the route of Dunkirk, Furnes, St. Omer, Calais.

Charles London: The Germans ignored us completely, not even bothering to shoot flak at us. The only significant happening involved our Group Exec, Lieutenant Colonel Joe Dickman, whose wedding anniversary it was. His cylinder head temperature gauge had been reading real hot and he thought it was an erroneous reading, but it turned out not to be. He blew a cylinder head over Calais and we followed him down as he bailed out two miles offshore and struggled into his one man life raft. About out of fuel, we gave ASR a good fix and they went to pick him up. When he bailed out, he caught his right arm in the chute risers and dislocated it. He couldn't unfasten his raft from his chute harness and pulled out his knife to cut it. Well, he managed to drop it and poke a hole in in his life raft, and he spent the rest of the time trying to pump it up with one hand to keep it inflated. When he saw the ASR boat he waved his arm and blew his whistle, but they were coming at him very slowly with someone on the bow looking at the water, and he couldn't understand why. It turned out he was in the middle of a German mine field. They finally got him out of there and with his arm badly injured, he was sent home."

In defense of Lieutenant Colonel Dickman's crewchief, who suffered the first crew loss of a ship, this was a common problem of the P-47 at the time, in that the engine fuel mixture controls were not automatically connected and an unwary distracted

Major Robert Eby's "VEE GAILE" MX-H 41-6249 gives scale to the 82FS hangar. A 2 bay WWI Belfast type with a trestle roof that survives today. All DX buildings were painted camouflage colors. (Harry Dayhuff)

pilot could easily damage the engine to the failure point as was probable in this case.

Additional short range sweeps, maximum two hours, continued on April 15th, a two mission day on April 17th, April 21st. And April 29 ended the month's combat introduction with a mission strength of thirty-six aircraft, previous missions being of lesser totals. The Group was not yet able to put up a full forty-eight aircraft. A big contribution to the Group strength occurred on April 28, when the second large batch of pilot replacements arrived at DX. This 100% U.S. P-47 trained contingent of eighteen pilots came via Dale Mabry Field, Florida, Camp Kilmer, New Jersey, and the Stone CCRC.

Other personnel vital to Group operations also arrived during April.

Allan B. Cowart: "Having flown in high school and being a licensed pilot, I was in flight cadet's class 42K and got through pre-flight okay, but then I was washed out at Maxwell Field due to a chest calcium condition. Along with eight other such men who were washed out cadets, we went overseas on the Queen Mary and were sent to an RAF training school. We worked really hard and I was one of the 40% who made it through this course for flight controllers. Then I went to hands-on training at Catfoss, near Hull, which was a Free-French Beaufighter base where we learned RAF aircraft controlling. This was far more complicated than just the traffic around an air base. Following that, another friend and I were assigned to an operational base at West Malling, down in Kent, where combat ops were going on. After several months there, having been blessed by the chief flying control officer, and certified to man a tower flying control office, I then went to Duxford.

"One of the first things I remember of DX was looking out of the tower across the field and seeing an absolute army of men marching down the far side. I was a brand new Second Balloon and I could not believe what I was seeing. The Forts from the B-17 fields all around us were just coming back from a big raid that day and I was talking to these guys calling 'May-Day', who were all shot up, and trying to steer them as best I could into our field, and then seeing this army of men walking across. Needless to

LtCol Joseph L. Dickman, Deputy Group CO , beside his P-47. His 84 FS aircraft failed on April 13, 1943, and he bailed out into the sea off Calais, France. ASR picked him up injured . (Robert Eby)

say, I was furious. I dispatched an airman in a jeep to tell whoever that was to get the Hell off the field and to report to me! Well, that's tall stuff for a Second Balloon. The airman came back and said he didn't know who it was but they sure scattered. The man who was leading them said he would call me back.

"About two hours later I did get a call while I was busy with an emergency returning heavy bomber. So instead of the usual phone answering, I could only say 'Hello' and then I jumped back into the microphone in my other hand. The first thing I heard over the telephone was, 'Is that any way to answer a military telephone?' but I couldn't do anything with him as I simply had to go on with the priority aircraft. It was a very unproductive phone conversation. It turned out to be General Murray Woodbury, our new Wing Commander - well, good going, Cowart!

"The next morning General Woodbury showed up in my tower unannounced, and he sat down in a corner and no matter what I tried to do for him, he would have nothing from me. He sat for a good two hours, doing nothing else but observing. Finally he said, 'Lieutenant, what rank does your position call for?' As a Second Lieutenant I wasn't too sure of myself and I said, 'I guess it was Captain, sir.' He said, 'What's your CO's number?' and he picked up the phone and called Captain Jones and said, 'I want you to put Lieutenant Cowart in for promotion immediately.' I never had such a nice apology in my life. That was super.

"Our job was multifaceted. Not only did we control traffic in the air and on the field perimeter, but we had to keep up on the secret TWXs tracking the barrage balloon locations around the country, as we had to sign flight clearances and we had better not route a pilot through them. We had to work closely with the pilot, checking the weather and signing him out on takeoff and find out what happened if he didn't show up at the proper time.

"We normally had two ambulances and a fire truck at readiness all the time by the tower. I had my Jeep parked there with our black and white checks painted on it and my gal's name, 'Pokey,' as the other guys named their planes after their girls. On top of the tower we had a mobile control cubicle that we designed to fold up like an accordion that was painted in black and white checks too, that we planned to use on our move to the continent that didn't take place. It bolted to the tower for high winds and had the neatest B-17 nose cone for a top which had a little trap door to fire flare pistols out of, if a pilot was coming in with his wheels up or we were launching a mission under total radio silence.

"One difficult thing about our traffic control at DX was that just two miles off the end of our runway was the 339th Fighter Group base at Fowlmere. Unless things were absolutely coordinated, we would take off and be right in their traffic pattern. This was classified information you couldn't talk about on the phone, so the FCO over there and I would run our trusted Sergeants back and forth on the twenty minute drive between, as there was no other way and you couldn't expose people to the danger of our making a west takeoff and they making a southeast takeoff at the same time. No one wanted to cause the repeat of a little eulogy ritual we performed whenever we would lose a pilot.

"The Officer's Club had an extremely high ceiling at least twenty feet with a grand big chandelier. We would form a pyramid of people and someone with a candle would write the name of the missing pilot on the ceiling in script with the candle soot. We all felt very deeply about this little exercise."

Before belly tanks, combat range was increased by refueling at advance coastal bases. Most of the 78th's Forty-eight aircraaft are shown at Land's End, RAF coastal base for a show to the Brest Peninsula. MX-G might be Col. Peterson's aircraft. April., 43. (USAF)

Chapter 7

Escort - Big Friends

May, 1943: The Group carried out uneventful missions on May 3rd, 4th, 7th and 13th; the 4th being their first occasion to employ a full forty-eight aircraft on a mission. May 14th however, was another story. On this day the 78th achieved their first solid contact of World War II with the Luftwaffe.

As the group approached their rendezvous with forty B-17s near St. Nicholas, Belgium, the bombers were under attack by FW190s on the sides of their formation. Leaving 84th Fighter Squadron as top cover the 82nd and 83rd Squadrons dove on the Focke Wulf fighters, chasing them into the bomber gunners' fire and enemy flak. The air fight ended in a draw with both sides losing three. Major James J. Stone scored the first 78th victory, flaming an FW190 in a diving attack which found him alone, evading other enemy aircraft and heading for home solo. Captains Robert E. Adamina and Elmer E. McTaggart, and Flight Officer Samuel R. Martinek were not quite so fortunate and all three were shot down in the dogfight with the FWs, McTaggart and Adamina after they dispatched a victory each. Only McTaggart avoided POW status to evade through Spain in June.

May 15th was an unproductive sweep to Amsterdam which was noteworthy for being the first show from an advanced base on the coast at Horsam St. Faith. It produced the loss of another pilot, Second Lieutenant Jack S. Sandmeier, to the dreaded North Sea.

The Group was sweeping the Flushing, Belgium area on May 16th when they ran into one hundred or more FW190s in several bunches. The 84th Squadron dove on about sixty enemy aircraft while the 83rd maintained top cover and the 82nd climbed to counter a high swarm of fifty or more Germans who attempted unsuccessfully to lead them inland. Thus the 84th bore the brunt of the fight with Flight Officer Charles R. Brown catching a string of three FWs. He blew up the tail-end "Charlie" and flamed the second FW before six bounced him. Brown was

Captain Robert Adamina in P-47 41-6219 "ROCKET JO" was the Group's first combat loss (POW) flying another aircraft. Note old type aircraft in-squadron number is being removed for new RAF style squadron codes. (Erwin Boettcher)

The 78th's first KIA, 2Lt Jack Sandmeier, with his crew L-R: James Whitaker ARM, Jay Williams CC, and Robert Conger ARM. The Sphinx proved to be a death symbol on MX-S 41-6218. (James Tudor)

wounded in the foot, leg, and head when his P-47 blew up throwing him clear. He parachuted and was picked up by a German destroyer off Walchern. Major John D. Irvin scored the third kill and First Lieutenant Andrew M. Barba limped home wounded but safe. A second show to Abbeville-St. Omer the same day was uneventful.

Eleven more missions were flown the remainder of the month. They were unfruitful although Second Lieutenant Richard A. Murray was KIA in the sea after bailing out on the 20th. The Group had received its full quota of seventy-five P-47s by the time U.S. Secretary of State Lovett visited the base on the 21st. British boxing champion Tommy Farr and singer Vera Lynn also visited the base during May.

Major James Stone, 83FS CO and his CC, T/Sgt. James Hallmark with their P-47 HL-Z 41-6373. (Robert Eby)

29

Typical of 78th escorted 8AF bombers is B-17F "CABIN IN THE SKY" FC-P 42-30338, a square J 390BG aircraft. Large brilliant recognition symbols aided assembly of bomber and rendezvous of escorts. (John Holzhauer)

But May 26th was the 78th's day to polish up. At 10:15 AM a maroon limousine and escort arrived at Group Headquarters and out stepped King George and Queen Elizabeth on their first tour of an American fighter station. They were met by Major General Ira Eaker, Eighth Air Force Commanding General and Brigadier General Frank Hunter, Eighth Fighter Command Commanding General and went on an inspection of the base. Major Stone's P-47 HL-Z, the first scoring Group aircraft was adorned with the often used wooden platform steps for visiting dignitaries. The royal couple then viewed a thirty-six aircraft Group massed takeoff and formation flypast. Perhaps by Eighth Air Force conspiracy, a formation of seventy-two B-17s was passing high overhead at the same time, one of the largest seen over DX till then. Having charmed the Group, the King and Queen took their leave for an Eighth Air Force Bomber Station. That evening Major Stone gained more attention on a BBC Broadcast to the USA.

With combat underway pilots were still piling up a host of new experiences.

Harding Zumwalt: "In the RAF I was taught to weave in formation, keeping a good lookout behind me. So on my first fighter sweep in the AAF, I flew as I had been trained by the British. Of course, everyone else was flying straight and level, and I needed nearly full throttle to keep up and hold my number four position, while weaving at the same time. I probably flew twice as fast as the others, but felt that I could see lots more of the air activity. However, by my next mission, I had developed the necessary confidence that cross-cover surveillance demands and held my position in the formation without weaving.

"Our procedure for departing on a mission was to assemble the entire Group of forty-eight or more aircraft at the east end of the field. By lining up eight aircraft abreast (i.e. two flights of four) and taking off at fifteen second intervals, climbing straight ahead for two minutes and making a 180 degree turn, all flights would be in formation. The Group Leader would then continue his climb on course.

"This was an extremely effective method of conserving fuel and forming up the Group quickly. Many times the weather was down to five or six hundred feet and we had to assemble quickly before we entered the clouds. The clouds were often so thick that a wingman could hardly see the aircraft next to him. It was up to each flight leader to maintain a constant rate of climb, heading, and airspeed, so that when we climbed out of the cloud tops, sometimes at 25,000 feet, we would be in some reasonable group formation.

"One thing we used to practice a lot in the RAF was 'tactical breaks', a maneuver used to avoid enemy aircraft. This was instilled in our very nature. You might say that we were programmed to react without thinking. On one mission over France for the AAF, when someone called for the flight that I was leading to 'Break', I automatically reverted to my RAF training and pulled the stick so hard that I snap-rolled and got into an inverted spin. When I pulled out, my flight was ahead of me, and I had some difficulty overtaking them. Needless to say, that never happened again. The next time I was more respectful of

King George VI (in RAF) Air Marshal's uniform) and Queen Elizabeth visit Duxford. Brigadier General Frank Hunter, VIII Fighter Command is at the Queen's left. (Alistter Raby)

the aerodynamic limitations of the Jug at high altitude, and made a brisk tight turn to avoid an FW190 closing in on us from our 9 o'clock position.

"Duxford aerodrome had a large grass landing field with no hard surfaced runways, and we simply took off and landed several aircraft at a time. On one trip mine was one of the first flights returning in pretty sorry weather, and we only had mobile control, which was normally used for gear check at the end of the runway, to assist us in landing. Normally we would receive vectors to the field from British radar and upon sighting the field, we turned to a runway heading, set our gyro compass to zero, made four left turns of ninety degrees each, and on our last turn into final, we would descend and land. You had to be familiar with the local area, while flying half instruments and half visual contact with the ground, to arrive in the right location for landing. This time after two unsuccessful attempts and on the third still north of the field, I realized that there were many aircraft up there low on fuel waiting to land, so I turned forty-five degrees to the direction of landing, dove for the field, and spiked the wheels on the grass. Applying brakes as much as I dared to keep from nosing over, I aimed for my parking area and managed to stop in time.

"Once I landed at a Martin B-26 base when I was short of fuel. It was the last time that I ever did that. They serviced our aircraft with an old hand-crank tanker which took forever and caused us to be too late to return to Duxford, where there were no night landing facilities. My flight and I spent a very uncomfortable night sleeping in tents. (A far cry from our plush quarters at Duxford.) After that I made every effort to land back at our home base.

"To further illustrate how critical our fuel supply was on extended missions: one day I ran out of fuel when our flight was in pitchout for landing. Since I was flying number four position, as the flight broke left, I broke right and flying a tight pattern landed before the lead aircraft. Another time I ran out of fuel on touchdown. These are unwise things to do in order to avoid going into other bases, because you have a tendency to be over confident and push the aircraft to its limits. Fortunately, it always worked out for me.

"You never knew with whom you would be coming home. Once my wingman and I were returning to our base alone, when we latched onto a badly shot up B-17 with one of his gears down and one of his engines out, so he was flying quite slowly. I slowed my airspeed and pulled up under his wing where I could see many of the crew waving from the windows. I sent my wingman up for top cover to keep an eye out for enemy aircraft, and we escorted our 'big friend' into a coastal base for a safe emergency landing. Sometimes we escorted or were escorted home by P-38s or P-51s or whatever friendly fighters happened to be handy to give cross-cover.

"After returning from a mission the standard procedure was to go into 'debriefing' and tell the intelligence types what you had seen and experienced during the mission: e.g. number of enemy aircraft destroyed, flak location and intensity, sky cover, etc. When you were finished they would give you a couple shots of bourbon; then you would get on your bicycle and ride back to the club, take a shower, have dinner, go to the bar a while and then go to bed. We were usually pretty tired after flying three or four hours above 25,000 feet so it took little coaxing to get us to go to bed.

"We were closely monitored by the Flight Surgeons and if you stayed too long at the bar at night, they usually figured that you were ready for a rest - and off you went to a 'flak home'; usually a lovely old estate or private home where the wonderful British people or the Red Cross would entertain exhausted air crews and rehabilitate them for returning to fight the air war. I spent a week or two at two different rest homes during my tour. One of them was a large estate in southern England, and the other was a lovely private home in rural Scotland, where the

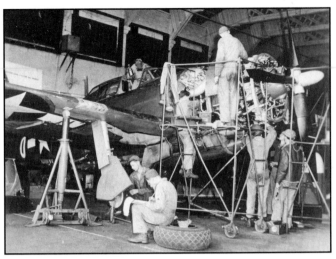

84FS hangar crew giving a Jug a periodic inspection. Airframe men do brakes, engine men have the cowls off, and a painter touches up the cockpit. (Duke Morrison)

83FS communications work on a Jug radio. L-R: Ben Wrenn, Garland Flowers (Comm. section chief), and Charles Powers. The work, laid out in schedules, forms and hourly inspections never ended. (Samuel Beckley)

Instrument maintenance section enlisted men calibrate the pitot tube (wing) with the cockpit airspeed indicator. P-47 42-22482 HL- "5PO" (slang for British money) carries new 200 gal. unpressurized "Baby" belly tank. (Samuel Beckley)

lady of the house prepared my bath water with flower petals in it. I had an extremely good time during both stays - playing golf and doing a bit of fishing. At twenty or twenty-one years of age, we played hard day and night, and did everything with much gusto, very much like the Australians that I had known in the RAF. Because those Aussies played so rough, I made sure to hide all fire extinguishers and any throwable items under the bed before they returned from a night out on the town. This was a matter of self survival. However, I really liked them very much."

June, 1943 : The last day of May 1943, the RAF Operations Book was closed at DX and the base came under full Eighth Air Force control. The first Group parade and decoration ceremony was held on June 3rd with top brass doing the honors. General Frank Hunter handed out the first Air Medals and Purple Hearts to the pilots, while General Eaker and General Longfellow watched along with a distinguished guest, British Secretary of Air, Archibald Sinclair.

The following day the 51st Fighter Control Squadron arrived from the U.S. taking up duty at Sawston Hall with the forming 66th Fighter Wing Headquarters which had arrived the previous day. June 10th marked the departure of the last RAF tenant from DX, the AFDU photo section and five days later Wing Commander S.L. Matthews formally turned the base over to AAF control in a noon parade ceremony. On June 25th the big brass were back to show off the Eighth Fighter Command to their guest, Sir Anthony Eden. The Group's P-47s received the new red border to the U.S. insignia on the planes commencing on June 29th.

During June the pilots went on fourteen missions, nine of which were uneventful. Near Lumbres, France on June 13th the Group ran into twenty enemy aircraft at 10 o'clock above and a fight ensued which left the 78th on the loss side with one pilot KIA and one pilot POW, and a few shot up P-47s limping home.

The services of the 82nd were taken from the group on June 20th when the squadron left for two weeks of offensive patrol training with the RAF. Major Dayhuff took seven aircraft and pilots to Kenley, Captain Oberhansly took seven to Biggin Hill and Captain L. Marshall took seven to Tangmere.

Arriving over Walcheren Island, Belgium on June 22nd to provide withdrawal support to B-17s, the 78th found Focke-Wulf 190s picking away at the straggling bombers and knocked down three for no loss. Two days later on a sweep, the Group was bounced by ME109s between Lille, and Ostend, Belgium and scored one kill. On June 29th the Group took off from Ford Air Base and flew to a rendezvous point over Rouen, France, to

The "Kingpost" leader, Col. Arman Peterson, in his P-47 "Flagari" MX-P 42-7948, named after his hometown, Flagstaff, AZ. He was KIA in this aircraft on 7-1-43. (Noel Assink)

meet the 1st Bomb Wing attacking Villacoublay Aerodrome and escort them home. At the rendezvous they found B-17s in heavy flak under attack by ME109s. Captain London scored his second and third kills by chasing enemy aircraft through the bomber formation and flak and exploding them with his P-47's firepower.

Occasionally supply problems arose with higher Headquarters.

Morris Lee: "The flamboyant Frank O.D. Hunter was Commanding General of the Eighth Fighter Command down at 'Cushy Bushy', the name applied to Bushy Hall. It seems the 87-90 octane aviation gas came under a very short supply situation. So short that Eighth Fighter Command Headquarters issued an order restricting its use. This kinda' struck me in a sensitive place, because I was using our C-78 so extensively I considered it my own personal airplane. The restriction threatened my freedom of action in getting around the Midlands, chasing parts to Wattisham, picking up forced down pilots at coastal airdromes, or just ferrying Headquarters personnel around in the 'Bamboo Bomber' as we called it. Not to mention a few other not so public uses for social calls.

"Shortly after the restriction came out, Colonel Pete got a call from Eighth Headquarters saying we were not complying with the order. He thought a minute before giving them an answer. A few days earlier when the squadrons went to Land's End for refueling on a show the pilots noticed one of General Hunter's aides down there in his private C-45 getting crabs for their Sunday dinner. When Pete referred to the General's airplane being seen at Land's End, the caller hung up the phone and we never heard any more about 87-90 octane gas."

The pilots continued learning of their hostile environment.

Harding Zumwalt: "The British aerial maps were excellent for low level flying. They were so detailed as to even show the location of wooded areas, and houses and other structures. Good maps and good map reading ability were essential to safe low level flying, especially when flying in or near the London area. There were many barrage balloons within that perimeter which were located to protect key installations from strafing attacks by enemy aircraft. These same balloons were also a hazard to allied aircraft, if the pilot was not aware of their location - especially when they were hidden in an overcast.

"One of the things I liked about flying at the northern latitudes was the lower contrail altitudes. Contrails point their misty fingers at friend and foe alike. However, I felt that it was more beneficial to us, since we were operating over the enemy's domain; an enemy who had radar assistance, while we did not, an enemy who could be vectored to oncoming bombers and fighters, while we were outside of our British radar range. The contrails were a great help to us in identifying incoming enemy aircraft.

"On one of my missions I could have sworn that I saw 'pink flak' which I had never seen before. When I returned for debriefing, I carefully avoided the subject completely (for obvious reasons). Apparently other pilots had also seen it, and we began discussing it among ourselves. Finally it was brought to the attention of the intelligence types. Later we found that the German ack-ack crews were using the pink color as marker flak, and we pilots were happy to know that we were not 'ready for the flak farm'."

Allan Cowart: "Peter Pompetti was a favorite of everyone, including me. He did a few things which were not kosher and we loved him for it. Being less disciplined than the AAF would have liked, they could have used a few thousand more like him. When he first joined the group, he was flying number four in a flight. He spotted an FW190 down very low, and kept calling his flight leader, but not getting any response. Finally he just thought, 'The Hell with it,' and broke off from the formation and spit-essed down on the German. When he got back home they just raised Holy Hell with him. Pete kept saying, 'Well, I thought that's what we came to do. Didn't you hear me calling?' They said, 'Yes, but you broke formation and left somebody exposed.' Pete said, 'Exposed to what? My God, we were at 30,000 feet.' This was not the only time he acted in the right spirit of a fighter pilot, but against some of the more conservative regulations which sometimes governed our Group."

July 1943 : July 1 was one of the blackest days in the 78th's history and the men who were there never forgot it. The Group took off at 1510 hours with thirty-two aircraft of the 83rd and 84th led by Lieutenant Colonel Arman Peterson in his P-47 MX-P 42-7948 'Flagari' radio call signed as "Kingpost Leader". The mission was an ordinary RODEO (fighter sweep) under Field Order No. 60. The Group was at 29,000 feet doing 210 mph as they approached the Dutch coast just south of the Hague near Hoek van Holland. Aircraft were spotted higher up ahead, but they turned out to be the 56th also on this sweep. Another large group of aircraft was seen off to the right about 5,000 feet lower. The 78th turned ninety degrees right into them and they were called out as Bandits.

Lieutenant Colonel Peterson leading an 84th flight, dove after an enemy flight of four FW190s as Major Roberts and his flight took on another four 190s flying right of Peterson's targets. It was a dive and zoom attack and after firing, but missing his FWs, Peterson pulled up into a zoom climb straight into the late afternoon sunlight. The sun's glare hid him from the rest of his flight and they lost sight of him. It seems fairly certain that at this decisive moment, when he did not have any wingman to cover him, that he dove again at the enemy and was killed instantly by an unseen enemy fighter bouncing him in his dive.

He gave no farewell on the radio and no one saw his aircraft plunge into the North Sea off Ouddorp, Holland. One moment he was their beloved commander diving with them into a pack of enemy aircraft and the next he had vanished forever. Captain Harold Stump did report a P-47 passing him in a steep dive as he pulled up from his first attack and several others called out parachutes, but they were probably from enemy aircraft shot down by Lieutenants Madole and Byers, and Captain Davis as the fight went on and the Group chased the enemy aircraft southwest across the Dutch Islands.

Captain John Irvin and his wingman, Lieutenant Pat "Max" Maxwell got into compressibility speed in their dives after their quarry. Irvin pulled out quickly, but Maxwell was caught in the demon clutch until he almost crashed. He was only able to save himself by the last ditch attempt of firing his guns, which changed the airflow over his wing enough for his controls to grab the air and allow his recovery. After scattering in the chase, the Group made their way home to DX landing at approximately 1750 hours.

As the word quickly passed around the base that 'Colonel Pete' was gone, the whole Group took on an air of personal grief. No 78th Commander was ever so well-liked and admired as the pleasant young twenty-eight year old Colonel had been. For the next week pick-up flights of P-47s left on futile sea searches. The score tally of three destroyed, one probable and two damaged was small recompense for so great a loss. Major James J. Stone was promoted to Lieutenant Colonel and made acting Group Commander until the new man arrived and Captain Jesse C. Davis was promoted to Major and took over the 83rd from Stone..

The following day the 82nd returned from their detached service to join the mourning Group, and then Bob Hope and Francis Langford brought their USO show to DX. Bob played one of his toughest houses during the show as pilots got up and left to take their turns on search patrols.

Colonel Pete's callsign, 'Kingpost', was permanently retired and the missions went on as before with Lieutenant Colonel Stone now leading them as 'Graywall Leader'. On July 12th Lieutenant Colonel Melvin F. McNickle arrived to take up command of the Group.

Lieutenant Colonel McNickle was an able leader and pilot who had experience in England from Autumn of 1941 when he was an observer/liaison officer to RAF 601 Fighter Squadron at Duxford. His twin brother commanded the 350th Fighter Group in North Africa.

On July 14 Major Harry Dayhuff led the Group to Hornoy, France where they made rendezvous with B-17s bombing Amiens/Glisly Aerodrome. Near Montreiul as he led the 82nd and the 84th into a large group of FW190s heading for the bombers at LeTouget more enemy aircraft joined the fight. First Lieutenant Donald Jackson was killed when he was believed to be struck by gunfire from the bombers in the chase.

In the ensuing fight, Second Lieutenant August DeGenero was bounced by two Focke-Wulf 190s that shot out the right side of his canopy and instrument panel causing shell splinter wounds in both his hands, ankles and right knee. At first he thought he was going to die but he quickly recovered and got damned mad, diving to 2,000 feet into a swarm of FWs where he shot one down from 100 yards, probably destroyed another and damaged a third. Then he lit out for the English Channel, ducking into low clouds to evade three more FWs that followed him almost to the coast. All this time DeGenero was flying his plane with no instruments and controlling it with forearms only. The right aileron was gone and the right wing and tail were badly damaged. A crash landing was out because he'd unhooked his safety belt in combat and couldn't re-hook it.

Afraid to bail out over land for fear his plane would fall on the coastal town of Newhaven, which he could see below, he spotted a fishing boat offshore and headed for it. The canopy was jammed by the FWs' shell hits, so he was obliged to batter it open with his injured hands. He finally left the plane, managing to pull the ring and hit the sea near the fishing boat,'Little Old Lady'. The crew quickly pulled him aboard and headed for shore. Had the fishermen not responded promptly DeGenero might have drowned because he was unable to undo his chute harness and was suffering considerable blood loss. Later in hospital he was awarded the DSC for valor and sent home to recover from his wounds.

Bob Hope and Francis Langford try out Bob Eby's MX-H "VEE GAILE" 41-6249 during their USO show visit to Duxford. Playing just after Col. Peterson's loss, they found a tough audience. (Eby/Assink)

Captain George Hays' polished WZ-K "PAPPY" 41-6243 slides in close for a B-17 photog. The Jug sports the flashy red-edged US star/bar later changed to a blue border. (Robert Eby)

The Wolves' Den, a Luftwaffe Airdrome in France is seen far below the bomber stream altitude. The enemy enjoyed excellent permanent facilities on their captured French fields. Hangars and technical shops are grouped upper left. (Garry Fry)

Chapter 8

Babies - Belly Tanks

Ten more routine and uneventful missions followed in July until the 30th when events took a sharp upswing. A few days previous a large number of big crates arrived, which yielded the new two hundred gallon unpressurized auxiliary gas tanks, belly-tanks, or "Babies" as they came to be called, which were being debuted by Eighth Fighter Command The planes were rapidly modified to accept the tanks which would permit a round trip range thirty miles deeper into enemy airspace than the 8th's fighters had previously gone.

Early P-47 missions without belly tanks averaged one hour and forty-five minutes to the maximum of two hours and five minutes. With the seventy-five gallon pressurized tanks, missions were from two hours thirty minutes to two hours and fifty minutes. The 165 gallon tanks gave another forty-five to fifty minute range and with two 108 gallon wing tanks the Group flew shows up to five hours and thirty minutes. The 165 gallon tanks were metal and in short supply. The treated pressed-paper 108 gallon wingtanks gave further range, but they also caused some problems. The grass field at DX was uneven and it was not unusual to punch a hole in the tank on takeoff. The paper tanks were sometimes difficult to drop in combat, because they occasionally froze at high altitude. One of the tricks used to jettison a recalcitrant tank was to have a wingman slip his wingtip between the tank and the wing, and knock it off the pylon. Late in 1943 the Group was using about 480 tanks a month and tried to keep a six to eight mission backstock on hand. Fighter units were assigned their escort relay points by the size of the tanks they carried on the show, which dictated their range.

As the pilots went into briefing at about 0800 hours on July 30th, they knew it was going to be an unusual mission. The ground crews knew that the new drop tanks denoted a long mission. The 4th Fighter Group had broken the ice by going into Germany two days earlier. The big briefing map showed it was to be withdrawal support for one hundred eighty-six B-17s going to Kassel, Germany. Lieutenant Colonel McNickle was leading the show which took off at 0854 hours. As the Group approached the enemy coast, the new belly tanks were dropped fifteen miles offshore of Hoek Van Holland and the 78th climbed to penetration altitude as they coursed over Rotterdam and Nijmegen, entered Germany near Kleve, and headed for the Rendezvous Point at Haltern, Germany. Nearing the rendezvous, the bombers were sighted at 11 o'clock twenty miles north and the Group turned left at 28,000 feet, four thousand feet above their charges and began to take up station.

Shortly after the turn, the 78th lost its second Group Commander in less than a month. Lieutenant Colonel McNickle was flying WZ-M 42-7961, the same aircraft in which Lieutenant Maxwell had experienced a compressibility dive. Whether that incident left the plane with an inherent problem no one knows, but the oxygen system failed and McNickle lost consciousness. His aircraft collided with his 84th Squadron wingman, First Lieutenant James Byers, near Winterswijk, Netherlands. Others saw Byers bail out, but he died in the mishap. When McNickle regained consciousness, he was still strapped in his cockpit in the wreckage of his up

LtCol. Melvin F. McNickle assumed command of the 78th after Arman Peterson's loss. (G. Fry)

side down, crashed P-47, with the Dutch Underground working at his removal. He had two broken shoulders and other serious wounds. After radioing England for directions, the Resistance turned him over to the Germans for medical treatment. Proper care was denied for several days in an attempt to get information. Finally he was treated and confined in a POW camp until VE-Day.

The 78th had no time to think on their leader's loss, as about one hundred enemy aircraft were attacking the B-17s from the front and the rear. The rear attackers were firing their new rockets into the bombers as the 84th came diving in behind and upsun. Deputy Group CO Lieutenant Colonel James Stone, also flying with the 84th eased in behind an ME109 and blew him up as his wingman, Lieutenant Maxwell, flew through the pieces of the kill. Captain Jack Price exploded an FW190 and then he and his wingman, Lieutenant John Bertrand, each shot down another Focke Wulf in their second attack on the same batch of enemy aircraft. Major John Irvin flamed two ME109s in formation abreast firing rockets far behind the bombers. Flight Officer Peter Pompetti made another attack on three 109s. The right one dove away and the leader took hits and just floated along on his back as Pompetti turned to the left man, pulling in behind at fifty yards and firing with the few guns he had yet working. Smoke poured out of the Messerschmitt and pieces fell off. The pilot was probably dead as Pompetti pulled up to avoid colliding and lost sight of the disabled enemy aircraft.

The first 8AF, Ace, Capt. Charles P. London, 83FS, and his CC , T/Sgt. Percy M. Scott, on the port wing of their P-47 "EL JEEPO" HL-B 41-6335. The aircraft was lost on 2-22-44 over Holland as HL-A. (Charles London)

Technical Sergeant Glenn Rowe assists his pilot, Major Harold Stump in their P-47 "BAD MEDICINE" WZ-C 41-6259. Broom symbols denote fighter sweeps and bomb symbols define bomber support missions. (Russell Hunter)

Major Norman Munson, 82FS, in his MX-C. The nude artwork was soon censored and supplied with an evening gown, the better to impress a constant stream of visiting VIPs. DX was luxurious for a base and near to HDQRS .(Robert Eby)

Major Harry Dayhuff, 82FS FS CO, on his P-47 "HUN RAMER" MX-Z 41-6618. A kill cross for his 7-30-43 victory and a new cartoon increase its markings. (Warren Kellerstedt)

Major Jesse Davis, 83FS CO, with his CC, M/Sgt. Alberf Ron, and his ACC, S/Sgt Roderick Wallace, as they ready their P-47 "OWLEY AND TOBE" HL-X 41-6402. (Robert Eby)

Major Jack Price, 84FS, in his P-47 WZ-A 41-6270 "FEATHER MER-CHANT". Jack did a 78th tour, went home, and came back to the ETO to lead a squadron in the 20FG. (Russell Hunter)

Major Eugene Roberts recovered from the first dive behind the bombers and flew alongside the bomber formation heading for the front attackers. He came up behind an FW190 going in the same direction and shot him down in flames. Continuing on, he repeated the kill on another FW with the same result. Reaching the front of the bomber formation, Roberts caught an ME109 peeling off to attack head-on at the B-17s and also sent him down in flames. As Roberts was dispatching his target's wingman, Flight Officer Glenn Koontz set fire to another which went into a death dive.

The 82nd had followed the 84th diving on the enemy aircraft. Major Harry Dayhuff found an ME109 making side attacks on the bombers and blew him up. The German pilot must have been a rookie as he was totally oblivious to the P-47s early firing. First Lieutenant Arthur Richie dove after an FW190 and fired all his ammo into him, leaving the enemy aircraft belching smoke in a dive.

The 83rd was right with the others and Captain Charles London, their top scorer, came up dead astern of two FWs at 26,000 feet exploding one which went down in flames. Then London climbed back to 28,000 feet and dove on an ME109 which also blew up. First Lieutenant William Madole caused an enemy aircraft to dive away with his first attack. Climbing back up in a vertical bank, he saw an FW on a P-47's tail and rolling, he raked the FW with hits, nose to tail. Pulling up and going into his second attack on the enemy aircraft Madole witnessed the pilot take to his parachute.

Running low on fuel by this time, the Group was forced to break off escort and head for home from near Tiel, Netherlands. Lieutenant Quince Brown was chased to the deck by two FWs which he soon out-distanced. Following the rail lines near Leiden, he saw a train and shot it up in what likely qualified as the Eighth Air Force's first strafing attack of World War II. Crossing the coast Brown dropped so low to the water to avoid the shore batteries that he hit the water with two of his prop blades, bending their tips, but still making it home.

First Lieutenant Paul Lehman was on his way out of enemy airspace when flak struck his engine. The staunch P&W held together long enough for him to get out over the sea to bail out. The British ASR was there in about an hour and a half with one of their cherished Walrus amphibians. Lehman got back to DX over two hours after the rest and received a riotous reception. First Lieutenant William Julian was forced to belly-land his damaged P-47 at West Wickham successfully. Second Lieutenant Warren Graff was shot down in the air battle and evaded capture to return in September.

When Intelligence finished debriefings, they knew this near three hour mission was one for the record books. The string of pioneer "Firsts" was significant and included the following: first Group belly tank show; first Group penetration of Germany; first Eighth Air Force Fighter Ace, Captain Charles Pershing London; first Eighth Fighter Command strafing attack, Lieutenant Quince L. Brown; first Eighth Air Force Triple Victory, Major Eugene P. Roberts; highest Eighth Air Force mission victory score to date (sixteen); and the first Eighth Fighter Command Group to score in double digit figures. Major Roberts was shortly awarded the DSC for valor during this mission.

The statistics for July showed the increased pace of combat with nineteen missions, twenty-one victories, five missing in action, one wounded in action, two crash landings, and two air-sea-rescues.

The Group was not ignored by the visiting firemen either. On the 29th Edward V. "Captain Eddie" Rickenbacker stopped off on his way home from the USSR and gave the personnel a grand pep talk.

Sad as the month was in some respects, there was also a little humor.

Allan Cowart: "A little put-down occurred. A very high ranking person who shall have to remain nameless, flew with the Group. He was going to come over and show everyone how to win the war, I guess. He went off on his first fighter sweep, which was, as I recall, at 30,000 feet some place around Belgium or further inland a little bit. This person was flying the Number three position in a flight, as protected as he could

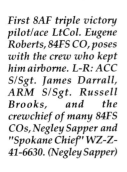

First 8AF triple victory pilot/ace LtCol. Eugene Roberts, 84FS CO, poses with the crew who kept him airborne. L-R: ACC S/Sgt. James Darrall, ARM S/Sgt. Russell Brooks, and the crewchief of many 84FS COs, Negley Sapper and "Spokane Chief" WZ-Z-41-6630. (Negley Sapper)

be, and when he hit the contrail level, and started pulling streamers, he began yelling on the operational channel, where radio silence was supposed to be observed. He was calling to the leader saying, 'You're on fire! You're on fire!' This goes on for a little and finally someone in the back, it could have been Pompetti (I don't know, but I wouldn't put it past him) says, 'You idiot! Shut up! Those are contrails!' Well, this person never got overanxious again."

August 1943 : The first few days of this month, attended by bad weather, were spent reorganizing the Group leadership again after Lieutenant Colonel McNickle's loss. On August 4 Lieutenant Colonel James J. Stone moved once more into the Group Commander slot from his role as Group Executive/ Deputy Group Commander, and three days later Harry J. Dayhuff was promoted to Lieutenant Colonel and given the Group Exec./Deputy job. Dayhuff's command of 82nd Squadron was assigned to new Major Jack J. Oberhansly. A new support unit for the 78th arrived from the States on August 12th in the shape of the 23rd Station Complement Squadron, but the big news of the day was Lieutenant Colonel Stone leading his first show as permanent Group CO. The planes carried new metal seventy-five gallon belly tanks to meet the bombers at Heinsberg, Germany and provide escort back to the Dutch coast at Flushing/Antwerp, where a few enemy aircraft attempted an easily thwarted attack on the bombers which resulted in a scoreless draw.

.On August 17th, just as the 84th was breaking escort near Aachen, Germany to head home, nine twin-engine aircraft were spotted trying to sneak up below and behind the bombers for a rocket attack. Major Eugene Roberts and Flight Officer Peter Pompetti were able to catch an ME110 and ME210 respectively and shoot them down. Lieutenant Koontz collided with Robert's victim and lost eighteen inches from his left stabilizer, but flew his aircraft home.

Major Eugene Paul Roberts became the second 78th ace on August 24th. The mission was to escort B-17s hitting an Air Depot at Villacoublay/Paris, into the target from Dieppe on the coast and back out, with a sideline escort to a small force neutralizing the German airfields at Evreux in the same vicinity. At 1800 hours on the leg of Rouen to Evreux, Roberts attacked two enemy aircraft climbing parallel with and at 1 o'clock from the bombers. Engaging the FW190 on the right he registered many hits until breaking off to avoid colliding. This enemy aircraft broke into flames spinning down. Roberts quickly switched his fire to the left enemy airplane hitting it from behind causing it to smoke and explode.

Even routine flights carried an element of danger. During staging to a coastal airfield for refueling on the show of August 27th, Second Lieutenant Robert F. Brower got into a spin in clouds and crashed to his death near Henlow airfield by Letchworth.

August 29th was noteworthy because the 78th received a new top boss when Lieutenant General William Kepner took over the Eighth Fighter Command from General Hunter.

Weather played a part in keeping the month's missions at eleven and plain luck kept the scoring to five kills.

At this stage of the war the supply lines in England were not always as efficient as they later became. The infant Eighth Air Force was still struggling in some ways.

Charles London: " Amazingly enough we couldn't get new spark plugs. We had to use reconditioned spark plugs in our P-47s and they were only supposedly good for about twenty-five hours. Normally after one mission they'd have to change them and with that big heavy engine cowl, it was horrendous to have to change them every time they were taken up.

"So we found out that six miles from us was a big bomber base called Bassingbourn, and that they used the same spark plugs we did. We used to escort them and I went over and talked about our problem with one of their squadron COs. He said, 'Well, you fly over here for lunch at the Officer's Club and when you go back, we'll have a whole bunch of spark plugs on the floor of your airplane.' So whenever we needed plugs for our Jugs, I'd fly over there and have lunch and when I came back, we had all the brand new spark plugs we could use. What a hell of a way to have to fight a war, but that's the way it worked out! We had a little saying there, 'In God and Pratt & Whitney we trust!'"

September 1943 : General of the AAF, "Hap" Arnold was in England inspecting the Eighth Air Force and getting a first hand look at the European Theatre air war. He arrived at DX on the morning of September 4th to check out the 8th's prime exhibit station and to inspect a complete selection of AAF and RAF aircraft types which had been flown in for his review. A squadron of the 56th flew over and landed at DX as an added attraction. General Arnold was introduced to the three leading Aces of the American forces, Eugene Roberts and Charles London of the 78th, and Gerald Johnson of the 56th. General Arnold presented Bulova wrist watches to all three.

A couple of days after General Arnold's visit, a Polish Spitfire pilot of the RAF climbed into his Spit parked next to the control tower, warmed the engine slightly, and took off full throttle toward the south end of the 84th flightline. He almost cleared the western-most crew shack, but his tailwheel caught the roof and cartwheeled his aircraft into the ground minus its tail assembly.

Ernest E. Stroud: "Being close to the crash, we 84th crews ran to help. A small amount of smoke was coming from the overturned Spitfire and reaching it , we found the pilot strapped in upside down, somewhat dazed and being rapidly drenched with leaking aviation gas. We quickly pushed the harness release button and pulled him from the cockpit while the guys lifted the fuselage a bit to get him through the side hatch. Then the emergency equipment arrived and we backed off. Later the pilot came around and thanked us for dragging him out of the plane before it caught fire. I picked up a set of RAF wings that came off his uniform as we pulled him from the plane"

The shack, an obstruction to the flying area, was shortly torn down.

Missions during the first three quarters of September were a mixture of sweeps and escorts, and were mostly uneventful, although losses still occurred. The September 22nd mission return over the North Sea saw Second Lieutenant Quentin Charlton run out of gas and bail into the ocean. ASR failed to locate and he perished.

The next day, thirty of the most senior pilots were decorated with the Distinguished Flying Cross.

This 83rd FS P-47C-2-RE named "UP STAIRS CAT" was flown by Lt. James E. Stokes. CC was S/Sgt Beauchamp and Sgt McCord. (J.E. Stokes)

Chapter 9

Germany - Deep Escort

At 0845 hours on September 27, 1943, forty-five Thunderbolts led by Lieutenant Colonel Harry Dayhuff took off from Hethel advance base as one of six Eighth Fighter Command groups assigned to give withdrawal support to two hundred forty-six B-17s of the 1st and 3rd Bomb Divisions attacking industrial targets at Emden, Germany. The Group was flying for the first time with new 108 gallon paper composition belly tanks, which increased their range to 400-plus miles (200 odd miles into German territory with an additional ten minutes or so of dogfighting gas available).

The 78th crossed into Holland at Den Helder, 130 miles from the United Kingdom and headed for the bomber rendezvous point ten miles west of Emden at the usual escort heights: 83rd at 27,000 feet; 84th at 29,000 ft. and the 82nd at top cover of 32,000 feet. Routine radio jamming interference by the Germans was making the bomber-fighter channel difficult to decipher.

As the Group approached the B-17s which were making a wide 180 degree swing away from the targets, two large fireballs fell from the bomber formation. As the fighters came in over the rear bomber boxes, they saw approximately thirty enemy aircraft firing rockets and making 6 o'clock attacks. The German fighters were at the bomber altitude of 25,000 feet, several thousand feet below the 78th as all three squadrons plunged to the attack.

The 83rd got to the enemy first. Everett Powell and Jesse Davis both hit their ME109 targets with flashing white armour-piercing incendiary strikes in cockpits and wingroots, sending the Messerschmitts spinning down out of control in flames. With so many enemy aircraft milling about the two pilots then quickly pulled up and left their victories to regain essential altitude.

Next the 84th Fighter Squadron reached the enemy and Harold Stump shot up an ME109, but couldn't stay on him.

Colonel Stone in the briefing room giving same. He uses the map and mission data board to provide mission details. Times, R/T callsigns, compass-headings, etc. fill the board for withdrawal support from France. Intell. Off's watch right. (Robert Eby)

After a group briefing, 83FS pilots pile into a Dodge Personnel-carrier and head for a small squadron briefing. L-R: G. Boteler, H. Askelson, two unknown, D. Wilkes, R. Knapp, M. Putnam, C. Peal, (William May)

His wingman, Pete Pompetti, finished off the disabled Messerschmitt, setting it on fire with hits all over the aircraft. Stump continued on under another 109 and pulled up firing. The 109 seemed to stop in mid-air and exploded as Stump zoom-climbed past the target. Pompetti next caught an ME110 picking on a straggling B-17 and scored hits. Pompetti skidded up above to the right and slowed to look down and see the pilot slumped over the stick, and the gunner out of sight. The ME110 went into a slow dive away toward the earth.

Meanwhile John Irvin got astern of an inverted ME109 and gunned him, lots of white smoke issuing from the enemy aircraft. Irvin broke off to get back up into another 78th flight with cross-cover. Quince Brown was following his leader, Eugene Roberts, who couldn't get into good position on an ME109. Brown, however, was able to get good deflection, closing to dead astern, and scoring hits. The enemy aircraft spouted flame and black and white smoke, pulled up into a stall, and fell off as Brown quickly rejoined his flight.

The 82nd Fighter Squadron was giving top cover and dropped last on the enemy aircraft. Jack Oberhansly blew some chunks off of his first ME109 as a probable kill, and saw another 109 below to his right. He swung around and down, raking him nose-to-tail with strikes. The German plane reared up vertically and fell into a vicious spin with smoke and flame coming from its engine.

The Duxford Jugs regrouped as best they could and stayed with the bombers beating off attacks until they got low on fuel and then broke escort forty miles off the Dutch coast. Rather split up and short of fuel, the 78th returned to scattered British coastal airdromes. The mission results showed the Group with nine kills and no losses, top scorers among the four Eighth Fighter Command groups engaged in action this day. It was Lieutenant Colonel Dayhuff's last mission for a while with the group, as he went on detached duty to Eighth Fighter Command, and Eugene Roberts took over as Group Deputy/Executive Officer. Major Jack C. Price moved up to command the 84th Fighter Squadron. September ended with fourteen shows, nine kills, and one KIA. One very welcome benefit from the new belly-tanks and increased range, was that they allowed the fighters to retrace the escort routes more than once and aid straggling bombers unable to keep up. This comment appears often in the month's records.

High octane aviation gasoline was important to the group in many ways besides keeping the planes flying. One enlisted man noted that, "We used to drain twenty-five gallons of 100 octane into a fifty gallon can from the flightline tanker-truck to clean our clothes. They dried in thirty minutes and no one gave any thought to the possibility of lead poisoning in those days, and it did an excellent job on the clothes.

"However, one day some cook spilled twenty-five gallons of 100 octane in front of our radio shack out on the east end of the field. Some guy flipped a lit cigarette on it and it burst into flame. Geez, you should have seen us go out the windows. The tower saw the flames and sent the fire truck down, but by that time the gas had burned off about thirty square feet of field and gone out. The firemen came up and said, 'Where's the fire?' and we said 'What fire?' because we weren't supposed to be using 100 octane to clean our clothes. The tower was flabbergasted, but our clothes were clean."

Donald Silveus: "Our 84th armament shack where I was armament inspector, was literally soaked from walls to floor with grease and flammable solvents from cleaning the squadron machine guns day and night. On this particular day one of the guys drew his cleaning rod out of a gun barrel so roughly that a spark was thrown off which fell to the floor. In an instant the sodden floor ignited in a flash fire and everyone bailed out of the shack for dear life as it swiftly became totally engulfed in an inferno. By the time the firemen got it under control the shack had burned to the ground."

October 1943: The first four missions of October were routine with little of note to report. October 10th produced better activity. Scheduled for withdrawal support, the Group arrived at the rendezvous point near Ochtrup/Rheine, Germany at 1530 hours. Radio interference was very bad and the bombers had been attacked heavily before the rendezvous. They were broken and scattered. The 84th found fifteen twin-

Armorers of the 78th thread 50 cal linked ammo into a Jug's wing trays. Ammo loading was about 425 rounds a gun. The shell sequence was 2 armor piercing, 2 incendiary, and 1 high explosive. Ammo finish was warned by 5 tracers 50 rds from empty. (AFM)

engined and eighteen single-engined enemy airplanes picking on straggling B-17s at fifteen to twenty thousand feet and whipped into diving attacks to clear them away.

Philip Larson picked out an ME110 and waited slightly for two P-47s to clear in front of him and then blew large pieces out of its right engine and fuselage, leaving it in a slow death dive. Charles Silsby chased another ME110 into the bomber propwash and saw the enemy aircraft emit smoke, then swung over onto an ME210 exploding its right engine. Eugene Roberts found an ME110 abusing a stricken B-17 and closed fast in a dive smothering the enemy aircraft with strikes before breaking violently to avoid a collision. Pulling up to 18,000 feet Roberts dove again on an ME210 positioning to hit a Flying Fortress and closed to point blank range getting hits all over the enemy. Again Roberts had to pull up sharply to avoid ramming as the ME210 fell apart on its right side and its tail broke off. Pieces of wreckage damaged Robert's wingman's aircraft flown by Glenn Koontz. The victories brought Robert's score to eight making him top Eighth Air Force ace.

October 14th went down in history as BLACK THURSDAY, the day Eighth Air Force lost sixty bombers on the infamous Schweinfurt Raid. The 78th was unable to fly that mission due to bad weather preventing its takeoff. A bit of the day's horror came back to the base when a B-17 force-landed at DX with shot-up landing gear, a missing wheel, and carrying a dead bombardier. This day the Luftwaffe employed a new tactic of engaging the escort fighters on their landfall forcing them to drop tanks early, thereby limiting range. However, the Eighth Air Force quickly countered this tactic by allowing only a limited number of fighters to break off against the enemy.

The 78th was recalled at the French coast on October 22nd, due to a late field order putting them too far behind. The aborted show was the first time the Group flew as two thirty-six aircraft, 78A and 78B Groups. Each Squadron put up twenty-four aircraft with one Squadron and half of the third in each A-B Group. As the pilots assembled prior to the second A-B Double Group mission on October 24th, they received a morale boosting pep talk given by Marshal of the RAF, Lord Trenchard. The mission was a novel first in that the Group was escorting fast Martin Marauder B-26s on their target area route. This concluded the month's combat tally of nine missions, seven victories, and the loss of two pilots, one in combat and the other on a training flight.

By late October, 1943, the buildup of Eighth Fighter Command groups was growing at a healthy rate.

Captain Jack Oberhansly, 82FS Ops Off., in the cockpit of his MX-X 42-7883 "IRON ASS", with his CC, T/Sgt. John Kovacovich (L) and ACC, Cpl Conrad Gerhardt(R). The aircraft was lost 2-10-44. Note tiny sweep symbols on cowl. (Robin Gray/AFM)

First Lt. Peter E. Pompetti, 5 1/2 victory ace, on his P-47 WZ-R 41-6393 "AXE THE AXIS" Very aggressive and well liked in the group. He spent a year and a month as a POW after 3-17-44. (Duke Morrison)

Morris Lee: "My old P-40 flight commander from Hamilton Field, Colonel Avelin Tacon, had arrived in England on October 19th with his own 359th Fighter Group at East Wretham. Through sources I learned of Tacon's whereabouts and I, a Captain, decided to go visit the Colonel. To set the stage of this story, it should be known that Wing Headquarters also had a C-78 based at DX that General Woodbury used for commuting to Fighter Command Headquarters and for inspecting his 66th Fighter Wing stations.

"On the appointed day for my visit, I just took off in our Group C-78 without a flight plan and without notifying Colonel Tacon that I was coming to visit him. As I circled his field and got a green light for landing, I noticed the airplanes neatly arrayed on the flight lines and everything appeared unusually shipshape.

"I didn't give the field condition much thought and just landed and taxied up to where a crew chief was directing me to park near the control tower. While filling out the form in the cockpit, I looked out the side and suddenly decided I'd better forget bookkeeping until later. A staff car had pulled up to my left and a half dozen officers in full dress uniform were alighting from it. I thought I'd better get out and see what's going on. As I got out of the plane to see a little better, here was Colonel Tacon with a cortege of officers behind him. He took one look at me, and with a half smile and half frown, said,'Maizie, you son of a bitch!'

"After a good laugh and an introduction to his staff, he explained that General Woodbury was due by air to inspect his station. They had mistaken my C-78 for the General's. As soon as the explanation and a few short reminiscences were over, I decided I'd better get out of there before the real impostor showed up. I managed to get back in the air before the General arrived."

The airplanes were the pivotal link between the crews and the pilots. Sometimes the crews had to protect the plane and the pilot from himself. One sergeant noted, "There were times when, after working all night on an engine change, you'd see this ship supposedly being flown for 'slow-timing' come barreling across the field pushing fifty inches of mercury. Then while trying to restrain the crewchief and take away the wrench he was threatening to use on the pilot, you'd see little white vapor puffs trailing the ship. At this point you realized a horrible truth and could only say, 'My God, now he's playing with the water injection!

"Some pilots were just big kids with a big plane. Generally the crew chiefs knew how to handle them, especially the older chiefs. In one incident a chief called for me to help him fix a sluggish prop. I went out to the flightline and determined the

Captain Paul W. Saffold, 84 FS B-Flight CO in his WZ-Q 42-7894 "REBEL". His crew is L-R: ACC S/Sgt. Gerald Shope, CC T/Sgt. Frank J. Kulis and S/Sgt. Donald Ring. (Paul Saffold)

prop governor was not working properly. We drew some gas from the tank petcock into a bucket to try and soak the governor's shaft free. According to tech orders you were supposed to put a metal plate over the prop opening when you had the governor out to work on it, and I had left the plate in the shop. I was going to get it when I saw the chow truck coming and the chief said to forget the plate and just put a rag over it to keep out the dirt and wire it down. We'd let the governor soak and check it after chow. He pulled the status sheet and red-lined the aircraft to show it was not to be started.

"On the way in he told me that this new pilot was driving him crazy by always fooling around the ship. The kid had already changed the gun convergence pattern a couple of times since he started flying the ship. After chow as we were coming up to the ship we saw the prop turn over and the engine rev up. I yelled to the chief to get it stopped. It was too late as a geyser of oil shot into the air and all over the ship and into the cockpit. finally the pilot cut the engine and as he got out we saw he was covered with oil. He just stared at us with a surprised and dumbfounded look on his face. I thought, 'Boy, now we are in big trouble.' The next thing I knew the chief jumped on the hood of the jeep and pointed his finger at the pilot and yelled, 'You're going to be in big trouble, Lieutenant, when the Engineering Officer hears about how you damaged my ship. Damn it! Didn't you check the status sheet?' Much to my surprise the pilot apologized and asked the chief to avoid telling anyone about it. Of course the chief had no intention of telling anyone and let him off with great magnanimity. We drove the pilot back to the BOQ and then we cleaned up the ship which was undamaged. I told the chief it was lucky he had red-lined her. He laughed and said he always did that to protect himself from those crazy kids. He was glad it happened because now he wouldn't have any more trouble with this kid.

"We were always looking for innovations to give the pilot an edge. One such was 'The Great Wastegate Conspiracy'. Taking a hypothetical case to protect the innocent, it first started with a jeep pulling up to the hangar and a pilot and crewchief getting out and looking around like they were selling hot watches. The pilot motions one of the hangar crew to the jeep and the conversation goes something like this, 'Sergeant, I understand you guys know a way to increase engine boost. I got jumped and couldn't shake the Kraut even with water injection. He stayed right on my tail.' The sergeant says to the crew chief, 'You know what can happen to your ship, first we are breaking regulations by exceeding war emergency power for the engine, second we can all get busted,

and third, suppose he blows the turbine or a cylinder, even if you get back the ship will be a wreck.' The pilot says, 'If I get a 20MM shell in the ass, the ship will be a wreck anyway.' They both look at the pilot and nod their heads. The Sergeant says they'll do what they can and to bring the ship to the hangar. The pilot says thanks and off they go.

"The ship comes in and the stops on the exhaust wastegate are reset so the valve almost closes, the linkage is adjusted, and the ship is run up, and back it goes to the line. A couple of weeks later the pilot comes in and hands the Sergeant a fifth of scotch for the gang and says, 'Boy, you guys really did a great job, I got on this Kraut and rammed it home. I hit seventy inches of mercury and it was still going up when I got him. He was flat out and I caught him like he was standing still.' Later in the war this adjustment became standard operating procedure and they got it up to ninety inches of mercury with modifications."

November 1943 : The middle of November brought the pilots grudging news from Eighth Fighter Command to the effect that henceforth pilots would not be allowed to complete their combat tours at two hundred hours, but would have to remain on duty. All squadron and flight leaders with more than one hundred seventy hours of combat would only be allowed to fly every sixth mission.

On November 15th, Lieutenant Colonel Harry Dayhuff returned from detached duty at Eighth Fighter Command and resumed his post as Group Executive Officer. Three days later a hint of things to come took the form of all Group armament men beginning on-base training in five hundred pound bomb deployment and loading.

The Eighth Fighter Command undertook the new tactic of fighter-bombing on November 25th when 78A and 78B Groups provided close and high cover escort to the 353FG bombing St. Omer-Rouge airdrome in Artois, France. General Murray Woodbury, 66th Fighter Wing CO, flew with the 84th to observe the 353FG bombing which became widely scattered due to heavy Flak dispersing the formation.

One of the officers participating in the event gave this account: "I will never forget the November 25th show. We were flying cover for the 353rd. I was near Colonel Loren McCollom Group CO of the 353rd as he came up to the target area with his squadron of bomb-loaded P-47s. His plane received a direct hit by flak and the explosion peeled the skin right off the side of plane right in front of my eyes. He was seen to get his chute open and he survived the war as a POW."

Seventy-six aircraft of 78 A&B Groups took off at 0927 hours and headed for mid-channel on November 26th, where they made rendezvous with 128 B-17s of the 3rd Bomb Division. After taking up escort above the bomber stream, the force flew

Captain J. Patrick Maxwell, 84FS, with his crew. L-R: CC S/Sgt James Tibbs, and ACC unk. Their WZ-O 42-74742 "WAR EAGLE" (Auburn University team name) has 36 sweeps, bomb symbol for bomber escort. (Patrick Maxwell)

First Lieutenant Norbert G. Lentz taxies on steel runway mat in his WZ-F 41-6333. Note the new 108 gal steel belly tank now giving 325 miles of range. (USAF)

the route of Dieppe-Montford-Evreaux to the target, a bearing industry at Montdidier near Paris. As the Forts made their turn for the target east of Paris, about thirty German fighters went into attacks on the bomber's front and rear ranks. The 78th fighters quickly positioned themselves to meet the attack and went after the enemy.

Major Jack Price started firing at an FW190 from 550 yards to prevent it making a head-on pass at the bombers. He got good strikes all over the German and closed to one hundred yards before he had to break off to avoid running into the bombers. The enemy aircraft stalled and went down trailing smoke. Next Price caught a climbing ME109, came in astern at three hundred yards and exploded it in flames.

Howard Askelson closed to two hundred yards with an out-of-the-sun astern run at three ME109s near bomber level and sent one straight down in fire and lots of black smoke. The battle went on in a running fight until the force reached the Beauvais area, where Warren Wesson took a long six hundred yard shot at the line of flight of an FW190 and held his trigger down as the German passed through his fire. The victory was confirmed by another pilot who saw the FW crash.

The 78th left the continent at Cayeux at 1120 hours and headed for England, where three of the Group's P-47s crashlanded at southeast coastal airfields. Behind the 78th left three pilot losses in France. John Herrick and Wayne Dougherty were shot down in the airfight and became POWs. Ralph Cormier was killed in action.

A small measure of revenge for these losses was gained on November 30th when Major Jack Oberhansly led the 78th Group to cover withdrawing bombers near Aachen, Germany. They finally rendezvoused with the late bombers at Eupen, Belgium, where Oberhansly came in behind an FW190 trying to finish off a straggling B-17. Someone called out the enemy aircraft as a P-47 and Jack had to pull up from his attack to correctly identify the plane, then did some flick rolls with the FW, firing down to two hundred yards before he overshot the plane, then in a smoking dive. Arriving back over England in a heavy overcast 78A Group led by Major Roberts called on the radio for a homing and let down into the soup using that homing from Duxford. They broke out of the overcast over central London fifty miles south of base. Thus ended a rather fruitless weather plagued month of eleven missions, six victories, and three combat losses.

Random incidents from this time period were remembered by various members of the 78th.

Allan Cowart: "While I was in the tower in November,

1943, a Tiger Moth aircraft came flying between my tower and the hangar line. The Tiger Moth ran into and through some communications cables and got them all wrapped around his airplane. The airplane flew on and I didn't see him because at that moment I was in the front of the tower and the lines were in the back of the tower, but someone reported that a Tiger Moth cut them. I would have killed him at the time, as my tower was my life.

"Almost forty years later while sitting across the table from a friend who was in another Fighter Group during World War II (at a retired officer's dinner at Eglin AFB), I overheard him bragging about the time he and Glenn Duncan of the 353FG over at Raydon, were buzzing an airfield in a Tiger Moth. They had to make a forced landing because they'd hit some wires and they had to get them unwrapped from their aircraft before they could go back to their base. I let him finish the story and we had a lot of fun over that incident. What a strange thing that we should be sitting across from each other and I found out who did me in forty years earlier."

On December 1, 1943, members of the 78th Fighter Group celebrated their first anniversary in the European Theater with a big evening dance held in the base theater. It provided a good escape valve for the nervous tensions built up that day on the mission to Duren, Germany.

The 78th had met the bombers at the Dutch coast near Overflakkee Island and carried on a running engagement to the Aachen area where low fuel forced a return. James Wilkinson and Charles Keppler destroyed an ME109 and FW190 respectively in the half-hour of skirmishing. Three other pilots got probables and three others survived return crash landings at UK coastal bases of Gravesend, Pelden, and Manston.

Then the weather went sour until the 10th, when the 82nd carried out practice fighter bombing costing the life of Melvin Wright, who misjudged or was unable to pull out of his dive.

Lieutenant Colonel Eugene Roberts, the Group's top ace (nine) and most decorated pilot, left the 78th on December 18th for a job at Fighter Command, as an operational troubleshooter. When he left his log was 190 hours in combat in 87 missions, and he took with him a silver cigarette case inscribed from his crew headed by Technical Sergeant Negley Sapper. He returned for a second tour in January, 1945 as the commander of the 364th Fighter Group at Honington and often visited the 78th.

December 21, 1943 was a black day for the 78th because through poor aircraft recognition four RAF Typhoons were shot down by mistake in a bounce during a B-26 area support near Doullens, France. It should also be stated that in the same fight, RAF Spitfires also shot down one of their own Typhoons, making five in all lost to faulty identification. After three days of investigation, the pertinent intelligence officers were disciplined and the four pilots involved were transferred from the Group along with others who were suffering combat fatigue and nervous problems. In one and one-half years of the early combat period of the Group, only five or six pilots left for this reason.

On a happier note, the Thunderbolt Band and the members of the Group attended an Anglo-American Christmas Eve Dance that evening in Cambridge's Guildhall, which was broadcast live on a U.S. coast-to-coast hookup by BBC. During the day the Group had given a Christmas Party for the local children and several unofficially adopted war orphans.

On December 30th, 1943, the teletypes pounded out the day's mission. Over 700 bombers of the now mighty Eighth Bomber Command were going to Ludwigshafen, Germany to attack the oil refinery complex. At 1036 hours 78B Group led by Major Harold Stump took off and flew to Folkstone, then across the Channel to Boulogne, France and caught up with the long-outbound bombers near Amiens providing penetration support to Traben/Trarback, Germany. They broke escort at 1215 hours and returned to DX via Walcheren Island, Netherlands and Harwich, United Kingdom.

An hour and a half later 78A departed from DX proceeding to make landfall at Cape Gris Nez, France at 1236. At 1311 hours they reached their rendezvous point with the returning bombers to provide withdrawal support near St. Mihiel, France. As usual, the bombers were being sniped at by enemy fighters trying to pry loose a straggler. William Julian spotted an ME109 sneaking up on a B-17 out of formation from up-sun and spiraled down on him. Pulling in dead astern, Julian hit him in the right side of the cockpit, wing root, and engine. The Messerschmitt released streams of black smoke and half-rolled in a vertical dive, which continued in a 2,000 foot drop into low overcast. Scoring similar victories on ME109s were Warren Wesson, Manuel Martinez, and William Hegman.

Flight Officer James Eastwood was a new replacement pilot in the 83rd on his first mission this day. His navigation was not yet as good as it should be and the winds aloft were much stronger than reported at mission briefing, (not unusual for the European Theater) and as he reached a point in the English Channel fifty miles south of Beachy Head, his aircraft ran out of gas. James bailed out and the others in the squadron saw him get into his dingy, but their gas was also low and they had to head for land. Air-Sea-Rescue failed to find Eastwood and he became the last 78th death of 1943.

The Group finished the month of December with nine missions, eleven kills, and two losses. The year 1943 had produced the following statistics: 113 missions, 71-13-27 victories, (destroyed-probables-damaged), and twenty-nine losses, from approximately 3800 sorties having 270 aborted flights.

On the social side, the Group welcomed in the next year of war on New Year's Eve attending a dance at 66th FW Headquarters at Sawston Hall. Providing the music was Corporal Bob Bravin's "Bobcats" dance band, otherwise known as "Woody's Wildcats".

Others spent the holidays off base if they could. A Staff Sergeant recalls, "Since I was going with a Scotch girl, we arranged our leaves together and stayed a week at her parent's home in Scotland, near Glasgow.

"When I went to the commissary with my barracks bag as the orderly room suggested, they proceeded to stuff my bag with everything imaginable. I couldn't believe it, for a one week sojourn, two pounds of tea, ten pounds of sugar, cans of peaches, pears, soups, and pineapples among other things. I said to the clerk, 'Wait a minute, I'm only going for a week and I can't possibly lug all this weight all the way to Scotland.' He said, 'Shut your mouth, flex your butt muscles, and get going.' I got my orders.

"Well, after my friend and I rode trains to Glasgow for about sixteen and a half hours mostly standing or sitting on the floor, no seats were available, I said to myself, 'Never again.'" If I went on another leave like this, it would only be three miles from the base.

"Anyway, after I was welcomed by the family when I entered their home, I put the barracks bag on the table and I told the mother that the least I could do to compensate for staying here is to give you this. When she opened the bag and started to bring the items out one by one, she began crying. She said her tea ration for the month was one pound and she hugged those two pounds of tea as if they were gold. Same with the sugar, they receive only five pounds a month and it's made from beets. The kids looked at the labels on the cans of peaches and pears, asking Mommy what they were. They hadn't seen any in their lifetime. After that emotional scene, I even had tears in my eyes, and I vowed I would do that all over again next year, regardless of the hardships, and I did."

Lieutenant William Madole, 83FS B-Flt. CO, in his HL-A 41-6540 "SKONK HUNTER. He transferred to MTO after his tour. The aircraft was MIA on 12-30-43. (Robert Eby)

Chapter 10

Battle for the Sky - Victories and Losses

January 1944: The 78th started 1944 off with a bang on January 4th, when they made rendezvous at Ahaus, Germany southwest of Munster to give withdrawal support to the Third Bomb Division hitting that city. The 83rd got the party going by Yellow flight's dive from 26,000 to 15,000 feet to bounce five FWs. Harry Roff reported, "We missed in the first pass, and I pulled in behind an FW which overshot me in his attack. I was diving and rolling with him firing repeatedly, getting many hits, flashes and pieces flying from his engine and fuselage. Half-rolling up over him, I saw his canopy go and the fuselage darkened from interior fire, then the open chute nearby so he must have got out." James Stokes, also in Yellow Flight saw Black Flight chasing an FW and got between them to fire on the enemy aircraft. He got strikes, saw smoke, and the FW split-essed, the pilot bailing out.

Quince Brown, leading Bayland Blue Flight with the 78A Group dove on twelve plus enemy aircraft and fired at an FW down to fifty yards, hitting him in both wing roots and in the belly. It was very badly afire as Brown pulled up and watched the smoking Focke Wulf spin down. Brown made a sharp right turn to come in behind an FW290 that was lining up on four P-47s. He shot at thirty degree deflection and one ring of lead. The FW290 took hits and poured flames from both wing roots as it pulled up and to the right before spinning down out of control smoking heavily.

Pete Pompetti, Number four in Quince Brown's flight dove on two aircraft that turned out to be P-47s. He continued turning and called out sixteen enemy aircraft attacking a B-17 straggler at 20,000 feet. Pete was closing very fast in a twenty-five degree dive at 300 mph on an ME109 in a vertical bank to

the right, so fast that he fired from fifty to five yards and jammed his stick forward to miss the ME by inches. The German flew through Pompetti's left gun's fire and then right, taking strikes over the whole aircraft. The canopy and large pieces of the ME flew off over Pompetti's P-47, some of them hitting the right wing.

On the way home, James Wilkinson scored the 78th's first locomotive victory near Dorsten, Germany. Joseph Scheibler, also of the 82nd made the 78th's first use of the water-methanol injection installation on the P-47 engines to out-run a pursuing FW190.

Manuel Martinez's wingman took a flak hit near Munster and Manny was nursing him home near Antwerp when eight enemy airplanes came in on their tails from the left and two enemy aircraft from the right. The P-47s broke into the attack and started a "Rat-Race", but when more enemy aircraft showed up to join in, the 82nd pilots dove for the deck into the clouds. Martinez came out of the clouds on the treetops near Antwerp and spotted an ME109 dead ahead with its wheels down, on final approach for an airfield. Manny's fire ripped into the ME's belly, and the plane exploded and crashed off the runway on its back. The explosion splattered oil on Martinez' aircraft and when he regained view, he was over the middle of the airfield with a parked ME110 dead ahead. The 78th's first ground victory claim was filed there as the ME110 was soundly strafed. (Later it was reduced to a damaged.) Martinez wisely lit out for home on the deck. His wingman also made it back to Duxford.

The following day, January 5th, while Major Oberhansly's 78A Group had a routine uneventful mission, Major Jack

Technical Sergeant William Jensen scrubs drag-producing dirt off of his WZ-J 42-74753 "OKIE", the mount of Major Quince Brown. Note checker wheel cover, pitot tube cover ribbon, taped up guns. (Negley Sapper)

Major Ralph F. Himes, Grp. Ops Off, in his P-47 WZ-M 41-6532 "CALI KID". He served as Ops. Off from California days, of '42 until going to 8FC in March, 1944. (Robert Eby)

Captain George Hays joined the group in Feb., 1943. His WZ-U 41-6201 "PAPPY" was earlier coded WZ-O. Broom sweep symbols are for aircraft, not all by one pilot. (Ernest Stroud)

Major John Irvin's P-47, "UNMENTIONABLE" WZ-B 41-6367, was later named "GERONIMO". Irvin moved from B-Flt. leader to 84FS Ops Officer, before going to 8FC in March, 44. (Negley Sapper)

"PERCY" was a distinguished aircraft in 83FS. Its pilot, Robert Knapp, temporarily lost control in a combat dive and reached 840 mph, reported the US newspapers. Its CC, S/Sgt Stanley Crawford, got the Legion of Merit for crewing 2-47s 137 shows/365 combat hours without aborting. (Robin Gray/AFM)

Technical Sergeant Odis Cunningham, Major John Irvin's CC, rests on their P-47 WZ-B 41-6367 "GERONIMO", which had earlier been named "UNMENTIONABLE". (Negley Sapper)

The 78th Brass R/V at the Officers' Club bar during an evening at DX. L-R: Lt.Col. Harry Dayhuff, LtCol Erlath Zuehl, Major Jack Price, Major Jack Oberhansly, Lt.Col. Olin Gilbert, and Col. James Stone. Two officers far right are unknown. (Harry Dayhuff)

Price's 78B Group had an eventful and sad mission. After the Rendezvous at Pougeres, France, Clinton Black Section of the 84th bounced four to six enemy aircraft behind the bombers and ME109s were destroyed by Philip Larson and Quince Brown. For some reason, probably due to the late arrival of the relief escort, the Group tarried twenty-five minutes past the break-escort point and turned for home dangerously low on gas. Concentrating on their fuel problem their vigilance distracted, a force of enemy fighters approached undetected in back of the top cover near Nantes, France. The Germans came in dead astern out of the sun and shot down three P-47s in one Flight and one P-47 in another. Three more FW190s bounced another element out of the sun and shot them up. One went down and the other limped home. The tactical commander's mission report states that haze over the continent restricted vertical visibility, but the horizontal was good, and the contrail level was very high up. Of the five pilots, Kenneth Hindersinn became a POW, and George Hartman, Melvin Putnam, Major Leach, and Arthur Granger were killed in action.

The 83rd Fighter Squadron received a new CO on January 18th when Major Jesse Davis returned to the U.S.A. and his command was assumed by Major Olin Gilbert.

The bombers aborted a mission on January 24th due to 10/10ths high and low clouds with few breaks, and the 78th A and B Groups carried out an alternate diversionary patrol of the Malmedy-St. Vith, Belgium area. Show spares, Robert Knapp and his wingman, Edward Downey, were bounced by FWs and Knapp shot down one which was blindly following Downey. The 78B Group was split up somewhat on the way home when they stumbled on three ME110s. Churchtime Blue leader, John Hockery, destroyed one of them as they dove for low clouds.

Robert Eby: "I was leading the element in Red Flight and on the way home I identified from French checkpoints that we were drifting west while holding course on our flight plan compass heading as briefed before the show. The aloft winds were much different than we expected. I called the Flight leader and he invited me to lead the flight as he had more confidence in my navigation than in his own.

"We eventually caught up with two of the squadron planes in Black Flight who were throttled back because one of them had apparently been shot up and neither of their radios were working, as we couldn't contact them. They were headed on a course at least thirty degrees left of us when they spotted us and we throttled back also and they tagged along for a while. Evidently they decided we were on the wrong course for home and they turned thirty degrees west again and we were unable to get their attention or contact them about the strong aloft winds affecting their course. They drifted far enough west that they were actually over the Atlantic Ocean instead of the English Channel and British radar tracked them west of Dieppe, France heading out to sea where they ran out of gas and perished."

The day had gotten off to an unlucky start earlier.

Earl Payne's Diary: "Big fleets of bombers are already taking out for Germany. One B-17 flying over near our field happened to blow up in mid-air this morning before crashing into the hills beyond the flying field. I saw six of the crew bail out and it seemed to take a long time for them to get down. Four of them landed out of sight, but two of them landed near the roundabout out of Whittlesford. Our crash crew went to the aid of the fallen bomber. Four of the crew crashed with the plane and were killed. One of them tried to bail out, but his chute failed to open because it was burned and didn't work. The poor fellow landed on his feet, which were driven clear up to his stomach and burst his lungs, his entrails coming out of either side of his body beneath his armpits."

On January 25th, Colonel Stone led 78A off at 1423 hours on the first Group "Thunderbomber" dive-bombing show with Major Gilbert leading 78B as top cover. They went in over Walcheren Island, Holland and approached the target from the Southwest. There was a solid low overcast at 7,000 feet and a wall of cirrus 15-25,000 feet right over the target which made it impossible to bomb and the middle clouds made it hard to cover and keep contact with the two groups. Finding no targets of opportunity in the clear, the 78th brought their bombs back home.

The Group provided penetration support on January 29th. Rendezvous Point was reached at Malmedy, Belgium and continued until the bombers reached their I.P. at 1120 Northeast of Coblenz, Germany. Soon after, Lieutenant Colonel Dayhuff's 78B Group shot down three FWs which were making attacks at the rear of the bomber formation. As the Group left for home, several of their flights were bounced by nine ME109s and eight FW190s vectored to them by German radar. The enemy hit two P-47s. Milton Ramsey bailed out over France to become an evader, and Claude Godard, though wounded

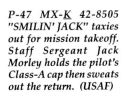

P-47 MX-K 42-8505 "SMILIN' JACK" taxies out for mission takeoff. Staff Sergeant Jack Morley holds the pilot's Class-A cap then sweats out the return. (USAF)

in the knee by 20mm fragments, returned his plane to Bottisham, United Kingdom.

The next day at 1320 hours near Rheine, Germany, Quince Brown swung around the last bomber box and spotted a lone aircraft 8,000 feet below. The stranger was flying in the sun and approaching from behind. Quince thought at first it was a P-51 and flew alongside it. Realizing it was an ME109 with a belly tank, he whipped around in a chandelle and closed to eighty-five yards spraying it with hits. The ME dropped its nose taking more hits in the belly. Fire shot out of the plane and it fell burning into an inverted spin through the cloud deck.

The first 78th dive-bombing mission finally took place on January 31st when the 82nd Fighter Squadron and half of the 83rd led by Major Oberhansly as 78A, took 35 x 500 pound bombs to Gilze-Rijen A/D. in Holland. Major Himes led 78B as top cover.

One pilot said, "I was very perturbed about them having us dive-bomb an area so heavily protected with flak. I was bitching to Jake Oberhansly about the poor choice of the Eighth Fighter Command and he kept kidding me that there wouldn't be any flak at all. Sure enough, we came into the target from the southwest to northeast at 8,000 feet and he peeled off in a sixty degree dive with his four planes and released their bombs at 3,000 feet and there wasn't a shot fired at him! As he pulled up, he called on the radio, 'Ha,ha - I told you there wouldn't be any flak!' About that time I was in the middle of the dive leading the second flight down, when I got a direct flak hit and all I could think about was that damned bomb exploding before I could drop it. The hit was in the oil cooler and flap area and outside of oil leaks, I made it home all right. I still can see that red-red flak map of the Dutch coast."

During January, the 78th was selected by the Eighth Fighter Command to experiment with bare metal finish and some of the planes had their paint removed. This first month under General Jimmy Doolittle's Eighth Air Force leadership produced twelve missions, fourteen kills, and eight losses.

Allan Cowart: "In early 1944 the B-26s were coming over with fuzzy-cheeked youngsters flying them. (The 78th was two years older and it made a big difference in those days.) One of them got lost and I heard him calling on the radio, 'Hello, Darkie, Hello, Darkie' which was the radio call if you were lost but not in an emergency. The ultimate distress signal was 'Mayday'. I helped this B-26 find his way into our field and he landed with no fuel left. He was bone-dry. He had flown up from Africa and was trying to find Land's End. He had totally missed everything and the wind had blown him off course, flying through balloon barrages and everything else.

"When we got him landed he was so grateful, and he had an airplane loaded with fresh oranges! Well, I can guarantee he didn't draw a sober breath while he was at Duxford and we - heh heh - ate all his oranges. The pilot was a big guy, a Big League ball player and his co-pilot was a little fellow. I kinda kept in touch with the co-pilot and we were all pretty friendly. I learned much later that the pilot had gone berserk coming back from a raid and the young 120 pound soaking wet co-pilot had to take over the B-26 and get it back."

Fifty plus 78th P-47s viewed from the tower looking southwest. Marshaling the aircraft so saved time servicing and gas taxiing. At this time, the group was putting up two 36 aircraft missions at once. (Robert Eby)

Chapter 11

Aerial Supremacy - Target Luftwaffe

Low level buzz jobs by aircraft large and small was pervasive. Here a 55th FG P-38H buzzes Duxford. A similar incident on February 10, 1944 led to tragedy. (Warren Kellerstedt)

February, 1944 An indication of the air war's heightened intensity was the Eighth Fighter Command's announcement on February 3rd that pilots may be kept in the European Theater indefinitely after their 200 hour tour, and to underscore that fact, Lieutenant William Hegman's orders home were revoked and he was transferred instead to duty at Eighth Fighter Command.

February 6th produced a truly significant escalation of General Doolittle's campaign against the Luftwaffe, when the Groups were briefed to strafe enemy airfields on the way home from their escort assignments. In accord with this welcome unleashing of the hounds, 78th pilots shot up four airdromes after they chased the enemy to the deck near Troyes, France. This action also introduced the pilots to the variety of light flak guns at Orleans/Bricy, Beaumont, Chartres, and Evreux Airdromes. The result was two ground victories added to the two aerial victories this day.

The mission of February 10th started out with serious consequences.

Allan Cowart: "As the squadrons were lining up on the field to take off, a pilot who had been asked to leave the squadron, had come back in a P-38 and he was buzzing the airfield. You can imagine how that hurt him, to be transferred from an operational squadron to a ferry command. He was buzzing the heck out of the field and I couldn't shoot him down or do anything about it. There was radio silence on the operational frequency for takeoff, but I was yelling at him on the common non-ops frequency and everyone taxiing out could overhear me and they knew who he was.

"As he came across the middle of the field, his propeller tips hit the ground and he lost power, caromed over the hangar, went into a turn, and skipped across the highway to belly land in a field northwest of the base. As the P-38 crossed the road, its wingtip sliced off the cab of a passing British Army truck and sadly and horribly, the driver was decapitated.

"The smoke and oil came up but he escaped from the plane. In the meantime the Group had a rendezvous to make and they couldn't delay takeoff. All the pilots saw the smoke and they wondered how this person had made out. When they were about fifty miles away from base heading toward the Continent, I just said over the radio in the blind, 'The pilot's okay.' and that was all. When they got back to base someone said that was a nice thing to do and they were glad to know what had happened to him, and it was something that wouldn't be on their mind to worry about in combat, and I felt that way too."

On this day's mission 78B could not make rendezvous with their bombers, so they proceeded along the bomber route to Dummer Lake, Germany and carried out an area patrol until 1151 hours. On their way out of the continent, they strafed Haaskamp and Hilversun airdromes with claims for a damaged JU88 and a coaster strafed off the Dutch coast.

A Group, led by Colonel Stone, had a much livelier time of it. As they arrived for rendezvous at 1056 near Meppel, Germany there were thirty to forty enemy aircraft getting ready to attack the rear of the lead bomber box.

Grant Turley: (who had not seen a German aircraft in fourteen previous missions, tells about the battle in a diary he kept for his family) "Thursday, February 10, 1944, Dear Folks, Took off this morning for just an ordinary escort mission, but it turned out that I got two ME109s. We were bounced at 26,000 feet by these jokers. Well, yours truly and his wingman finally got on their tails and followed them down. I fired short bursts on the way down. When the leader leveled off on the deck, I got in a second burst from dead astern. He blew up and went into the deck from 300 feet. Looked like one big splash of flame when he hit. I then got on the tail of the second one and he crashlanded in flames. My wingman followed me to the deck but became lost before my second encounter. There was another P-47 around and he covered my tail. I would like to meet that pilot and thank him.

Technical Sergeant Clarence Koskela paints on his pilot's sixth kill. First Lieutenant Warren M. Wesson is in cockpit of their P-47 MX-I 42-8530 "JEANIE V.O.S.. VOS meant "victory over separation". (USAF/Tom Ivie)

"We then came home from Osnabruck on the deck. Saw one Messerschmitt coming out, but he didn't see us. I was out of ammo by this time. Boy! I was glad to see England"

Warren Wesson hit his FW190 so badly in the wing roots and fuselage that its pilot bailed out. Y.V. Jones helped chase some FWs to the deck and then shot up an ME109 which crashed and exploded before Y.V. himself was killed by a German pilot.

The 83rd also reaped victories in this fight. Harry Roff closed to sixty yards on an ME109 and shot him into a flat spin where the pilot bailed out. A double was scored by Harold Barnaby, the first, an FW190 crashed in a flaming spiral with the pilot aboard, the second, an ME109, took two good bursts in the engine before the pilot bailed out. Edward Downey blew up a FW190's belly tank, causing it to spiral down burning. William Waldheim hit compressibility in his dive and came out behind an ME109 at 4,000 feet with a forty degree deflection shot. The enemy aircraft crashed and burned.

Grant Turley's Diary: "Well, what a day. The only losses were Lieutenants Jones and Ludwig, both my roommates. Ludwig was seen to ditch in the North Sea. Guess he has 'had it'. Jonesey shot down a 109 and was heard to be O.K., but he never came back. So it is - one never knows who will be next. Good night everyone. Right now it worries me that I have murdered one man and probably another. <u>War is hell</u> . I guess I'll get callous, however it is nice to say 'planes destroyed' and not think of the pilots."

On the way home, Richard Hewitt and Donald Ludwig crossed the enemy coast at Egmond, Netherlands low on the deck. Coastal flak emplacements opened fire on them and Ludwig took a hit. His turbo began smoking and then his propeller froze as the P-47 smashed into the grey-green stained sea. The thick haze and low ceiling of an approaching coastal storm quickly hid his final resting place.

The following day, February 11th, was almost a repeat performance. Shortly after takeoff, as the Group climbed to altitude outbound, Flight Officer Archie Daniels felt the propeller of his P-47 break its governor and begin to run away. With no power to keep it airborne, HL-T, heavy with gasoline and ammunition, dropped from the formation as Archie struggled to effect a forced landing at the nearest field, he tried to deadstick the Jug into what seemed an open meadow. In a fatal mistake, Archie did not realize the meadow was on a hill. The aircraft slammed the ground at a disastrous angle of approach, causing it to explode, killing the pilot instantly.

Continuing on to the rendezvous point near Verdun, France, the Group surprised ten to twelve enemy aircraft getting ready to launch an attack on the bombers. Once again the Germans fled for deck with the P-47s racing after them. John Hockery caught an ME109 with a burst at 300 feet. It nosed down smoking and crashed on the edge of a woods. Gerald Brasher used his P-47s new water-injection modification to catch and hit his ME109. It chandelled up to 1,000 feet where the pilot bailed out.

Grant Turley's Diary: Friday, February 11, 1944 "Dear Folks, Forts raided Frankfurt today. We escorted them out from North Central France. Just after rendezvousing with the bombers we ran into about twenty ME109s. I was number three in Lieutenant Hockery's flight when we went into the middle of them. My wingman lost me (a bad habit my wingmen have had lately), but I bounced a 109, followed him through a cloud, and got in a good burst. Saw strikes all over the cockpit and wing roots and a lot of smoke. He went straight down out of control. I am sure that the pilot was dead. I pulled back up through a cloud layer and went around and around with another one. This Jerry had one yellow stripe on his fuselage indicating that he was a squadron leader. He was plenty good. I only got a couple of ninety degree deflection shots at him.

"Came home on the deck. Shot down a Focke-Wulf 190 that was taking off. The flak and tracers were really buzzing around. I got lost and was sweating out my gas when I found that I had flown way out over the Brest Peninsula. I didn't know where I was until they started shooting flak at me over the Guernsey Islands. I really prayed to God coming across the water. I was at 2,500 feet. They shot flak all around me. I could hear it go 'whump' about ten different times. That's getting pretty close. I really kissed the ground at Warmwell, the base I landed at. I had only seventeen and a half gallons of gas left. The weather was bad and my radio was dead, but I started on to Duxford. I was forced down by the weather at Chettingford. Spent a bad night under wool blankets in a Quonset Hut. It was rough and cold."

Donald Morsch and William Swanson were both killed in the air battle in an unknown manner, perhaps by a mid-air collision. Mission time was three hours, forty-seven minutes.

Throughout the strategic daylight bombing campaign Eighth Air Force had suffered terrible losses when its bombers reached beyond the range of escorts. And despite enormous claims by bomber gunners for the destruction of German attackers, Luftwaffe strength seemed undiminished. In a desperate attempt to stop the flow of replacement aircraft to German fighter units, the Eighth concentrated a series of air raids against aircraft production plants in the heart of Germany over the period February 20-25. This campaign became known as "Big Week" and the 78th was in

Archie Daniels,83FS, was killed in a post-takeoff crash on Feb. 11, 1944. His prop ran away and he made a fatal forced landing. (John Elam)

the thick of the fighting. Meeting a formation of Flying Fortresses on February 20th the Group scored three victories.

Grant Turley's Diary: "Dear Folks, Bad weather all week. No flying at all until today. Well, we escorted B-17s out from Central Germany. Eight FW190s were encountered over Belgium. Yours truly got one bringing his total to five. Well, I'm an ace now. It is a thrill and yet not nearly as much as I thought it would be. Sometimes I wish that we didn't have them outnumbered so badly. But in war, you can't let your feelings get the upper hand. After all, it is he or you!"

On February 22nd, Major Jake Oberhansly led 78A Group in at Knocke, Netherlands and arrived at the rendezvous point thirteen miles east of Cologne, Germany. The second box of bombers was under attack by thirty to forty enemy aircraft as the escort closed. Evidently the enemy saw the approaching Thunderbolts as they turned away and dived for safety inland. The Group tore after them, fighting from 22,000 feet to the deck. Despite an oily windscreen, Major Oberhansly got dead astern of an ME109 and blew him up with hits in the cockpit. Max Juchheim finished off a diving ME109 that went straight in. William McDermott got into a Lufberry circle with his flight and some FW 190s. Mac made passes across the circle from above on the FW190 and let him fly through his gunfire hitting him in the canopy and wingroots. The German pilot dumped his canopy and bailed out at 700 feet.

Kenneth Dougherty chased four enemy aircraft to the deck and found himself chasing two with four others behind him, two on each side. He kept after the front two and left one pouring white smoke and glycol and rolling on its back at fifty feet. Kenneth turned into the rear four in succession, going over the top of them trying to run them into the ground. This tactic put him behind them and he finished off his ammunition on one, leaving the ME109 streaming smoke and glycol at ten feet high, about to crash. When he got home, Kenneth praised his new paddleblade propeller and water-injection modifications which allowed him to pull up over the enemy aircraft when breaking into them with a 4,000 foot per minute climb at 230 mph.

Coming home near Gelze-Rijen Airdrome, Netherlands, Major Oberhansly found a limping FW 190 with one wheel down and blew it into pieces with a two second burst of fire. As Oberhansly and his wingman, Courtlyn Hotchkiss, crossed out over the Dutch coast, they were bounced by two FW190s and dove to 1,000 feet at 450 mph ready to break into evasive action. However, they witnessed the two enemy aircraft colliding in mid-air 800 yards astern. One lost a wing and fell into the sea and the other's fuselage was cut in half and fell onto the beach. None of the four victories Jake was involved in got out of their aircraft before crashing and the last two were too low to bail out anyway. Jake and his wingman went home and filed claims on the two colliders. John Johnson, Red four, did not avoid the bouncing tactics at the coast and spent the rest of the war in POW Camp, having to wait until 1945 to file his FW190 kill claim for this day.

Two days later on February 24th, it was 78B Group's turn to make a repeat performance with seven victories. Twenty miles west of Dummer Lake, Germany at Furstenau, the Duxford Jugs bounced twenty to twenty-five enemy aircraft making head-on passes from above the bombers and chased them down to the deck. Near Dummer Lake, Grant Turley found a CV-W coded P-47 six hundred yards above an ME109 firing at it, but not getting any closer or getting any hits on it. As the 359th Fighter Group P-47 quit shooting, Grant closed up to 150 yards on the Jerry and lit up his wing, canopy, and engine with hits. Pouring smoke, the 109 rolled over and the pilot bailed out to have his picture taken on gun-camera film in an excellent pose with his chute.

Max Juchheim followed two ME109s to the deck, hitting one steadily with a pair of two second bursts at 200 yards. The Messerschmitt's canopy came off and the plane crashed in a field.

First Lieutenant Grant M. Turley with his crew. L-R: ARM James Sterner, CC Alfred Turrow, ACC Albert Costelnik. The Arizone cowboy flew MX-D 42-7998 "KITTY - SUNDOWN RANCH". (John Lambert)

Pulling up on the second one, Max chased him over a little town where he streamed black smoke and rolling inverted, crashed in a small woods.

Robert Wise closed up astern of an FW190 to fifty yards and exploded him with fuselage hits. The ME109 that Charles Peal was hitting in the fuselage and wing roots, flattened out on the treetops with his prop windmilling and crashed and disintegrated into the ground. Walter Tonkin's FW190 took a long burst at fifty feet altitude, flashed, smoked, and hit the ground in flames. Tonkin's wingman, Randal Hathaway, saw three P-47s chasing an ME109 around a church steeple and joined in the chase. Closing to ten degree deflection, fifty feet off the ground, Randal got heavy strikes in the enemy's fuselage and wingroots, causing the 109 to hit hedges along the street and blow up into flames as it hit the ground.

Coming back from Mannheim, Germany the next day, February 25th, Pete Pompetti and his wingman made a strafing pass at an airdrome near St. Wendel, getting two ME109s with good hits.

Peter Pompetti: "As I banked around the building, I saw soldiers run out and fire rifles at us. I leveled off and looked to the right and saw a staff car with four German officers stopped along the road. They had gotten out and were watching us shoot up the airdrome. One officer had field glasses. I flew parallel to them about fifty yards away and could see them plainly. I called this off to Lieutenant Lang and then made a sharp turn and came back at them. They did not run until I fired at them. Evidently they thought I was making another pass at the airdrome. They ran into the fields on both sides of the road. Due to the trees and my closeness to the ground, I do not know whether I hit them."

Kenneth Dougherty: "An ME109 tried to bounce Stedman Yellow Flight. My wingman and I chased him to the deck using water-injection and after getting hits lighting him up like a Christmas tree, overshot him going too fast. He kept turning into us until he crashlanded and then both of us strafed him until he disintegrated. The pilot did not get out."

Second Lieutenant Ronald C. Orr would remember the last show of the month, February 29th, an area support over the old Western Front trenches at St. Quentin-Lille, France. His engine caught fire and and froze, whereupon he rode the ship down to 12,000 feet and bailed out to be a POW. The month's tally for fourteen missions: thirty-four victories, seven losses.

Fighter Group Tactical Commander reports for February, 1944 point up the state of European Theater war operations at this juncture in the air war. "The bombers are often late and flying on the wrong courses either north or south of the briefed route,

The end of the "BIG WEEK" attacks hit the Messerschmitt works at Regensburg, Ger. B-17G 42-37859 "ESKY" is from 385BG at Great Ashfield, Suffolk. The 15AF from Italy has hit the far target earlier. (AFM)

taking the quickest course out of enemy territory instead of the Field Order course. This takes them away from the escort making rendezvous and protection hard. The bombers fly wide-front boxes instead of columns as briefed. Columns make for easier protection as the fighters can just go along the columns to reach their assigned boxes and flying down the column scares the enemy away and makes it easier to identify who is being attacked. New modifications to the VHF radio sets finally got rid of radar noise. This modification also improved fighter-to-bomber contact and allowed ground control to be heard much further inland than before."

Due to the double-Group missions being put up during this period, it was necessary to maintain a large staff of pilots in the Group.

Richard M. Holly: "I actually came overseas with the the 14th Fighter Group from California in the second batch to fly P-38s across the North Atlantic. Being in the tailend squadron, we got as far as Iceland and were sidetracked there for almost a year and a half. Then we were sent down to England where they were going to make a photo reconnaissance group out of us. After flying the Mosquito Mark III a couple of times, I didn't like that idea very well.

"I had heard that Colonel Jim Stone had command of the 78th Fighter Group only about ten miles from where we were stationed, so one day I borrowed a bicycle and found my way over to Duxford. In an audience with Colonel Stone, he remembered me because we had been together briefly back in the States. Well, I requested that I be considered for transfer to the 78th. He said, 'By all means. Have you got any more guys over there who want to come?' I said, "Yes, I think I've got a couple.' Jim said, 'It's time for all my experienced pilots to rotate and I'd sure like to have two or three guys over here who've got some flying experience even though they don't have any combat experience.' I said I'd see what I could do and went back to talk with Doug Lawhead and Bill Guilfoyle. They both agreed they'd like to go to the 78th and

so, about ten days later we all transferred to the 78th, where we each ended up in different squadrons. In approximately six months we each had completed a combat tour in the 78th.

"That first day at DX was a memorable one for me. After my talk with Colonel Stone, I thought I had better fly one of these P-47s because they were the first example I had ever seen. They had come out after we left the States and being marooned in Iceland, we never had a chance to see one. I looked up John Irvin, Operations Officer of the 84th, a former classmate of mine at Luke Field in the class of 41I. When I asked him if I could fly his plane, he said, 'Sure, I'll take you out and show it to you.' Having borrowed a parachute, we went out to where it was parked, and that's what my entire check-out consisted of. He showed me where the stick and throttle were and that was about it. He forgot to tell me how to get the landing gear up. In the P-38 and other aircraft I'd flown, all you did was throw the handle up and the gear retracted. The P-47 was different in that you had to pull the handle out first and then throw it up. Anyway, I fought that thing for about ten miles after takeoff, straight out of Duxford, getting up to two or three thousand feet or more before I finally figured out how to get the gear up. All of a sudden I was lost. What John did remember to tell me was how to get back to the field by calling on the radio and getting a vector from them. That worked very well, as a matter of fact, I got right over the field and I was still asking where I was. Whoever was in the tower said, 'You're right over the base', and looking down, sure enough I was but I couldn't see it."

March 1944: After four minor missions in early March, the show on the 6th saw the 78th giving penetration support to the first large force strike at Berlin. Colonel Jim Stone led A Group's thirty-six aircraft to the rendezvous point with the First Air Task Force northeast of Dummer Lake, Germany. The relay escort route was completed and the Group turned for home along the bomber stream near Celle, Germany at 1205 hours. Five minutes later twenty to twenty-five enemy aircraft bounced the 83rd high squadron and the bomber stream in the Barenberg area. Flight

Officer Edward J. Downey was attacked by an FW190D in the initial clash and KIA. Instantly the combats went from 24,000 feet to 4,000 feet in the Steinhuder Lake region. Robert Spaulding closed up astern of an FW190 whose pilot bailed out as soon as hits were received in the cockpit and wingroots. Bob almost struck the FW's wing as it went past him. James Wilkinson shot the canopy off another FW190 which crashed with its pilot aboard.

Eighty-second Ace, Grant M. Turley chased several FWs to the deck and then three more jumped his section. Grant got on the tail of one and into a turning Lufberry Circle with another one on his tail. He destroyed the FW190, his seventh victory, but by the third turn, the FW190 behind him was able to pull deflection on Grant. Dick Hewitt saw the German scoring strikes on Grant's P-47 and the tall cowboy from Sundown Ranch at Snowflake, Arizona ended his twenty-one years and a combat tour of forty-seven missions and 113 hours as he crashed in his Thunderbolt.

Coming home from Hannover, Germany on March 15th the 84th saw another fighter unit being bounced by twenty plus enemy aircraft above them at 25,000 feet. First Lieutenant Quince Brown took his flight toward the only hole in the overcast to catch the residue of enemy aircraft going for the deck. Sure enough, he and Raymond Smith caught two ME109s at 10,000 feet and easily out turned them from there on down to 2,000 feet. They used water injection to outclimb and maintain height advantage. Leaving the enemy aircraft in flames the P-47s pulled out at the overcast to avoid a collision.

The action moved back to France on March 16th. Near the rendezvous point southeast of Strasbourg, Richard Hewitt took a long-range six hundred yard, twenty degree shot at an ME109 which flopped on its back and went straight into the ground and burned. Walter Tonkin chased an FW190 to the deck and while turning with it there, he clipped the ground with his wingtip and cartwheeled, the P-47 exploding. At 1325 hours in the vicinity of St. Dizier airdrome Pat Maxwell's Flight was passing under a B-24 formation which was being attacked by ME109s. The 109s split-essed down on the 84th from 11 o'clock high as Maxwell's boys dropped their tanks and climbed in a head-on firing pass. As the antagonists merged Pat split-essed back in a position for a deflection shot at a 109. The enemy aircraft flew through his gunnery pattern and exploded.

At the same time, Quince Brown led his flight down to the deck to check on an enemy aircraft he had spotted and found an ME109 in the landing pattern at St. Dizier airdrome. Chopping throttle and skidding to slow down, Quince got astern at fifty yards and fired, scoring hits. The 109 flamed and crashed to the left of the runway. Quince then saw a parked JU88 ahead of him and torched it with a short burst.

Climbing to 7,000 feet above the cloud deck, Brown met two FW190s coming at him from 9 o'clock. As he got into a lefthand Lufberry Circle with them, the enemy wingman deserted his leader, who kept trying to outclimb and outturn the P-47. Brown used water-injection to defeat this tactic. Finally the FW190 dove through the clouds followed by the P-47. Keeping the German in his sights and firing at 350 yards, Quince Brown watched the FW190 roll on its back smoking, and crash into a small creek.

With his wingman, he again climbed through the clouds and discovered two ME109s trying to tag them from behind. All the opponents went into a Lufberry turning battle and again the German wingman split from his leader. The leader then tried to outrun the Americans on top of the clouds, but they stayed with him without resorting to water-injection. Quince cut him off from a hole in the clouds and shot him up nicely. The German leader was last seen going vertical into the clouds with heavy smoke streaming from his engine and wingroots. Quince Brown was awarded the Silver Star for this four kill mission.

The weather was too bad for bomber operations on March 17th so the Group took part in a Wing field order to strafe enemy airfields in France. By the time the boys got to the Reims-Chalons area, the visibility was so poor that everyone had split up in

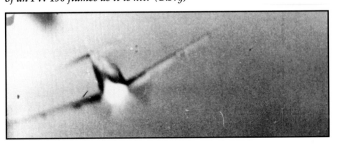

Combat film clips from 78th gun cameras show (above) a German Messerschmitt 109 after a P-47 while being filmed and shot at by a pursuing 78th pilot (Erwin Boettcher); and (below) the rear fuselage tank of an FW 190 flames as it is hit. (G.Fry)

separate flights looking for targets at 1,000 feet. As Boyd Sorenson was crossing Reims, a turn forced him to 500 feet and he saw a DO217 parked on an airdrome. He and his wingman, William Waldheim put their bursts directly into the cockpit and engines to burn it in clouds of black smoke. Courtlyn Hotchkiss wasn't that lucky, getting his prop hit by flak and saying he'd had it over the rendezvous point and bailing out.

Peter Pompetti and his wingman, Ernest Lang, left on their own in the split-up wandered over Beauvais Airdrome and flamed a parked HE111. Pompetti's P-47 was set on fire by a flak hit in the attack and he pulled straight up and bailed out, coming down in a marshaling yard. He was in the safe hands of the Resistance for a short while, but the Germans captured him later that evening.

Back in England, Estel Ulerick was making a test flight with a P-47 named "Little Demon" when it began leaking fuel. The fumes caused him to pass out just as he made an emergency landing at an English bomber base. The aircraft crashed and Estel was severely burned in the face and neck before he was rescued from the flaming cockpit.

The bomber escort to Steinhuder Lake, Germany, on March 22nd was thankfully uneventful after the miracle which took place during the mission takeoff phase. As Captain Charles DeWitt's P-47 lifted to 100 feet slightly astern of his flight, it was caught in their turbulent propwash and lost its lift, going into a left wingover out of the stall point. The Jug cartwheeled into the ground, totally destroying itself. DeWitt's squadron mates had counted him dead as they flew off to the continent, so upon their return they were awed to find him at the bar nursing only a few bruises.

Boyd Sorenson: "We were petrified with amazement to find DeWitt standing at the bar in the Club after we debriefed. This was the opposite extreme to watching Gennaro Riccardo make a perfect wheel-up belly landing and running over to find that he

A non-combat loss. Estel Ulerick's P-47 sprang a fuel leak and he passed out from fumes just as he landed on an RAF base. He crashed and was badly burned before getting out alive. "LITTLE DEMON" 42-8476 was the aircraft. (Roberet Eby)

had been killed because he had forgotten to lock his shoulder straps and had gone head-first into the gunsight."

The next day, March 23rd, the Group was in Germany when Quince Brown's Bayland Black Flight chased four enemy aircraft through a hole in the overcast near Goch at 1130 hours. Brown lost the Germans but going north a mile he met an FW190 coming head-on. Quince got on its tail as it passed and commenced zooming up and breaking for the deck with the enemy, but he couldn't get him in his sights. The Jerry went to the deck below the treetops and tried to outturn Quince, zooming straight up and skidding, but Quince stuck to him despite his water-injection not working. During one skid maneuver Quince almost rammed the German aircraft, then fired at close range, hitting all around the cockpit and engine roots. The Focke Wulf exploded showering pieces all around Brown, who did a violent wingover to 500 feet to avoid the debris.

Coming home, Quince escorted two B-17 stragglers with their wheels and bomb-bay doors down, one after the other, across to the English coast. Stedman White Flight circled for forty-five minutes over a B-17 marked Square-A 42-31120 down in the sea and Colonel Stone and his wingman dropped their dinghies to the crewmen in the water.

Lieutenant Luther Abel had to abort the mission after takeoff to get the elbow tubing of his belly tank fixed then took off to catch the Group. By the time he had reached Melsbroek Airdrome near Brussels, he hadn't found his outfit, so he contented himself with making 550 mph east to west strafing passes at the airdrome. He found four ME410s all lined up nicely and hit them, burning at least two, although the Wing Victory Credit Board would only confirm one.

Coming home on March 24th near Paris, John Hockery saw the shadow of an aircraft on the ground and went down to check it out. He found a JU188 flying very low and attacked. John fired quick bursts at 300 yards as the bomber took violent evasion

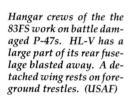

Hangar crews of the the 83FS work on battle damaged P-47s. HL-V has a large part of its rear fuselage blasted away. A detached wing rests on foreground trestles. (USAF)

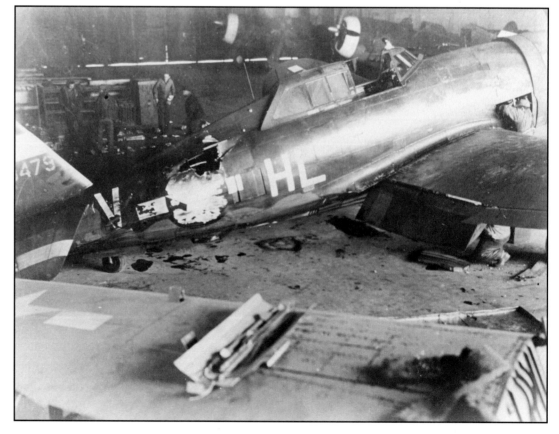

54

around trees and hills. Immediately pieces came off the enemy aircraft and it crashed and exploded in a field in a 300 foot ball of flame as Hockery's wingman, Karl Wagner, went through the blaze.

March 26th was noteworthy for two reasons. The 66th Fighter Wing CO General Murray Woodbury, accompanied the 84th on a fighter sweep of targets around Roye, France, and the 82nd had a P-47 stolen from their flightline while its crewchief was reporting it out of commission. The thief was apparently a highly skilled infiltration intruder taking part in a security exercise.

No bomber operations were laid on for March 30th so the Fighter Command sent three Groups to strafe airfields in the Low Countries. About 1515 hours, the 82nd entered the continent at Overflakkee Island and went to Volkel airdrome where no suitable targets could be found. One flight of four sank two barges and tugs on the Rhine River and then blew up two gilder bombs in a field. The other squadron flight destroyed four locomotives east of Wesel, Germany.

The 83rd burned an ME109 on Venlo Airdrome and bagged four locomotives at the rail yard in Vierson, Germany just before

Then the checks were marked off using several sizes of sheet-metal stencil squares. These squares were connected by pencil laterally and vertically, and the black coat was hand-brushed by a steady handed hangar painter. It was all freehand with no masking done. Future P-51 checks were done the same way.

The weather in the first part of April was atrocious and pilots called the April 12th mission the most fouled up they had flown to date. The Group stuck with the 2nd Bomber Division until southeast of Aachen, Germany where the bombers aborted, the last division to do so. At 1310 hours Quince Brown was leading part of 78A near Duren, Germany when thirty plus FW190s and ME109s emerged above heavy clouds going in the opposite direction. Quince's 84th turned and pursued in a steep climbing turn that overtook the enemy formation. The German squadrons scattered and dove for the deck.

Brown picked out an FW190 with a belly tank and at 5,000 feet, raked the FW from left wingtip to cockpit. The enemy aircraft exploded, Quince flying safely through the flame and debris. Later near Malmedy, Belgium, Major Len Marshall along with Karl Wagner, Robert Baker, and George Lundigan chased

Jugs of the 83FS form up for takeoff on the large steel matting at the east runway end, as the Group launches a show. The 84FS is ready to roll eight abreast. Forty aircraft missions generally got off in just five minutes. (Robert Eby)

eight ME109s bounced Olin Gilbert. He was badly shot up but escaped pursuit to limp back to Duxford.

The 84th split into two flights at Dieren and one flight went to Deelan Airdrome where results were nil. After leaving the airfield a locomotive with flak firing cars behind it, was left issuing clouds of steam. The other 84th flight swept in over Twente/Enschede Airdrome where everyone queued up to blast a luckless DO217 caught in the traffic pattern. It was promptly dispatched. Heading on to Coesfield, Germany, Quince Brown's flight found a suspicious factory building which detonated violently under their concentrated fire. The cost of the above Rhubarb mission was the loss of Albert Werder, who bailed out at Venlo Airdrome from flak hits. Both his aircraft and his parachute were aflame as they plummeted to the earth.

As Spring approached better weather produced twenty-one missions for the month, with twelve air and nine ground victories at a cost of nine pilots lost and two wounded. A new victory column was opened for various ground targets destroyed by strafing. (This text will only report the locomotive tally, nine being destroyed in March)

April 1944. The first seven days of April saw the 78th's P-47s receive their colorful and immortal black and white checkerboard nose cowlings. These were applied for two reasons. The 56th Group had had some varied success in fooling the Germans with colored nose paint, and the mighty armada now roaming the enemy's skies was so large that for ease of recognition between bombers and escort fighters at longer ranges a new form of unit identity marking was needed.

The application of 78th aircraft cowling checkers was done as follows. First a base coat of white was sprayed on the cowling.

several FW190s to the deck. Marshall overshot his, allowing Wagner to get in two long, wide angle deflection bursts which caught the FW as it was belly landing. The FW's left wing broke off and it flipped on its back and exploded. As Wagner passed the FW's remains he saw the pilot lying off to the side where the explosion had thrown him.

About the same time, a section of 82nd pilots composed of Captain John Hockery, John Lamb, Ben Watkins, and Dan Hagarty, stumbled onto a shooter's feast near Sedan, France, when they spotted a bandit going down through the clouds and followed. Emerging from the overcast, they found a half dozen plodding JU87 Stukas beneath them milling around Ensheim Airdrome with another fifty plus parked on the drome. The Thunderbolts had trouble trying to hang behind the slow birds long enough to take their shots, but the outcome was never in doubt as each bagged one before giving the airdrome a quick squirt.

Three days later the Command launched an airdrome strafing exercise, which went to central and western Germany in terrible weather. The weather was primarily responsible for thirty-three pilots being lost, a poor tradeoff against the meager fifty-eight air-ground victories scored. The 78th's quota of death took Captain Charles Silsby and Flight Officer Joseph Mundy. Midway across the sea climbing in close formation through solid overcast at 21,000 feet, Silsby was seen to go into a steep climbing wingover and fall into a vertical dive with Mundy sticking close to him. Nothing further was heard or seen of them. Back at base, Martin O'Connell was on a local flight and crashed to his death within sight of the field.

On a much happier note, April 19th saw eight of the Group's old hands depart for well deserved sixty day stateside leave.

A three part gun camera sequence shows the pursuit of an FW190 at treetop level by Captain William E. May, 82FS on April 9, 1944. May's fire detonates a fuel tank (center) and the German plane disintegrates (bottom). (Robert Eby)

Harry Dayhuff, James Cooper, William May, Eugene Roberts, Norman Munson, Charles Peal, Charles Clark, and Philip Larson were delighted to miss U.S. Secretary of War McCoy's visit to DX with his platoon of Generals Doolittle, Lee, Kepner, McMann, Spaatz, and Woodbury, to review a collection of Allied aircraft.

James Stallings Diary: "Today, April 29th, we had a long mission using the big belly tank. Rendezvous point was made with 660 bombers in eleven boxes, four boxes of Libs and seven boxes of Forts. We looked after all the stragglers at the rear of the formation, most with one or two engines feathered. Coming pretty close to some of them, the crews waved at us. They were darned glad to see us, as they probably made it back without being shot down. After staying fifteen minutes later than scheduled, we started home, low on gas and losing altitude. A stiff wind blew us further south than our course. Passing over Dunkirk at 4,000 feet (20,000 too low to suit me) they gave us a good reception of flak. The first three bursts hit just under my tail and knocked holes the size of my fist in my left wing and behind the motor. It went through three thicknesses of metal before stopping, making more work for my poor crew chief.

"I received this plane from Major Munson after he finished his tour. The name of the plane is 'Lady Yvonne', but I'll rename it 'Millie B' soon. It gets more gas than lots of them and I landed with almost one hour's supply while some of the fellows had to land at the coast. Getting that belly tank off makes a big difference in consumption, averaging about eighty-five gallons per hour."

The following day, Major Olin Gilbert was leading 78A with his 83rd Squadron at the bomber stream's most forward point, when "Snackbar" radar control called out many enemy aircraft ahead and moving to 12 o'clock high on the bombers. Instantly climbing, Major Gilbert saw twenty-five plus FW190s approaching him from 20,000 feet and led the squadron head-on into them breaking up their attack and splitting their force. Half the FWs went for the low box of bombers and the rest performed the regular German trick of trying to draw the defenders to low altitude. Gilbert fired at one from long angle and range, causing the enemy to pull up and bail out.

Captain Alvin Juchheim got behind a Focke Wulf and scored hits, also causing the pilot to hit the silk. Spotting another FW attacking a squadron mate, Juchheim did a head-on pass causing the German to abort the attack. Reefing into a reversal, Alvin gained the 6 o'clock shot spot on another 190 and then ran out of ammunition before he could finish him off properly. By then the two fighters were tearing along just off the deck and never a man to quit in the advantage, Juchheim put his P-47 on top of the FW and dropped his nose a bit. This caused the German to clip the ground with his propeller and in panic, he tried to turn away. Digging a wingtip into the ground, the plane crashed and exploded.

First Lieutenant Andrew Barba's WZ-E 42-74694 "JOKER" with CC S/Sgt. James Darrall. A tribute to its crew, the aircraft will become the longest surviving P-47 in the 78th. (USAF)

Meanwhile Frederick White and William McDermott were pursuing an FW low across the landscape, having already blown off the belly tank. The 190 pilot misjudged an oncoming hillock and clipped the top of it, ripping off one wing and expiring in a fiery explosion. When this mission landed, the Group's monthly score for twenty-two shows stood at seventeen air kills, twenty-nine ground kills, twenty-eight locomotives and seven pilots lost to all causes.

Harding Zumwalt: "At the end of my tour, I was assigned to the 495 Fighter Training Group, an Operational Training Unit at Atcham, training new pilots from the states who had no combat experience. This duty could be perilous and was heavy with responsibility. On one occasion I was leading a flight of four, when just after takeoff one of my students reported fumes in his cockpit. Following recommended procedure, I immediately declared an emergency and turned the flight back to our home station. However, before he could take corrective action by going to 100% oxygen, the pilot veered out of formation and went straight into the ground. Apparently he had waited too long before reporting the fumes and was too far gone when he called me. The accident emphasized the importance of a pilot keeping alert to the presence of fumes in the cockpit and to the value of using 100% oxygen."

Harold Barnaby: "At the end of my first tour of combat in the 83rd, I was reassigned to Eighth Fighter Command Headquarters (AJAX) as assistant A-3 on the mission planning staff. AJAX was located in an old red brick building, formerly a girl's school, called Bushey Hall, in the village of Bushey and Oxley, northwest section of London, near Watford. It was reached from downtown London on the Bakerloo North tube line. I was billeted in a private home of a British family some one quarter mile distance from our Headquarters building.

"My duty was to assist in planning fighter cover for bomber missions, fighter-bomber attacks, and ground strafing sweeps. These plans were drafted in minute detail with separate orders for each group, then sent out on the Telex, not to arrive later than 4:30 AM. These field orders told each group of their assignment, the routes to and return from target, check points and arrival times, altitudes, and other pertinent data. Some of these Telexes would be fifty feet in length for complex missions.

"Mission planning is an extremely rigorous task requiring the staff to remain on duty in 24-hour shifts, from midnight to midnight. Because of the complexity of a plan involving up to two thousand aircraft, the staff had to stay on duty during the execution phase, to react to any necessary changes. After 5:00 AM the scene changed from the planning room to the operations room, where RAF WAAFs plotted the show progress on a large table map of the European continent. They plotted location, numbers, and altitudes of both Allied and German aircraft, obtaining this information from ground monitoring stations on the coast. We had radio contact with our aircraft by means of relay aircraft parked over the European coast at high altitude. However, there was a limit to effective range of these systems, so that on big mission days into East Germany or Czechoslovakia, there were times when we would be out of contact.

"It would be early evening before the normal mission was completed, the pilots debriefed, and the results compiled. This data was Scramble-Phoned to Headquarters where we would prepare the final report. The time was now 9:00 P.M. or later, almost time to hold the first weather conference to prepare for the next day's mission."

Major Quince Brown's WZ-J 42-74753 "OKIE" backstops 84FS pilots. Top L-R: Harold Stump, George Hays, Macie Marlowe, Ernest Lang. Bottom L-R: Gray Doyle, Quince Brown, Edward Fleming, Dorian Ledington. (Negley Sapper)

78th Little Friends (center high) weave over a combat box of 96 BG B-17Gs as the bomber stream roars across Germany leaving tell-tale vapor trails in the frigid air. (Carl Moschel)

Chapter 12

Extended Tours - Flak Bait

May1944: Early May brought grumbling from the pilots when the Command increased combat tour time from 200 to 300 hours and thirty-four P-47s were transferred to Ninth Air Force cutting each squadron back to twenty-eight aircraft, or sixteen per mission.

James Stallings' Diary: " On May 8th we made rendezvous with the first box of Libs just west of Hanover, and dropped off Black and Green flights continuing to the rear bomber box to protect stragglers. We were pulling contrails all over the sky and it was beautiful. As usual our squadron saw no enemy aircraft but the lucky 83rd were bounced by ten plus Bandits and lost one pilot who was too far from the formation. The Germans also got two bombers in the pass. They are smart and don't attack unless they have the advantage.

"May 9th We didn't see any flak at the coast when we came out. Everybody was P.O.'ed because they had to pull so much manifold pressure to stay with the Colonel. Unusual number of aircraft operating along the invasion coast from Cherbourg to Fresian Islands, many A-20s and B-26s were seen going in to keep up their good work - pounding Hell out of the Germans."

On May 12,1944, twenty-five miles southwest of Coblenz, Germany, Captain James Wilkinson as 78th A Group leader had his four flights of Surtax (82) Squadron 1,000 yards ahead and above the lead bomber box, just crossing their flight path north to south. At this moment 100 plus FW190s appeared closing on the lead bombers at 12 o'clock level. The first two Surtax flights turned into the oncoming enemy and split their force in half, going into a diving chase after the Germans who hit the deck for home. Wilkinson's two flights pursued enemy aircraft fleeing southward and groundward. James secured hits in an FW's wingroots and cockpit at 200 yards causing it to catch fire and dive into the ground with no bailout.

Triggering his guns at 400 yards, Robert Baker's target poured black smoke and the canopy popped off to show flames in its cockpit. The German came out in a squatting crouch and he bounced on the ground right below Baker before his chute could unfurl. Daniel Hagarty set his first FW on fire and it crashed into the hills south of Coblenz. Although he had become separated from the rest of the squadron, Daniel chased another FW190 to deck level where he blew up its left ammo bay with the last of his bursts. This ripped off the Jerry's wing and he snapped end-over-end into the trees below and exploded. With no ammo and alone, Hagarty was unable to avoid being shot down himself and went into captivity for the remainder of the war.

The remaining Surtax flights broke into the rest of the enemy at altitude and caught up astern where Merle Capp opened on an enemy aircraft at 200 yards, inducing its canopy to fly back and strike Merle's right wing. Capp fired up to fifty yards and broke off to watch his target crash in the Rhine river south of the city, and then he shot film of the oil and debris in the water. Benjamin Watkins closed out the inning by hounding his victim FW190 for twelve or fifteen minutes at 10,000 feet prior to tearing large pieces off of him at 400 yards. The

enemy pilot immediately exited over the side and jerked his ripcord, causing Ben to report that "the Kraut sailed back and hit my left wing and I returned with part of his chute caught on my wingtip."

James Stallings' Diary :"12th We turned back over Metz at 4,000 feet and for about two minutes it seemed as if the flak wouldn't let me out of town. I'd heard that if you can hear the flak it is too close. Today I heard at least fifty bursts and felt very certain I would never get away alive, but the Lord looked after me and I got away with no holes in my plane. Was very short on gas and had 300 miles to go, so I leaned out the mixture and cut my RPMs to 1900 to conserve fuel. Made it home with about twenty minutes left, logging four hours for the mission. We lost one of our best flight leaders, who had done a tour in bombers and who was almost through his tour here. He had flown about 2,000 hours when lost [Dan Hagarty]. This is our third man in two days, which isn't good!"

Richard Holly: "A few days prior to May 19th, 1944, Colonel Stone held a pilot's meeting and announced that the Group had 198 confirmed victories. Somebody had donated or we had acquired a nice big silver loving cup for the lucky pilot who downed the 200th enemy plane. The instructions were that whenever we were on a sortie and we claimed a kill, that we be sure to jot down the time so we'd know who actually got the 200th one. A couple days later the Command called to release us from operations the following day and every pilot recalls what used to happen when we were given a release. The Officer's Club opened early and everyone went in and had a gay old time, knowing we didn't have to fly the next day. It has been known for some Jug Jockies to tip a few when they had a day off flying. So we had this magnificent party on this memorable evening and I don't recall what time I got to bed.

"Lo and behold, about 3:00 AM our operations officer awoke me and said, 'Hey, we got a mission to fly!' I wasn't feeling too good and tried to run him off, but it didn't work. Finally it got through to me he was asking for help in rounding up enough pilots to fly a mission. I got dressed, but I couldn't find anyone in the sacks they were were supposed to be in and I also couldn't find anyone sober. First thing I did was to call the mess hall to brew a lot of black coffee, and then I went around all the barracks gathering up enough guys to go on the show, but no one felt very well at all.

"After soaking up some black coffee and half-sleeping through briefing, we got out and cranked the planes up. We got the Group into the air, but the formation we were flying was something to behold, they were scattered all over the sky and nobody seemed to care too much. We had just caught up to the front of the bombers when somebody called out 'Bandits at 12 o'clock!' Well, that bunch of drunks really woke up about that time."

At 1230 hours on May 19th B-24 bomber boxes of the Third

The 78th acquired its distinctive Group colors in April 1944. Earl Peterson sits in his WZ-D 42-74657 "VICKY" boldly adorned with the new black and white checkerboard nose marking. (James Peterson)

Air Task Force were nearing the Dummer Lake area of Germany on course to attack air industry targets in Brunswick. The 78th Group was 11 o'clock level with the lead box of 300 bombers when a large gaggle of sixty plus Messerschmitts and Focke-Wulfs in two waves came at the nose of the great formation spread out abreast to increase their firepower.

James Wilkinson: "We got behind the first wave of thirty FW190s attacking the bomber boxes abreast and in front of the second wave of thirty FW190s. We broke up the first wave and turned back into the second wave. More P-47s came in above and together we broke up the second wave. My wingman and I broke into a third wave and I hit one at 200 yards from astern. He split-essed and bailed out. I had gotten some 20mm hits in my own tail during the first wave attack."

When the first enemy wave turned away to 10 o'clock from the bombers, Merle Capp closed in quickly to 150 yards dead astern of an ME109 and exploded it with a long burst. The German pilot bailed out. Lloyd Covelle dropped his tanks and climbed into the gap between the waves of enemy aircraft. Some of the Germans broke for the deck and some headed for the 78th escorts. The P-47s had no problem turning with the attackers and closing with them as they climbed and dove to evade the Jugs. Covelle tried some bursts at 300 yards and his German's prop windmilled at 7,000 feet. As another burst hit him in the cockpit area, his wheels dropped down and he streamed smoke and tumbled, rolling straight into the ground.

Myron Woller's flight spotted the first thirty to forty bogies coming in parallel to the P-47s. He was turning his unit into the enemy when another twenty to thirty enemy aircraft approached behind the first formation. As this second squadron came ninety degrees to Woller, his mates dropped tanks and broke into them, scattering the German fighters. Woller closed on one on the deck and his second burst resulted in hits, loose pieces, one wheel down. Continuing through a turn, the Jerry nosed into the ground and exploded. Woller took his photo, then went for another ME109, which was evading three P-47s in and out of the clouds. Again Woller's second burst drew cockpit strikes and the ME109 spun through a cloud layer and blew up on the deck. Once again Woller photographed the wreck.

In the German's attack on the P-47s, Herbert Boyle got separated from his flight and his wingman, and when an FW190 spun past him from above found himself below a Lufberry circle. The German recovered his spin and took no evasion on the deck so didn't realize that Herbert had followed him down. After firing three bursts scoring hits in the canopy, fuselage, and wingroots, Boyle drew alongside the enemy aircraft, its prop windmilling as it traveled along just off the treetops. Herb saw the dead pilot in the shattered cockpit and pulled up as the doomed ship dug its right wing into the ground and disintegrated. Later back at base, Boyle found oil splashed all over his own ship and blood on his cowling and canopy.

When the first German attack was called out, William Hunt was with Colonel Stone's flight. Stone radioed his unit not to drop their tanks as they were right in the bomber's path and had to pass out to the right of the bombers before they could get rid of the "babies". This effectively omitted the flight from the first scrap, but five minutes later as Steinhuder Lake approached, thirty plus enemy aircraft attacked the bombers from 9 o'clock. Hunt waited to see if Colonel Stone would break into this attack and then went ahead and broke himself, but the Jerries were on the opposite side of the bombers and they had too much lead for him to stop the attack. The enemy fighters came in close abreast to put maximum firepower into the bombers. Hunt saw four P-47s coming up behind the bombers when two of the 47s flamed and fell smoking. He broke into the P-47s and saw the trailing ME109 that had shot down the two Jugs. The German saw him coming and headed for the deck with Hunt taking a wide deflection shot. Going straight down, Hunt got lots of strikes in the 109's cockpit and wingroots. Pulling up at 6,000 feet, William last saw the German tumbling out of control going straight in.

William Luckey followed his leader to the deck after the 109s and fired at the number two plane when his leader fired at the German lead. Luckey exploded ammunition in the German's wing. The wing sheared off and the victim flipped and tumbled to the ground.

Richard Holly put hits into an ME109 which cleared the bottom of some clouds spinning upside down. The German bailed out as his ship exploded. Paul Holden had just gotten in gunshot proximity to five enemy aircraft and was lining up on a target when to his astonishment, the "bloke bailed out". Frederick White was in a Lufberry with an ME109 near Lingen, Germany getting strikes on him when White stalled out. As he lost altitude he saw the German also diving to avoid other P-47s. White tried again and got to fifty yards firing on the German but overshot him. Fred did a 360 degree chandelle onto the enemy's tail for another try but the German pilot bailed out before Fred could fire again. In the same vicinity, Robert Ealey was at the rear of the bombers at 25,000 feet as forty to fifty ME109s attacked from 2 o'clock high. Ealey chased and peppered one watching as it spun down spewing smoke and glycol streamers and finally saw the pilot parachute.

Perhaps the luckiest man this day was the 82nd's Harold Beck. Near Dummer Lake three ME109s put several 20mm hits into his supercharger and air ducting. Manifold pressure dropped to thirty inches, hydraulic pressure dropped, and his gyro compass and airspeed indicator went out. Soon four ME109s were taking turns blasting away at Beck as he attempted to avoid them. Oil was covering his windscreen and smoke came out of his engine when a hit in his right engine side started a fire. The R.P.M. went down to 2500, oil pressure to ten pounds, oil temperature went to maximum, and with three ME109s still behind him, Beck dove vertically to 2,000 feet blowing out his engine fire. Two ME109s left, apparently out of ammo, and Beck watched the last ME109 continue to fire at him as he struggled to evade. After three minutes the German vanished from his rearview mirror but then Harold found him flying off his right wingtip in close formation. Beck tried to shake him but he stayed right there just observing. Presently he flipped Harold a salute and split-essed for home, evidently out of ammunition.

Having fought the four Germans for twenty minutes (1235 to 1255 hours) Beck headed for home using needle/ball/compass. Even his trim tabs were shot out. Crossing the enemy coast oil pressure went to zero and cylinder head temperature went to maximum, Harold was forced to let down over the sea from 12,000 to 4,000 feet in solid haze and overcast on his meager instruments. Nearing the English coast, he took a heading left for an emergency field and then his engine froze solid at 2,000 feet in poor visibility. Searching below he spotted an airfield and by shaking his wheels down and undershooting he slipped into the field. Once on the ground he had no brakes and using S-turns he got his ship stopped. A count disclosed ten 20mm hits and many smaller caliber holes, a prop holed, and the tops shot off of two engine cylinders. Beck declared the Republic P-47 the best aircraft in the USAAF.

Richard Holly: "In a matter of a few seconds there were planes going down every direction you turned. The whole thing lasted about five minutes and it was all over and we were reforming again. We all marked down the times we'd gotten our victories and when we got home everyone compared notes. Most of the guys had the same times on their claims, so the Colonel decided to put our names in a hat one time for each victory. Then they drew Holden's name for this 200th victory silver loving cup. The funny part of it was that the guy, Holden, never even broke the tapes on his guns that day."

The tally for the four hour, sixteen minute May 19th mission was twelve victories without loss.

On May 21, 1944, Colonel James J. Stone turned over command of the 78th Group to Colonel Frederic C. Gray, Jr., 33, and returned to the US for leave before reporting for duty to a new job at AJAX. Another arrival was the new model P-47D-25RE, a bubbletop, 360 degree vision canopy equipped Jug to replace the old Razorback.

On May 24th, the Eighth Fighter Command attempted a new attack method as the 78th flew its first "Droopsnoot" bombing mission. This consisted of a P-38 Lightning fighter equipped with a glass-nosed nacelle bearing a bombsight and bombardier, who signaled by radio to a following fighter/

Released to strafe targets of opportunity on the return home, Peter Pompetti, at a very low level, smothers a loco with strikes. (Peter Pompetti)

Captain Richard M. Holly, 84FS CO, and his crew, L-R: S/Sgt. Melvin Armstrong ACC, and chief, S/Sgt. Henry Bauer. P-47 WZ-Y 42-25871 "NIGGER II" was nicknamed after his always suntanned wife. (Richard Holly/Henry Bauer)

bomber formation when to drop their bomb load on target. Major Harold Stump flew the Droopsnoot P-38 lead ship to the target, a railway bridge over the Oise River south of Creil, France. The first bomb run was aborted but the formation did a 360 degree turn and dropped their bombs from 18,000 feet demolishing half of the bridge.

Earl Payne's Diary: "On May 26th I was standing in the bus queue waiting, when the M.P.s told us all to go the hangar for an announcement by our new CO, Colonel Gray. He announced extensive defense preparations going on in the event of a German paratroop attack on our base. All planes have been removed from the far perimeter area at night and the place is oozing with guards. A certain number of men have to sleep in the dispersal areas at night as well. All passes have been canceled and there is a permanent alert force of forty-nine men and one officer at all times. Everyone has to carry his rifle at all times, but no one is grumbling about this because we all feel it is high time that we found out how to defend the place in an attack."

The following day an 82nd armorer, Sergeant John P. Hartman, who had been in a bomber squadron, was bicycling back to his old base to check on his pay records. Six miles east of Duxford he saw a P-51 buzzing the 409th Bomb Group base at Little Walden. Just then the P-51 collided in mid-air with a departing A-20 bomber. Hartman ran to the crash site and, with the help of a passing nurse, rescued one of its gunners. They went back to help more of the bomber crew and just at that moment the plane's bombload exploded, blowing Hartman and the nurse over forty feet. The nurse died instantly and John Hartman succumbed to his wounds seven hours later in hospital. He was posthumously awarded the Soldier's Medal for heroism.

At 1415 hours on May 28th, one of the 78th's highest scoring aces, Captain Alvin "Max" Juchheim, was at 22,000 feet near Gardelegen, Germany maneuvering to attack an enemy aircraft, when a P-51 of the 363FG suddenly entered his flight path coming head-on at him. The P-51 collided with Max's P-47, which had its wing sheared off and went into a spin. With the impact, the P-51 exploded in flames killing its pilot. Captain Juchheim was able to extract himself from the spinning remains of his Jug and get his parachute to deploy properly for his descent. However the descent was almost fatally interrupted by a German ME109 diving on the chute.

Luckily for Juchheim (who was about to become a POW) his fellow flight members, William "Mac" McDermott and Frederick White were covering his descent for this eventuality. They saw the enemy fighter diving past 2,000 yards away and chased it to 1,000 feet off the deck where White got many strikes on it before the glycol streaming from it blinded his windscreen and he was forced to overshoot. McDermott then attacked it, placing his second burst into the German's fuselage side which provoked a flaming explosion and crash.

James Stallings' Diary: "May29th: An uneventful trip, though we had a couple of chances to go down on trains. It was Lieutenant Bernhard's last mission and he said he'd be damned if he'd get shot down on his last one down on the deck after a train. Yesterday we lost three men in this most dangerous of all sports - strafing."

Earl Payne's Diary: "May 30th: An ammunition dump near Great Chesterford blew up and I've never experienced such terrific concussions. It lasted until mid-afternoon and we had to keep all the windows opened in case of a new and bigger blast. The dump is a series of Nissen huts and a

Captain James W. Wilkinson in his MX-L "PIN-UP GIRL". His crew is, LR:unk. ARM, ACC S/Sgt. Eugene Carter, and CC S/Sgt. Ismal Boase. James scored 7 air and 2 ground before he crashed into a South Wales mountain. (Eugene Carter)

pyrotechnic signal exploded and set them off by sympathetic detonation. Many people were killed but the newspapers wouldn't acknowledge it."

At 1613 hours that same day Major Stump led a mission to bomb the railroad bridge at Beaumont-sur-Oise, France, where 50 x 500 pound bombs dropped from twenty to fifty feet altitude scored good hits on both ends of the bridge. During takeoff a 500 pounder with an eight second fuse dropped from George Rickett's plane blowing a four foot crater in the runway. When the mission returned, another bomb that had failed to release over target, fell from a landing P-47, but failed to explode. Colonel Gray would not allow anyone near it until he had ridden around it on his motorcycle to check the fuse position. Later in the day an RAF bomb disposal crew dealt with the ordnance.

The stage was set for the Second Front as the month of May,1944 ended with statistics of twenty-five missions, nine losses, twenty-five aerial victories, four ground victories, and twenty locomotives destroyed.

Captain James W. Wilkinson, the acting 82nd CO had been fairly successful in strafing locomotives and the RAF people wanted him to demonstrate his theory on a real locomotive target in Wales. The Silver Star, DSC-ribboned pilot held that hits in the right spot put a locomotive out of action for months rather than only days. This test range loco-shoot was arranged for June 4th but bad weather enroute held up his flight clearance. In order to get airborne, Wilkinson told the authorities he was going up for a local test flight and then he headed for Wales to strafe the locomotive target. Tragically the ten victory ace was killed when his P-47 struck a mist-shrouded mountainside near Llandoverry, Carmarthenshire, South Wales. His place at the 82nd helm was taken by Captain William A. Guilfoyle for four days until Captain Benjamin I. Mayo of the 84th was assigned CO on June 8th.

Brand new P-47D-25 WZ-E 42-26590 issued to crewchief T/Sgt Negley Sapper, and flown most often by First Lieutenant Lawton Clark, who was KIA in it on 9-10-44. Later it will be painted dark green/sky blue with the artwork, "THOROUGHBRED" by its canopy. It carries a 150 gal tank. (Negley Sapper)

Chapter 13

D-Day - Normandy Invasion

Warren Kellerstedt: "They didn't tell us when D-Day was going to be, but the night before we could smell something in the wind. They closed up the post tight and wouldn't let anyone on or off and right after supper on June 5th they ordered black and white stripes painted around the wings and fuselages of the planes. We armorers were kept busy all evening lugging bombs from the bomb dump out to the dispersal area to stack next to the planes. I worked till about midnight and then got two hours sleep in an air raid shelter before I went out and pulled guard from two until four AM. It was a beautiful night with a full moon that made everything as bright as day. All night long the bombers went out, first the RAF, then ours. They all had their navigation lights on because there were so many of them and the sky looked like a Christmas tree, full of red and green lights.

"Well, that started it for us. It was the same thing day after day for us. We were up before three in the morning arming the planes for an early morning takeoff. All day they flew back and forth dive bombing and strafing everything of Jerry's that moved. When they landed from a mission we hopped on the planes, re-armed and bombed them, and cleaned as many of the eight guns as we had time before they took off again. Between shows we prepared new ships to take the place of planes shot down or battle damaged. Finally we would put the ships to bed for the night and crawl into our sacks all set for a good rest and just get to sleep when the damned loudspeakers would start blaring out, 'Attention, all personnel, Air Raid message Red! Buzz Bombs!' Then you lay in your bunk sweating and straining your ears to tell if it's coming your way. Sometimes they were miles away and you hardly heard them, but every so often they would line us up right on the nose and then you really sweat and prayed she wouldn't cut out right overhead. After a close one we'd all get religion and head for the shelters, but then after a while we'd get lazy and stay in bed and trust to luck until the next close one. We never did get one on the field although they hit on all sides of us and came close enough to rattle the windows and vibrate the whole barracks. On a clear morning we could see the vapor trails they left while climbing up and once in Croydon, one of their pet targets, I had half the ceiling plaster come down the back of my neck from a close hit."

James Tudor: "When D-Day arrived all the crew chiefs were issued a Thompson submachine gun and .45 caliber pistol. You wore your pistol all the time on the flight line and kept the machine gun close by. We were also required to pull guard duty on our own aircraft at night for a period of time. This meant 24-hour duty a day."

Richard Holly: "The thing started for me around 7:30 PM the night before. Somebody came around and said we've got a briefing, tomorrow's the day we invade the continent. I thought, 'Well, we've been waiting a long time for it. At the briefing we were told that the Allies were massing and they would hit the beaches at a certain time. Our takeoff time was about 3:20 AM for the first mission. By the time I got out to the line the crews had the black and white stripes painted on the planes. Our job was to line up all the thirty-two aircraft plus spares that were going on the mission in position for takeoff at the end of the runway. I was leading the very last flight of four planes, in 78A Group, made up of 83rd and 84th's sixteen aircraft each.

"After we'd gone back and gotten a few hours sleep, we returned to the airplanes and got them cranked up and checked over. By this time it was just pouring down rain. I'm sure visibility was less than a mile. When the Colonel took off I noticed he had just barely cleared the end of the runway

A 78th armament crew send a 500 lb. bomb and appropriate message to the Wehrmachat's transportation system. Note size of underwing star/bar and D-Day stripes for recognition. (Duke Morrison)

Lt. R.L. BAKER in mx-R 33	June 6, 1944 "D" Day			
Start Engine 5⁴²	Take Off 5	Set Course 5⁴⁸	Alt 3000	
TO XRDC	MILES	CC	ETA	ALTITUDE
EAST CHURCH	57	163°	6:04	8,000
RYE	32	702°	6:13	9,000
ST. VALERY	73	705°	6:32	15,000
BERNAY	55	713°	6:45	17,000
ECOUCHE	40	253°	6:55	,000
BERNAY	40	49°	7:04	,000
LV. AREA	-	-	9:15	,000
ST. VALERY	55	11°	9:20	,000
HOM:	155	35		

A D-Day mission card prepared by each pilot from Intelligence section briefings. Each pilot also carried maps, escape materials, and his flight equipment. Mission card info included check points, miles between, compass-courses, estimated time of arrival and altitudes flown. (James Tudor)

Captain Richard Holly's P-47 WZ-Y 42-25871 "NIGGER II" in its new dark green and sky undersides camouflage paint, shows D-Day recognition stripes to good advantage.. (Negley Sapper)

when he went out of sight. I watched these flights of four take off and it seemed like each time they went out of sight quicker. When it came my turn, I looked down the runway and I just couldn't see anything, so I instructed the guys who were with me that we were going to make a quick takeoff and I would just set my gyro and they were to follow me. That's the only actual instrument takeoff I ever made in World War II and also the only takeoff I used water injection on as well. We cleared the end of the runway all right and climbed on up through about 7,000 feet of rain and overcast, broke out on top and I swear we weren't in it more than a minute and a half! We got separated going up through the clouds and my second echelon couldn't find us and we never did find anyone else.

"Starting across the channel it was pitch black and all of a sudden I began seeing little orange balls all over, and as my eyes focused a little better I found out that the two of us were right in the middle of a formation of Lancaster bombers! They, of course, were all painted black. I looked above me and that seemed like the quickest way out, so we just peeled straight up and out of that formation. Crossing the channel and in our assigned patrol area we were in and out of clouds most of that first mission. I did not see anything on the ground, but the red glow down beneath the clouds told us it was Omaha Beach, because we were a little ways north of there in our area. As it got daylight the red glow went away but we knew from the smoke and haze there was still plenty going on down there."

During D-Day, June 6th, the 78th put up three shows by each squadron. The first and last were combined efforts with a sister squadron and the middle mission was a split effort by single squadrons. A and B Group designations were used during the efforts flown from 0323 to 2315 hours. Thus in effect, squadrons were taking off and landing all day long as the line crews kept up the flow of fuel and ammunition to the planes. Fighter Command labeled the day's operation, "Fullhouse", "Stud", and "Royal Flush" after the giant gamble the Allies were conducting. Perhaps as a treat and souvenir of the great day, the pilots were issued the new B-8 flying goggles with polarized lenses and wide angle view.

Single squadron strikes flew through midday from 0945 hours to 1430 hours as fighter bombing efforts with eight aircraft bombing and eight aircraft giving top cover and then reversing roles. The 83rd bombed a railroad bridge forty miles northwest of Paris while a bit later the 84th mission put fourteen 250 pound bombs into the Alencon marshaling yard damaging some seventy rail cars and causing a large explosion

in a nearby ammunition dump. A little after noon the 82nd carried out a bombing and strafing Rhubarb of rail lines in the area.

The only contact with enemy aircraft during the day came on the third mission by the 83rd Squadron which was led by Colonel Fred Gray. Fighter Command called for a fighter bomber effort to St. Valery Airdrome and Mayenne marshaling yard. As the squadron approached Mayenne, France at their assigned altitude, eight FW190s were called off on the deck below and 83rd flights bounced them. The enemy turned away from another 83rd unit and came towards Peter Caulfield's flight in their attempt to evade the Thunderbolts. Peter singled out one and got into a turning Lufberry with him. Drawing up to a sixty-ninety degree deflection angle, Peter hit him heavily with his bursts and the Jerry snapped, rolled, spun, pulled out, turned, and hooked a wing on the ground, destroying the plane.

Colonel Fred Gray and his wingman, Vincent Massa, joined the chase across the French countryside after the fleeing FW190s and tagged onto their tail-end Charlie. They hauled the German right in after they both turned on their water-injection boost. Fred admits to some sorry deflection bursts, but they did serve to keep the enemy honest going straight, until Fred hit him with four bursts which blew his canopy off as his engine quit. Correctly keeping his speed up in a fight, Fred then overshot the German and skidded out to the side as his wingman, Vince Massa, pulled in to get off a final burst. The German pilot slowly crawled over the side with his helmet and jacket on fire, getting a good chute deployment after a 600 foot lag.

The last mission of the great day took off at 1822 hours with thirty-two aircraft plus spares to patrol the area Chaillone - Coulonche, France. Flights by the 82nd in the northern sector of the area found no targets and departed for DX at 2130 hours. The 84th flights in the southern area sector were more fortunate, strafing a twelve car petrol train which exploded sending flying debris into several P-47s. Wallace Hailey's WZ-F was so hard hit he had to part company with it over the Channel, where ASR picked him up unhurt. Two other Jugs damaged as well, landed safely at Ford, UK advance base.

Allan Cowart: "One humorous note of the dramatic day. A South African friend of mine, an RAF squadron leader, had flown in on June 5th in his Spitfire to make arrangements for our Thunderbolt Band to play a dance at his airfield. Because the Germans had so many of our aircraft with our our markings on them, the invasion force aircraft received the big black and white recognition stripes so we wouldn't get ambushed by our own planes. Everyone on the field worked all night painting stripes around everything and he got the D-Day bands on his Spitfire. It was somewhat embarrassing for him to come out and find it all painted up, because the stripes were for operational aircraft and his was a training squadron and he must have been heavily ragged when he got back there."

This passionately intense period in Group history reached a crescendo four days later when the 78th suffered its most grievous operational day since inception. The first mission of June 10th was another fighter bomb effort along the railroad system in the vicinity of LeTouquet-Evereux-Conches, France. The Group arrived in the area at approximately 0720 hours and proceeded to skip dive-bomb and strafe every military target: bridges, marshaling yards, rail cars, trucks, tanks, and flak towers. No one in the 82nd saw Robert Baker disappear, but it is believed that flak struck his underwing bombs while he was low-level strafing and he was blown out of the sky. Squadron mates did see Richard Kuehner go, without a hope of escape when his P-47 struck a pole on a bomb-run and crashed in an explosion with its full bomb load. When the 84th got back to England Daniel Loyd had to belly in his flak damaged Jug near Duxford.

The second mission of the day took off at 1245 hours led by Major Harold E. Stump, 84th CO, a 78th vet on the first mission of his second combat tour. They arrived in the area south of the Normandy beachhead bomb line at Bernay-Lisieux-Argentan-LaFerte Mace, France, shortly before 1400 with about forty P-47s. Eight aircraft of the 82nd Fighter Squadron continued along the rail lines toward Rennes looking for targets per field orders.

Major Stump led the 84th and 83rd in a dive bomb attack onto a railroad bridge southwest of Argentan. The first five Jugs had released their bombs and were pulling up, when suddenly over twenty ME109s painted in D-Day white-stripes with fake British roundels superimposed, came screaming out of low clouds right on top of the diving 84th Jugs. The rest of the 84th Squadron cut loose their bombs and racked their aircraft back to break up and into the Germans. For Major Harold Stump, Major William Hunt, and Second Lieutenant Daniel Loyd, it was too late, as they were shot down and killed early in the engagement. Instantly the sky space under the cloud deck was a swirling maelstrom of careening aircraft and tracer smoke trails cut by propwash.

Dorian Ledington had just pulled up at 4,000 feet from his bomb run as the Germans broke on him, and he reefed onto the tail of an ME109 whizzing past. He triggered bursts into wingroots and fuselage prompting the German pilot to bail out at 300 feet. Luther Abel dropped his tanks and bombs as the bandit cry clamored in his headphones and dove into the milling rat race. Spotting an ME109 slightly off alone, Abel followed him through thick clouds and claimed hits at long range, causing the pilot to bail out. Finding himself outnumbered in the thick of it, Robert McIntosh got an FW190 in his sight and forced the German to take to his parachute. Shortly after Robert bounced another German and was himself shot down in the protracted engagement. Like McIntosh, James Casey was also downed and taken Prisoner of War.

The 83rd was some distance out of the main action when Franklin Pursell saw the scrap and headed for it. Although outnumbered by fifteen plus, he got in a climb-turn duel with an FW190 and scored hits in an overhead head-on pass. This caused the enemy to bail out. Robert Ealey also outclimbed the enemy aircraft and dove for an ME109 attacking a lone P-47. He got several bursts into the 109 before being forced to look away to save himself form another 109 on his tail. Taking a glimpse back, all he could see of the first 109 were falling aircraft pieces and a chute.

Donald McLeod was pulling hard" Gs" breaking into flashing ME109 snouts and finally worked his way behind one to give it a two second burst. He scored heavy hits on cockpit and engine which blew the 109 apart. Shortly after this McLeod pulled deflection on another ME109 for a short burst to good effect. The German flicked on his back and dove vertically from 800 feet pouring black and white smoke. Again Donald had to quickly break visual contact to avoid an enemy attack.

A bit later, McLeod was himself shot down trying to rid a P-47 of three enemy aircraft. Donald was able to evade German ground forces and link up with French resistance people, who several days later, allowed him to walk over the ground of the big June 10th air battle and view the crash sites and wrecks to verify the results of his kills. One of the wrecks may have been of Vincent Massa, a fellow 83rd pilot, shot down and killed in the flight.

As the fatigued survivors straggled across the English coast for home, Herbert Boyle crashlanded his damaged P-47 at Manston Emergency coastal base.

Not that the woeful day was over, for yet another mission was assembled and dispatched from Duxford at 1730 hours, using thirty P-47s and what daylight remained to strike at an ammunition depot south of Falaise, France. During the outbound climb through overcast toward the south coast, two 83rd planes collided near Southminster, south of London. Francis Kochanek was able to get his parachute open in time and only suffered a broken ankle on ground impact. William McDermott was a fatal casualty trapped in his HL-E as it plunged to earth. The group flew on to bomb the railroad bridge north of Falaise and some Monfort canal barges.

Lt. Louis Dicks, 82FS, models new B-8 flying goggles with polarized/wide angle lenses. A-14 oxygen mask is fastened to his RAF Type-C helmet. His chute harness tops an RAF "Mae West" life preserver and an AAF B-15 jacket. Note glove insert for mission card. (James Kinsolving)

This batch of replacement pilots arrived in the Spring of 1944 to fill the voids left by rotation and casualties. Top row L-R: Lynn Hosford, Harold Beck, Don Swankowski and Harry Slater. Bottom row L-R: Louis Dicks, Ruben Wilkinson and Richard Steele. Slater and Dicks would be lost. (Lynn Hosford)

Along with other Allied fighters, the 78th interdicted German supply lines after the Normandy Invasion. Right, a strike on a marshalling yard produces an explosion and, left, German armored units are strafed while moving by rail. (G. Fry)

Chapter 14

The Battle of France - Low Level Work

Lynn Hosford's Diary: "June 13th: The climb out through the clouds turned out to be hazardous when my Red Flight Leader stalled us out in the propwash of the flight ahead. I did a stall recovery on instruments and my wingman recovered from a half turn spin, as we narrowly missed colliding with each other. On the way in, our radar controller told us there would be enemy planes in our area and sure enough, we saw them. 'Ginfizz' an English radar station, gives us courses to fly to find enemy aircraft. These boys can tell us when enemy aircraft are up and their altitude as far as a hundred miles inland from the coast.

"About thirty plus enemy aircraft escorted us at 11 o'clock high and level, waiting for a good opportunity to bounce us. We were in close battle formation, and this saved us. From time to time, the Huns would slide in to see if we were still in good formation, but as we were, he got tired of waiting and went home when we reached the target still carrying our bombs.

"Arriving back near home base, we ran into the worst weather I've ever flown in. It was raining with low scud clouds down to 100 feet. Had to fly very low to see the ground. I was cut out of the landing pattern once, but succeeded in getting down the second time after skimming over the rooftops to stay out of the clouds, and to miss other landing P-47s.

"June 14th: Guess it was too good to last, because this is another dive bombing show with two 500 pounders. Target is of special importance, we are to hit a camouflaged building northeast of Chantilly, France that houses the German Fighter Direction radar center. We located the target exactly with about 7/10th overcast and dive bombed through a hole. We peeled off one after another in string formation and went Helling down, but I didn't have a good pass, so I racked my ship around in a tight climbing turn to the left at 400 mph to miss the aerial field of 20mm flak coming up, pushed everything to the firewall and climbed back to 10,000 feet. All the way up in the climb I could see the flak bursting just behind in my rearview mirror.

"I had on almost full throttle in this dive, so I was really going fast. I dropped my bombs with good success, broke right, and zoomed back up into the clouds, thus evading the flak. Having lost my flight leader due to the second pass, I tacked onto two 47s from home and returned with them. All this time enemy fighters were reported in our area, but we didn't see any, probably due to keeping well together and deploying some top cover planes high over the target. The Luftwaffe won't attack us unless we are outnumbered, in sloppy formation, straggling, or he has a great altitude advantage. He generally hits and runs from out of the sun, and dives into the clouds and streaks for home. At debriefing we counted up two hits on the main fighter direction building and twenty-six on lesser buildings.

" June 22nd: This mission was a combination Type -16 area support and fighter bombing targets of opportunity. The 'Big Friends' were happy, so we went down looking for targets. Captain Conner's No. 2, James Stallings, saw a locomotive and was given the O.K. to lead the flight in shooting it up. Once below the clouds we found two locos and accompanying trains. Stallings and Conners got the locos on the first pass, and steam blew out of all the holes. My wingman, Bosworth, and I concentrated on a flak car near the end of the train that was shooting at us, getting a few hits. The next pass we all took on the flak car and set it on fire so that the shells were going off like Roman candles. Stallings was so intent on hitting the flak car that when he pulled up he flew through four cables on a high-tension electric line next to the track. The cables cut into his wing and broke his pitot tube nearly off which knocked out his airspeed indicator. He was very lucky!

"Conners shot up the other loco which was throwing up some 20mm flak. Then we dive bombed the first train, getting some close hits. Leaving the area, the loco was billowing steam, dark smoke was rising from the whole train, and the flak car was furiously burning.

"Streaking for home we spied a doubleheader train and dove down to strafe it. Captain Conner and Stallings took out

The P-47 Pratt & Whitney R-2800-59 Double Wasp engine with a Curtiss Type-836 paddleblade prop, instead of the usual Hamilton-Standard. Here S/Sgt. Stoney Wiseman works on his 42-76584 WZ-H P-47-20-RE model. (Negley Sapper)

the loco and my element shot up the boxcars. On my second pass I started shooting at extreme range, which probably saved my life, because after my bullets hit the cars, there was a terrific explosion and four or five boxcars flew into the air. I banked sharply left, but still flew through smoke and pieces of flying boxcars. There was a huge hole in the roadbed where the cars had been. Doubtless they had been carrying some kind of explosive. Upon landing I discovered a hole in the left wing, elevator, and one under the belly. My wingman also was hit by flying pieces and both of our aircraft were scratched and dented."

Robert Eby: (Group Operations Officer) "June 25, 1944 I was leading a flight on the return home from escorting bombers to southern France, when I took a direct hit from the first sign of flak we'd seen all day. Two engine cylinders were knocked out and my flaps were damaged, causing smoke and excessive loss of fuel and oil and the oil on the windshield eliminated forward vision. My first inclination was to bail out as the oil loss was great and the fumes were quite bad in the cockpit. I rolled the canopy back and prepared to exit, but as I had reasonable lateral vision I decided to stick with it a while.

"We had been advised of five emergency airstrips which had been built near the beachhead. I called my wingman and advised of my forward vision problem and that I wanted to try and make one of these emergency strips, and not chance the channel crossing with such a heavy oil loss. So he in effect flew my plane for me and I flew formation on his wing. He took me into a strip which turned out to be B-5, a British strip three miles from the lines and five miles from Bayeux. The Germans shot at us as we crossed the lines and then the English shot at us, but he hung in there and lined me up on the runway and did a beautiful job of throttling back and making a 'no flaps' approach to the short runway. He told me when I was over the end of the runway and I chopped the throttle. He called me to advise I was running out of runway and still going at a good clip. I unlocked the tailwheel lock, kicked hard left rudder and brake and did a 'snap 180', groundlooping the good old Jug, which backed up the last few hundred feet into the brush at the end of the runway. The landing gear would have been wiped out on any but a Navy carrier plane.

"My next problem was to bum a ride home as the P-47 was a candidate for spare parts. I found a British war correspondent who was going into Bayeux, which was an interesting experience. You'd never have though the war was going on to watch the French natives who had been liberated a few day's previous. Eventually I bummed a ride over to Strip B-

2 and hitch-hiked a ride home in an English Anson, via Thorney Island, Northolt, and Duxford."

James Tudor: "I was assigned crew chief on one of the earlier model P-47s, MX-C. The insignia 'SQUINT' was painted just below the cockpit and "T-BOLT' was painted near the engine cowl firewall. This aircraft had a very ragged olive drab paint job on the upper wing surfaces, and with official approval, we removed the upper mainwing paint, leaving it a natural silver Alclad metal finish. It was one of a kind, the first tutone P-47 in the Group."

Richard Holly: "Our squadron got several brand new Jugs and I had a nice silver unpainted one assigned to me. We gave it a shakedown and my crewchief, Dusty Bauer, told me it was ready to go. I took it on the mission and as we were starting home we ran into bad weather. We were not very high, probably around 6-7,000 feet, so we began climbing on the instrument gauges. There were only four of us as the strafing had split up the squadron. All of a sudden all Hell broke loose. The flak gunners had us zeroed in and the shells were bursting right outside my canopy. We quickly broke formation and evaded, but I could tell my plane had been hit. I couldn't get away from the flak and nothing had come into the cockpit, and there didn't seem to be anything wrong with the ship, but they had me so zeroed in I was seriously considering bailing out. I couldn't see where I was going being on the gauges, and I couldn't tell which was the quickest way to get out of there. Sticking with it I finally got out of the flak and I looked around the plane. I could see flak holes in the wings every place I looked, but there seemed no serious structural damage.

"Getting above the overcast, I formatted again with the other three pilots and we resumed climbing for home. We still couldn't see the ground and at around 30,000 feet we came over another heavy flak concentration which got hits on three of the four of us even though we were split up but still staying in visual contact. Evidently we'd flown over the postgraduates of all flak gunners. I got the plane home from its first trip across the channel. When my crew finished counting holes there were thirty-two of smaller size knocked in there.

"Each hole required a patch and it just seemed a shame that a brand new airplane like that was all patched up. In a couple of days it was back on the line and I took it on the next mission, which was a low-level show in France. We were shooting up trains and flak towers and I took a cannonshell smack in the leading edge of the left wing, jamming two of the wing guns.

First Lieutenant Robert Baker with his crew, L-R: Acc Cpl. Arthur Christensen (behind canopy), and CC S/Sgt. James Tudor (on wing). P-47 MX-C 42-8471 was a tutone Jug, with a camouflage fuselage and NMF wings. (James Tudor)

It didn't seem to be too bad, but I knew a cannon shell had exploded inside the wing. I brought it home with no problem and when the crew got to inspecting it, they found it had a busted main spar. This called for a wing replacement. There didn't seem to be a silver wing in the whole European Theater, so they ended up putting an olive drab wing on the aircraft. I flew it like that for the next two or three weeks, and finally decided that it was kind of showing off a little too much, so we painted the rest of the plane to match and I lost my pretty new silver airplane. Each time I brought that shot up silver plane home, I thought poor ole Dusty Bauer was going to have a heart attack. He was a great crew chief and kept that aircraft flying, no matter what happened."

Sergeant James Aicardi: "The P-47 could shake off 20mm shells and come back. One 83rd Jug came in by himself, flying kind of crazy. He landed and taxied to his revetment with the whole ship vibrating so much we thought the engine would shake loose. When they brought it into the hangar we saw the damage. Two of the prop tips were bent way back, there was telephone cable wrapped around the prop shaft, there were small tree branches and leaves jammed down the cowling scoop, and dents in the cowling and leading edge of the wing. How he got it back with that out of track prop was a miracle."

James Tudor: "During this period we changed an engine on one of our P-47s, which required a test flight prior to releasing it for service. The pilot test flew it and came in *wheels up* for a belly landing. When he was asked if the cockpit warning horn sounded as he approached for a landing with his wheels up, he said that the horn was so loud in his ears that he forgot to put the wheels down!

"Some young pilots coming into the outfit gave us mechanics a fit. While flying your plane on a mission, they would get as far as the English Channel, when all of a sudden the engine would begin to act up, so back to base they came. The familiar write-up in the Form-one was: 'Engine runs excessively rough,' or 'prop surges at a given altitude'. Some guys we hated to draw once we got to know them, because you could predict an 'abort' with a high degree of accuracy. Some overcame it after a few trips, others never did."

Ernest Stroud: "One day in the summer of '44 I was doing some post mission work on our P-47. Hearing a most unfamiliar noise overhead, I looked up and saw a B-24 making a low pass across the field. It turned and made another low pass, only this time the flaps were down and the bomb bay doors were open. As it came abreast of the control tower, I saw this small parachute drop from the bomb bay. Having work to do on our plane, I returned to it but I was still wondering about what took place.

"A short time later a Jeep pulled up to our plane and in it were two people, an M.P. and the Officer of the Day. They came up to me and asked me my name. I told them and with that I was presented with a cigar box with my name on it and a small parachute attached. They asked me to open it as they were curious as to what was so important that it had to be delivered by a B-24. Upon opening the box, guess what was inside? Well, inside were seven bars of Palmolive soap. At this time quite a few of my buddies had gathered and at that sight we all had a good laugh. Needless to say I took a lot of ribbing from this.

"The pilot of the B-24 was a close friend of mine from Richmond, Virginia. I had visited him at his base and during our visit I just mentioned that we were having a shortage of soap. I had forgotten about it until I opened the cigar box that arrived by four engine bomber special delivery."

The month of June, 1944, translated into statistics of: approximately forty-five Group missions, (because they often

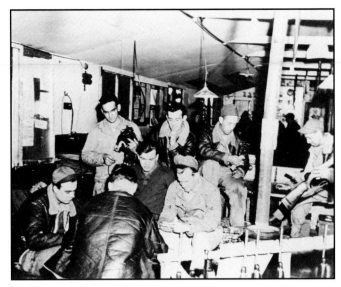

Sweating out the return of a mission, 84FS crews catch a breather. Note rifle rack with weapons to defend the base from rumored German para-troops. (Charles Clark)

involved only separate squadrons or portions of squadrons, it is difficult to call each a group mission): twenty aerial victories, one ground victory, thirteen locomotives, sixteen pilot losses, one evader, and the loss of a crew chief, Tech Sergeant Montell Riddick, who fell off his bicycle directing a taxiing P-47, and was clipped on the left arm and leg by the propeller. After blood transfusions and surgery and two months in hospital, he was sent home and invalided out of the service.

The 83rd Fighter Squadron statistics provide a more defined picture of June, 1944 operations. They include: 639 aircraft dispatched, fourteen aborts, eight failed to take off, 97,363 rounds of ammunition fired (78,000 in combat, 19,000 in practice), 78.9 tons of bombs dropped, 617 sorties, 1984.30 combat hours, 78 hours per pilot average, 2,145.30 hours with training, and 215,500 gallons aviation gas used.

July 1944 : The month got off to an inauspicious start right on day one.

James Stallings' Diary: "This mission was by far my closest call to date. To begin with we had two 250 pound bombs on each wing, a full belly tank, and a bad cross wind for takeoff. Two of the first eight ships that took off collided just after liftoff and crashed about a quarter of a mile off the end of the runway with a big explosion and fire. Edward Kitley and Cleon Raese were both killed instantly. I was already sweating out the takeoff because of the load. We took off over the burning wrecks and didn't feel very good about it. A couple of days ago I went to a crash and saw what was left of the pilot and it was an awful sight.

"We climbed through three layers of clouds and proceeded southeast towards our target, tanks and barges on the Soissons to Reims canal. When we crossed the enemy coast at Furnes, we were only at 9,000 feet, much too low an altitude and started to climb. Our radar controller 'Oilskin' notified us there were bandits at 23,000 feet at point H, which our code for this trip indicated as St. Quentin. We were at about 12,000 feet in this area when the first bandits were seen very high and preparing to attack, so we jettisoned our bombs and tanks. Half a minute later I saw five ME109s coming in behind at 300 yards. I called for my flight to break left as I broke also.

"Seeing that they were still able to hit me, I tried an old stunt Hosford had got away with on an occasion very similar to mine. I pulled the stick back hard into my belly and kicked bottom rudder, going into a violent spin to the left. There isn't

This Jug shows the results of a 20mm cannon shell exploding in its port wing flap. Another example of how the P-47 shook off battle damage to return. (Robert Eby)

a pilot living who can hit a guy in a spin and when I recovered about 3,000 feet below, I didn't have any elevator trim tab control. I surmised a hit had severed the cable. In fact, I'd taken two 20mm cannon shells in my tail surface and was darn lucky my controls weren't completely gone. I had to keep a lot of forward pressure on the stick to fly straight and level."

Lynn Hosford's Diary: "Starting a climbing left turn, I saw an ME109 in a spin and smoking. All this time there was a fight on up ahead of us and the radio was jammed with warnings and calls to 'break'. As I tried to look in every direction at once, I saw a 109 get hits on a P-47 slightly high on me at 8 o'clock. The 47 rolled over and split-essed and the 109 turned toward me. As I broke into this Jerry, I saw he had three 'T-Bolts' on his tail and was only trying to get away.

"Just then my flight leader, George Lundigan, reported that he'd been hit. I looked for him, but the sky was broiling with 109s diving for the clouds and almost all of them had three or so 47s after them. There were some P-51s in the area also chasing the Huns. After landing I learned Lundigan had gotten back to England all right, but his ship was shot up beyond repair. Fred Sharp was bounced by eight 109s and had most of his instruments shot out. He is still in the hospital with some 20mm cannon shell fragments in his left leg and right shoulder."

Combat was not always necessarily with the enemy. On July 5th, Jack Miller, 83rd Squadron, had to abort the mission over France when his P-47 developed failing oil pressure. He got separated from his escorting wingman in the clouds over the Seine Bay just before several British Spitfires bounced him and shot his P-47 out from under him, causing an immediate bailout into the Channel. Later he was picked up by an Allied beach patrol and flown back to Duxford from a beachhead strip. Other than some mental upset and physical exhaustion, he was unharmed.

The black and white checkernosed 78th Thunderbolts were particularly aggressive on the following day, July 6th. Captain Richard Holly led 78A Group off at 0440 for an early morning attack on the German/French trains running out of Orleans, south of Paris. The Group made their familiar landfall at LeTreport on the French coast at 0600 hours and headed south in the corridor between Rouen and the western fringes of Paris. Fifteen minutes past the coast at 15,000 feet the 83rd formation tally-ho'd an enemy gaggle of twenty-five FW190s approaching at 7 o'clock high and turned into them head-on. The enemy went into their standard defense and split-essed for the deck near Rambouillet, southwest of Paris. Foy Higginbottom caught up to one of the FW190s near the

ground and began firing bursts at it, but the pilot skidded his fighter each time Foy pulled the stick trigger. Foy caught on to his trick and made the adjustment that got strikes on the German's canopy. The enemy promptly bailed out.

Franklin Pursell put his P-47 into a vertical dive after one of the FWs and quickly got himself lined up in a zero degree deflection shot at 450 mph straight down. His shooting was right on the FW and Franklin pulled up out of the dive at 8,000 feet, while the FW went straight on into the ground without its pilot bailing out.

One of the 84th's flights kept up the pursuit of two fleeing Germans along the Paris suburbs. Harry Lay leading the flight noticed that the FWs were trying to lead their P-47s between two flak towers on the outskirts of the city and turned to evade the dangerous towers. A swift reappraisal of the situation revealed ten to fifteen more FW190s circling higher up at 9,000 feet waiting to bounce the Jugs. As Lay put it, "We climbed 'Balls Out' to 7,000 feet and the Germans headed for us. The three of us attacked them." Lay got on one's tail and followed its evasive aerobatics until he got strikes forward of the German's cockpit. The enemy pilot bailed out at 800 feet showing a good chute.

Paraphrasing Charles Parmelee's report of the action: "Twelve to fifteen enemy aircraft attacked us from 3 o'clock above and we got into a Lufberry circle with them. I stalled and spun out and started to climb back up, but there were no

This gunfilm shows an ME109G pulling vapor streamers in the warmer lower air as it plunges to its destruction. The canopy is gone, the pilot having just parachuted. (Robert Eby)

Captain Peter Caulfield watches S/Sgt Everett Chappell, 83rd photoman, unload his gun-film post mission. The radio hatch is off of HL-K 42-26543. The aircraft was shot down 9-1-44. (Everett Chappell)

friendly aircraft in sight so I dove away to the north. I saw two FW190s in the mirror following me, so I pulled up left with water-injection on before they could fire and outturned them. They pulled up in climbing turns and I hit the number two man with 70 degree deflection at 150 yards in his wingroots and cockpit. He burned and bailed out."

John Putnam got into the Lufberry circle with the ten plus enemy aircraft that came out of the Paris flak defense. He dove on the last pair of Germans to leave the Lufberry and caught up to one on the deck taking violent evasive action. John finally got him in a left bank with some thirty hits in the cockpit. The Focke-Wulf crashed into a block of houses. The remaining FW came in on John's tail, but was outrun in a five minute chase.

Lynn Hosford's Diary: July 8th: " We were up at 0345 hours to breakfast and at briefing at 0400 hours. Our area was near Compiegne, acting as aerial watchdogs for five boxes of B-17s attacking in that area. The moon was full and very pretty, and I was more in a loving than fighting mood. The moonlight helped on takeoff and it was light enough to see the bombers forming up overhead. As we reached Herne Bay at 10,000 feet, I looked over toward London and saw a great orange flash and then a puff of black smoke rose above it. No need to say what it was. I was astounded by the apparent size of the V-weapon blast."

Lynn Hosford's Diary: July 12th: "As we crossed in the enemy coast, we were shot at through the clouds and Lt Brown's plane was hit, getting about thirty holes in it from the count later at home. We were two miles up traveling about 200 mph over a solid cloud cover, so it's quite obvious how accurate their flak is. The 'Big Friends' were coming out as we went in. I saw a 'Big Friend' circling the clouds and then it dove into them. I imagine the crew was bailing out, but it was too far away to be sure. Our flight relieved four P-38s that were guarding a B-24. This 'Lib' we called , 'black and white tailed B-24 'K' for Kitty.' We escorted him out to the channel. I switched to 'C' channel on the radio and listened to the chatter between the 'Little' and ' Big Friends'. The stragglers, especially ones with engines shot out, were glad to see us and almost implored us to stay with them, which we did. They were extremely appreciative of our protection and told us so.

I heard some of the fighters oblige the bomber crews with some aerobatics, much to their enjoyment judging from the whoops of applause on the radio. Came home feeling like a Boy Scout who'd done his daily good deed."

Lynn Hosford's Diary (an aborted mission): "I have one 108 gallon paper drop tank under each wing of my P-47. Mine is the number one plane on the left of my echelon and as the wave ahead departs, I wiggle Mike Xray-Oboe's ailerons to alert our wave for takeoff. Throttle and turbo levers interconnected, about 3/4 power set and holding, gauges in the 'green', brakes released, full power and take-off roll started. Holding steady heading so as not to crowd ships on the right, quick check of the engine instruments - all O.K. tail off ground, speed increasing, first bounce, second bounce, third bounce (par for a Duxford takeoff) and airborne. Gear coming up and stick shaking from side to side. STICK SHAKING FROM SIDE TO SIDE?? I grab the stick with my left hand and brace with both arms, but the oscillations can't be stopped. Check trim settings and they are nearly neutral, indicators show gear to be up, but ailerons and wings are fluttering up and down at about two cycles per second. Visual inspection from cockpit reveals no cause for this 'rock and roll'. Call to wingmen elicits responses that the gear is really up, fairing doors closed and everything appears 'normal'. I hope they are referring to my ship and not to my flying!

"Climb speed and position in squadron are maintained amid this mystery and thus on into the overcast with wingmen tucked in despite the 'shakes'. Through three thin cloud layers to 14,000 where Phoenix Leader levels the lead squadron to enable the other two to join. Airspeed increases on level-off and wing flutter also increases in rate and amplitude. I brace against the stick with hands and knees but to no avail. Don't want to terminate this mission, but since I don't know what is wrong with the control system and the situation may get worse, I give the code word for an abort.

"Dropping down out of formation, I start a slow turn to the RTB heading. Reducing speed close to a stall as a test indicates control and stability are essentially normal. The stick shaking diminishes at low speed, but does not entirely stop. I decide to keep the drop tanks and fly a four-engined pattern around Duxford and a long, powered final approach. Both saturated drop tanks stay on the racks during touchdown attesting to the necessary careful landing.

"Three surprised, perplexed, and crestfallen ground crew guide MX-O to the hard stand. The puzzled crew chief is on the wing before the prop blades stop turning to inquire with concern, as to why I've aborted. The crew's hopes of getting three day passes after twenty-five consecutive completed missions have just been jeopardized by my early return. We search for the control problem and find it under the right wing. The 'U' shaped fairing covering the front of the wing rack had broken loose on its right side allowing the slip stream to catch and bend it inward and back to lodge between the wing, rack, and the drop tank. In this position it directed air against the underside of the right aileron forcing it up and through the control linkage, pushing the left aileron down. Then the slipstream airflow repeated the cycle. Ironically, it would have shortly broken loose from the internal dzus fasteners and solved the problem itself. The dejected crew begins to drain the gas tanks and I head for the operations room to report and reflect. The P-47 was a great bird, but it really didn't need to flap its wings to fly."

The middle of July brought a fresh flow of leadership changes in the 78th. On the 13th Lieutenant Colonel Robert Eby took off his second hat as Group Deputy CO and remained Group Operations Officer. Lieutenant Colonel Olin Gilbert stepped up to Deputy Group CO. Major William Julian took over as 83rd CO from Gilbert. Major Benjamin Mayo took over the 84th from acting CO, Captain Richard Holly, and Major Norman Munson came back from U.S. leave to resume as 82nd CO, replacing acting 82nd CO Major Mayo. However, Major Munson was killed five days later and Captain Charles Clark was assigned as 82nd Commander.

Pilots and dogs go together like kids and teddy bears. In the 78th there was a particular dog whose name was "Major". This German Shepard was originally owned by Second Lieutenant Ora Brown, of the 82nd who was killed in action on June 13, 1943. After his loss, the dog was befriended, or took up with various pilots, many of whom, whether through the law of averages or plain bad luck, were lost in combat. Once this fact became apparent, a lot of superstitious pilots were reluctant to associate with Major, although he remained in the Group's canine corps.

Major eventually took up with Captain Harry Lay, of the 84th, who had done his first tour in the 91st Bomb Group at Bassingbourn. Lay signed up for fighters so, "I could shoot back at the Jerries for a change". The mornings of his missions, Major and Harry would walk together out to the Captain's plane. On the morning of July 17, 1944, they changed their routine and rode together in a Jeep out to his plane.

Major Olin E. Gilbert (LtCol), 83FS CO and later Group CO, on his HL-X. Note Style 2 crew name panel of black names on yellow square. Usual Style-1 was reverse colors. Collar whistle was to call ASR with salt swollen throat. (Olin Gilbert)

Major Benjamin I. Mayo, acting CO of 82FS and 84FS during June-Sept, 44. His P-47 was crewed by: CC S/Sgt. James Tudor, ACC Cpl. Arthur Christensen, and ARM Cpl. Robert Thuot. MX-X 42-26671 had "NO GUTS - NO GLORY" painted red/yellow with Style-2 crew panel. Note new D-Day stripes on wings. (Duke Morrison)

By 1018 hours, Captain Lay was strafing a German troop train near Liffel-le-Grand, France. His P-47 was quickly crippled by AA fire, and he had to take to his parachute, which dropped him safely into a field, and he was seen to run into some woods to the east. Troops from the train swarmed after him as the circling P-47s held them back with their wing-guns. Inevitably the Thunderbolts ran out of ammo and regretfully headed home. They were forced to leave Captain Lay to the mercy of the avenging troops. Harry Lay's exact fate was never determined, either through the Red Cross or post-war graves registration efforts. At the end of the war, Ora Brown's father, Major's first master, came to England and took the dog back to America with him.

July 19th was a day that would be marred by tragic deaths. Major Ben I. Mayo, 84th Squadron CO, took off at 0705 hours leading the three sixteen ship squadrons plus spares on a penetration escort job. An hour later the group crossed the enemy coast and seventeen minutes later they made visual contact with the bomber-stream headed for targets in west and southwest Germany.

Turning in above some B-24s, they passed along the great armada until they arrived at the lead box of B-17s to take up their escort assignment slot. Shampoo Squadron (84) was weaving in their escort pattern at 0915 hours when they spotted an airdrome below with many parked aircraft. This was Eutingen, near Coblenz/Limburg. The squadron carried on with their escort duty making a mental note of the sighting. Ten minutes later the P-51 relief group swung in to take over and the 78th broke away heading for that plump airdrome full of targets. Cargo Squadron (83) was behind when they turned, so they became leaders in the race for the drome.

The Group let down in a wide circle to the north of Eutingen and hit the deck west of the target lining up on the checkpoints they had picked out five miles west of the airdrome. The leading flights came in across the airfield four abreast with each man picking out a target. They pulled up from the attack two miles to the east and since there was very little flak, another pass was made from northeast to southwest. Mayo almost ran head-on into a flight coming in from the west, so he radioed for everyone to use a sun pattern of southeast to northwest. Still there was little flak and he called for a third pass. By this time smoke was covering the field so badly it was hard to see and the attack was broken off. Circling out around the field, Major Mayo observed every enemy aircraft on the drome was burning. Eleven of the Group pilots had destroyed seventeen enemy aircraft, mostly JU-188s with some DO-217s, JU-87s, and ME-410s. On the way home the 83rd disposed of a locomotive caught in their path.

Ernest Lang hits a Leo-453 French bomber on an occupied French airfield His leader's P-47 just ahead is also seen by the gun camera. (Robert Eby)

A German DO-217K starts to light up from a 78th pilot's bursts as he strafes an enemy airfield. (Robert Eby)

Major Norman "Doug" Munson, on his fourth show of a second tour, was leading Surtax Squadron (82) some distance from the other two squadrons on the escort, and when the turn for home was called, his squadron found another airdrome at Freudenstadt, a grass field near Stuttgart. On his first pass he destroyed one JU-52 and James Kinsolving got another one. As he finished the first pass, Major Munson radioed he was going to make a second pass and came west to east across the field. He got good hits on another JU-52 and it caught fire. Then his P-47 appeared to take a flak hit and it nosed down and struck the ground at a slight angle and flamed. The wreckage of his ship slid along the airdrome and into an adjoining field. The squadron turned for home to report the loss of their popular commander and took some slight vengeance on a locomotive enroute.

The day's mission landed shortly after noontime and the group went about their duties. No one knew the tragedy that was about to unfold.

Lynn Hosford's Diary: "After returning from the mission, Lieutenant Stallings and I went to our room when we'd finished lunch to catch forty winks. At about 2 o'clock we were awakened by a series of loud noises followed by a big explosion that shook our building. I rushed to the window and looked out. About 100 yards away in our barracks area I saw a terrible sight. There was a huge column of black smoke rising high into the air from a great roaring fire, and I could see the wreckage of a plane near one of our buildings. We rushed outside to watch just as the ammunition started to go off."

An 83rd Squadron member relates more of the story: " A 401st Bomb Group B-17 from Deenethorpe came to the base to visit. Its co-pilot was a close friend of two 84th Squadron pilots, John Putnam and Martin Smith. As usual the pilot was persuaded to give rides. He took aboard the two 84th pilots and his own crew. They buzzed the field at breath-taking altitude for a bomber, circled, and came back toward the hangarline at all but naught feet. Many personnel were out watching and all sensed an unavoidable crash as the bomber drew close to the hangars with very little gain in altitude. The bomber did lift over the 84th hangar, but on top of the hangar was a neon light beacon which flashed the station code letters at night in Morse code. The B-17 caught its left wing on this blinker light and sheered off twenty feet just outboard of the engines. The broken wing folded back and tore off the left stabilizer and part of the rudder. The stricken bomber rolled inverted to the left, dropped the stabilizer on the lawn of the Officer's Club, its wing section on the Club roof, tearing up a big patch, and dumped a fuel tank on an empty hut. In a careening scream it passed over a corner of the ball fields back of the Club, causing the ballplayers to take off like professional racers, and crashed into the roof of the 83rd enlisted men's barracks. The bomber hit with a full load of fuel

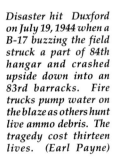

Disaster hit Duxford on July 19, 1944 when a B-17 buzzing the field struck a part of 84th hangar and crashed upside down into an 83rd barracks. Fire trucks pump water on the blaze as others hunt live ammo debris. The tragedy cost thirteen lives. (Earl Payne)

and the gas and flames were thrown over the two story brick structure, destroying a major portion of it, killing Sergeant Ernest Taylor, and badly burning two other men."

With the help of the Cambridge Fire Department, base firefighters managed to extinguish the blaze, but only after it had raged for three hours, mainly due to exploding ammunition. Few who were there could forget that thirteen men had died needlessly and about a half million dollars damage resulted from a pilot trying to show how good a flier he was. Shortly after the incident a stiff order went out from Fighter Command about the penalties for buzzing. Chaplain Zink became the first Eighth Air Force chaplain to win the Soldier's Medal for his heroism in trying to rescue victims in the barracks. Martin Smith, who died in the B-17, had only eight hours left to finish his combat tour.

The following day sections of the Group were returning from Frankfurt separated and mixed in formation from dodging heavy flak, when they saw a B-24 circling at about 7,000 feet near Brussels. On closer inspection they could see the bomb bay doors were open, but there appeared to be no one in the plane. The crew had apparently bailed out for some undiscernible reason. It gave the pilots a weird feeling to watch this pilotless bomber circling above the clouds all by itself on automatic pilot. The Group leader took a picture of The Flying Dutchman, and then turned for home.

Robert Eby recalls a near miss he had in July, 1944. "On the 30th, we were on a Type-16 mission for targets of opportunity and I was strafing a marshaling yard when I got hit by flak. It was a tracer so I could see it coming and I instinctively ducked as it seemed to be heading right for my forehead. The bullet penetrated the windshield, hit the bulletproof glass and ricocheted out the top of the canopy. Outside of the glass fragments flying around and the

A German train blazes far below on the French countryside after 78th pilots have sharpened their gunnery on it. (Robert Eby)

momentary scare, there was no damage done, but it did require a new windshield, bulletproof glass, and part of the glass canopy replaced after I got back.

"In reflecting on the incident I laughed about my instinct trying to duck being quicker than the closing speed of the bullet, but it probably helped keep flying glass fragments away from my eyes."

Major revisions in the Group's aircraft markings took place during the latter part of July, 1944. Before D-Day the Eighth Fighter Command considered that some groups would deploy to the continent and directed the painting of aircraft upper surfaces in camouflage colors on the natural metal finish aircraft. Because of the hectic pace of operations during the invasion and immediately after, the 78th did very little aircraft repainting. When the late July order from the command to remove the black-white invasion stripes came in, the 78th began to comply with the earlier order, as aircraft inspection routines permitted. Also, many pilots felt that a camouflaged aircraft stood out less against the terrain from above than a silver aircraft. The recent heavy losses during June and July low level missions from German fighters with altitude advantage, supported this belief. So from this period on, the Thunderbolts of the 78th slowly acquired dark green upper surfaces and sky blue undersides. However, the D-Day Stripes were retained under the wings and aircraft belly and never did disappear during the aircraft's service in the 78th.

Statistics for the month of July included twenty-eight missions, eleven combat losses plus three killed in the base B-17 crash, against a tally of nine aerial victories, twenty ground strafing victories, twenty-one locomotives, and the usual host of railroad cars, trucks, autos, barracks, and every type of enemy transportation target on which the Group could bring its guns to bear.

Lieutenant Colonel Robert E. Eby, 78th Ops Off. shows the 13mm tracer hit on his canopy, which showered his cockpit with flying glass but missed him on July 30, 1944. (Robert Eby)

August 1944: The 82nd Squadron lost their second CO in less than two weeks, when Captain Charles Clark became a POW on August 2nd. The squadron was bombing and strafing in the Beauvais-Compiegne area when his P-47 received a flak hit on a run over a rail yard. He stayed with the aircraft for a time, attempting to nurse it home, but it became non-flyable and he parachuted safely. His place at the 82nd helm was taken by Major Joseph Myers, a newcomer to the Group.

On August 19th, Captain Charles Peal was leading his flight along a railroad line near Saarbrucken searching for trains when he spotted twenty to thirty HE111s and JU52s hidden under camouflage nets in the woods beside a large grass field at Chateau Salines. Eleven 83rd Squadron pilots left fourteen of these bombers and transports blazing from their gunnery runs.

Harold Beck and his wingman, Wilbur Grimes, put their bombs into a roundhouse full of locomotives at Conflans rail yard and also found a nearby airdrome. They destroyed two JU88s between them and Grimes was hitting an ME109 when it blew up as he passed over. His P-47 received wing damage and it mushed along in the treetops at near stall speed, but he kept it airborne and returned to Duxford.

The Group went out again in the late afternoon on a transportation target area mission against marshaling yards at St. Menehould, Valmy, Tagnon, Fagnieres, Suippe and Epernay. A train of fifty oil tank cars was hit and burned. When the day ended, the Group had destroyed eighteen enemy aircraft on the ground, blown up ten locomotives, and turned scores of vehicles and rail cars to wreckage, for the combat loss of Lieutenant Louis Dicks.

James Kinsolving: "Knowing I had a little 35mm camera, Louis Dicks asked me if I would take pictures of him and his plane. Normally a very pleasant smiling man, he was very serious. We were good friends, and I kidded him a little. 'Want some hero pictures for the home folks, huh?', I said, or words to that effect. Still unsmiling, he said, 'No, but I'm not going to get back alive, and I want them to have the pictures.' Shortly after, maybe a week, we were on a mission together. We were strafing a train in a sort of draw, an Epernay Forest wooded slope on the far side of the track. He was in front of me and to my left. I could see the smoke puffs from his guns as he strafed. He crossed over the train, but didn't pull up, crashing in flames on the slope. Just a coincidence I'm sure, but it was a bit eerie."

Fred Bolgert: On August 10, 1944, I was number two man in Warren Van Dyk's Flight when we spotted rail cars on a siding near Rheims-Epernay, France. I flew a wider than normal right-hand pattern in an old razorback 47 coded MX-F, when all Hell broke loose just as I came into range! Two 88mm flak guns opened up on us at very low altitude. I pulled up taking evasive action, but the bursts kept leading and bracketing us. I distinctly heard two that were extremely close. Off to my right at ground level, I saw a ball of black smoke indicating that one of our aircraft had crashed. Suddenly my aircraft rolled slowly to the right. With reflex action, I pushed full left stick and dropped the nose, as I considered pulling the canopy to bail out. It seemed like an eternity, but as the airspeed increased, the aircraft gradually leveled out, and the 88s stopped firing. The aircraft would fly with full left stick and aileron trim at cruising speed, but would vibrate periodically. The right aileron was flapping in the up position destroying any lift to the outer right wing.

"As I gained altitude and headed for England, I experimented with reducing speed, but it caused the aircraft to roll over to the right. I couldn't make a coordinated turn left - only right. The landing gear operated OK as I came into

Two of August's many flying mishaps. Above, Captain Wallace Bennett lost power on takeoff and his HL-O crashed at Duxford. Below, Lt. Herb Boyle's "OLD SMOOTHY", WZ-J 42-26624, sustained battle damage that took away most of the vertical stabilizer and crash landed at DX on its return. Both pilots survived. (Robert Eby/ James Darrall)

Manston on the coast at 240 mph, touching down in the first third of the runway. Riding the brakes over the last half of the runway, the end was coming up fast, so I ground-looped the aircraft, blowing out the tail wheel tire. We found three holes in the aircraft, two in the right rear tail section, and one in the lower right wing. This one and one half inch square flak fragment had severed the aileron control tube. The vibration had cracked all the gun mounts in that wing. The old razorback was repaired and flew a few more weeks until someone dropped it in from seventy-five feet and washed it out."

On August 12th, the 82nd Squadron clobbered five locomotives at the Fourmies, France, rail yard while the 83rd destroyed two more and torched thirty-five oil tank cars. But the fireworks belonged to the 84th Squadron when their strafing set off a train of twenty ammunition freight cars, whose explosions and fires wiped out the entire rail yard at Breuil, France.

One of the pilots recalled: "On one of the early August missions I was leading my flight back from a target and one of the practices was to follow a railroad track in the general direction of home, and when we spotted trains we would go in and strafe. This particular day we discovered a line of cars and as we set up on our first pass I was just getting squared away at about 1000 yards, getting ready to fire, when the sides of the boxcars dropped open, and I never saw so many muzzle flashes at such close range in my life. There must have been at least eight or twelve 40 mm Pom-Poms zeroed in with a no deflection shot at me and my flight. It didn't take but a split second for me to give them a ninety degree deflection shot, because I was not about to trade eight fifties for all the lead

P-47 WZ-G 42-74694 "JOKER" with a 100 plus mission symbols and test fitted with 5" rocket tubes. Staff Sergeant James Darrall's aircraft was probably the most senior Jug in the 78th. Andrew Barba finished his tour in it in May, 1944, but the aircraft was on operations for over a year. (Duke Morrison)

they were putting up. This action was in line with a recent Command warning to avoid this tradeoff and possible combat losses thereby."

The Group's arsenal received a boost the next day with the trial installation of 4.5 inch M10 rocket launchers on a few P-47s. The first was WZ-G "Joker", one of the longest serving Jugs in the Group.

The 13th of August was mortal bad luck for Lieutenant Billy V. Smith of the 82nd. His P-47 lost power on the morning takeoff, could not lift off, and washed out in a vicious ground-loop which he survived at the runway's end. On the afternoon mission to Boudan, France his aircraft controls were damaged by flak and he gingerly nursed the aircraft back to Duxford. As he turned in the landing pattern to approach the field, his last control cable parted and he died when his P-47 dove straight into the ground three miles from the field.

August 14th started out as a repeat of the previous day. As Captain Wallace Bennett took off, his aircraft refused to climb, mushed into the runway, and skidded along catching fire and exploding when it came to rest. Fortunately for Bennett, he was quick enough to jump out as it skidded and didn't get hurt. The crash delayed the mission takeoff for an hour. That day's fatal bad luck claimed long serving Charles Peal. His P-47 was last seen in heavy flak after his bomb run over a train near Noyon, France.

Another first for the 78th occurred on the 15th as the boys flew fighter escort for Royal Air Force Lancasters and Halifaxes bombing Deelen airdrome southeast of Amsterdam. The Jug jockeys were helpless and greatly saddened to see so many of the big RAF birds stricken by AA fire and sent flaming to earth.

James Stallings' Diary: "Well, August 16th, my 24th birthday, and we're taking 1,500 heavies on withdrawal from targets around Leipzig and beyond. Crossed the Zuider Zee to Steinhuder Lake where we turned southeast and picked up the bombers. We had a straggler escort and continued to the end of the Task Force and then started home with them. I led Surtax Blue Flight and we picked up a B-24 Lib straggler and stuck with them to keep off enemy aircraft. They kept calling on "C" channel asking us to stay with them. After the third time we reassured them we would stick with them, they threw out all their guns, ammo, and everything they could to lighten

the plane. They were then able to gain a little altitude as they were too low for comfort. They were fearful of not making it across the channel, so we stayed until the English Coast. I then pulled up alongside and waved goodbye. They were waving like mad and were really joyful. Those boys really made us feel appreciated. I started to land with them to see them, but decided to come on home."

Colonel Fred Gray, Group CO, inaugurated new P-47 under wing rocket launchers on August 18th during a mission under MEW control to targets at St. Valery, Rouen, and Reims, France. The results and the accuracy of the rockets was very poor as they all missed the aiming point. One new wrinkle to the mission was all the flak fired at the P-47s from desert-camouflaged trucks bearing international Red Cross markings. The Group managed to wreck sixty-five to seventy rail cars.

The weather intervened and the next show didn't take off until August 23rd. Colonel Gray gave the rockets another test on the Lille - Tournai, France marshaling yard but they were again a good deal wide of the mark. The remaining Group ordnance must have been in sympathy, because eighteen of the bombs slung into the rail yards also failed to explode.

Lynn Hosford's Diary: "On August 25th, I led Blue Flight and had five ships as the spare ship joined up with me. Going in we got some flak from the Frisian Islands and also from Heligoland, a real hot-spot, just one big flak gun! Crossing in at 20,000 feet we spied a crippled B-24 going home and radioing for fighter protection. Captain Conner, Squadron leader, told me to escort him home with Blue Flight.

"As we crossed out, the B-24 and the flight got some more flak and I tried to contact the Lib on 'C' channel. As I wasn't sure I was talking to the right bomber, I left the flight up at 19,000 feet and descended to 11,000 to identify the B-24 and call him on the radio. As I flew near, the crew was throwing things out of waist hatches to lighten the ship. This was very necessary as both right engines were stopped with the props feathered. They informed me that they were losing 500 feet a minute flying on two engines. It was easy to establish positive contact with them as the B-24 had two horizontal yellow stripes on the rudder fin with the call letter 'B' between. I told them my whole flight would stay as long as we could. They weren't sure of their course, so I called my Blue three upstairs to get a fix, but the whole flight could not contact 'Oilskin'. I told the bomber to steer 240 degrees and to follow me if his compass was out. I headed 240 degrees and he turned in behind me. After a while on this heading I was getting way ahead of him and I circled to the left to come back alongside.

"When I was about 7 o'clock to him, I saw him suddenly start a steep climbing turn to the left and then he reversed it to the right and then stalled out going dead. The ship went into a dive and although it turned a little, the dive became steeper, and he went straight in, crashing in the sea amid a geyser of flame and water. I saw no chutes leave the ship and I dove down very quickly to look for any possible survivors. I saw pieces of metal that looked like cowling, falling past me. It is my belief that one of the overworked engines blew up, throwing the bomber out of control.

"There was a spotty cloud layer 400 feet over the sea, and I flew over the burning water at 100 feet under this three times trying to see a sign of life. Nothing was visible but yellowish-green oxygen bottles and debris, no sign of a survivor. After climbing back up and rejoining the flight we escorted a lone B-17 home.

"Seeing the B-24 go in has made me feel bad all day. Even though I talked with them only a few minutes, I feel as though I'd lost some close friends. It's a terrible helpless feeling watching men plunge to certain death unable to help them. My hat is off to the bomber crews."

Two days later the Group carried out a noontime bomb attack against the marshaling yards around Metz, France. The 84th found a yard with seventy five to a hundred cars within its confines. An investment of the first two bombs produced a sympathetic explosion which demolished the entire rail yard's contents and sent smoke columns billowing up to 10,000 feet. The locomotive claims upon return to Duxford amounted to seventeen engines.

August 28, 1944 initiated a new era in the ETO fighter war when the 78th claimed the first victory in aviation history over a jet powered aircraft.

Their second mission of the day was a fighter bombing show against rail lines fanning out to the west of Brussels, Belgium. The Group arrived in the area at 1755 hours and began to follow railroad tracks shooting up rolling stock. Major Jack Oberhansly's 82nd Squadron was serving as top cover for the Group strafers when, near Charleroi, Belgium he caught sight of a gray JU88 low down on the deck heading northeast. "Jake" dove from 11,000 pulling up 200 yards from

the twin-engine bomber and firing down to fifty yards before breaking off. He scored numerous strikes on the enemy aircraft which crashed into a small field and blew up into many small flaming pieces.

Working their way north around the western fringes of Brussels, Major Joseph Myers, 82nd Surtax Blue leader, was providing top cover for the Group. At 1915 hours near Termonde, Belgium flying at 11,000 feet, he saw what he thought was a B-26 going south very fast and very low. Joe dove at forty-five degrees registering 450 mph and got right above the bogie at 5,000 feet noting that it was painted slate blue with no markings. The bogie began doing wide ninety degree evasive turns as Myers cut him off from above, right astern, in his 450 mph dive to 2,000 feet. Closing to within 800 yards, it became apparent the stranger was not a B-26. Myers recalled a similarity between the aircraft and ME262 recognition plates.

As he prepared to fire from 500 yards astern, the jet slowed and crashlanded in a plowed field. Myers started shooting as it touched the ground and continued pumping strikes into it down to 100 yards getting hits in the cockpit and both engines. The German jet skidded over a field, stopped, and caught fire. The pilot, Oberfeldwebel Hieronymous Lauer of the unit, Kommando Schenk, jumped out and ran as the rest of Blue Flight came in strafing. In his strafing run Blue Four, Lieutenant Manford Croy, hit the pilot as he ran away from the jet. The Messerschmitt had been transferring from Juvincourt, near Reims, France to a base at Chievres, Belgium when the encounter took place.

As Group flights began turning for home, they left behind Lieutenant Colonel Olin Gilbert, the 78th's Deputy Group commander, whose P-47 was struck by flak while strafing Charleroi airdrome. Olin managed to belly land HL-X safely and began his successful evasion via the Resistance. He returned to England in a fortnight. Lieutenant John Lacy was not so fortunate. He was with 84th squadron strafing a train of fifteen flatcars near Beaumont, Belgium. It appeared as though two cylindrical objects on the cars might be V-1 buzz bombs. The bombs went off with a mighy blast which damaged Lacy's fighter so badly he had to belly it in. As he walked away to become a POW, the rest of the Squadron strafed and destroyed his wrecked WZ-O. The Group also left behind over two dozen dead German soldiers.

The loss of Lieutenant Colonel Gilbert dictated some changes of command. Jake Oberhansly was promoted to Lieutenant Colonel and assigned as Gilbert's replacement and Major Richard E. Conner assumed command of Oberhansly's 82nd Squadron.

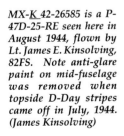

MX-K 42-26585 is a P-47D-25-RE seen here in August 1944, flown by Lt. James E. Kinsolving, 82FS. Note anti-glare paint on mid-fuselage was removed when topside D-Day stripes came off in July, 1944. (James Kinsolving)

Gun cameras of the 78th record the damage or destruction of a variety of ground targets: above left, a German fighter control radar; above right, a Dornier 217 bomber; below left, a French Breguet 693 bomber, employed as a trainer by the GAF; and below right, a Junkers 88G nightfighter. (Robert Eby)

The next day's mission destroyed twenty-five locomotives and large amounts of rail cars, plus twenty-two trucks. The grand total of 143 locomotives for the month was achieved in twenty-four missions for eleven combat losses, with five enemy aircraft destroyed in the air and twenty-four ground victories.

September 1944 : After the last mission of September1st, landed at dusk, there were some very happy pilots to be seen in the club. They were celebrating their final mission which they didn't know about until they landed. Command had just shortened the required combat tour to 285 hours from 300 hours. So they were spared the agony of sweating out that last combat flight, a welcome anti-climax to a tour. Many of them saved that last mission card as a cherished memento. This little card was carried on each sortie. It gave the following notations: the code letter of each ship in the flight, the flight color, order of squadrons in formation, start engine time, check points enroute with compass course and estimated time

of arrival and the letter code of the day for major checkpoints along the route.

The Group was treated to an outdoor concert in a light drizzle of rain on September 2nd. It was worth the wetting to see and hear Bing Crosby's U.S.O. Troop perform at the hangar entrance. Bing had a sore throat and they didn't want to get him sick in the rain. On his arrival everyone had a chance to meet the famous Hollywood star at the Officer's Club. The Group photographer forgot himself and snapped a photo of Bing with a drink in his hand which caused Bing to frown and whisper something to the Group Commander, who walked over and took the photoplate from the photographer. After the concert Bing was escorted off to Wing Headquarters for a luncheon at Highfield House.

Another non-combat tragedy struck the Group on September 3, 1944.

Allan Cowart: "I saw a British Halifax bomber in a flat

spin from the tower, and then the smoke of its crashing into the ground not too far from us down toward Wing Headquarters at Pampisford on the edge of Sawston. First Lieutenant William Shoemaker, our Engineering Fire-Fighting Platoon commander was with me in the tower at the time. Super guy that he was, he got in his Jeep and took his fire-fighting crew down to the crash site. While the aircraft was spinning down we had the glasses on it and we could make out the markings on it. I got on the phone to RAF Flight Operations to find out if the plane was operational with a bomb load, and the answer came back that it was not loaded but only a a training flight. Had Shoemaker been there I would have told him this, but in fact it really was on an operations mission.

"Just about 1645 hours he got there and was trying to locate survivors, when the plane exploded its bombload. He was killed instantly in an act of bravery that so frequently goes unnoticed because the visibility of his action was just not there. Also killed in this explosion were our base Provost Marshal, First Lieutenant Louis Streb, 989th M.P. Company, and his driver, Sergeant Wayne Marsh, as well as Major Clyde Kennedy, 66th Fighter Wing Headquarters. Three others were struck by a flying tree trunk, but escaped serious injury. Five members of the plane's crew perished in the crash."

Three days later the top ace in the Group, Major Quince Brown with thirteen victories, was killed on the 136th sortie of his second combat tour. While scouting Vogelsland airdrome near Weirmuehle, Germany his P-47 was hit by flak. He managed to bail out of stricken WZ-Z near Schleiden Germany, but soon after landing a German civilian shot him in the back of the head with a pistol. In 1946 the War Crimes Trials executed the civilian for his crime.

After one of the longest combat tenures in the Group's history, Major Robert Eby finished his tour and received new orders. He was promoted on September 8th to Lieutenant Colonel and assigned a desk job at Third Air Division Headquarters. His new responsibilities would be as Director of Fighter Operations for this giant Air Division. His old job as Group Operations Officer was assumed by Captain William May.

On September 9, 1944 the 78th was on a dive bombing and strafing mission in the Giessen-Frankfurt-Fulda area at 1730 hours. Visibility was good at 5/10ths low cloud cover and a 4,000 foot base. The area was loaded with locomotives and trains going in all directions.

Major Ben Mayo's White Flight shot up eight locomotives and passed up ten more due to being low on ammunition. Mayo spotted eight FW190s twenty miles north of Frankfurt headed east on the deck and took his three ship flight down in a bounce from 7,000 feet. He knew he had only about seventy-five rounds left in four guns and he determined to close to point-blank range before firing. Ben was unable to close on the far right aircraft - looked left - and saw another FW190 dropping behind the pack. He swung over in trail on him and gave him a couple of short bursts. Observing strikes all over the plane, he watched the German nose over and go straight in from seventy-five feet. Mayo swung in behind another one and started firing with only one gun still operating. This produced two or three hits in the belly and the enemy aircraft started smoking - chandelled sharply up to the left. At 1,000 feet the canopy flew off and the pilot climbed out. The enemy plane half-rolled and went into some woods and burned, while the pilot fell, his chute unopened.

In a beautiful example of how a wingman protects his leader, Lieutenant Wilbur Grimes described his role in this airfight. "Major Mayo, White Leader, called out bogies on the deck heading east southeast near Butzbach, Germany. We came out of the sun at 6 o'clock and chased them east for twenty minutes full out. I was left of my leader ninety degrees going toward him. An FW190 chandelled from my right to left and got on my leader's tail. I threw my plane into a ninety degree left bank and allowing deflection, I set my sights on my leader's plane and opened fire. I continued firing until I had to check my nose down to go under my leader's tail. Glancing up to the right to observe the enemy aircraft, I saw my strikes start at his canopy and go out to his right wingtip. His plane did a violent snap to the right, changed direction 180 degrees and headed down about twenty-five feet off the deck out of control. I racked my plane left to stay with my leader and lost sight of the enemy aircraft I had fired on, but Lieutenant Dunham of the 82nd, shooting at the same plane, hit the enemy pilot as he was bailing out and the aircraft exploded into a hill."

Howard Scholz was near Giessen, Germany at 1725 hours with Surtax Yellow Flight when they spotted twelve FW190s in the process of takeoff from an airdrome. He did not attempt to fire on the first ones taking off because of the intense flak, but closed on the last three enemy aircraft to get airborne. His gunnery quickly caused two of them to crash and explode. Howard was getting numerous strikes on the third one, but had to break off as it was leading him back into the airfield flak barrage.

Surtax Yellow Four, Wayne Coleman, picked one of the FW90s rising from the field and pulled up on its tail firing. The enemy pilot bailed out and the FW crashed and exploded west of the airdrome. Just then another FW190 came headon at

Captain Richard A. Hewitt starts off his second tour with a picture flight in MX-E 42-26635. (George Letzter)

Wayne on the deck, but Wayne could not get into a firing position. The German broke sharply left, got into a spin at low level and crashed, scattering debris. Then Coleman pulled up and made a pass at an FW190 to shake him off of another P-47's tail. The German broke off his attack and slowly lost in a turning match with the P-47. The enemy headed out running due east on the deck. After a five minute chase Coleman slowly drew into range and obtained strikes on the enemy's wings. The German chandelled up to 200 feet, rolled twice, and crashed, causing the belief that the pilot had been hit.

About this same time Herbert Shope found three ME109s parked on the airdrome in a rose petal fashion with their noses together. He dove his pair of 250 pound bombs directly into the center of this grouping, blowing all three to bits. For good measure he blew up another enemy aircraft, a JU88, on an airdrome southwest of the first field before he headed home.

September 10th, 1944 saw the 78th destroy almost as many German bombers as the whole RAF on some of the better days of the Battle of Britain. The day's tally was forty bombers strafed and burned in a Rhubarb mission to airfields in the Aschaffenburg-Mannheim, Germany. The airdromes were Mainbullau and Gernsheim, and the mission ran four hours and forty-two minutes. Top strafer on the sweep was Captain Raymond E. Smith with five HE111s and three shared victories.

However, the show was extremely expensive. Charles Parmelee was belly landing his aircraft near Wiesbaden Germany from a flak hit when it ran into a hedge that was hiding a stone wall. The P-47 blew up killing him. William Lacy was hit by the intense flak at Mainbullau, rolled on his back and fatally crashed and burned. The squadron suspected that Lawton Clark was hiding a poor depth perception problem because he had been flying though a lot of treetops when strafing. On this day he was shooting up a marshaling yard when he flew into the top of a train destroying pilot and plane.

Those pilots who ended up as Prisoners of War were a lot more fortunate. Robert Clague fell victim to the airdrome flak, lost his oil pressure, flew a course for home for five minutes, and then bellied in southwest of Darnestadt, Germany. No one saw what happened to Paul McKenney after he left Gernsheim airdrome in his flak-stricken Jug.

On September 12 the Deputy Group Commander slot reverted back to Lieutenant Colonel Olin Gilbert when he returned from his successful evasion behind enemy lines.

"MARGARET'S MACE" MX-O 42-76351 was flown by second cycle pilot, Lt. Lynn H. Hosford, 82FS A-Flt Leader. The tour reduction to 285 hours from 300 hours enabled him to go home by 9-1-44. (Lynn Hosford)

First Lieutenant Hayden Richards with his crew, L-R: ARM Cpl. Cecil Sellers, CC S/Sgt. Tauno Koski, Hayden, and ACC Cpl Kenneth Christopher. Behind is their MX-T 42-76557 "JUDY". (Hayden Richards)

Second Lieutenant Joseph Jackson and his chief with their "FAST ACTION JACKSON" Note NMF canopy frame and redone code letters (Jack Miller)

First Lieutenant James B. Stallings readies for a show in Fred Sharp's "ROUGH EDGE" The pace of ops saw his tour start on 4-10-44 and finish on 9-12-44, roughly 5 months for 285 combat hours. Multi show days did it. (James Stallings)

Chapter 15

Arnhem - Flak Busting

The six missions of September 17-26,1944, earned the 78th its first AAF Distinguished Unit Citation. They consisted of flak-suppression and air support sorties during the enormous albeit disastrous OPERATION MARKET-GARDEN, the Allied airborne assault across the Netherlands Escaut Canal and thence to the Rhine at Arnhem-Nijmegen.

At 1207 hours on September 17th, the 78th Fighter Group made landfall at Haamstede-Westhoofd on the Dutch coast led by Lieutenant Colonel Joseph Myers. Flying along the routes to be used later by transport aircraft the Group sent a flight down to 2,000 feet to draw enemy flak. Once the enemy gunners opened up, the rest of the Group came down and dropped 260 pound fragmentation bombs on the gun emplacements. From 1227 to 1330 hours the Thunderbolts destroyed sixteen multi-gun sites and damaged thirty-seven others by the use of these tactics.

After all guns were knocked out or had quit firing the flights went back to the coast to escort the first glider towing C-47 transports. No anti-aircraft was received by the gliders as they landed. Several flights escorted paratroop carrying C-47s of which ten to twelve were shot down by flak sites 78th pilots could not locate to neutralize. Five C-47s were seen to bellyland in fields at Best, Belgium. Three C-47s were downed south of Nijmegen and three more east of Dordrecht. One C-47 ditched in the North Sea. On the way home, Herbert Shope destroyed an ME109 on the ground at Gilze-Rijen airdrome. Donald Hart was hit by flak and was forced to bail out into the sea enroute home, being picked up safely by ASR.

The next day Lieutenant Colonel Jack Oberhansly was up front as the Group went back to Holland in late afternoon to patrol the Dutch airborne supply drop areas. Twelve light flak positions and a twenty to thirty truck convoy were put out of action. In some spots the overcast closed down to 500 feet and this produced a very hot flak reception in the target areas. The 56th Fighter Group lost sixteen aircraft in these treacherous conditions. The 78th's losses were considered heavy with one pilot KIA and four pilots as POWs. At approximately 1630 hours Eugene Wood's P-47 was set afire by flak hits while strafing in the Nijmegen area and he crashed to his death. John Fee was hit by flak at the north end of Nijmegen bridge and squadronmates saw his P-47 spin into a lake from 2,000 feet. Unseen, Fee had parachuted into captivity. Both John Loegering and Richard Snyder were forced to belly in their flak damaged fighters at Goch and Rotterdam respectively, while Russell MacDuffee took to his parachute after some heavy caliber flak downed him near Turnout, Netherlands. He was last seen afoot running rapidly east. Somewhat luckier was Allen Rosenblum, who managed to get his aircraft inside Allied lines at Brussels before plowing a field furrow with it.

Poor weather on the 19th kept most Command groups grounded including the 78th. The following day Major Richard Conner led the Group to their Dutch patrol area at Hertogenbosch. Finding no suitable targets they went north of Arnhem to bomb five light flak positions and then west of Nijmegen where they attacked six more sites. Along the route they strafed a troop convoy whose soldiers returned fire from the shelter of a wooded area. In the same area pilots witnessed

several RAF Stirling bombers with paratroops aboard hit the ground and explode. Arnhem's deadly flak also claimed several more C-47s.

Colonel Fred Gray took off at 1421 hours on September 23rd with the next mission to neutralize flak in an RAF resupply drop-zone, without knowing that the British troops had been withdrawn some time previously. Circling Arnhem, the Group approached from the south and turned ninety degrees west to Kasteel, where they met a terrific barrage of 20-40mm light AA from the hedgerows and woods north of town. Colonel Gray took a squadron and temporarily silenced these guns while another squadron suppressed guns in a church south of the woods.

Just after completing these attacks the Group witnessed a formation of C-47s from the south at extremely low altitude. The transports dropped supplies into the woods the pilots had just attacked. Three C-47s approaching were shot down by some of the guns which resumed firing in this marred effort. Immediately the third squadron attacked the remaining guns and destroyed them, as two more wings of C-47s and Stirlings appeared and dropped more supplies into the midst of the German defended woods. No flak met the transports on this operation despite their very low approach altitude.

In another area where the 78th had not been assigned to flak suppression, four Stirlings were hit heavily and went down in flames. German AA units were very well hidden and held their fire until the fighters had passed and were banking away. When the 78th planes turned back to attack them, they, of course, ceased firing. The supply drop was doubtlessly captured, but scores of transports were saved from the approximately twenty-five multi-gun emplacements. During the first dive at the flak batteries just west of Heteren, Netherlands, Colonel Gray's wingman, Dunstan Hartley received a direct hit and went straight into the ground. The

Air and ground leaders of the 78th, LtCol Erlath Zuehl (L), Grp. Adjutant, and Col Frederic Gray, Grp. CO. Behind is Col. Gray's "MR. TED" HL-Z 42-26391 with his one-half kill and a Style-1 crew panel. Gray was a USAF Brig/Gen (ret). (Erlath Zuehl)

Group returned to base with thirteen fighters bearing battle damages.

A weather stand-down from operations on the 25th allowed time for a change of squadron commanders in the 84th. Major Ben Mayo finished his tour and turned the squadron over to Captain Leonard Marshall before returning to the States. Lieutenant Colonel Olin Gilbert left the Group and Lieutenant Colonel Jack Oberhansly moved back as Deputy Group Commander.

Leading his new command, Leonard Marshall took the Group on their final Arnhem support mission on September 26th. Patrolling the area at 2,500 feet from 1531 to 1630 hours the only activity was one flak burst at Arnhem, meager flak at Hertogenbosch, and some C-47s landing and taking off from a strip in the area. A bogie report northwest of Dusseldorf yielded nothing.

The 78th was awarded the Distinguished Unit citation for its 237 sorties over the Arnhem - Nijmegen battlefield but that noble effort was insufficient to save large portions of the British First Airborne Army trapped north of the Rhine and forced to surrender.

Late in September 1944, the Germans added a new terror to their bag of horrors.

Allan Cowart: "About this time the German V-2 rockets produced a scary prospect. You just didn't know what would happen then. Those things would come in all of a sudden and there would be a double explosion, blowing the air out and then the air rushing back in. I was in London with a bad tooth ache, walking to the nearest hospital, as I was really in bad shape. I was walking west on a street on the way to the hospital, and all of a sudden I found myself walking east along the street away from the hospital. A V-2 had exploded maybe two blocks from where I was. There were some big buildings in between which protected me, but somehow the concussion had gotten me on the other side of the street. Perhaps I was knocked unconscious, but I was still mobile after it happened, and there was no dirt on my clothes. I just found myself walking the other way."

As a result of the abundance of low-level strafing and the Arnhem support missions, the group finished the month with almost a casualty per mission. Flying twenty missions, the Group suffered eighteen losses while claiming thirteen aerial victories, forty-seven ground victories, and eighty locomotives. Three group members were also killed in a bomber crash rescue near the base.

Major Benjamin Mayo's 84FS P-47 artwork. Crewchief S/Sgt Sam T. Snoddy is on the wing of WZ-V 42-26567 "NO GUTS.....NO GLORY!" The same art was on his 82FS P-47. (Richard Ballard)

Third cycle pilots of the 78th began to arrive through Aug-Sept. 1944 to replace the heavy casualties of the Summer months and tour completions. Captain Huie H. Lamb, Jr. just joined 82FS, with the P-47 MX-O 42-28422 he shared with another pilot. (Huie Lamb)

MX-K 42-27378 was flak-damaged on the Sept. 23 '44 Arnhem show and was sent back to the depot. Captain Wilbur Coss flew it that day. Note chief has full back-stick to keep tail down while testing motor. (James Kinsolving)

Chapter 16

Top Cover - Escort Resumes

October 1944: The October 7th mission called for the 78th to provide penetration and target support for the Heavies attacking Leipzig, Germany. The group crossed at the Hague and made rendezvous at 26,000 feet at 1158 hours near Northeim, Germany. Fighter Control warned of approaching bogies northwest of Jena and west of Naumberg, as the bomber stream was west of Leipzig. Major Richard Conner was in the vicinity of several bomber boxes at 1220 hours flying at 24,000 feet looking for the reported bandits southwest of Hannover, when he saw two aircraft at 12-14,000 feet. Going down with altitude advantage, he still could not close on them and this made him realize they were jets. Evidently the jets were short of fuel because they began to circle an airdrome north of Osnabruck allowing Conner to catch up and make an attack. The jet target outran him and came back head-on. Conner was able to turn inside of the enemy fighter and score some hits. Continuing for the airdrome, with Conner pursuing at full power, the German jet lowered his wheels to land. Richard got one quick shot from dead astern at the slowing jet and overran him to do some quick evasive action in the intense accurate light flak coming up from the field. Conner's wingmen saw the German jet fighter crash on the drome and explode.

Near the same locality west of Leipzig, Lieutenant Colonel Joseph Myers was proceeding down the line of bombers at 27,000 feet when a gaggle of fifty plus Germans approached at 10 o'clock slightly higher. Radioing their position, Joe called the squadron to full power and started a climbing left turn to gain altitude. Reaching the enemy's level with four aircraft, Joe attacked the force of ME109s causing most of them to split-ess for the deck. Joe's section jumped the remaining enemy aircraft climbing away using fifty inches of mercury and closed rapidly on them. Firing on the far left German from 300-150 yards, Joe found his K-14 gunsight producing no results.

Closing to fifty yards dead astern, he gave the German a burst using his fixed sight and observed about ten flashes around its oil cooler. The enemy aircraft started to burn as Joe skidded aside to avoid ramming. As he broke off the attack the German jettisoned his canopy and crawled out to parachute.

Robert Bosworth got into a Lufberry with one of the Germans who bounced the Thunderbolts in their climb. Bosworth raced the German down to 10,000 feet without scoring any good hits, when suddenly the German pulled up steeply and bailed out. The Germans did not depart empty handed however, as they downed six B-17s in their attack. The eighteen bomber crewmen descending in their parachutes were subjected to light AA practice by German gunners.

On the deck heading for home, P-47s knocked out three locomotives, but lost Robert D. Smith. After his second firing pass at a locomotive his fighter was seen to mush into the trees of a wood northwest of Neustadt, Germany. The pilot was killed in the impact and explosion. The Leipzig mission had been the longest to date. Some pilots were airborne for five hours, twenty minutes

The 83rd squadron experienced a change of command on October 9th when CO, Major William Julian, took U.S. leave and his post was assumed by acting CO, Major Samuel Beckley. A higher echelon change of command took place on October 10th. Eighth Fighter Command moved to the continent assuming duties of a fighter direction center, while 66th Wing groups were then assigned for operations to the Third Air Division.

German jet fighters then operating against Allied bomber forces were particularly vulnerable during their takeoffs and landings, therefore, the Luftwaffe made a practice of flying piston-engine fighter top-cover over the jet fields to protect their ME262s from patrolling Allied fighters. This was the stage set for the combats of October 15, 1944.

P-47 WZ-S 42-28878 is 1LT. Frank E. Oiler's "EILEEN" in new dark green upper and sky blue lower paint job. Also note new squadron rudder markings. (Frank Oiler)

Lieutenant James Mattern's MX-P 42-28740 lands from a show with underwings stained by gun smoke from the shell ejection chutes. Note long gear extension minus aircraft weight. (USAF)

At 0845 hours, Cargo Red Leader, Captain Julian Reems, was passing over the German jet field of Bohmte northeast of Osnabruck. The weather was 4 to 6/10ths cloud with base at 2,000 feet and tops at 5,000 feet and a heavy haze from clouds to deck.

Julian Reems: "We saw bogies circling the airdrome and bounced a flight of four Longnose FW190Ds followed by a flight of two more. I took the right one of the two and pulled up to check him out as they were painted like us - grass green on top and light blue underneath. We surprised them and he didn't break until I was right on his tail. He did a tight turn, rolled out, three quarter flick, rolled out in the opposite direction at 2,000 feet and dove to the deck and pulled up in a sharp chandelle. I fired with no result until I got him with a deflection concentration at the top of the chandelle in the cockpit and wingroots. He did a tight turn, roll, dove to the deck, and leveled out. I fired as he leveled out, hitting the ground around him, and he struck the ground and blew up.

"Then I jumped one of two circling FWs, one a fine flier who went through exhaustive low level evasion for fifteen minutes, with me getting many good strikes. At this point Robert Green came in on his tail and struck him good, as did another P-47. I fired through a flick-roll and a roll as he bailed out and I must have hit the pilot as the chute didn't open at 800 feet. I took film of the fire."

Lloyd Eadline "Four bandits were called out on the deck and we bounced. I closed in and got strikes on one on the right. He started to smoke and broke left. After another burst his canopy came off, he broke right, and I gave him more bursts until he crashlanded bursting into flames. I was in very heavy flak at the time. I was using the K-14 sight and just put the pipper on the aircraft canopy and ignored lead. I like the sight very much."

Robert Green: (Cargo Red Three element leader who ran up the most victories for the day): "As we passed over Bohmte airdrome at 15,000 feet, bogies were called at 2,000 feet at 2

First Lieutenant Robert Laho's "MY BABY" WZ-X 42-28615 was crewed by: CC S/Sgt. Gerald Shope, ACC PFC Charles Ketterer, and ARM Sgt. Michael Sheehan. An RAF Spitfire rearview mirror was mounted on most 47D-25-plus model aircraft. (Charles Clark)

o'clock. There were two FWs and I took the left one closing very fast. I was unnoticed as they did not break. I cut loose and observed hits on his cockpit and engine, which poured white smoke. He went down in a forty-five degree dive and crashed and exploded in some trees as I broke up in a chandelle and spotted two FW190s in a left turn trying for a headon pass at me. I pulled around and took a ninety degree deflection shot at the rear enemy aircraft and got hits on his wing, fuselage, and cockpit. I was closing so fast I had to rack it around and throttle back. He straightened out and I positioned myself nearly dead astern. Gave him a long burst, passed on the left and climbed up. He fell off to the right minus his canopy, went over on his back and exploded into the ground.

"I climbed up and saw four more FW190s at 1,000 feet ahead and below. I took the number three man who tried a couple turns, a chandelle, and rolled for the deck. I got in two short bursts on the way down, which must have killed him, as he went straight in and disintegrated.

"Circling up, I saw a P-47 (Reems) fighting an FW190 on the deck and I told him I'd give him top cover. The enemy pilot was an old hand doing half snap rolls and the two were about even, so I decided to lend assistance. My first burst achieved many strikes on his fuselage - cockpit - engine, and his canopy shot off and he went in and exploded.."

It was almost time to head back to England at 1045 hours, when Huie Lamb of the 82nd spotted an ME262 jet from 15,000 feet near Osnabruck. Diving to the jet's level at 4,000 feet, Huie

didn't think he could make it home and joined the rolls of 78th POWs. The long mission had lasted just minutes short of five hours.

Late in October Colonel Fred Gray tested a new modification on his P-47, the installation of a 20mm cannon attached to each underwing pylon shackle. Gray gave a negative report on the results of his test, saying that the recoil shock of firing the cannons was too great for the Jug to withstand their use.

Frank Oiler recalls a novel use of a regular component on the Jug that pilots periodically employed. "We used to crank out the engine-cooling cowl flaps on the Jug as air brakes when flying in a formation. For instance, if you were speeding up too much and moving out of position, you'd deploy the cowl flaps out as far as they'd go and they would create drag and slow you down."

Two 83rd squadron pilots were unable to take off on the October 26th show because their fighters became mired in the mud of the soggy runway at DX. The grass surface was proving to be a severe handicap to operations due to Autumn's heavy rains. This problem set in motion arrangements to lay down a hard surface runway in the following month.

During the fall of 1944 the green and sky-painted Jugs of the 84th acquired a flowering of "nose art" which for some unexplained reason, did not reach such heights in the other two squadrons.

Gas men of the 84th: Cpl James Wenninghoff, standing and S/Sgt Sylvester Heytman and James Tolleson atop the tank. Oil truck is a GMC Deuce and a one-half 6 x 6 with a 700 gal Columbian built tank body. (Charles Clark)

closed to within 1,000 yards in a steep dive at 475 mph. The jet began to pull away and Huie was able to close very slowly using water-injection. Once in range Lamb took a shot and the jet turned left, allowing the P-47 to easily turn inside and score many strikes. The German did a 180-turn and led the P-47 back over an airdrome, through an intense curtain of light flak. The jet pilot finally threw off his canopy and the plane caught fire as it flipped on its back and exploded. Huie watched the flaming wreckage crash to the ground.

On the days debit side, Jack LaGrange, 83rd squadron, collected some flak damage in a strafing pass at Fassberg Airdrome near Munster, Germany. Twenty minutes after heading out for home base, he called on the radio that he

Richard Baron: The first P-47 I was assigned was WZ-A and I had the name "Mrs. Blue" painted on it. The name evolved from my name of Baron and the fact of a top-name dance-band leader back in the states who was using the stage-name "The Blue Baron". And in addition, I was using the radio callsign,"Shampoo Blue leader", when I led my 84th Flight. Ergo, the guys all took to calling me "Mr. Blue" and so I gave my airplane the name "Mrs. Blue". For young pilots it all went together quite logically.

"When we gave our old D-series P-47s to the Ninth Air Force I ferried "Mrs. Blue" over to Paris and bid her goodbye. Next I received a new silver D-25 bubble-canopy P-47 coded WZ-A and I called her, "Mrs. Blue II". While I was in London on pass, my crewchief needed an air test done with WZ-A and a brand new squadron pilot fresh from the States was assigned to take her up for the test. I have a snapshot of what she looked like after he landed her. It shows the twisted and smashed fuselage laying on its back standing on the vertical stabilizer. The main wings, entire engine assembly, and the horizontal stabilizers are completely ripped off. He could thank the sturdiness of the Jug that he survived the crash landing. After that I was forced to fly my last few missions in just-junk airplanes that were spares. Boy, was I angry. But I finished the tour okay and that's what really mattered the most."

By this date in the war certain commodities were hard to come by in the UK, but the ingenuity of the American G.I. was always equal to the challenge. One sergeant related, "Hard drinks were difficult to buy in England, so we had to improvise some way of getting some into the country. Scotch and Gin were about all there was and then in very limited quantities, except if you could wangle something from the Officer's Club personnel.

"I heard somewhere that it could be brought into the country by a unique way that even the censors could not detect. I sent a letter to my uncle through other means than military mail so nobody would find out what I meant to do. I told him to get some good aged liquor, such as Schenley or Calvert, and also some bottles of Aqua Velva after-shave lotion and Kreml shampoo. I told him to dump out the Aqua Velva and Kreml, wash the bottles out very clean and to fill them up with the good liquor , and also specifically to seal them up with the same color tape as the labels. These bottles came through all right,

"For a while, the boys were taken aback, because instead of using the contents of these bottles on my hair, I was drinking it. They didn't catch on until a little later when I was staggering a little bit and my eyes were getting shiny."

Going back to almost strictly bomber escort duties in October, '44 caused a great reduction in pilot losses, and it was duty the pilots were much happier to perform. From this period on, the fighter/bombing role was left to the Ninth Air Force and the other Allied Tactical Air Forces. Pilot losses in October were only two combat and one flying accident for seventeen missions, producing twelve aerial victories, one

ground victory, and twenty-four locomotives claimed. Since the 78th's combat debut, the Group to date had scored 239.50-22-119 aerial kills and 142-2-117 ground kills for 16,621 sorties.

November 1944 : Colonel Fred Gray summoned the entire Group to the base theater on November first and dropped a blockbuster announcement on them. They were being re-equipped with the North American P-51D Mustang fighter aircraft and their beloved Jugs were leaving them. This was greeted with mixed feelings. For the ground crews the change meant learning to service and maintain a completely different airplane, going from an air- cooled radial engine to a liquid cooled in-line engine. For the pilots it meant increased range, although not as much as some thought, because the P-47 had been greatly aided in range by new tanks and the use of bases on the continent. The P-51 had greater maneuverability, but a great deal less endurability, as it had nowhere near the Jug's flak tolerance. The P-47 could be counted on to get you home, but not always so the Mustang, as many would later learn to their regret. Personally Colonel Gray was heartbroken and declared they'd have to drag him from his Jug with his heels furrowing the concrete. The reason for the change was General Doolittle's desire to have his fighter forces all using the same aircraft for many reasons of compatibility.

The early part of November saw a markings change on the Group's P-47s. Eighth Air Force fighter forces began using colored rudders as an aid to squadron identification within the groups. Squadron painters sprayed the 82nd Squadron's rudders red, the 83rd's white, and the 84th's black. At this time the Group was able to average eighty-six aircraft ready for a mission, and they began to fly A and B group formations again on occasion along with many other Eighth Air Force units. By mid-month the Group was receiving 215 gallon drop tanks for use in helping them keep up with the fast-advancing ground forces on the continent.

To begin the transition to Mustangs, the Group was issued several old war-weary P-51B and C Models for pilot training in off-mission hours. Support for these P-51s came when the 84th Air Service Squadron received a thirty day supply level of P-51 parts, which were stored in the base theatre until shelf space became available. Coinciding with the pilots' training, an engineering school of P-51 maintenance was opened on the base for ground crews.

Jug MX-S 42-27339 flown by LtCol. Joseph Myers was the first fighter to down an ME262 German jet. The Grp.'s aircraft line out behind on Bassingbourn bomber field, their temporary home. (USAAF)

Chapter 17

Bassingbourn - Temporary Base

By November first heavy rains had made Duxford too soft and muddy for flight operations. Therefore, Group aircraft were moved to the 91st Bomb Group's Base at Bassingbourn. This airfield was located fourteen miles west of Duxford just three and one half miles north of Royston. Ground crews and armorers still living at Duxford, were awakened three hours before mission takeoff, had a quick breakfast, and climbed into trucks for the half hour ride to Bassingbourn to prepare their aircraft. Each squadron's engineering and supply section had a single pyramid tent on the bomber field with a direct phone line to Duxford so parts could be sent for quickly. As the days were cold, a big fire was kept stoked in front of each tent. Perimeter parking at Bassingbourn was also muddy and congested and aircraft often got stuck, but no takeoffs were missed or delayed while the Group flew from there.

With the Thunderbolts out of the way, Army Engineers began to lay down a 3,500'x150' pierced-steel-plank main runway between the two steel mattings laid down in 1943 at each runway end, for a total of 4,100 feet of runway. The work at Duxford went slowly due to the fact that most of the matting supply had been sent to France for airfield construction, it being deemed no longer needed in the UK. Work went around the clock under lights. One evening an RAF night bomber dropped a small practice bomb on the lights and sentries fired their rifles at the supposed intruder, but no one was hurt on either side.

The first mission from Bassingbourn on November 21st was a target support escort job to Hamburg, which took off at 0940 hours. The Group made rendezvous at Nordholz, Germany, escorted through the target, and left the bombers at Itzehoe at 1240 hours.

Black Flight of the 82nd was in the area of Hannover at 1220 hours, when fifteen plus ME109s approached out of the sun at 10 to 12 o'clock high. The flight turned into the attacking MEs and a fight started with everyone breaking into the German assault. Richard Hewitt's five second burst into an ME109 caused it to lose control and go straight into the ground from 4,000 feet. Allen Rosenblum fought a 109 for ten minutes before his strikes sent it into a spin on top of the clouds and spun it into the deck. Robert Holmes saw an ME109 on Richard Conner's tail, climbed at full power and turned inside, closing rapidly with hits into wingroots and cockpit. He quit firing as it rolled over and dove into the ground. Conner easily caught up to another Messerschmitt crossing in front of him and sprayed strikes on its engine as the pilot bailed out. Turning into a gaggle of 109s, Conner's several bursts produced strikes in the fuselage, wings and engine of one which went into a vertical dive losing its canopy. The pilot did not get out before it crashed. On the way home the 82nd strafed Gutersloh airdrome scoring two ground victories.

On the loss side, Harry Thompson belly landed his P-47 southeast of Munster, Germany, set it on fire and walked off into a prison camp.

The mission of November 25th, 1944 observed a foreboding sight, new in military history and an evil omen for mankind's future, the liftoff and climb-out of a V-2 rocket. Three "Big

Officers of the 83FS pose just before show time at Bassingbourn field. L-R: Capt. Joel Meyer (83 Eng. Off.) LtCol Sam Beckley (83 CO) Capt. Duncan McDuffie 83 Ops Off.) and Captain Peter Caulfield. (Samuel Beckley)

Ben" contrails were seen at Coblenz, Germany. One actual projectile was seen. It rose slowly to 30,000 feet and then went up at terrific speed into the fringe of outer space to fall back on a target in England. As the war went on this would become a routine mission observation.

The next day's mission was an escort for the First Bombardment Division attacking Osnabruck, Germany with 400 B-17s. the 78th flew the penetration-target-withdrawal leg of the bomber stream. At 1100 hours the 82nd was vectored by control toward a forty plus formation of enemy fighters approaching the bomber forces.

Donald Hart: "We were vectored to a gaggle of Germans and I picked one out at 25,000 feet. My first burst started coolant coming out of his engine and I fought him down to the deck and across an airdrome. As he straightened out I hit his engine. He pulled straight up and bailed out and the plane crashed."

Harold Liebenrood: "We ran into ME109s in the Rheine area. One overshot me and pulled onto my leader's tail, so I pulled up on his tail and got some strikes on his fuselage. Then I pulled in dead-astern and got many strikes all over his plane. He caught fire and smoked badly, falling off on one wing and went down through the clouds flaming and covered with smoke."

Manford Croy saw ten ME109s above in the sun and climbed up towards them, engaging two. The first 109 was hit with numerous strikes in the cockpit and wingroots. It caught fire and the pilot bailed out. Manford chased the second 109 down to the deck around a small town where AA batteries were producing intense light flak. Firing from dead astern, Croy saw pieces fly off and the enemy aircraft burst into flame. As he drew up alongside the plane, he saw the pilot slumped down in the cockpit just before it nosed over and crashed into a field.

John Hockery describes the events leading up to the end of his combat flying and passage into POW camp: "Spotted thirty plus ME109s attacking the bombers and I led my flight into them. I caught one in a deflection shot getting strikes on his canopy and wingroots. Pieces came off and I fired again. Then he flamed and went down. I spotted another 109 with Staffel Kapitan chevrons on its side and followed him to the deck. He led me to an airdrome where we did a Lufberry at 1,500 feet right over the field. They were throwing up lots of flak, but I stayed on the enemy. All of a sudden there was a big explosion on the 109 and his wing came off, flicking him into the ground. I think his own flak shot him down.

"I broke off and started home, then started to climb into a fight above, when the three FW190s passed me coming down. Getting into a rat-race with them, they turned out to be better pilots than I expected. My water-injection ran out and they started to catch me, so I turned on them to fight it out. Just as I got strikes all over one of them, an explosion behind me blew off part of my wing and I crashed into a field. I got out and hid in a ditch as two FW190s strafed my P-47 wreck. I was taken POW shortly after."

Ten minutes later as the 83rd was passing south of Dummer Lake, Germany, Robert Bonebrake was pursuing German planes headed for the bombers when he saw two more enemy aircraft going to join a fight at 25,000 feet. Diving from 31,000 feet he split the latter pair and then pulled inside the wingman who stayed to fight. At 450 yards at 400 mph he got concentrated strikes in the German's engine, roots, and cockpit. The Focke Wulf emitted coolant smoke, rolled slowly inverted, and spun into the ground and exploded, its pilot still aboard.

Philip Larson of the 84th aborted the mission at 1200 hours with an oxygen leak and circled Vorden airdrome until all the bombers had passed before starting for home. He spotted a couple of enemy aircraft in the landing pattern and chased them to Hesepe airdrome where the hot flak caused them to turn into his gunbursts. He saw one make a floppy turn down to the left and later, Philip made out gashes in the ground and the burning wreckage of an FW190.

The 82nd lost Troy Eggleston in the air fights, but no one saw him crash. Back in England while the fighting was taking place, Herbert Shope lost the Group's first P-51 when he was force to bail out of one of the old war-weary training ships.

The Group closed out the month with fifteen regular missions and two small escort jobs, accounting for four combat losses, one killed in a flying accident, thirteen aerial kills, six ground strafing kills, and forty-seven locomotives blown off the railways of western Germany.

December, 1944 Work on the new runway at DX lagged on into December, not being finished until the 11th at which time the P-47s were flown back from Bassingbourn to resume normal operations.

More command changes took place on December 2nd, 1944 when Major Joseph Myers became acting 82nd CO. The regular Squadron CO, Major Richard Conner, and assistant Squadron Operations Officer, Captain Winfield Brown, left on thirty day U.S. leave at the finish of their tours. The following day Major Harry Downing came over from the 84th to assume command of the 82nd from Myers, who moved up to Group Headquarters staff as Group Deputy commander and Group Operations Officer. Group Deputy CO Lieutenant Colonel Jack Oberhansly was transferred to the Fourth Fighter Group at Debden to work for his old 78th buddy, Colonel Harry Dayhuff, commander of the Fourth. Group Operations Officer, Major William May, dropped back to Assistant Operations Officer to make room for Myers who held seniority in rank.

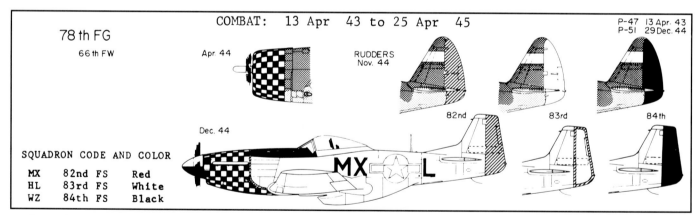

Markings of the 78th Fighter Group from the book, Eighth Air Force Story, by Kenn C. Rust. Courtesy Kenn Rust and Aviation Heritage - Sunshine House, Inc., P.O.Box 2065, Terre Haute, IN 47802

Chapter 18

Mustangs - New Mounts

December 16th the P-51 "SPAM CANS" as 78th Jug lovers called them, arrive at DX. Foreground, P-51B MX-F is a war weary aircraft issued for transition in November. Right P-51D will be first one lost. All Ds are unmarked at this point. (Samuel Beckley)

The dubious day arrived on December 16th when approximately thirty North American P-51D Mustang fighters flew in from the air depot and parked around the control tower. Hangar crews of the 82nd squadron collected them for maintenance, inspection, and modification before turning them over to the line crewchiefs. Radio technicians, armorers, and 84th Air Service Squadron men also got in on the work performed on the Mustangs. A few of the tasks, were installing wing tank pressurization kits; G-Suit hookups; guns sighted in; invasion stripes removed; engine boost set to draw seventy two inches; landing gear switches modified; compasses swung; blower switches installed; K-14 gunsights mounted; making fifty pairs of P-51 wing covers, forty-one seat covers; repacking 155 dinghies; 112 type S-1 and 170 type B-8 backstyle parachutes; and sewing up ninety-eight silk pilot scarves.

Another item needing attention was the application of the group markings to the new fighters. The noses were painted white and the black checks were laid out and hand brushed in as had been done on the P-47s. There were eight rows of checkerboard with a red two inch border aft. The prop spinners were half white and half black, which produced a flickering effect in motion, something to disconcert the enemy.

The 82nd Fighter Squadron went into pilot training with the new planes and turned their P-47s over to the 83rd and 84th Squadrons to use on combat missions, although the weather was bad and prevented much flying or operations until December 19th. Meanwhile on the continent, the German Army had taken advantage of the sour weather to launch their huge Ardennes counter offensive in Belgium. The Battle of the Bulge had begun.

Things were becoming desperate in Belgium as the Germans over-ran portions of the American Army and laid siege to pockets of resistance. The weather in England on December 19th was bad at most fighter bases and the 78th was the only Eighth Air Force Fighter Group able to get airborne.

Forty-one P-47s of the 83rd and 84th took off at 1130 hours, with John Wade crashing on takeoff but surviving uninjured. Forging on through the foul weather, the pilots made a late rendezvous with the meager bomber force able to find their way to the Initial Point near Trier, Germany. Escorting through the target, the Group was vectored by Nuthouse Control to the east, but made no contact with the enemy. There was solid overcast from 10,000 feet to the deck with fog 300 feet thick on the deck. An attack on Baben-Heusen airdrome was aborted and the Jugs attacked the railroad from Siegen to Giessen. Fifteen trucks were destroyed from Bonn to Duren.

At 1515 hours the 83rd Fighter Squadron climbed to engage thirty plus ME109s that appeared out of the thick clouds at 7,500 feet north of Coblenz, Germany. The Germans were not very eager and split up into ones and twos running for cloud cover. Just as the P-47s were wading into the 109s approximately twenty FW190s came into the fight from the east.

Cargo Black Four, John Kirk, sighted the enemy at 3 o'clock high and started upward. As an ME109 dove on him, he pulled up in an eighty degree climb, hung on his prop quickly sighted an eighty-eight yard head-on shot, and fired until he passed. Many rounds hit the German who dove straight in, pulling streamers while trying unsuccessfully to pull up. A lone FW190 crossed Kirk's nose and he broke into a Lufbery out-turning the enemy aircraft. Suddenly the German pilot leveled out at 300 feet and bailed out.

Francis Harrington broke into several enemy aircraft bouncing the squadron from 9 o'clock. Turning with one German, he got many hits and drew white coolant smoke. The 109 rolled over with its wheels extending and hit the ground at fifty degrees, still inverted. Harrington climbed to chase three FW190s and fired at one inverted, following it down. Pulling out of the dive he got hits from one wingtip to

Pilots of the 78th clown for the camera to show how they feel about flying the P-51. Frank Oiler (center) models the Mae West life preserver many will need after their Mustangs go down in the dreaded "Drink" WW43-6593 is an old P-51B.

the other. Its canopy popped off and the Focke-Wulf burst into flames, flipped over and mowed down a patch of trees, setting them afire.

Entering a Lufberry with three 109s Robert Bonebrake saw concentrated strikes in one's cockpit. It smoked, began to roll and went straight in from 6,000 feet with no chute. Next Robert glimpsed a 190 heading east and fought a running battle until he put rounds along the whole side of the enemy plane. It leveled out with its cockpit on fire and the pilot bailed out, doing some fancy flips until his chute opened.

Yellow Leader, Frank Fish, chased four 109s which dropped their belly tanks. After a series of pull-ups, Frank got a 109 hard in the cockpit. The German bailed out, his plane blowing up on impact.

One of the Group pilots related, "A pilot got on an ME109's tail that was trying to get away in the clouds. The pilot had a wingman - how this man even got his wings I don't know - he was a poor individual, but an even poorer pilot. The Jerry made a sharp turn and the pilot turned with the Jerry toward his wingman. Instead of the wingman going on in back of the leader's P-47 correctly and sweeping around so he'd be on the outside of the turn, the wingman allowed himself to go in front of the leader. Just then the pilot had the German in his gunsight and he started blasting away. The German popped into a cloud and got away free, while the wingman almost collided with his leader and flew through the line of fire getting his oil cooler shot up. The wingman was escorted back to an Allied base right across the lines. He made a forced landing in a bomb dump, scattering 500 pound bombs all around and why he wasn't killed, I don't know. The next day when he returned to home base he was shipped out and that's the last we ever heard of him."

The disappearance of enemy aircraft left the Group with just the miserable weather and a 350 mile return to their base. Many of the pilots did not try to make it home, twenty aircraft electing to land on continent bases, and nine landing at Castle Camps, Essex. Only eleven made it back to Duxford.

General Jimmy Doolittle, Eighth Air Force Commander sent a commendation to the 78th for the December 19th mission, thanking them for a job well done and for being the only Eighth fighter unit to get airborne in support of heavy bombers. General William Kepner endorsed the commendation. For the next eight days a heavy fog settled on the East Anglia Plain and the Group was unable to launch another mission until December 28th.

The 83rd received their replacement quota, thirty-one new Mustangs and gave their P-47s to the 84th. Around Christmas

Day the 84th received their share of P-51s and all Group pilots tried to squeeze in as much flying to acquaint themselves with the P-51.

Lieutenant Colonel Gilbert returned from his U.S. leave and resumed his Deputy Group CO post from acting Deputy, Lieutenant Colonel Joseph Myers, who continued as Group Operations Officer. A number of 78th enlisted men had a close brush with death on December 22nd when the Army truck they were riding in missed a curve half a mile from base and rolled over three times. They had been returning from evening passes in Cambridge. There were no fatalities, but a number of men went to hospital with back injuries.

On December 25th, the 78th was ordered to fly a maximum effort by Eighth Air Force Headquarters in support of the Ardennes fighting. The weather was too bad to get to Belgium, but Headquarters stated they only wanted the 78th to cross the coast and return to qualify for a sortie. Because the bad weather had so delayed P-51 training, Colonel Gray, siding with his pilots, refused to fly, resisting the Headquarters numbers game. The base was socked in anyway, so the mission never took off. In any case, the group put on a nice Christmas Party for some war orphans.

Finally the mists and fog cleared enough on December 28th to allow an all 84th show of thirty-six P-47s led by Colonel Fred Gray to patrol the Coblenz, Germany area. The mission proved to be uneventful.

The briefing for December 29th detailed a 78th A, B, and C group. C Group would take off first at 0940 hours and be comprised of thirty-two 84th P-47s divided into two sixteen aircraft sections. A and B Group would take off at 1030 hours flying the first 78th Group P-51 show using thirty aircraft from 82nd and 83rd squadrons. The 84th's Thunderbolts flew to Malmedy, Belgium and then were vectored around chasing Ninth Air Force aircraft near Coblenz and Luxemburg, before returning home. Escorting bombers, the Mustang show visited the Frankfurt and Ashaffenburg rail yards and headed home at 1413 hours from Ghent, Belgium.

Near Frankfurt, Huie Lamb's wingman, John Childs, signaled his radio was going on the blink and they turned for home with Lamb escorting. They were a dozen miles from the UK coast when Lamb's P-51 engine began to lose its coolant. In mere seconds the engine was melting its manifold pipes and on fire. Huie loosened his straps to bail out, but his canopy jammed until he was too low to jump. Lamb saw the whitecaps coming up at him, pointed the nose into the wind, dropped flaps, and stalled out just off the surface as slow as possible. The tail hit first, a wave caught Huie's right wing, and the plane cartwheeled. With his safety-belt loose, Lamb smashed the gun sight with his face. The impact blew off the canopy as Huie shot out of the seat and pushed away from the plane to avoid the suction. In three or four seconds, the nose plunged under in a burst of steam and sank "like a granite rock". In the numbing cold water he first inflated his Mae West, then the dinghy, but the sea kept him from getting into it and he just hung on for dear life.

It had all happened in a flash. John Childs saw Huie's plane going down with the nose in flames. It seemed to dive straight toward the water and John thought he might be gone. He circled around Huie rocking his wings as a signal he was going for help. John's radio wasn't working but it was later learned that Huie's May-Day call had gotten to the ASR control center. John headed for the English coast and dropped down to 500 feet over the Orfordness, Suffolk lighthouse. By some miracle he spotted an airfield with a big old twin-engine Walrus flying boat of the British ASR sitting there, engines running. They had heard Lamb's May-Day call and were preparing to takeoff. John quickly landed and rolled right up to the Walrus, jumping out and yelling at the pilot to follow him. The RAF pilot obliged, but the Walrus could only go about 150 mph and Childs had to keep circling back to stay with him at the Mustang's 280 mph lope. Heading back toward the lighthouse, they were soon over water again.

Next came the biggest miracle of all. In all that vast expanse of water, Childs saw Lamb and his dinghy bobbing like a fishing cork. John couldn't believe it, but there he was. The Walrus landed into the wind gingerly and circled Huie counter-clockwise. The radio operator had trouble hauling him and his sodden wet kit into the plane, but they finally managed it and after several attempts, the Walrus took off for the nearest airfield at Martlesham Heath.

The only thing Lamb could remember about the rescue was being grabbed out of the water into the Walrus and having his clothes ripped off. They loaded him down with hot-water bottles and blankets. Once in the base hospital, his temperature was found to be ninety-three degrees and his pulse very weak. Doctors later told him he was extremely lucky to be alive. Lamb attributed his survival to will-power, not quitting in the weakened struggle, and God's help.

Huie Lamb was the first 78th pilot to ditch a Mustang into the sea and one of the few Eighth Air Force pilots to be successful.

The next day was a repeat of the previous day's show. Major Leonard Marshall took twenty-five 84th squadron P-47s to Duren, Germany at 25,000 feet as 78C Group. Arriving at 1119 hours they spent their combat enduranace being vectored around by the controller after friendly Allied aircraft. Ground forces slugging it out in the Bulge far below the 10/10ths clouds were invisible to the pilots.

Captain Huie Lamb after he survived a miraculous 40 minutes in the North Sea. His new P-51D MX-V 44-11631 "ETTA JEANNE II" is named for his younger sister. The victory emblems are an ME109 and an ME262 jet. (Huie Lamb)

Meanwhile, bomber forces were hitting rail yards and communications targets in Western Germany in an attempt to assist troops in the Ardennes. Thirty-five P-51s from the 82nd and 83rd Squadrons made up 78A and 78B groups under the direction of Lieutenant Colonel Joseph Myers. They met and escorted their charges through the targets and out to Rheims, France.

The last 78th mission of 1944 rose from the field at 0930 hours on December 31st. Captain Patrick "Max" Maxwell was at the front in Len Marshall's old Jug, WZ-Z, with thirteen P-47s of the 84th behind him to give free lance bomber support in the Hamburg area on this Sunday morning. "MEW" control vectored them around the area of Dummer Lake, Bremen, Hannover, until 1230 hours when they turned for home.

Pat Maxwell: "I saw a train just below headed west. I peeled off with my wingman following. I made one pass from the south, but I was going too fast and only damaged it. I pulled up to the north and when I was at 2,500 feet I saw an FW190 1,000 feet below me going south. I called him off and

A story in a picture. Lt.Col. Leonard Marshall's new P-51D "THE FACE VI" WZ-Z 44-63212 P-51D in a bay with a P-47D-25 which will soon be sent to the air depot for re-issue to the 9AF or a French AF tactical sqd. (Negley Sapper)

Colonel Fred Gray (L. Frt), presents the 78th's 400 victory silver beer mug to Capt. J. Patrick Maxwell (R. frt.) as 82FS pilots watch. Officers fifth and third from the right are Captains Charles Christ aand Richard Hewitt respectively. (Patrick Maxwell)

peeled after him. My closure was very fast from dead-astern. When approximately 800 yards behind him, he saw me and broke up to the left. I put the dot on the canopy and opened fire at 400 yards from eighty degrees deflection. I began getting strikes in the engine, cockpit, and wings. His belly tank blew up and a long stream of fire shot out of the engine. He flipped on his back and fell like a rock from 400 feet, leaving a long stream of smoke and fire behind him. His aircraft hit the ground with a terrific explosion. The pilot tried to bail out at 200 feet but his chute opened just as he hit the ground and as he didn't move, I think he was killed."

After Pat Maxwell landed from this, his last mission of his second tour in the 78th, Colonel Fred Gray awarded him a silver beer mug honoring the outfit's 400th combat victory.

And so the T-Bolts passed from Duxford, the adieu of an airplane the Group had grown to love as an old friend - one which rarely let them down in a jam. The 79th Air Service Group of the 78th recorded their work on the Jug during its tour with the Group. They had performed major and minor repair on 227 P-47s including 103 wing changes, forty-one engine changes, and twenty-three aircraft disassembled for shipment to depot.

While the 84th was flying its last wartime squadron size P-47 show, the 82nd put up fifteen P-51s led by Captain Dick Hewitt, and the 83rd flew seventeen Mustangs behind Major Sam Beckley as B leader. They toured Emden, Hamburg, Munster, and left their B-24s and B-17s at Namur and Knocke, Belgium. After Major Beckley landed, he resumed his job of Squadron Operations Officer, handing the CO's reins back to Major William Julian, just back from his U.S. leave.

Besides training Group pilots to fly the P-51 in December, the Group had assumed the job of giving operational conversion training to all the new incoming pilots. Previously this training would have been conducted at Atcham and Goxhill. However, these old Operational Training Units were now being used differently, and each Eighth Air Force fighter group had to start its own, "Clobber-College", as they became labeled. The 78th closed out the old year of 1944 with December's seventeen missions, a wondrous zero loss in pilots, eight aerial kills, no ground kills, and one locomotive destroyed.

January 1945 : On New Year's Day the 82nd and 83rd flew an A and B Group show to support the Third Air Division attacking Bonn and Frankfurt. Meanwhile four P-47s of the 84th took off to fly the Group's last actual combat Thunderbolt show. Captain Wilbur Grimes led the Jugs to escort the last mission flown by the "Aphrodite Operation", a radio controlled robot bomber unit. This last mission of the "Castor" B-17s loaded with 22,000 pounds of Torpex was directed at Oldenburg, southeast of Emden, German. Thus the old Jug helped the Group start its third year of overseas service before being shipped off to Ninth Air Force units.

By January 5th the 84th had received enough P-51 conversion training to join the other squadrons for their first Mustang mission. Captain Dorian Ledington led to Bad Kreuznach, Germany leaving the Big Friends near Saarbrucken. Their Mustangs had seemed to work well.

However, the Group had been experiencing some mechanical trouble with the P-51 and the next day it was the 84th's turn to feel its bite. During takeoff Thomas Reeves could not get any power out of his engine and crashed at the end of the runway. After Captain Raymond E. Smith got his P-51 airborne, the engine froze and he made a crash landing a few miles from the base. He received facial cuts and other slight injuries, which resulted in his cultivating a goatee for some weeks.

When the squadron reached the target at Speyer, Germany, Captain Wilbur Grimes took a flak hit in his engine which froze from an oil leak at 1,200 feet. Wilbur took to his parachute, landing in a tree half a mile northeast of Marche, Belgium. Although he injured his leg and face, he was able to successfully elude the Germans with the help of the Belgian underground, and returned to operations sometime later. The 82nd Squadron's Gordon Weston, was not so fortunate and made the full sacrifice when his Mustang clipped a tree in the fog and crashed twenty miles from Duxford on the return.

Edward Briski: "About January 8, 1945, we had a snowstorm that created a lot of havoc. I don't think we'd seen a snowstorm in England until then and it was a feeling of celebration for us northerners on the base. When it came down a lot of us had or took the time to go out in the snow and play like a bunch of kids. It was no holds barred when we had a snowball fight. A Colonel could sock a Private in the head with a snowball and vise-versa. In fact, it was like a battleground. You would see a Jeep driving through with someone delivering a message or running an errand, and he would have a stick tied to the windshield of the Jeep with a white cloth tied to the top of it. Apparently he was clobbered so many times by snowballs trying to do his job, and he was trying to look as presentable as possible when he got to where he was supposed to be.

"We had a mission scheduled for the day it snowed or the day after. We had just laid steel matting for the runway and the wet snow on that was very slippery. When the first flight started to pick up speed down the runway, one or more aircraft ground looped and they had to scratch the flight and clear the mess. After wrecking five airplanes, they decided to abort the mission."

Allan Cowart: "Late in the day we had a big snowstorm and a raid of B-17s was returning. One was calling 'Mayday, Mayday!' and I was trying to guide him into our airfield. He thought he had it spotted, but in the poor visibility it was very hard to make out. He thought he had the approach okay and I could hear him, but he decided to go around again in the pattern. Why he decided this I don't know. But he did and all of a sudden there was total silence. I had no idea what had happened to him and I couldn't see any smoke or fire because the visibility was so bad. He vanished.

"The next morning, (it had been snowing very, very hard) sitting on the hilltop across the field from the control tower, was that B-17 resting on the crest of the hill just totally undisturbed, just nestled in the snow. The crew had gotten out and gone to some farmhouse and made contact with their base. They were not sure where they were at that time in the

Duxford's Mustang graveyard. WZ-H 44-15692 is William DeGain's 1-10-45 takeoff crash. WZ-B 44-11693 is Ray E. Smith's 1-6-45 crash. (USAF)

storm and I couldn't identify our location on the radio. All I could use was our call sign, "Rutley Control". Later the B-17 crew came to see us and they were very grateful for our assistance."

The next mission got off on the 10th of January after the weather cleared up and the crews had cleared the runway. The high snowbanks lining the runway proved to be a hazard to the 84th's Peter Keillor, when they tore off one of his landing gear doors on takeoff and he had to abort the mission. His squadron mate, William DeGain, had an even nastier surprise when ice covering his left wing spoiled the wing's airfoil shape, resulting in a lack of lift on takeoff. His Mustang ended up in a heap at the end of the runway. Three days later the squadron lost Herbert Elin because his Mustang had instrument failure in heavy clouds after takeoff and he crashed to his death near Royston.

On January 14th, Willard Warren of 82nd Squadron was in the Cologne area at 26,000 feet when he sighted fifteen plus bogies down on the deck. Getting permission to investigate same, he dropped tanks and took his wingman, William DeGain, 84th, down on a bounce. They barreled right through another fifteen enemy aircraft they had failed to spot and jumped the original bunch. Pursuing three of them, Willard opened on an FW190 with hits in the cockpit that killed its pilot and caused it to flick into the ground. DeGain was doing 450 mph and seeing that his leader was clear, he moved up behind an ME109. His bursts caused its canopy to fly off and its right gear to drop. Passing it, DeGain saw the pilot standing in his seat just before the enemy aircraft pulled up and its engine exploded, spinning it into the deck. Meanwhile Willard caught an FW190 positioning on DeGain, and rolled over onto it firing a deflection shot. His hits in its canopy caused the 190 to crash and explode.

When the bogies were called out at 1210 hours Robert Smith was sent to bounce a single bogie going north over Cologne. They played a merry chase of hide-and-seek from fog bank to fog bank, hopping over churches and tall

The snow on 83FS' HL-N 44-11695 indicates this winter was the worst in many years. The crews toiled to free runways and planes of snow and ice. Accidents increased. Aircraft in foreground named "BOUKA" later crashlanded inside Russian lines. (Warren Kellerstedt)

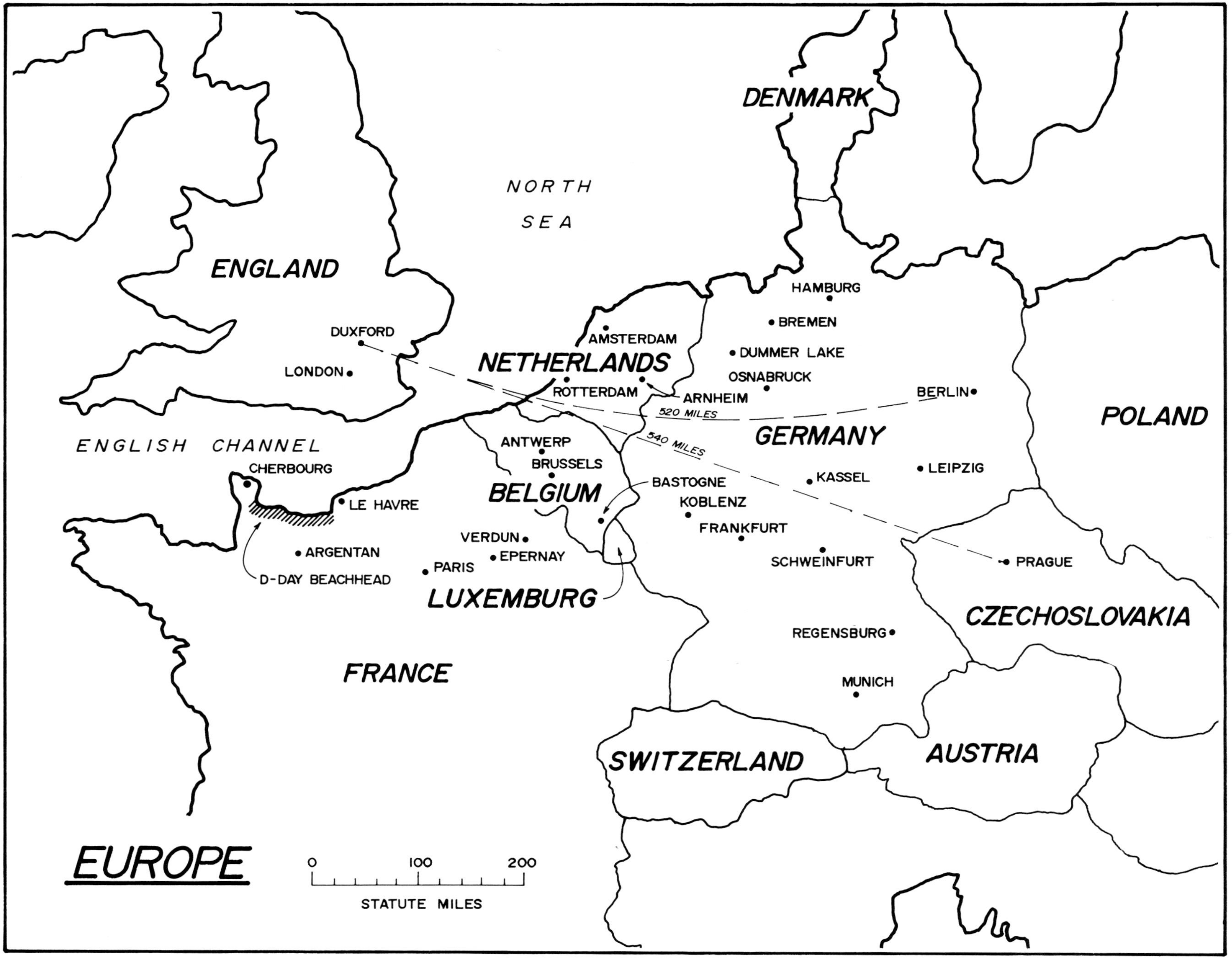

EUROPE

DENMARK

POLAND

CZECHOSLOVAKIA

AUSTRIA

• PRAGUE

• BERLIN

• LEIPZIG

GERMANY

• HAMBURG

• BREMEN

• DUMMER LAKE

OSNABRUCK

• KASSEL

• SCHWEINFURT

• REGENSBURG

• MUNICH

SWITZERLAND

ARNHEIM

520 MILES

540 MILES

NETHERLANDS

• AMSTERDAM

ROTTERDAM

• KOBLENZ

BASTOGNE

• FRANKFURT

BELGIUM

ANTWERP

BRUSSELS

LUXEMBURG

VERDUN •

• EPERNAY

PARIS •

NORTH SEA

ENGLAND

DUXFORD •

LONDON •

ENGLISH CHANNEL

CHERBOURG

LE HAVRE

• ARGENTAN

D-DAY BEACHHEAD

FRANCE

0   100   200

STATUTE MILES

Map of Northwestern Europe showing relative distance from Duxford to various 78th targets.

buildings, with Smith eventually tagging him with hits in the fuselage. At fifty feet over northern Cologne, the FW's left wing went down and it crashed and exploded in a three gun heavy flak position.

The 78th C Group leader on this day was Major Leonard Marshall, 84th Fighter Squadron. The Group was near their first check point at Giessen when Nuthouse control reported enemy activity around Cologne. Leonard started chasing three bogies he thought were enemy aircraft but he soon found one to be a P-51 pursuing two ME109s. One Messerschmitt broke left and tried to belly in when he spotted Leonard behind. Hitting the ground at 300 mph, the 109 made a huge cloud of snow and smoke. A wing came off and pieces flew in all directions. Turning his attention to the other 109, Leonard saw the P-51 was having trouble with it, and at Marshall's approach, the 109 turned and fired a burst head-on. Both P-51s got in position behind the German and fired, one from 400 yards and Marshall from 800 yards. Leonard did not get any hits but the attack of the other P-51 caused the enemy pilot to parachute. Louis Hereford flying the other Mustang, quickly broke off because he thought Leonard represented another German on his tail.

Turquoise Red leader, Richard Spooner of the 83rd Squadron tagged onto an ME109, one of the twenty plus enemy aircraft trying to form up for a mission. Closing to 200 yards, Richard shot him and the German bailed out as his plane spun in. As Richard was trying to film this kill, another enemy aircraft appeared and he gave chase. Closing to 400 yards on the deck, Richard ran out of ammo and, deciding to bluff the German, he closed to less than 100 yards. The German broke right, hit some power lines, and crashed in flames.

Earl Stier got into a tight right-turning duel with one of the 109s heading east on the deck. When the Jerry reversed his turn, Earl put strikes into him causing a stream of coolant and oil. The German pulled up in a steep climb and bailed out. Earl was just getting good strikes on another of six ME109s when 20 mm went flashing over his canopy and he broke from three 109s on his tail. The last he saw of his second German the enemy aircraft was gliding down in trouble.

Frank Oiler: (Turquoise Yellow Three) reported after the Group landed: "We dropped our tanks and split-essed down on them. Rainbow Squadron split up the gaggle and Turquoise Squadron attacked them as they split up in twos and threes. My leader and his wingman took out after two bandits going up a creek bed. An FW190 went between us firing, so I turned on his tail. I lost him over some woods, but picked up an ME109 and two FW190s being chased by a lone P-51. I called to the P-51 to take one and my wingman and I took the other. The 190s broke opposite directions and the ME109 went straight up. I got into a Lufberry at 1,100 feet with the FW190, and with the use of flaps I got on his tail in two turns. I got in a three second burst at about thirty-five degrees deflection, and observed many strikes in the cockpit, fuselage, and wing roots. Pieces flew off the enemy aircraft and he did a half snap and went in upside down."

Mark Wilson closed astern of an ME109 and had little trouble shooting off its left wing three feet from the fuselage. This resulted in its spinning and snap rolling into the ground without a chute showing.

Having trouble dropping his right wing tank, Willis Lutz had been left above the fight by the rest of his flight. He tried to fire his guns to shake off the tank but none of the guns would work. Deciding to go home, he saw three planes come out of the forest shading and thinking they were P-51s, dived down to form on them. As he came closer he recognized them as FW190s. Looking back something caught his eye. Three more enemy aircraft were coming down on him from 5

o'clock. Thinking they might not have seen him, he tried to sneak away turning left, but they came in behind him. Pulling his turn in tight, the four of them were in a Lufberry. Willis pressed his gun-trigger as hard as he could and was delighted to find four .50s working. Gaining on the Germans in the turn, Willis hit one and the pilot jettisoned his canopy and bailed out. He gave another enemy aircraft a long burst causing a fire in its right wing. The FW190 flipped on its back at 100 feet and crashed.

Looking about, Lutz saw two FW190s coming after him from the north. They all quickly got into another Lufberry and again Lutz managed to outturn the enemy aircraft. After a couple of hits on an FW's canopy he ran out of ammunition and the German pilot disengaged. Lutz ran a bluff on the remaining FW190, which also ran off to the east.

Once more Lutz resumed his course for England. Patches of ground fog kept him on the deck. He crossed Allied lines south of Aachen, Germany and recognizing the area, climbed to 350 feet for a better view. As he leveled off, Allied anti-aircraft guns opened fire on him and hit him with their first burst. Gas and smoke poured into the cockpit and he could feel heat on his legs. Willis climbed until the engine quit, popped his canopy, and as the ship fell into a spin, he jumped, coming down safe but injured near Hauset, Belgium.

Louis Hereford was also returning alone with a bad engine and finally was forced to belly land at Merriville, France.

A second mission for this date ran the day's kill tally to 14-0-14 when the 83rd Squadron's red flight bounced four FW 190s in the traffic pattern of an airdrome north of Diepholz, Germany. Peter Caulfield chased several of them around the airdrome flak defenses, firing bursts without effect. Getting behind another which strayed away from the safety of the flak, he chased it back to the drome where it hit the ground, bounced, and exploded.

First Lieutenant John A. Kirk, 83FS Flt. Ldr. managed to survive his tour, although two of his roommates did not. His P-51D was HL-C 44-63620 "SMALL BOY HERE". (Samuel Beckley)

John Kirk: "Probably the scariest and most dangerous thing we pilots faced in combat with the Eighth Air Force was the channel. Strafing was certainly dangerous, especially in the P-51, with your coolant lines running underneath you and halfway the length of the airplane. They were very easy to shoot down. But that's something I accepted and I figured I could give as much as I took, so that didn't worry me too much. But the "DRINK" as we called it, was wild and terribly cold, and you couldn't last very long in it, it was so cold. I lost two roommates to it, two extremely good men.

"I lost the first roommate, Gerald Boner, on the mission of January 17th, 1945. We'd just gotten Mustangs and of course we were all new to them, pilots and mechanics alike. We'd had a lot of engine trouble, a lot of engines stopped. It turned out from what I heard that they had a wrong percentage of glycol coolant in the things.

"Anyhow, we were flying over the drink, just a short section going toward the rendezvous point at Heligoland, enroute to Hamburg, when Gerald Boner's engine cut out and stopped cold. He was a good friend of mine and I asked permission to pull out and escort him back. Well, we turned back, but he probably would have been smarter, since we were close to the continent, to try and make it to that coast. But he turned back. Of course you go down fairly fast in a Mustang. He got down to 5,000 feet and he decided to get out and I saw him bail out. I followed him down and I saw him hit the water. His yellow life raft popped out as I made a big turn and I saw him just trying to crawl into it, and I lost sight of him. By the time I completed my turn and came back he was gone - nothing - I couldn't see anything anymore! It was that fast.

"My other roommate, Jack Hodge, was lost on the show of March 11th, 1945. We were taking the bombers to hit northern Germany and we were taking them north over Denmark to avoid the flak on the way in. It was a long flight over water heading toward the coast of Denmark at 20,000 feet, when the weather socked in at maybe 10,000 feet down low and you couldn't see the ground any place. Jack's engine quit and he kept going down toward Sweden, trying to start it up, but it never started. I kept calling to him to bail out. Well, the last I saw of him, he was heading into the clouds and that's the last anybody ever heard of him."

A big party was held in the Officers's Club on the evening of January 30th as Colonel Gray's hail and farewell. His tour of combat was completed and he was being transferred to Eighth Air Force Headquarters as director of fighter operations. His successor as 78th commander, Lieutenant Colonel Olin E. Gilbert, presented him with the ritual silver beer mug as a token of best wishes from the Group. Gilbert's second in command as Deputy CO was Lieutenant Colonel Joseph Myers.

Nineteen missions had been carried out in January with nine losses, fourteen aerial victories, twenty-one locomotives destroyed, and six non-fatal P-51 crashes. There were approximately eight P-51 engine failures in January which resulted in crashes and some deaths. The ground crews were changing spark plugs on the engines after every second mission to alleviate one of the problems. Some of the planes were also being fitted with the new tail-warning radar sets, and K-14 gunsights were slowly being installed on all Mustangs. For the third time, combat tour hours were adjusted by higher command, this time increasing from 270 to 300.

Charles Clark: "One day in January, one of our line Corporals started up a P-51 to check out its engine, and the throttle stuck wide open. The Mustang jumped over its wheel chocks and crashed into a Cletrac tow tractor. The authorities made him sign a statement of charges for damage to the Cletrac, but not for damages to the Mustang. For about six months they took sixty or seventy dollars a month out of his paycheck and about six months later they rescinded the charges, canceled them, and they paid him back all the money they'd charged him!"

Allen Clapp: "The P-51 I was crewchief of developed an oil leak and at the time we were changing the outboard spark plugs after a mission and the inboard spark plugs after the next mission. This time it was required of us to change the inside engine bank plugs. At this period we used 100 octane gas as a solvent to clean the engines. I asked my assistant crewchief to wash the engine down due to this oil leak. I forgot the plugs were out of the bank and as he poured the five gallons of gas over the engine, you could see the gasoline go gurgle, gurgle into those cylinders and pistons. I yelled, 'Hey stop!' and then I said,. 'Blow it out!'. Well, I wasn't thinking too clearly. That's evident. So he rolled the starter and the engine energized and engaged. As soon as it engaged, the engine had coils that would spark, because the magnetos weren't turning fast enough yet. Well, all of those inside leads were sparking - and it just took one - and - Bang! That thing went off. There was fire and a cloud of black smoke went shooting up. The fire trucks came racing over and I jumped off the plane and got a fire extinguisher and it didn't have anything in it. Charlie got one and it didn't have anything in it. Cecil brought one up and it was empty. The fire truck arrived and they snuffed it out.

"That plane made the next flight. Luckily the weather socked in and we took it up to the hangar that night and

The new 78th look, an 84th P-51D WZ-K 44-11763 assigned to Lt. Henry Slack. Both Slack and the Mustang made it safely to VE-Day. Cowling oil streak is from crankcase overflow. (Negley Sapper)

Captain Earl Stier, 84th Sqd. almost lost a major portion of his tail over Luneburg, Germany on February 3, 1945 but returned "BUM STEER" to DX. (G. Fry)

changed the engine, and got it back on the line and slow timed it. By the time the weather cleared up it made the next combat mission. I was a Staff Sergeant at the time and I got demoted from Staff Sergeant to Private in one fell swoop, and on the same order I got promoted from a Private to a Sergeant. The next month I was back to Staff Sergeant again. So they taught me a lesson."

February 1945: While many other fighter groups had been on shows to the Reich's capital over a year previous, the 78th had never been able to claim that distinction until February 3rd, 1945. The group rendezvoused with bombers at Zwolle, Netherlands and left them two and a half hours later near Ulzen, Germany.

Harry Downing, leader of the Group gave everyone permission to go down on the deck and strafe on the egress route. The 84th Squadron lead spotted a train with its steam already shut down and as the flight approached, an airfield appeared nearby at Luneburg. Climbing back to 6,000 feet the cry was given on the radio to bring the rest of the squadron to the found pickings. They positioned up sun of the drome and came at it full throttle on the deck. Jerry hadn't been caught napping as a terrific wall of flak quickly revealed. Leon Grisham, Blue one, took their full converging fire and survived it, but his fourth pass proved unwise as he was shot down and became a Prisoner of War. Red Flight's Warren Sawall also succumbed to the murderous flak and also joined the POW ranks. Salvation from further losses were low clouds which allowed the Mustangs to quickly elude the flak on pull up.

The vicious AA almost got Earl Stier as well. His WZ-Y took a blow right behind the cockpit and his armor plate saved his life. Another hit on his tail section blew away most of the rudder's top half and damaged the horizontal stabilizers. The shell's impact dropped one wingtip, which nicked a tree, but Stier resisted the force of gravity and pulled up from the treetops. To his wonderment he was able to fight his P-51 "Bum Steer" for 450 miles and two and one half hours while it corkscrewed through the air constantly trying to fall off on the left wing. When he arrived over Duxford the squadron CO gave him a choice of bailing out or bringing it in to land. After coming this far he wasn't about to quit, so he made his erratic approach.

James Aicardi: "He came in low over the field, flying very unsteady and trailing smoke. We thought his hydraulic system was gone and he would have to belly land, which, for a P-51, wasn't too good. Somehow, he got the gear down and made a very rough landing with the 'meatwagon' following him down the field. When we got to the ship the pilot was sitting there very shaken. The chief helped him out while the ship was dowsed in foam.

"He had taken at least one 20mm hit in the side of the ship (just above the oil cooler scoop and behind the cockpit). It had started a small fire from leaking hydraulic fluid - the hole was big enough to put your head in. Shell fragments had torn a lot of holes in the fuselage, tearing up the oxygen equipment. The armor plate behind the seat saved his life. He also took several hits in the tail, as the whole top of the rudder had been shot away. The elevators looked like a sieve. He did a lot of good flying to get that wreck back."

While the 84th fighter squadron was destroying fifteen enemy aircraft on Luneburg airdrome, John Kirk, 83rd Fighter Squadron had wandered off on his own a bit.

John Kirk: "We were up against a competent enemy and weren't always the aces we thought we were. Getting separated from the Group, I decided to go down and strafe an airfield at Potsdam, which was situated on the edge of a lake. So I came screaming across the deck, chewing grass. I didn't see any airplanes right on the runway, so I blasted some buildings as I was swooping across. Reaching the outer limits of the airdrome, I saw some planes in revetments in the woods. Making a 180 degree turn I came diving back down with only time for a quick shot and went right over the top of them. I didn't see any burning. Meanwhile I'm getting plastered with Ack-Ack from the field and I'd have been wiser to keep right on going on the deck. But it made me mad I'd risked my neck to get this airplane, so I swung back and allowed myself more room. Aiming, I let him have a real long blast, and I kept in, kept in, and finally at the last second I pulled up. I looked down close and it was a DUMMY! Just a wood dummy with glass around the canopy so it reflected off like a real airplane. By this time I'm over the airfield again chewing grass and the only thing I could see was a barracks. I thought, 'Damn it, I can't do anything else, at least it's wintertime and I can give those German soldiers pneumonia!'. So I hit the guns, kicked the peddles, and I sprayed the building from one end to the other. I know there wasn't one window left in the building when I went home."

Every pilot logged over six hours on the Berlin mission. The mission of February 14th, was the occasion for an

First Lieutenant William DeGain in his P-51D WZ-H 44-63632 "LEE D", with armorer, Cpl Nicholas J.Vale on the wing. Girly illustrations like these Vargas were often clipped out of magazines and doped onto 78th P-51 cowlings. (Nicholas Vale/AFM)

unusual occurrence. Andrew Innocenzi, 83rd Fighter Squadron was west of the target at Chemnitz, Germany when his engine generator began to malfunction, knocking out his radio, compass, and coolant controls. Using hand signals, he explained his predicament to the flight leader. The leader detailed James Peterson to escort Innocenzi toward Russian lines to the east as far as his fuel would permit. They left the formation and headed east sixty degrees from Chemnitz. James stayed with Andrew all the way to Inowroclaw, Poland behind the Russian front lines, where they made their landings. Peterson's P-51 landing gear collapsed on landing. They used their U.S. eagle badges and Russian language cards to identify themselves and both returned to DX on March 22nd.

The 82nd Squadron command changed hands on February 17, 1945 when Major Richard Conner returned from his U.S. leave. Acting squadron CO Major Harry Downing moved back to squadron operations officer.

A couple days later hair triggered Allied flak gunners shot down another 78th P-51. Austin Miller was limping home in his battle-damaged Mustang across the Rhine river when AA fire forced him to bail out. Another 82nd pilot, Robert Blossom, had to take to his silk umbrella behind Allied lines the next day. His Mustang struck a brick factory smokestack while strafing in the Wiesenburg-Wurzburg, Germany area.

Operation Clarion, a full scale assault upon enemy communications systems took place on February 22, 1945. For the 78th it was nothing more than they had been doing all along, shooting up German rails and roads on mission returns. It was an A and B Group show, with Colonel Fred Gray coming down from Eighth Air Force Headquarters to lead 78A and get in his month's flight pay.

It was also this date that the 78th got a new Commanding Officer, Lieutenant Colonel John D. Landers. Lieutenant Colonel Olin Gilbert stepped back to Deputy Group CO and the Deputy, Lieutenant Colonel Joseph Myers, transferred to the 55th at Wormingford, UK.

Landers came to the 78th with a magnificent combat record. He had become an ace in the Pacific Theater in 1942, scoring six kills with the 49th Fighter Group of the Fifth Air Force. After a stint in the U.S. training P-38 pilots, he flew a second combat tour in the European Theater with the 55th and 357th Fighter Groups scoring five more aerial victories. Once more he had gone home on leave in late 1944 and then had returned to England for his third combat tour to lead the 78th. Colonel Landers would finish the war as one of the top U.S. aces with fourteen and a half victories in the air and twenty on the ground. His decorations would include: two Silver Stars, three Distinguished Flying Crosses, the British Distinguished Flying Cross, the Purple Heart, twenty-one Air Medals and the French Croix De Guerre. He was the second youngest "Bird-Colonel" in the USAAF.

On February 24, 1945 the Group escorted bombers to Hannover, Germany and then strafed their way back to the Zuider Zee. This strafing was a constant source of pilot fatalities and losses this date were exceptionally above the norm. Edwin Anderson was not seen after strafing the Dummer Lake rail yards, but survived to be a Prisoner of War. Lucian Bibeau was hit by enemy fire at the same location and went straight into the ground. Louis Musgrave was killed near Einbeck, Germany. Flak from barges in the Quackenbruck, Germany area claimed Lloyd Eadline and he died after parachuting into the Zuider Zee. The next day flak knocked down Charles Oldfield and Mark Wilson, evaders, who joined together and worked with the Dutch Underground until April 21st.

Marvin Bigelow: "I was on the February 26th mission when Charles O'Brien and Leonard Olson were lost. O'Brien developed electrical trouble near Berlin and started home with Olson escorting him. I got the full story several years later when I ran into Olson as I was leaving the dormitory at the University of Colorado. O'Brien had to belly land his P-51 in Germany and Olson crashed his Mustang in an attempt to land and pick him up. Both were captured. In his belly-in, O'Brien had hit his head bad and was at times violent. Olson and the German guard aboard the train taking them to POW camp could not control O'Brien. O'Brien was worrying so much about his wife and her reaction to his loss and capture that he leaped from the train to escape and broke his leg in the process. He was forced to turn himself in to the Germans to get it reset. Several days later he escaped again and was shot to death about sixty miles behind the German lines."

John Kirk: "I saw this train and decided to knock out the engine first from the side and then I could go back and strafe the train at my leisure. So I came in from about 1,500 feet with my nose down and got a good sighting on the engine. I don't believe I even got any shots off. All of a sudden my right wing exploded and flipped the plane half up on its side. This dropped me down to three or four hundred feet and I leveled the airplane, keeping on the deck until I got past the train. The wing still seemed to be on, although the aircraft was vibrating very badly. I looked over and saw the gun covers were blown off, the gun ammunition belts were all flipping back on the trailing edge of the wing, the wing was bent, the skin had been blown away from the ribs, and the wing was so wrinkled it looked like a washing board.

"I unfastened everything to get out, because I didn't know how long it was going to last. I pulled the nose up so I could get up to four or five hundred feet before I bailed out. As I rolled the canopy back to start out, the plane was still flying, so I thought I'd go up to 1,000 feet to make a good safe jump. At 1,000 feet it was still flying, although poorly, of course. I decided to get my wits about me and see what the heck was going on before I made any further decisions. Climbing to 2,500 feet it required full rudder and the stick all the way over in the corner to keep it flying. I had it going fairly fast because I knew I'd lost a lot of lift in that wing. I experimented with a stall and it stalled out at about 130 mph. Thinking I'd try and get at least to France, I found my compass wasn't working from the hit in the wing cable. I was in a spot. A busted up aircraft, no compass, late in the day, separated from the rest of the group, and still fairly deep in Germany.

"As I plodded along I thought about when I was a Boy Scout and how they taught you to look for tree moss on the north side of a tree, but that was out. Then you look up to the sun and that's what I did. I headed my nose in the direction of the late sun in the west. Kept my eyes outside looking for Germans as I was almost defenseless. Another idea came to me and I got on the radio asking someone to point his nose into the sun and give me a heading. I got an answer back and set my gyroscopic compass to that heading and climbed to 12,000 feet out of small arms range, but not too high where I could be seen too well. Continuing on, I finally hit the coast, and I knew exactly where I was because I knew it by heart.

"Crossing the channel I contacted my base and told them my problem. They told me to head out over the drink and bail out. I said, 'Noooo,' I wasn't going to do that as I wasn't particularly fond of bailing out of an airplane. Coming over the field I tried a landing up in the air to see what my stall speed with wheels down was, and what would happen when I slowed her down with flaps. I came in real hot, made a good landing, and taxied up to my revetment.

"My chief and I looked it over. A 20mm cannon hit the wing from underneath blowing a great hole in it and severing the spar right in half. It blew the skin off and that's what gave the flying trouble. The crew chief asked me what I'd gotten and I said the truth was I didn't get a darned thing. He was mad as Hell because he said, 'You go out and get all that damage and I got to spend the whole night changing this wing and you didn't even get anything!'"

The Group put up eighteen missions for the month, and due mainly to the Nazi flak crews, the losses were extremely heavy. They included seven men Killed in Action, ten Prisoners of War and four evaders. The Luftwaffe had been totally absent in the air. There were no aerial kills and all agreed that the fifteen ground kills and 103 locomotives destroyed were dearly purchased.

First Lieutenant Robert Blossom's P-51D MX-A 44-72237 "KEEP KICKIN II", with chief, S/Sgt. Robert Wilson on the wing. The armorer was Sgt. Donald Baker. The first edition was lost when Blossom hit a smokestack. (USAF)

A formation of Flying Forts from the 379th BG heads for the Continent. The near aircraft is a G model. (USAF)

B-24 Liberators of the 467th Bomb Group just at "Bombs Away" over Austrian target, the Alps below. (Allen Healy)

Chapter 19

Beginning of the End - Final Dogfights

March 1945: As March dawned the Allied ring was closing on Germany and the Luftwaffe fought final desperate battles over their homeland, often over their own airdromes.

The 78th was assigned to an unopposed escort mission on March 1st. Leaving the bombers north of Lake Constance, the group dropped down to search for targets. Southwest of Stuttgart, Cologne, and Kassel, Germany, Ernest Boehner took a flak hit at 500 feet, crashed, and exploded. Boblingen airdrome flak got Roy Higgins on his second pass and his chute failed to open before he struck the ground. Near Heimsheim, Germany, William Townsend's Mustang caught a wing tip on a truck and exploded into the ground next to the Autobahn.

The Group more than evened the score the following day. Lieutenant Colonel John Landers was flying with the 83rd squadron near the head of the bomber column at 1010 hours midway between Berlin and Magdeburg. Between the First and Second Combat Wings at 21,000 feet, the Group sighted twenty-four plus ME109s below at 15,000 feet. The Germans appeared to be forming for an attack as they climbed through a hole in the clouds. They were flying in string formation in flights of four with belly tanks.

Landers circled the Group around to approach the Germans out of the sun and proceeded to attack. The German flight leaders were experienced aggressive pilots who dropped their tanks, but the rest appeared to be novices who kept their tanks and played follow-the-leader tactics. Most of the Germans bailed out eagerly after one or two strikes on their aircraft. At one point in the battle nine parachutes were counted.

Landers' guns would not fire at first and his wingman, Jack Hodge, had to take on the first German they encountered. The enemy pilot parachuted. Only four of Landers' guns worked on the next 109, producing modest hits in the German's wing before two guns quit firing, but again the enemy bailed out even though his plane wasn't smoking. Pulling up behind another Messerschmitt, Landers' guns refused to work again. Breaking away he managed to get one unjammed and jumped another 109 with a belly tank. Without even scoring any visible hits, he pulled up around the Messerschmitt, and to Lander's amazement the German also hit the silk at a low altitude. Another ME109 skidded in between Landers and Hodge firing all its ammunition without result. Hodge only had one gun working by this time, but it was enough to get hits on the rookie and cause him to take to his chute. Back at Duxford the veteran Landers termed all four kills as freaks.

After chasing several Germans with no result, Foy Higginbottom went head-on at a 109 and got good strikes as it dove for the deck, where it crashed in flames. The confusion of the milling dogfight had everyone taking snapshots. William Julian finally maneuvered behind a 109 at fifty yards and registered many good strikes, causing pieces to fly off. The German aircraft smoked and spiraled to a crash. Chasing another 109 through clouds, Julian got it smoking and the German took to his chute. Richard Kuehl tightened his turn after a 109 wingman and dumped flaps to stay with him. Kuehl's canopy strikes made the 109 stream white smoke and roll into the ground exploding. Hubert Davis turned 360

First Lieutenant Roy P. Higgins, 84FS sits on his P-47 WZ-G 44-19934 "GINNY" waiting for morning takeoff. Roy died on Mar 1, 1945 when he bailed out too low over a German airdrome. (Charles Clark)

degrees after two 109s coming at him and got one in a climbing turn with a thirty degree deflection shot. The German spiraled straight down pouring dense black smoke and its gear dropped before it hit and exploded.

However, the day's shooting master was Duncan McDuffie. He quickly dispatched two 109s with short bursts and dropped below the clouds on another unsuspecting ME109 which received a long burst. It became enveloped in flame and plowed into the ground. Duncan sighted his fourth 109 at 7,000 feet and played tag with it through the clouds, until after five passes, it streamed glycol and slid off in a steep dive. His ammunition almost gone and catching flak from an aerodrome below the fight, McDuffie climbed up to rejoin Cargo Squadron. All told, the 83rd came home with thirteen kills from this battle near Burg airdrome. The cost was Henry Staub, a POW whom no one saw go down.

Peter Keillor: "The airfield proper at Duxford was not the best landing field in the world. I supposed the reason the 78th stayed on there was due to the excellent living quarters on

base. There was a huge bunker at the end of the runway that was easy to run into on takeoff. In a three point landing on the rough field, the front wheels bounced as you touched, and the aircraft would crow-hop about three times before you got down to stay. On the third hop you may have been ten feet in the air with no speed, so you poured on the throttle, and the torque of the P-51 twisted the aircraft. I picked up grass stains on my wing tip one time when this happened." [This may explain Lieutenant Colonel Lander's habit of using a P-38 style main wheels only landing technique at DX rather than a three point touchdown.]

On March 19th, the 78th was briefed as free lance support for the First Force, Third Air Division's withdrawal from Plauen/Ruhland, Germany. Colonel Landers led, making landfall at the Hague, Netherlands at 1219 hours. When the Group reached the German border west of Lingen, a pair of ME262s and a lone ME163 began making faint attacks out of layers of stratus clouds from 8,000 to 18,000 feet, attempting to force the Group into dropping their combat tanks. The ploy didn't work as the 78th kept the jets at bay by making brief turns into them. At 1220 MEW control reported there were

Little Friends ahead, but when the 82nd Squadron reached the Osnabruck area at 1230, they sighted four ME109s at 3 o'clock level at 8,000 feet. At first the 82nd thought the 109s were Spitfires because of the elliptical wings and the cross on the wings appearing as roundels against the camouflage. As Captain Richard Hewitt, Surtax Leader broke into the ME109s more and more enemy aircraft began to appear and make attacks toward the Squadron. It quickly became evident that the group had stumbled upon upwards of 125 enemy aircraft forming for bomber interception over their airfields in the triangle of Hesepe-Vorden-Achmer, Germany. Immediately the 83rd and 84th Squadrons were mixing in what would turn out to be an hour long swirling air battle as other and larger enemy gaggles joined in. Most of the "Dummer Lake Boys" airborne this day were Staffels of Jagdegeswader 27. At the beginning of the fight there were twenty-five plus FW190s above a thin layer of cirrus at 14,000 feet. They soon descended on the 78th as well. The Germans were willing to engage and showed no tendency to run or bail unless badly damaged in the fight that ranged from 15,000 feet down to the deck.

Richard Hewitt opened fire and simultaneously jettisoned his wing tanks. Since he had forgotten to switch fuel tanks, his

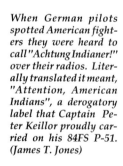

Captain Ivan Keatley's MX-Y 44-72352 "CUTIE II" He has his oxygen mask and goggles off mugging for the pix. (USAF)

engine sputtered and kicked in again in time for an Immelman that brought Dick behind his first ME109 victim. A short chase later and many strikes saw the German bail out. By this time there were 109s all over the area and he fired ninety degrees into another German's cockpit. The 109 snapped three times and spun tightly into the deck, pilot with it. Hewitt's Number Three, Walter Bourque, climbed after four 109s, 3,000 feet above, one of whom came down firing head-on. Doing a 180 turn onto its tail, Walter blew off its right stabilizer and the German bailed out.

Surtax Red Leader, Ivan Keatley, attacked a 109 intent on bouncing White Flight. The 109 streamed coolant, its canopy came off and the pilot jumped. Ivan lost his wingman in an unheard break and started climbing after two plus 109s at 12,000 feet. The first bravely met Ivan head-on, going over his top and streaming coolant. Another short burst astern induced him to bail out. Out of ammunition Ivan located his wingman and, with two other 51s, headed home.

Red three, Allen Rosenblum, fought a 109 for ten minutes at 400 feet over an airdrome and gave up due to the flak it stirred up. Joining James Parker on the deck, he helped hit an Arado 234 jet. Allen chandelled upward as the German fighter struck a farmhouse and exploded. Reforming with Yellow Flight, they were making head-on passes at ten 109s when Rosenblum's tail warning radar sounded. Looking back, he broke into a dozen FW190s going head to head firing. Allen's target flew right through his line of fire and crashed into the deck.

James Parker, Yellow Two, got on the tail of the AR234 jet that seemed to be stooging along on the deck. He was blasting the jet's tail, engines, and fuselage as Rosenblum joined to get hits. The jet pilot crawled out of the cockpit to bail out, but Parker's bullets knocked him forward over the wing. A bit later Parker split-essed onto an FW190 on the deck below, using a long ninety degree burst and sent it crashing into the ground. Captain Winfield Brown, Yellow Leader, quickly destroyed a 109 at 1,000 feet and pulled up to find himself astern of an AR234 jet. Brown and his wingman, Huie Lamb, set the jet aflame and it dove into the deck.

Surtax Blue Leader, Austin Miller, pulled his nose onto two 109s bouncing his flight and didn't think he hit anything, but one of them did a wingover and dove straight into the ground and exploded. In the same vicinity a few minutes later he got behind a 109 at 12,000 feet. An extreme range burst gave some flashes on its tail. The 109 went straight in with no chute. Blue three, Edwin Schneider, got in a short burst at 700 yards going head-on at a 109 which streamed glycol, leveled off, rolled twice, and went vertical to explode into the ground.

John Landers, Cargo White Leader, took his flight down on a low gaggle of 109s. He overshot the first pass and lost his

1Lt. Warren Blodgett in his WZ-X 44-72099 "LITTLE CHIX" flies formation over Cambridgeshire with Captain James Farmer in his WZ-H 44-15731 "MISCHIEVIOUS NELL". The crew panel on Warren's a/c reads: CC S/Sgt Allen Clapp, ACC Cpl. Thomas Stoker, and ARM Cpl Joseph Raths. The A/C carries the black tips of 84FS on wings and tail. (Edward Briski)

wingman climbing back up. His tail warning radar gave good service as he spent time clearing his own tail. When another 109 split-essed out of the fight, John cut out another P-51 and closed dead astern and clobbered the enemy aircraft. Circling on the deck he watched the damaged plane belly-in at Vorden airdrome, trying to reach safety.

White three, Howard Seeley, shot down two ME109s in a row using his ability to out turn them and gain the advantage. Following a 109 in a step dive to the deck, White four, Robert Talbot, made concentrated hits, and watched his target explode on the ground.

After a protracted chase and turn session, Red Leader, Foy Higginbottom and his wingman, Richard Kuehl, shared in destroying a 109 by damaging him enough to cause his bailout. Red three, John Kirk, found himself matched with a good Jerry pilot and went through a turning duel up to 15,000 feet before John caught him reversing his turn and scored strikes on the cockpit that sent the German diving into the ground.

Cargo Yellow Leader, Major Charles Christ, got into a daisy chain Lufberry descending to 7,000 feet with an ME109 between himself and another P-51. All three were firing at the other's target as they went around. Finally Christ got several strikes at minus 100 yards and the 109 pilot bailed out. Hubert Davis flying as Yellow Three, bounced a Messerschmitt 1,000 feet below him. He went through two turns before scoring hits on the German in a ninety degree deflection shot. The enemy aircraft was last seen, spiraling down, its pilot parachuting. Trying to join up with some P-51s, Hubert climbed up behind a 109 pilot who bailed out even before he fired.

Peter Klassen 83rd Blue Leader, saw four contrails heading for Red Flight above the thin cloud layer and climbed through after them. Breaking out in the clear, he was in excellent position on a 109 and scored many hits on its cockpit. Although the canopy came off, the pilot went in with his smoking aircraft. While climbing back up to the fight at 7,000 feet, Blue Four, Anthony Colletti, spotted two FW190s cross above and peel into him. He went head to head at one registering strikes nose to tail. The enemy plane began smoking and its pilot bailed out.

Shampoo White Leader, Major Harry Downing brought his 84th Squadron into the fight and jumped a 109, shooting it down. Just then the large FW190 gaggle came down on the Squadron from 14,000 feet. Major Downing was heard to say on the radio, "There's lots of meat here," and soon after that he indicated he'd gotten another German and that there were some twenty FW190s around him. His last radio message was "I'm hit and I'm bailing out. So long, gang."

William Degain, White Three, spotted eight silver FW190s at 11,000 feet bouncing a flight of P-51s. He circled a cloud and snuck up on a 190 who was too wide in the gaggle. William hit the German at 400 yards but didn't see him crash because a quick look astern showed a trio of 190s on his tail. Before

long there were five FWs taking turns potting at him. After ten minutes of this, William ducked into a cloud with an aileron shot out.

Shampoo Red Leader, Alfred Garback and his wingman Red Two, Thomas Thain, chased two 109s to the deck where they became separated. Garback and Thain each took on and destroyed a German. As Yellow Three, Henry Slack, approached a ten ship dogfight, he saw a P-51 going straight down trailing smoke. Henry latched onto a 109 diving out of the fight and chased him for five minutes on the treetops until he sent the German flaming into the deck twenty miles east of Munster.

Shampoo Blue Flight with Paul Ostrander leading, dropped tanks and bounced a 109 split essing out of the fight. Closing too fast, Paul cut his throttle and tried to lower flaps, but his ram-air knob got in the way and he skidded off to the side while two other P-51s ripped through his flight missing his 109 completely. Reversing his turn Paul put many hits on the German's canopy and the enemy plane hit the deck and exploded with no chute. Blue Three, James Moores, still had all his ammunition so he joined five Mustangs circling an airdrome. Spying a pair of FW190s 3 o'clock high, heading east just under a thin overcast, James climbed and tailed them in the bottom edge of the clouds. Closing in a five minute chase, James put his second burst into an FW190's engine and canopy. The German bailed just as Moores fired and no chute deployment was seen before the 190 exploded on the ground.

The Group filtered back to Duxford over a one hour period. When Intelligence Officers had completed debriefings it was apparent that the 78th had tallied one of the highest single mission scores in Eighth Air Force history and the best day the 78th would have in aerial victories. Claims were 32-2-16. Five pilots did not return from the bitter battle. James Bolen and Ralph Bush had made the supreme sacrifice. Those pilots finishing the war in captivity were Harry Downing, Thomas Reeves, and Elmer Nieland.

Just two days later 78th pilots proved to be expert "Jet Slayers", as well. The Group was on the board for penetration and withdrawal support to Ruhland, Germany. Forty-three checkernose Mustangs led by Major Richard Conner rendezvoused with the First Air Task Force of the Third Air Division at 0840 hours above Nienburg, Germany.

When the Group reached the Wittenburg area, an ME262 made a pass on the bombers and exploded two of them. As the escort fighters reacted, the 262 came back for a second pass at a crippled B-17. Cargo Blue Three, Edwin Miller, tried to scare him off with a 2,000 yard burst and got a few hits in his wing that made the 262 dive away for some clouds. Miller was clocking 500 mph as he chased the jet through a thin overcast and cut him off in a turn.

The German was in a dilemma. If he kept turning Miller would close faster and hit him with a deflection shot. If he straightened out it gave Miller a better shot, but at longer range and the 262's speed advantage might allow him to

Major Richard E. Conner, 82FS CO, leads the troops off in his P-51D MX-D 44-72233, the aircraft he crashlanded in his evasion to Russian lines on 3-21-45. (USAF)

First Lieutenant Thomas Thain's "SWEET AND LOVELY" rests on the east tower apron near the crash truck and ambulance. Note the tower Jeep of Captain Allan B. Cowart done in Group's black/white checkers. (Duke Morrison)

outrun the P-51. The German chose the latter, but he'd failed to reckon with the K-14 sight and Miller's shooting finesse. At 500 yards Edwin scored hits all over the Messerschmitt jet and it began to slow. This permitted Miller to close in tight and finish the job. The German plane was seen to strike the ground and explode.

Escorting fighters had reached the Dresden vicinity and Phoenix Leader, Major Richard Conner, observed Alt.Lonnewitz airdrome loaded with planes of all types. Taking his White Three, Conner dove to the deck and made a strafing pass at three ME262s parked at the end of the runway waiting to take off. Conner got good strikes on the first two and then put a short burst into the third. The ME262 must have had a bomb load, as it blew up with a large explosion and fire. At 22,000 feet the Squadron saw the huge explosion and then they heard Conner radio that he'd been hit by light flak and that he was taking a course for the Russian front.

Conner's cockpit filled with smoke as he took a heading for Poltava, the Shuttle Missions' base in Russia. His engine caught fire enroute but he made a successful crashlanding on the east bank of the Oder River. He was in a wooded no man's land between the lines and there were pockets of both nation's troops roaming about. Suspecting he was a German spy, none of the Russian troops would accept or aid him. He was getting very hungry, having eaten only his survival rations when he began rabbit hunting with his .45 pistol.

Eventually the Russians took him in and he spent a week at the front with them before being moved to a hotel in Lvov, Poland. A week later he finally arrived at Poltava and went on to Moscow. After being Missing In Action and stranded in Moscow fifty days, he returned to DX on May 10th.

John Kirk: "We were flying at 26,000 feet in the Meiningen, German area, maybe 2,000 feet above and to the right of the bomber stream. I happened to glance over and saw a B-17 explode. Right below it I saw a plane diving and recognized it instantly as an ME262. He turned off towards us in a forty-five degree dive toward the ground. Immediately I turned and dove almost straight down after him. I had full bore on the engine and was gaining speed rapidly. Red line was approximately 500 to 505 mph and I kept checking the airspeed so I didn't collapse my airplane. He didn't seem to be gaining, but neither was I. I decided to chance hitting him with a pot shot. My guns weren't supposed to be fired at Red-line as there was a hazard of pulling the wings off. I pulled my nose up a couple of radii above him and let go a short blast, and checked my wings, which were still on. So I took a couple more shots and some smoke came out of his right engine. That did it. It slowed him up.

"As the ground was coming up rapidly, he started pull out and I took a pursuit curve on him. Gaining gun range quickly, I used my K-14 sight and started blasting him. I could see hits

Major Winfield Brown, 82FS Ops Off. waits for mission takeoff in his P-51D MX-F 44-72191. Note the many maps needed for a mission, tucked into leg pocket. (USAF)

all over the middle of his ship and was approaching him real fast when all of a sudden the canopy flew off. He came out just like he had an ejection seat and the wind caught him and sent him flying back. He was so close I was afraid he was going to hit my wing. I looked at him as he went by in his leather helmet and jacket.

"I flipped over and followed the jet to the ground, and took film of it exploding. Then I went back up to 4,000 feet to film him in his chute. It was an odd ribbon chute that I'd never seen anything like. He thought I was going to strafe him and started wiggling back and forth as I pulled my nose toward him to film."

At 1215 hours Surtax Squadron was heading home on the withdrawal. Captain Winfield Brown, 82nd lead this day, spotted three ME262s taking off from Giebelstadt airdrome and took his boys down from 14,000 feet. Winfield closed in on one 800 feet west of the field and got some good strikes before being hit by airdrome flak and forced to pull up. Blue Leader, Allen Rosenblum, watching Brown pull up, pursued the same ME262. As he was getting strikes on the jet he looked out his left side and saw a P-51 sliding into his belly, so he broke off. He later saw the 262 explode on the field as he strafed a Wurzburg radar dish at the airdrome perimeter.

Walter Bourque, Blue Three, lost his jet and climbed back toward what he thought were three P-51s with tanks. They proved to be ME262s and all quickly became embroiled in a turning duel. Several 339th Group Mustangs almost cut Walter out, but he had greater airspeed, passed them by, and fired at one of the jets. His strikes exploded its left engine and it went down out of control flaming and smoking.

As others dueled, White Three, Robert Anderson cut off the last ME262 taking off. Getting into firing range on the jet just as it went over the airdrome, Robert was flak hit several times but still got strikes on the 262. Catching up again in a turn, Robert hit the jet in the cockpit at fifty feet altitude and it exploded on impact with the ground. Anderson headed for home with his rudder and elevator trim shot away.

The final tally for the Group was five German jets downed at the cost of Conner's forced stay in Russia.

On March 22nd, the 8th's bombers were out to shut down the German jet bases. Lieutenant Colonel Landers led the 83rd Squadron on ahead of the Liberators while the 82nd and 84th escorted them through the targets. Second Air Division B-24s were attacking airfields at Kitzingen, Giebelstadt, and Schwabisch-Hall, between Wurzburg and Stuttgart, Germany.

At 1300 hours near Ulm, Surtax Red Four Milton Stutzman picked up an ME262 approaching the Liberator formations and cut him off by turning into him. The jet broke and headed

south until apparently its pilot thought he had outdistanced his pursuers then turned gently ninety degrees right. This allowed Stutzman to gain on him and he forged ahead of other P-51s also after the jet. North of Lake Constance, the Messerschmitt led Milton across the middle of an airdrome. It was there that the Mustang pilot opened fire and started scoring strikes on the jet. Pouring smoke, the German jettisoned his canopy and bailed out. His chute didn't open before the jet veered off left and crashed beside a small road.

Cargo Squadron was doing combat air patrol duty over the jet dromes in case the bombers stirred the Jagdverbande to retaliate.

Harold Barnaby: 83rd Yellow Leader, relates what happened at 1330 hours: "My attention was attracted to Giebelstadt airdrome because of its long runway and number of jet fighters dispersed around the perimeter. Four ME262s were parked on the runway ready to take off. After calling this information to Phoenix Leader, I saw one of the jets taking off from east to west. From 10,000 feet over the west end of the runway, I closed rapidly in a slight left turn as the 262 cleared the runway. I was indicating 425 mph and was about 400 yards behind when I reached his 1,000 foot altitude. He was going 400 mph in less than three miles flying distance. My first burst hit his left engine, which caused an explosion, blowing off parts. Hits in the wings and fuselage were making it unhealthy for the pilot. Using his speed he pulled up to 2,000 feet. He bailed out. Unfortunately his jump was successful. The 262 half rolled to the right striking the ground vertically. The explosion made a spectacular sight about two miles south of the airdrome. The other jets were quickly dispersed after the tower fired a red flare."

The Lord Mayor of London visited the base on March 24th. He was on hand to watch some of the activity as the Group flew three separate missions. A,B, and C, in support of the ground forces in an area triangle of Lingen, Diepholz, Cloppenburg, on the North German plain. B Group did the most damage of the area strafing patrols. East of Amervort they caught a convoy of gasoline trailer trucks with red crosses painted on their tops and burned out some twenty-eight of them.

Finally, over the period March 29-31, 1945, the Group began to get some answers to the problems they had been experiencing since they switched over to the Mustangs.

James Tudor: (Crew chief) "My plane had accumulated a long streak of flying hours without a mechanical abort. My pilot aborted a mission one day while we were using 150 octane fuel in the Mustangs. It was colored purple with dye to expose fuel leaks, not green like the 100/130 octane gas. It was so powerful the valves had pounded the seats in the cylinder until there was hardly any valve clearance left. This resulted in an engine change. My pilot, Captain Robert Holmes, apologized for weeks about having to bring it back early. He was a fine young man, didn't smoke or drink. He spent lots of time on the line with us and gave us his scotch allotment. He was lost on the Prague mission just a few days before the war was over. His mother wrote me asking for details of what happened. It was amazing that the letter reached me. She addressed it: 'James Tudor, crew chief, somewhere in England'."

James Aicardi: "We had a problem with the American plugs in the 'Maytag Messerschmitts'. These fouled up quite a lot and we had to change all the plugs after every show. The rough running engines and power loss could be critical for the pilots. Then word got out that the British plugs didn't foul. This resulted in a lot of private negotiations with RAF types to swap plugs for 'other' items. Finally the Army caught up with reality and we were able to obtain them 'legally'."

Another member of the engineering staff recalled: "A problem in the P-51 engines was caused by the ethylene dibromide additive in the 150 octane aviation gas. It caused an improper manifold fuel distribution. This burned the valve stems in the front cylinders and cracked or broke the valve stems in the back cylinders. After fifty hours the valve stems in the engine often stretched 30,000th of an inch. About 250 hours was the maximum life of the Packard Merlin engine."

John Landers led the 78th again on March 30th escorting Third Air Division B-17s to Hamburg, Germany. After ushering the bombers out to the coast, John swung north toward Keil with the 84th Squadron. Near Rendsburg airdrome he spotted an ME262 1,000 feet off the deck heading south behind him. Landers and his wingman, Thomas Thain, diving from 7,000 feet bounced the jet and, thanks to the German pilot who did some suicidal gradual turns, both the 78th leader and then Thain, were able to queue up on him for cockpit strikes. The German tried to drop his gear and land on Hohn airdrome but crashed and burned without getting out.

Surtax Red Leader, Wayne Coleman, was sweeping the target area near Stendal, Germany the next day at 15,000 feet. He heard on the radio that jets were in the area and shortly spotted two ME262s flying parallel out to the side. They went out of sight and then several Surtax flights chased and lost another 262 in a distant smoke cloud. Wayne thought it was gone, but again spotted the jet over the leading edge of his left wing. A semi-split-ess drew Wayne into range to score hits in the cockpit and right engine. As he broke left, the 262 rolled right and went straight into the deck exploding. Undoubtedly the pilot had been hit.

After the Group left the bombers at Meppel, Paul Ostrander's Mustang took a light flak hit. Ten minutes out into the North Sea from the Dutch coast, his P-51 engine quit. Paul called over the radio that he had a draft in his cockpit and then said the plane was on fire and he'd have to bail out. He lost power immediately and flames began coming out the exhaust stacks. The use of the "B" emergency channel for casual fixes hindered his May-Day transmission as he was about to bail out. James Moores saw him jump at 5,000 feet and as his chute opened, his dinghy sailed away from him. Moores cut power, dropped flaps, and stayed with him going down and circled him in the rough water. An RAF Warwick and three other P-51s circled the spot, but Moores was unable to contact the Warwick. Wing operations had gotten a class A fix and vectored two P-47s and a Catalina to the spot, but Ostrander disappeared from view five minutes before they

arrived. Moores searched the area until his gas ran low, but Ostrander was never found. As soon as they could be refueled an 84th flight took off and continued the search until their gas gave out.

Two 84th Mustangs also flew escort for a lifeboat equipped B-17. Unable to find Ostrander the Dumbo successfully dropped its raft to a stranded bomber crew in three dinghies.

April 1945: Thus the book closed on a very hectic and action filled month. The Mustang was having an effect on the Group few could have foreseen. They were achieving more aerial success but suffering heavier losses. Twenty-five March missions with the bird brought fifty-four air-to-air kills at a cost of nine KIA, one KIFA, four POW, three evaders, and two wounded in action. Nine locomotives and four ground claims finished the slate.

The next heavy action took place on April 7. The Group was on escort duty north of Dummer Lake, when MEW reported bogies in the area. Francis Harrington, 83rd Blue Leader, observed three contrails coming from the southeast toward the bombers and climbed to meet them. At 23,000 feet he got into a tight circle with an ME109. Francis pulled into position astern and firing at 150 yards sent the 109 into a spin. Next Harrington noticed long stream contrails in groups of two and three coming in from the same direction as the first attackers. Climbing to 29,000 feet he was soon involved in another tight Lufberry with an FW190. After a few hits Harrington had the 190 doing wide barrel rolls going straight down. Both went through a cloud and Francis found the 190 flying close formation with him. The German eventually rolled, dove into the ground, and exploded.

Yellow Leader, Robert Green chased 109s making single passes from 6 o'clock on bombers. The Forts downed the first which collided with another bomber. After dodging pieces, Robert dove on a 109 at 6 o'clock low. He had to chop his

Captain Robert T. Green, 83FS D-Flt leader, with his P-51 HL-K 44-11573 "THE GREEN HORNET". The swastikas include four and one-half aerial victories, three and one-half in one day. The other two kill marks would be ground victories. (Samuel Beckley)

The control tower at Duxford. Portable B-17 Nose bubble control booth is on top of tower. (Russell Hunter)

throttle to stay behind and scored many hits on the Messerschmitt's fuselage. Closing to 200 yards, Green ran up close enough to see glycol streaming over the German's windscreen. The enemy aircraft pulled up sharply and spun slowly into the ground with its elevators shot out. Its pilot did not get out.

In the meantime, Cargo White Three, Richard Kuehl, found an ME109 stooging along in front of him crossing to the left. Richard rolled left and hit him as the Jerry did wingovers and rolls. The German pilot was seen to parachute.

About thirty minutes later 84th Shampoo Leader, Richard Corbett, saw an ME109 diving at his bomber box and firewalled everything in pursuit. Richard ran through the bomber's gunfire and started getting strikes on the 109 going straight down at 500 mph. He overran the Messerschmitt as it streamed smoke and coolant and ducked into low clouds. Corbett pursued through the clouds and found the 109 coming at him head-on. Firing quickly and turning, Corbett was again confronted by the German head-on. The Mustang was not hit but the 109 received strikes on its nose. Corbett's wingman, Henry Slack, took a firing pass at the same German and saw strikes in the cockpit. The German rolled over and dove vertically into a small pond without a chute showing.

Altogether, some thirty ME109s and FW190s had pressed aggressive attacks on the bombers, while eight all white ME262s had attacked singly from 30,000 feet. Seven B-17s went down in this area, two from collisions with German fighters. Robert Talbot and another 78th pilot were heard to say that they had been attacked by P-51s with German markings. Talbot was forced to jump and became a Prisoner of War.

John Kirk: "Comments about the P-51: It was a superb, beautiful flying airplane, it had no bad characteristics. The left wing did stall out first and drop on landings, you had to be a little careful of that. It accelerated extremely fast which was very helpful. What we liked about it after flying Jugs was the range. You could pull the mixture control back and the thing would just about breathe air, and you flew almost forever as far as the gas was concerned. Turning radius was equal to any German plane and I never met one that could turn inside you. I'm sure with good pilots they could turn with us, but they certainly couldn't out turn us. Climbing rate was fantastic. It was a rugged airplane and we used to put them through some strong aerobatics. We never had any structural failures I can recall. I never had a turn back from a mission because of mechanical failure. I had an extremely good mechanic. He kept my plane in spotless shape and he used to wax it. It was probably one of the fastest airplanes in the Group.

"At the time I shot down the German jet, my wingman had blown a gasket when he got home, from trying to keep up with us. So it was really a plane that made the pilot feel confident. I had no hesitation at all in meeting any situation in combat. There was one thing you had to be a little cautious of. The brakes were death on most North American airplanes and you had to be awful careful applying brakes. They overheated and tended to fuse. If you came up to your revetment after a hot landing and pulled your parking brake on, you just had a solid mass of brakes, and one mad crew chief. It didn't take a lot of muscle to fly it and swing it around. The controls were very responsive with an excellent rate of roll. The elevator wasn't sensitive and it turned easy, and you could push the stick down and it dove on you. It was an extremely all around well-flying airplane. I never had any trouble with discomfort while flying. I was usually warm enough, as we wore pretty heavy clothing to protect us from fire."

Chapter 20

Airdrome Strafing - The Death of the Luftwaffe

The 78th's second anniversary of European Theater combat operations was celebrated on April 8th with an escort mission to Plauen, Germany. Two days later, Colonel Landers with the 82nd Squadron, was leading a mission when they made rendezvous at 1404 hours and 17,000 feet near Osnabruck, Germany. Again the Third Air Task Force was going after the German jet fields around Brandenburg. After the bombers unloaded on Brandenburg/Briest airdrome, Landers gave the okay to strafe jet dromes in the vicinity. The 83rd Squadron went in first making tentative passes at Briest airdrome but the flak was considered too hot. Moving over to Burg airdrome near Magdeburg, which was still burning from bombing and strafing, Cargo Leader Foy Higginbottom made a solo pass on an ME262 which he damaged.

Landers had swept on to Werder Airdrome east of Briest and southwest of Potsdam, where he observed some P-47s burning ten to fifteen enemy aircraft on the drome. Landers radioed the others to converge on Werder airdrome as there were around seventy targets parked closely on the perimeter and in the woods on the west side. Both hangars were on fire and the smoke rising from the burning planes made spotting targets and strafing difficult. Pilots were occasionally in instrument conditions in heavy smoke. Up to twelve passes were made by 78th pilots and when they pulled away from the field sixty enemy aircraft were smoldering wrecks. The gunnery pattern was run from northeast to southwest with moderate to meager flak response. Enroute home the boys also made some courtesy passes at Gardelegen and Hustedt airdromes.

When the details were worked out by Intelligence Officers back at Duxford the ground claims came to 52-0-43. Squadron totals were 82nd Fighter Squadron - thirty three; 83rd Fighter Squadron - eleven; and 84th Fighter Squadron - eight. Colonel Landers destroyed eight, Carroll, Lamb, Harrington, and Slack scored four each, and the rest of the pilots claimed three down to one kill, with only three pilots having no score. The debit side was three officers Missing in Action. Roger Spaulding bailed out from a Werder Airdrome flak hit and became a Prisoner of War. The Briest flak got Richard Kuehl and he bailed out at Helmstadt, was captured for thirty-six

hours until he was freed by the advancing U.S. 84th Infantry Division. Five days later he was back on operations at Duxford. However, Herbert Stinson was killed by the Werder flak.

Wednesday, April 11th John Landers was introduced into British Society. The Lord Mayor of London invited him to London Mansion House, Earls Court for Easter Luncheon to meet the Diplomatic Corps.

On April 16, 1945 the 78th got in a final heavy punch at the Luftwaffe as the war wound down to its final days. This seven hour, forty minute marathon mission won the group another Distinguished Unit Citation.

To paraphrase the Fighter Command's citation: "After a long, wearisome, and hazardous flight deep into enemy territory, they successfully attacked five enemy airdromes in the Prague/Pilsen, Czechoslovakia area, and established a wartime Eighth Air Force record for ground victories. They braved heavy AA fire at dangerous low-level, to neutralize the enemy gun emplacements, and return in systematic waves of destruction to wipe out the dispersed enemy aircraft below. Although fatigued by many hours of combat, they continued until their ammunition was nearly expended and their return flight fuel was at its minimum. Their gallantry, sacrifice, and espirit de corps reflect the highest credit on themselves and the Army Air Force."

The assigned mission was to give area support to the 760 Flying Fortresses of First and Second Air Divisions hitting bridges and marshaling yards in the Regensburg-Straubing-Platting-Landshut areas. The 78th arrived at 1430 hours led by John Landers with the 84th. The 82nd was given permission to separate into individual flights and to check on strafing prospects at various area airdromes being patrolled. White flight led by Manford Croy made a pass on Straubling airdrome where Croy destroyed a single Focke Wulf 190 before flak hit him. He pulled up and bailed out, but was too low for his chute to open. James Parker and Eugene Peel each burned an enemy aircraft at this drome and then Peel scored another at Laudan airdrome. Peel was clipped by flak and forced to make a belly landing near Frankfurt.

Robert Holmes led Red Flight down on Straubling where he shot up two enemy aircraft. George Stilwell destroyed

A section approaches the pattern over Duxford's east runway. WZ-P 42-106886 (foreground) was an old P-51B that came to the 84FS as a trainer, but later flew combat. WZ-L 44-11747 was B-Flt leader Captain Peter Keillor's aircraft also flown by Captain Dorian Ledington, Squadron CO. He was WIA on 4-16-45. (Nicholas Vale/AFM)

First Lieutenant John Murphy, 84FS pilot, a gifted cartoonist, expressed the general abhorrence of low level work. (Frank Oiler)

three, but they would not burn, as many targets refused to do this day. The Luftwaffe was simply running out of petrol. Moving on to another airdrome, Holmes hit at least three enemy aircraft and Stilwell got two more. Leaving what was probably Marienbad, they strafed Ganacker airdrome southwest of Platting, Germany. Robert Holmes was last seen going into his pass at Ganacker and probably crashed to his death from a flak hit. Red three, George Elsey, also burned an ME109 on one of these airdromes.

Yellow flight headed by Donald Hart descended onto Marienbad airdrome where Robert Blossom hit a DO217 and burned it after four passes. Fred Swauger, Yellow Four, took a small arms hit and crashed. He was released from captivity by U.S. troops a short time later.

Lieutenant Colonel Olin Gilbert had again come down from Eighth Air Force Headquarters to fly on this show with his old outfit. His leadership of Blue Flight this day earned him a Silver Star. As the Group flew past the various dromes,

flights from the 82nd had been detailed to strafe and Blue Flight was still at altitude with the rest of the 78th as Landers led them away from the area of patrol. With bombers bound for home and escort duties completed, Landers headed towards the airfield complexes surrounding Prague, where intelligence had reported hundreds of Luftwaffe aircraft seeking shelter from the advancing Allied Armies. Still carrying their wing tanks allowed the P-51s on this flight to get almost an hour deeper into the shrinking Reich.

At about 1530 hours Phoenix Leader John Landers observed some eighty plus enemy aircraft of all types on Cakowice airdrome just north of Prague. The Group dropped down to 3,000 feet and flew over the field from north to south checking for flak response. Leaving 82nd Blue Flight as top cover, Landers took the 84th and 83rd on south until out of sight, made a 180 degree turn and hit the deck coming into the drome from the south to give the flak guns a tougher ninety degree deflection shot. Enemy aircraft were scattered all over the field in groups of two to five, with singles in outer revetments.

On his first pass, Landers picked out a row of four HE177s. Two lighted up as he fired and after pulling up, all four were burning. On his second pass from east to west he had two more HE177s burning. The first eight Mustangs across the field set thirteen enemy aircraft on fire. After four passes there were fifty plus fires on the perimeter and more going in isolated dispersals. The checkernosed P-51s set up an east to west pattern and methodically reduced every plane to ashes. Lander's third pass flamed two more. He destroyed three more in his next five passes. Damaged planes were finished off by other pilots coming in behind each other. When the 84th and 83rd Squadrons left the airdrome, only three enemy aircraft remained and 82nd Blue Flight went down and made it 100%.

Pilots who found the smoke too thick or the targets too scarce at Cakowice, moved over two miles southeast to Prague/ Letnany airdrome which was filled with fifty plus enemy aircraft. After two or three passes the half dozen AA guns quit firing and a nice, well spaced left hand gunnery pattern was flown for twenty-five minutes. Many planes hit repeatedly would not burn. Some pilots made ten to twelve passes at the

1LT. Harry Roe's MX-Z 44-72938 "MISS PAM", crewed by S/Sgt. Walter Cannon. The a/c behind, MX-U 44-73042, may be Capt. Wayne Coleman's bird, possibly a jet-killer. The yellow tip to MX-Z's fin may be a squadron flight color. (Walter Cannon)

First Lieutenant Herbert Stinson was KIA in his MX-Z 44-15556 "DOUG" on April 10, 1945 at Werder airdrome. CC S/Sgt Walter Cannon is by prop far left. The armorers have the guns out servicing them lower right. (Walter Cannon)

airdromes. Smoke became so thick wingmen left their leaders and carried out solo runs for safety. Clyde Taylor used his gyro-compass setting to keep score of his four JU52s, FW190 and three ME110s. All six of Anthony Colletti's destroyed claims were burning. He was the last pilot strafing at 1615 when the group recall was given on the radio. As he withdrew, he noticed a few enemy aircraft break out into flames while no one was shooting at them. He counted seventy aircraft burning. The group lost no aircraft or pilots during the Prague area attacks.

When 78th Intelligence had finally amassed all claims and sorted them out back at Duxford, the signal was flashed to Eighth Air Force Headquarters that a command record 135-0-89 enemy aircraft had been destroyed and damaged on the ground during the mission. Squadron claims were: 82nd Fighter Squadron 19-0-28; 83rd Fighter Squadron 58-0-28; and 84th Fighter Squadron 58-0-31. High scoring pilots of the day were: John Landers, nine; Clyde Taylor, eight; Edward Kulik, seven; and Olin Gilbert and Anthony Colletti, six each. Those pilots also now ranked as ground kill aces with five were; Donald DeVilliers, Dale Sweat, Duncan McDuffie, Gene Doss, Danford Josey, and Dorian Ledington. The only Group casualty was Dorian Ledington who was in a left bank over one of the fields when a thirty caliber projectile came through

his canopy, grazed his neck, and exploded fragments in his neck. One of his flight members escorted him safely back to base.

Surtax Squadron also flew an additional Black Flight on the mission which did not take part in the strafing. The flight was composed of an unarmed P-51D two seat Mustang flown by Captain Richard Hewitt, the squadron CO, and several escorting wingmen.

Richard Hewitt: "My rear seat passenger was Major Vincent of the Group intelligence staff. He wanted to go on a mission and it was an opportunity for him to see what it was all about from the air. It was over six hours and it wasn't any milk run. It was a real thrill for him and he thoroughly enjoyed it. Virtually no ground officers had ever actually flown a mission in a fighter. These guys did a tremendous job in their own right."

While the Intelligence Officers were still typing up the previous day's combat reports, the Mustangs were taking off for a show to Dresden Germany on April 17th. About fifteen miles north, northeast of Dresden, Shampoo Red Flight chased some bogies that turned out to be friendlies. When they reached the deck, Red Leader, William McClellan spotted an airdrome with thirty plus enemy aircraft. A quick test for flak found very little to speak of, and the flight proceeded to carry out a half dozen or so passes apiece. By 1530 hours the four P-51s had burned thirteen and damaged thirteen more enemy aircraft on the unidentified field. One was a captured B-17 painted with black crosses.

As the relief escort group arrived to make rendezvous with the bombers going home, the 82nd and 83rd squadrons turned back for a strafing sweep of the Prague area. Anthony Palopoli of Cargo Squadron flying as a spare with the 82nd destroyed an ME262 on the ground at Cakowice airdrome. Surtax Leader, Richard Hewitt and his flight bounced a couple of ME262s and chased them a long way before the jets ran low on fuel and headed for the single runway at Kralupy, Czechoslovakia. As the last one was on its final landing approach, Hewitt swept in and shot him down into trees off the end of the runway. The first ME262 was still rolling on the other end of the runway as Hewitt set him aflame.

By this time the flak was coming up furiously and Hewitt's wingman, Allen Rosenblum was hit as he approached the airdrome. His Mustang wanted to quit flying but by sheer strength Allen pulled up. His engine was dead and he knew

The interior of 84FS hangar. RAF wall sign says, "Gauntlet (1920s bi-plane) endurance 2 hours". What a contrast for the 6-7 hour range Mustangs then in the hangar. Foreground is Lt. Alfred Garback's WZ-G 44-63779. (Nicholas Vale/AFM)

The snazziest looking 51 at DX was Col. Landers' "BIG BEAUTIFUL DOLL". Note the checker wingtips, red-edged spinner, anti-glare panel, and red/black fin/stab. tips. (Nicholas Vale/AFM)

he had to bail out or belly in. He chose the latter, being too low for the former. As he looked ahead he saw a light German two place trainer, which he strafed until he crashed. Hewitt thought for sure that Rosenblum had met his maker as he watched the disabled P-51 slide across the airdrome going about 350 mph, careen through a couple of hedgerows and disappear in some trees. But even as the trainer burned, Rosenblum was taken Prisoner of War and set off on a road march into Germany. Another Surtax wingman, Alvin Rosenburg, had to bail out from flak west of Adorf, Germany.

Hewitt was not able to receive confirmation for the aerial jet kill, only the one on the runway landing. The former would have given him five aerial victories and ace status.

Eighth Air Force service units underwent a merger and reorganization on April 18th which involved veteran units based with the 78th Fighter Group being amalgamated into a new 443rd Air Service Group.

All 78th airdrome strafing activities ceased on April 20th, 1945 when the Eighth Air Force placed a ban on further operations of this sort. The strafing restriction frustrated the 78th the next day, when twenty plus German jets were spotted parked along the Autobahn southeast of Munich, Germany. Bad weather delayed the group's rendezvous until the bomber stream could be overhauled near Munich. After the bombers had dropped their loads on the marshaling yards the squadrons started for home at 1215 hours. Weather worsened and the Group began to let down from 18,000 feet. By the time the 84th had fought their way through the rain and thunderstorms, they were down to 2,000 feet west of Coblenz, Germany. There at 1340 hours, it became a solid front with ceiling and visibility zero.

Shampoo leader, Dorian Ledington, was flying on the deck at treetop level, looking for an airfield on which he could set down because his wingman, John Sole, had only ten minutes gas left. Black Leader, Earl Stier and his flight were

1Lt. William McClellan's WZ-U 44-63191 "LUCKY BABY" sits on the A-Flt. line near the hangar. The a/c has a red-edged canopy frame and fin tip, an individual marking, not a unit feature. CC S/Sgt. Sylvester Heytman, and ACC Sgt. Ira Bents. (Charles Clark)

An 82FS P-51B, converted to a two seater. This may have been the P-51 referred to in Major Vincent's 4-16-45 combat flight. Post VE it was painted red overall with buzz code underwing of 78FG. B-17 hulk in the background was General Woodbury's "Waldorf Astoria". (Nicholas Vale/ AFM)

following them. When they hit the solid front Black Flight climbed to 13,000 feet. About this time Stier heard Ledington radio that he'd badly damaged his left wing, hitting a tree. Nothing further was heard from Ledington and it was assumed he had already crashed to his death. Stier then told Sole, who was out of gas, to turn 180 degrees and climb and either bail out or belly in. Sole radioed back "Roger" and it was later learned that he bailed out at only 300 feet and his chute failed to deploy.

Group Leader, Lieutenant Colonel Leonard Marshall, Headquarters Squadron was also killed on this mission. His Mustang was last seen flying upside down in an overcast at 28,000 feet in the Mannheim, Germany area. Later his body and unopened parachute were found twenty miles north of Strasbourg, France. He may have been the victim of oxygen starvation or instrument failure. Gene Doss had to force land his Mustang at Valenciennes, France and was heard from two days later in a French hospital with a sprained leg. Further bad news advised that Harry Just's grave had been found in France and that the grave of Quince Brown had been located in Germany.

On a much happier note, four lost pilots who had been evading capture returned to Duxford safely.

Before the group crossed over the English coast on their last World War II combat mission, a final KIA was registered. On April 25th, 1945, Second Lieutenant Edward J. Carroll aborted the mission shortly after takeoff and turned back toward the base. Several miles from Duxford near Sawston, Cambshire he hit trees in a dense fog and crashed to his death.

The mission proceeded on across the North Sea and hit the Belgian coast at Furnes at 0650 hours. A rendezvous was effected with the wrong bomber force over Luxembourg at 0735 hours and the Group disengaged and swept on to the target alone. They found the correct bombers there and escorted them out to Stuttgart, breaking off escort at 1000 hours. This force consisted of eleven RAF Lancaster bombers of the famous 617 "Dam Busters" Squadron, who had just completed their World War II missions by dropping 12,000 pound "Tallboy" bombs on Hitler's mountain retreat at Berchtesgaden, Austria. After leaving the Lancasters, the 78th was vectored in a 180 degree turn back to Landshut, Germany where they rendezvoused with Second Air Division B-24s at 1025 hours. The Liberators were escorted back to Salzberg, Germany to flatten the rail yards filled with fleeing remnants of the German Armies. Escort was completed over the target at 1045 hours and the Group departed the Belgian coast at 1350 hours on the Belgian coast at Furnes. All 78 planes landed at Duxford at 1440 hours.

Once again the two seat Double Mustang had flown this mission with the Group, piloted by Huie Lamb, with 66th Fighter Wing Flight Surgeon Lieutenant Colonel Ben Pentecost, in the jump seat. Now that the war was finished for the fighter pilots, the Wing Flight Surgeon had gotten a first hand insight. Typical Army timing, down to the last gunshot.

And so the final month of World War II combat came to a close for the 78th Fighter Group. There were only five aerial victories but the 202 ground victories were testament to the ferocity of the strafing operations. The eighteen missions had cost seven lives. Six pilots were in temporary captivity, and one pilot had a painful wound.

Many enemy aircraft which pilots claimed damaged on airfields were actually destroyed. However, due to poor film,

"SCREAMING EAGLE" JD-Z 44-8007, a B-17 of the 384BG, coming home in the twilight. Spring, 1945 (AFM)

On June 7, 1945 officers and enlisted men of the proud 78th paraded one last time as their Mustangs stood in silent review. (Russell Hunter)

lack of visual confirmation, or insufficient internal fuel to get them burning, they were not observed outright to be destroyed. In fact, they were often too badly shot up to be repaired or they were never repaired due to lack of spare parts and labor to do the work. Even had they been repaired, there was so little petrol and so few pilots available. They were effectively neutralized without warranting a victory claim. Of course, the same holds true for aerial claims. It is probable that more enemy aircraft and pilots were killed than the stringent confirmation requirements showed. Many enemy aircraft damaged in air to air engagements never flew again. The loss of life among enemy flak crews and ground crews in strafing is also an overlooked statistic which is poorly revealed even at this late date.

The end of combat missions allowed intelligence sections to develop the final tally of the war concerning various aspects of this conflict in which the 78th had been engaged. They found that the pilots had taken part in 453 to 465 missions, depending on the size definition of mission. The penalty was 200 combat losses, sixty-eight by the 82nd, sixty-two by the 83rd and sixty-two by the 84th, with eight losses by other group sections. This loss tally broke down to 100 Killed in Action, seventeen Killed in Flying Accidents, seventeen Prisoners of War and sixty-five evaders. Included in the KIAs are other deaths of ground personnel. (See Appendix 4) Aircraft lost to all causes approximated 253; 164 being P-47s and 89 Mustangs.

In twenty-five months of unrelenting combat the 78th Group had logged a massive list of enemy aircraft and equipment destroyed or damaged. (See Appendix 5) And while the cost was high their kill ration against the Luftwaffe was 1 to 3.33.

With the advent of the Mustang, losses increased by almost 53% a month over the P-47 losses. However, equipped with the long range P-51 the Group's kill ratio was raised by a factor of almost two.

May 1945: VE Day was celebrated quietly at Duxford on May 8, 1945. There was free beer at the Officer's Club, and Sergeant's Club and at Duffy's Tavern, the enlisted club. An open air dance turned into a songfest for lack of women. Physical training and educational programs were put into effect both proving quite popular.

In June, 1945 low point men with fewer than eighty-five points began to transfer to other units and men with high points arrived, a sure tipoff the group was being readied to go home and not into combat in the Pacific. On June 7th, Brigadier General Eugene Eubanks, Third Air Division CO inspected the group. All personnel marched in review on the flying field in front of the Group's aligned P-51s. That same day P-51s arrived from other 66th Fighter Wing Groups to join the 78th's newest model Mustangs being mothballed and stored for shipment to depots. Colonel John Landers left on the 28th to train a group in the U.S. for the Pacific Theater. His replacement was Lieutenant Colonel Roy B. Caviness, former 361st Fighter Group CO.

Air Force Day on June first was celebrated at Duxford with an open house for some 5,000 visitors who filled the base to view exhibits of planes and equipment. About September first, the men were overjoyed to learn that their shipment date had been moved up to October, 1945 and that they would be home for Christmas. From September 7th through the 15th, the Group's last P-51s were flown away to the depot at Atcham.

Personnel still remaining with the 78th sailed from Southampton on October 11th on the Queen Mary, and glided past the Statue of Liberty on October 16th to berth beside the Welcome Home signs emblazoned on the Port of Debarkation, New York. Two days later, on October 18th, the wartime 78th Fighter Group was disbanded and inactivated at Camp Kilmer, New Jersey, the camp from which they had departed, one month shy of three years earlier.

Lieutenant Colonel Samuel Beckley remained in command at Duxford through November, 1945 preparing the base for return to British custody. He handed it back to the RAF's Wing Commander Alan Deere on December first, and departed for his new assignment with the Occupation Air Forces' 55th

Fighter Group in Germany. An RAF Fighter Wing from Andrews Field moved into Duxford.

On August 20, 1946, the 78th Fighter Group was activated again at Straubling Airbase, Germany, as part of the 70th Fighter Wing on an airdrome above which the old group had fought. But that's another story.

Many a pilot who flew the Pursuits,
Has winged his way to Heaven.
But I know the jock who led the Flight,
Was a kid in a P-47.

Unknown Prisoner of War

Mothballed, battle weary Mustangs from many 8th AF groups slumber at Duxford in June 1945 awaiting shipment. Some went to other U.S. units while others were sold to Sweden and various nations. "EVE" and "DIANE" foreground are both vets of the 55th FG. (Charles Clark)

The Thunderbolt All-American Swing Band

While fighting the brutal air war the 78th Fighter Group gave birth to a highly civilized and entertaining phenomenon, a dance band.

The early history of the band is rather sketchy, but it was conceived just before Christmas, 1942 at Goxhill. Captain Montimore "Monty/Doc" Shwayder, 83rd Fighter Squadron Flight Surgeon, got four players including himself together to provide music for the Squadron's holiday celebration.

From December, '42 until shortly after June 3, 1943, the band was a fun group of four, performing mostly within the group. Soon after Col. Murray C. Woodbury arrived at Duxford with his 5th Air Defense Wing, later known as the 66th Fighter Wing, he gave an order to 1Lt Allan B. Cowart, the base control tower officer, that Cowart should form a dance band for a celebration the Colonel was planning that month. Cowart at once began a search for musicians and the 83rd quartet was enlisted into a larger band of twelve members.

By August 19, 1943, the band was known officially as "THE THUNDERBOLTS" and its fame as the best Army band in England was known as far afield as the Chicago Daily News. Although 1Lt Cowart initially acted as the band leader, by August 19th he had handed the baton to Captain Shwayder whose higher rank put the band in a better perspective from the Army's viewpoint. It was a good move because it gave the leader more weight in dealing with higher authority. In fact, it had been necessary to get 8th Fighter

Command official permission to have officers and Enlisted Men performing together in the band. The members had been a mixture of amateurs and professional musicians in civilian life.

With the help of Army Special Services Branch and the American Red Cross, some instruments and a sheet music library were accumulated. Doc Schwayder was able to obtain many free orchestrations by visiting the British Music houses in London. Practice was usually in the base Officer's Club on off-duty time. The band played behind music stands made by the 78th's carpentry shop, which were painted blue and emblazoned with the Air Corps winged star emblem. Many Eighth Air Force bands were forming and they all played, Swing, Boogie-Woogie, and the contemporary hits.

The band traveled in two "Deuce and a Half" ton army cargo trucks and flew in a wide variety of aircraft when air travel was necessary. Large on-base dances were held in the Base Theater Hangar, "YE OLD BARN", and smaller dances were hosted at the Officer's Club or the Red Cross Aero Club. Captain Shwayder played second saxophone when not wielding the baton. During his college days at Stanford, he played sax and sang in a trio as a professional to help pay his way through college. Premature baldness caused him to choose medicine. He said he knew of very few bald band leaders.

The Thunderbolt All-American Swing Band. Members, L-R: Frank Kulis-bass violin; Stuart Warwick - piano; Thomas Vrabel - guitar; Wallace Kellig - drums; Monty Shwayder - 2nd sax (leader);Harding Zumwalt -1st trumpet;Allan Cowart - 1st Sax; Jack Miller - 2nd trumpet; William Thomas - 3rd sax; Stuart Strohman - 3rd trumpet; Norbert Anderson - trombone; Harvey Pritchard-4th sax; and a stag line of WAAFs. (Harding Zumwalt)

Captain Stuart B. "Stew" Warwick, 83rd Intelligence Officer, played the piano. Prior to the service he had been a classical concert pianist in California who wanted nothing to do with popular Jazz and Swing music. He turned down playing in the band at first, but eventually his reluctance was worn down and his patriotism won out. Slowly he was induced to jam a hot tune now and then.

The drums were handled by Sgt. Wallace P. Kellig, 84th Fighter Squadron, who also doubled as a vocalist. "Wally" was a pro who had performed pre-war with the Ted Weems Orchestra.

Staff Sergeant Thomas J. "Tommy" Vrabel, an 84th crewchief, chorded a potent guitar.

Another 84th member was crewchief, S/Sgt. Frank J. Kulis on the bass, a talented amateur from Berwyn, Ill who crewed a/c named "Mister Lucky", "Rebel", and "Lee-D".

First Lieutenant Harding Zumwalt, an 83rd Squadron pilot, played first trumpet and T/Sgt Jack L. Miller of 78th Headquarters Squadron played second trumpet.

Sergeant Harvey W. Pritchard, Headquarters Squadron, S-2 Section, and Corporal William R. Thomas, 84th FS, played fourth and third saxophones respectively. Third trumpet was owned by S/Sgt. Stuart E. "Stew" Strohman, 83rd supply section. Technical Sergeant Norbert D. Anderson, an 84th Flightline crewman worked the slide trombone. Other men who sat in from time to time with the band were 1Lt Russell L. Burgher, 83FS ground officer; Sgt. John A. Cerra 23rd Station Complement Sqd.; Sgt. Conrad S. Moore, 83FS; and Sgt. James F. Becker, 23rd Station Complement Squadron.

Thus the band was usually made up of three trumpets, piano, trombone, four saxophones, guitar, string bass, and drums for twelve pieces. The saxophones were one tenor, one bass and two alto.

Dangerous incidents stand out in wartime band memories.

Technical Sergeant Jack L. Miller vividly recalls: "During a date to play at Lincoln RAF base, the band was fog-bound for three days which made the 78th Group Commander, Colonel James Stone, most unhappy to say the least. When the weather finally cleared up, the band was flown back to Duxford in two old eight passenger RAF transport planes. These planes were flown by some young RAF student pilots. As our plane touched down on the slick grass field at Duxford, it struck the ground very hard and bounced back up into the air quite high. When we hit I looked out my side window and saw the runway come into view and go out at almost a ninety degree angle to the plane. My reflexes took over then and I closed my eyes awaiting the crash. Luckily our pilot quickly gunned the motor and kept enough flying speed to stay airborne, went around, and landed okay the second time. I thought we'd 'ad it that time!"

Before joining the RAF in 1941, Harding Zumwalt had been a professional trumpet player with several dance bands in St. Louis, MO. In late February 1943, he joined the 78th at Goxhill after transferring to the AAF from the RAF. His association with the band was a mutually beneficial arrangement.

First Lieutenant Harding Zumwalt: "Music (playing the trumpet) was my profession before I joined the RAF. I had started playing at the age of nine and later used my income from music to pay for flying lessons and aircraft hours. This flight experience made my forthcoming military career possible. It was a means to an end. Shortly after joining the 83rd I was contacted by our fight surgeon, Captain Mortimore Shwayder, who was organizing a Group dance band asking if I would play trumpet in the band. This sounded like a great way to let off steam in the evening so I agreed wholeheartedly.

"Not long afterward I was grounded for my corrective lenses problem until I had a re-evaluation by the powers-that-be at Headquarters. Monti, as my Flight Surgeon, went to bat for me, and soon afterwards I was back in the cockpit. I owe him a great debt of gratitude for his efforts. My flying career could easily have come to a screeching halt at that time had he not intervened."

If Harding got back to base too late at night from a dance, he was not allowed to fly the next morning's mission, so he had to watch his times. When he enlisted in the RAF, his trumpet went through the whole training system and the rest of the war with him. On more than one occasion he had to lock and chain it to his bed to prevent its being stolen. After he got to England he performed with the official RAF Band during one of its dates at his station. When he was on leave in London and in need of a good meal he was welcomed at the Orchard,

Embassy, and Slip-In Clubs to play for his supper with their bands. On other off-duty hours he regularly jived in Johnny DeGeorge's Band at a P-51 base west of Duxford.

Probably the best known of the band's wartime performances was on Christmas Eve, 1943. The Cambridge-American Hospitality Committee gave a Christmas Eve dance at that city's large Guildhall. The affair was broadcast on a coast-to-coast hookup live to the US where a special message was sent to a sister city, Cambridge, Massachusetts. The radio stations carrying the program were the BBC, US Forces Network, American Mutual Broadcasting Service, and General Overseas BBC. The guests, 150 American GIs and 150 British Auxiliary Territorial Service and Women's Auxiliary Air Force, were welcomed by Major Alderman Briggs of the city and Dr. Hele, Chancellor of the University. The BBC Master of Ceremonies was Gilbert Harding and the co-M.C. for the USAAF was Sergeant Pix Miller. Starring entertainers were the famous duo, Bebe Daniels and Ben Lyons. All band member's families in the US had been previously alerted by British Information Service cablegram to listen for the program. The band was enlarged to fourteen pieces for this evening. Another state-side radio broadcast by the Thunderbolts was played from the American Red Cross Rainbow Corner Club in London, during one of several dates there.

While being bussed to an engagement at Eighth Air Force Headquarters in London on another occasion the vehicle's exhaust system was faulty. By the time the band arrived to perform, they were all horribly sick from the toxic fumes leaking into the bus. No matter, the show went on.

Some of the fondest band memories come from the founder and first leader of the enlarged twelve piece band.

Captain Allan B. Cowart: describes the beginnings, the directive from Colonel Woodbury. " The Colonel said 'We're going to hold a dance at Duxford, a month from this coming Saturday and I understand you are a musician.' I had played in college, several years working my way through at Auburn University and had sat in on occasion with Dick Stabile's band. 'We're going to have a dance and we're all going to have fun and we're going to have our own band.' I thought, 'Well, that's just grand, Colonel,' because I thought he knew something I didn't know, and then he said, 'And you're going to lead it!' I said, 'Who's going to form the band?' he said, 'You, Lieutenant!' And that was the end of the conversation.

"Well, I scurried about and found all kinds of talent. So off we went and doggone it if we didn't play that dance a month later. I was never so surprised in my life. I had been diplomatic enough to ask Colonel Woodbury what his favorite tune was, I remember it very well, it was 'Beyond the Blue Horizon'. I think one guy in the band had heard it before. And so we jammed it a little bit. So when he came in the night of the dance, we were playing something, and I stopped the band, and we started to play "Beyond the Blue Horizon". I have never seen a man more amazed, and happier. He had some pretty gal on his arm and so a grand evening was had by all. That is how the band took off and we got better as we got going.

"We played many places in England, at the invitation of the RAF principally, because everybody got us for nothing, I think and we had to try and do these things between missions. It was hard to play a job without Harding Zumwalt, because he was so good and he really carried the section. We would get transported around anyway we could. They would send down junky RAF airplanes and fly us back and that was a big deal. We'd play these dances and they'd have the British and American flags draped across each other. It was kind of neat. We were always honored to do that. That made us feel pretty good. The quality of the band was all right. There were some very strong people in it like Zummie, and some weak ones too, but there is safety in numbers some times, so I guess all in all we didn't sound too bad.

"Another big trip for us was to go down and play the Rainbow Red Cross Club in London. That was always a joy. It's just a different thing. I remember playing down there once and I found myself during intermission at the top of some winding stairs. I guess everyone had gone up to go to the bathroom or something. I found myself standing beside an absolutely gorgeous woman! She was by herself. She asked me if I would escort her down the stairs and, you bet! So I did it in as elegant a way as I could. She didn't care about me. She needed a prop to walk down the stairs and be seen always with a man, I guess. She was a famous movie actress whose name escapes me right now. Things like that were always fun, a thrill to get away from Duxford and go down to London.

"Another little deal. There was a big bomber base to the west of us about twenty miles, Bassingbourn. We'd been asked to play a dance there one night, and we were playing along, and all of a sudden, I was sitting in my regular spot reading my music, it was dim light over there and you couldn't see too well, so I was struggling with the music a little bit, and I finally got a suspicious sense that someone was standing in front of me, staring at me, and I looked up and Darn! It was my old roommate from Auburn University! Ho,Ho, he was flying B-17s over at Bassingbourn at the same time. We still get to see each other now and than today. Another of those strange happenings.

"There came a time later after we started, when it seemed a little wrong for a Lieutenant to be fronting the band in which a Captain Monty Shwayder, was playing. You know the military caste system, and I've always believed in that very much. So, I suggested that Monty assume leadership of the band, which was appropriate. He was a bit reluctant in the beginning and it came out real good, and I think the band was better for that. I was able to pay more attention to playing lead saxophone, instead of worrying about the whole band all the time.

"The Interesting thing about this orchestra business is that, it was absolutely another hat for everyone. You were not excused for any reason, for not doing your duty. We took the jobs very very seriously. We were truly dedicated. I didn't know any people in the orchestra who would not travel all night to get back to the job if they had to. It was a joy playing and it was a good group of people."

A band closeup shows L-R: Wallace Kellig, unknown soldier background, Harding Zumwalt, Frank Kulis, and Jack Miller. (Jack Miller)

Eighth Air Force

78th Fighter Group

82nd Fighter Squadron

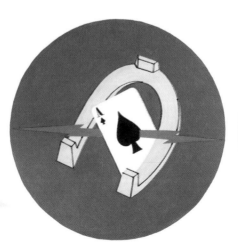

83rd Fighter Squadron

84th Fighter Squadron

Note: The 82nd and 83rd insignia were not approved until post World War II. Unit insignia were not carried on a/c in combat.

An early "razorback", P-47C-2-RE, Serial No. 41-6249, MX-H was Bob Eby's 82nd FS mount. The plane was named for Bob's baby daughter, Vivian Gaile who poses as a logger. Piloted by Lt. Don Ludwig, it failed to return from a 2-20-44 mission and was last seen over the Dutch Coast.

Representative of the "bubbletop" Jug era, P-47D-25-RE, Serial No. 42-26624, WZ-J was piloted by Herb Boyle of the 84th FS. Crew Chief for "Old Smoothy" was S/Sgt. G. Wahlstrom.

"Fly'n Time Bomb", P-51D-20NA, Serial No. 44-63712, was first flown by Ray Smith, 84th FS Ops. Officer. WZ-B was lost in action over Germany with Lt. John Sole, KIA, on 4-25-91.

A P-51D-20NA from the 82nd FS, Serial No. 44-64147, "Big Dick" was the mount of Dick Hewitt. Crew Chief was Sgt. Phil Doloway, Asst. CC Herb Trantham, and Armorer Cpl. John Montgomery. Also flown occasionally by Winfield Brown, MX-U survived the war.

P-47D-25-RE, Serial No. 42-26590 (above), belonged to 2Lt. Lawton E. Clark of the 84th FS. Kidded by 84th Squadron mates about bad eyesight, Clark had two trees he had flown through added to the scoreboard of "kills" later painted on the fuselage of his plane. While strafing a train in "THOROUGHBRED" on Sept. 10, 1944 he flew into the target affirming a belief that he had disguised a depth perception problem. (Negley Sapper)

Major Jesse Davis ' P-47 HL-X 41-6402 "Owley and Tobe" comes to grief in a belly landing. Pilots loved the Jug's safety in this eventuality. Note the red-edged US star/bar that replaced the yellow circled US star on June 29,1943. (Robert Eby)

Show preparations on the far east end of 84FS flightline. WZ-E 42-24459 is George Hartman's "Joker". Pierced steel plank matting became slippery with grass coming through it. (Negley Sapper)

84FS rolls on a mission takeoff. DX was unusual in its 8 airacraft abreast launches. Most 8 FC bases took off in twos. WZ-T 41-6386 is Lt. Robert Gore's aircraft. (Noel Assink)

When a mission ran through lunch hour, returned pilots needed a snack. Pictured are 83FS pilots in the squadron pilot's shack. (Robert Eby)

High over the East Anglian haze, Capt. Charles London curves his HL-B 41-6335 "El Jeepo". This P-47 was shot down over Holland on 2-22-44 as HL-A with John Johnson becoming a POW. (USAF)

MX-G 42-27607 comes home from a mission high over cloud cover. The upper surface D-Day stripes were ordered removed in July, being too visible to enemy aircraft against the earth. (USAF)

Another happy homeward bound pilot, 1LT. Kenneth C. Allstaedt, with his HL-W 42-25552. The 83FS flight leader had girly art just ahead of the Style 1 crew panel, otherwise the aircraft was a stock old bird that flew on until P-51 conversion. (Kenneth Allstaedt)

An east view of 84th D-Flt line. P-47 WZ-I 42-25698 "Jeanie" (left side art) is 2nd. "I"-coded sqd. a/c hence, bar below letter. New a/c. were arriving in NMF and were only waxed if time/weather allowed. No. 42-7899 behind was WZ-H and I later on. (Negley Sapper)

1Lt. Harold Beck, 82FS, in his MX-Q 42-26333 "Hun-Buster", July 1944. His crew is CC S/Sgt. Ray Sandve, ACC Sgt. James Whitaker, and ARM Cpl. Frank Penar. Lt. Louis Dicks was KIA in this a/c on Aug. 10, 44. (James Kinsolving)

1Lt Frank E. Oiler with his 84FS crew, CC S/Sgt. Charles Clark (L), and ACC S/Sgt. Donald Shope. Their WZ-S "Eileen" had one of the most colorful emblems in the 78th, and it was used later on their bubble top P-47. (Charles Clark)

"Zombie" MX-V 42-25742 rests on a British coastal base after one of the four 82FS missions on June 10, 1944. The a/c. seems undamaaged so it is likely a fuel visit. Ten pilots were lost in heavy combats this date. (AFM)

Each 82FS pilot had his own coffee mug with his a/c artwork on it, at the pilot's shack. Almost 35 pilots were on Squadron strength at this time., March 1944 (Harry Dayhuff)

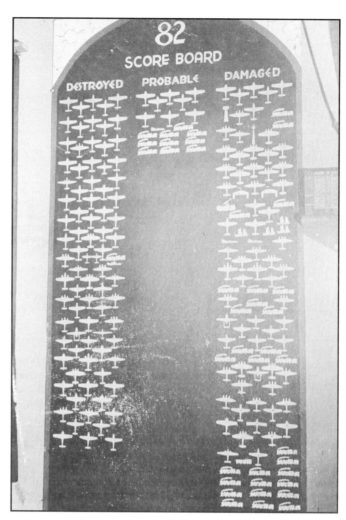

82FS victory score board in sqd flight shack. Score in May 44 is 82-8-65 a/c, 1-10-3- locos, 1-0-6 ships and misc. flak towers, lighthouses, and hangars. Pre D-Day ground attacks are shown by loco symbols. (USAF)

Capt. Alfred F. Eaton, 84FS Flt. Ldr., on his WZ-U 42-26682 "Ozark Queen". The art is, of course, a picture of his wife. The name colors follow standard 8AAF tradition, in red and yellow. (Alfred Eaton)

Posing in his new NMF P-47, possibly 42-25698 WZ-L, Major Quince Brown has his final tally of kills on this "Oakie". Soon after, he finished his tour and went home, returning in Aug, 44. (Duke Morrison)

Major Quince Brown got a new NMF P-47 and his old a/c here is recoded WZ-V. Note the revised and expanded score panel versus the old artwork. (Richard Ballard)

T/Sgt. Bill Jensen shows the new fighter-bombing P-47 profile, of 2-500 pound bombs and a 108 gal. belly tank. Major Quince Brown's "Oakie" is ready for a fighter bomber show into France. (Charles Clark)

C-Flt. line with "Roger the Lodger" WZ-Y 42-25871 being gassed. Its pilot was Lt. Charles Whitefield and his crew was, CC S/Sgt. Henry Bauer and ACC S/Sgt. Melvin Armstrong. The a/c were always topped off the night before a show. (USAF)

78FG Ace, Capt. Alvin "Max" Juchheim's "LADY JANE" HL-J 42-26020 ready for a mission. Two 108 gal. tanks mean a long escort show. Helmet, goggles, life jacket, and the auxiliary power cart mean the pilot is nearby waiting to mount up. Pitot cover comes off just before taxiing. (Clifford Glidewell)

Lt. Paul Ostrander's P-51D "PORCELAIN PILLBOX" WZ-J 44-11743 in January 1945 with 110 gal. metal wing tanks. This type of tank was used after the 108 gal. paper tank was retired. (Negley Sapper)

Capt. Robert E. Wise, 83FS B flt ldr., with his HL-U 44-63208 "THE HORRIBLE HOSSIER IIII". Crew panel names are: CC S/Sgt. Willis Beauchamp, ACC Cpl. Burt Monin, and ARM Sgt. Joseph Clithero. Art is offset from the exhaust where it would burn or be hard to keep clean. (Samuel Beckley)

Lt. Col Samuel R. Beckley, 83FS CO, just back from a mission in his HL-B 44-63178 "BECK-DOR". Name is a blend of his and CC S/Sgt. Robert Dorr. The ACC was S/Sgt. Edward Sweeny, and ARM was Cpl. Hjalmer Korte. (Samuel Beckley)

82FS P-51s being serviced in Feb 45. Capt. Robert Holmes was KIA in MX-R 44-63214 on the 4-16-45 Prague mission. MX-N is 44-11650 with cowl off. Lt. Austin Miller bailed out of MX-O 44-63256 on 2-19-45. (USAF)

"JUST HANG 'EN AROUND" WZ-G 44-15577 flown by Lt. John Murphy. 84FS EM: unk., S/Sgt. Sam Snoddy, and S/Sgt. Henry Bauer. A/C later had B/W checks around canopy . Note stencil style squadron codes. Spring 45. (William May)

"SCREAM'N DEMON" P-51D WZ-G 44-63779 was flown by section leader, 1Lt. Alfred Garback in 84FS. (Nicholas Vale/AFM)

84FS crews swarmed over returned a/c in B-Flt. WZ-X is Lt. W. Blodgett's 44-72099 "LITTLE CHIX", and WZ-C is Lt. R. Taylor's a/c. Armorers inspect repair, and the gas tanker refuels. (USAF)

Capt. Earl L. Stier's WZ-Y 44-63187 "BUM STEER". He flew this a/c 450 miles from Luneburg, Ger., corkscrewing through the air for 2 1/2 hrs. with most of his fin/rudder shot off. He landed safely to 300 cheering men. (James T. Jones)

1 Lt. Mark Clemons is the 84FS pilot known to have flown "FRANCIS DELL"WZ-W 44-72927 in combat, though it may not be his assigned aircraft. Olive drab paint on the anti-glare panel extends around the canopy frame, an 84FS trait in the 78th. (Charles Clark)

Top fighter leaders of the 8th AF gather at Duxford in spring of '45: L to R: Col. Fred Gray, 8th FC; Col. Claiborne H. Kinnard, 355th FG; Col Ev Stewart, 4th FG; Lt.Col. Erwin Righetti, 55th FG; LtCol. John Landers, (dark glasses) 78th FG; Col Ben Rimerman, 353rd FG; unk., unk., Lt.Col. Eugene Roberts, 364th FG; LtCol. Phil Tukey, 356th FG. (Landers via Bradburn)

On Mar. 26, 1945 S/Sgt. Galen Breshears and Sgt. Anthony Yaksta of the 84th Air Service Squadron converted 84FS P-51B 44-108876 to a two seat Mustang. WZ-S shown here on the line sports two standard B-model canopies linked together. Most of these conversions involved removing the fuselage gas tank. (James Kinsolving)

The 78th's 2-seat P-47 WW war weary 42-27606 post VE-Day. A British Malcom-hood was fitted aft of the P-47 canopy with another seat. The a/c appears to be painted blue overall with red cowl flaps and rudder. (Charles Clark)

The Opposition

A Messerschmitt Bf 109K, a late version of the most widely utilized German single seat fighter of World War II, shown here after VE-Day. 35,000 were built. (Merle Olmsted)

The less numerous Focke-Wulf 190 was produced later than the ME 109 in some 10 variants. Here is a captured F model. (Merle Olmsted)

The ultimate variant of the famous F W 190 was this long nosed Ta 152. The "DORA" was faster than any Allied single-engined fighter. (Merle Olmsted)

The formidable Messerschmitt 262, twin engined jet fighter might have devastated Allied bomber forces had it appeared earlier in the war. The fighter version entered combat in the Summer of 1944, but production problems and bizzare demands for their use as bombers prevented employment in large numbers. This unit appears on Rheine A/D in the Spring of 1945. (Merle Olmsted)

GLOSSARY OF TERMS AND ABBREVIATIONS

Abort	Turn back for home due to cause
A/C	Aircraft
ACC	Assistant Crew Chief
Ace	Pilot with five or more victories
A-Channel	R/T channel used by fighter operations controller
AD	Air Division
A/D	Airdrome, usually enemy
AF	Air Force
A/F	Airfield, usually friendly
Aileron	Wing control surface
ASR	Air Sea Rescue units either vessels or aircraft
Area Support	Fighter patrol in bomber route areas.
Arm.	Armorer
Assgnd.	Assigned, to duty, sqd., unit, job.
Baby	Drop-tank, usually a belly tank.
Bakehouse	R/T call sign, 78 FG B-group leader, 5-43 to 4-22-44
Bandits	Enemy aircraft
Barrel Roll	Medium speed roll on constant course.
B-Channel	R/T channel fixing system used by Air-Sea Rescue
BD	Bomber division
Belly-land	Wheels up a/c crash-landing
Big Friends	Allied bombers
Black Flight	Fifth flight in a squadron formation
Blue Flight	Fourth flight in a squadron formation.
Bogies	Unidentified aircraft
Bomber Box	Sixty bombers in aerial formation
Bounce	Attack on A/C from above
Boycott	R/T callsign, 78th C leader, 4-23-44 to 5-45
Break	Quick aircraft turn
BW	Bomber wing
Cargo	R/T callsign, 83FS A-group, 4-23-44 to 5-45
CC	Crewchief
C-Channel	R/T channel used for fighter-to-bomber and away-bases instructions
CG	Commanding General
Chandelle	A banking-climbing 180º reversal of direction with height gain.
Chock	Aircraft wheel stay block
Circus	Escort of a small bomber force to draw e/a up.
CO	Commanding Officer
Contrails	Vapor trails caused by exhaust heat on air moisture.
Darkie	R/T callsign for emergency directions - but not in danger.
D-Channel	R/T channel used for emergency homing-fixer.
Deck	Ground level/surface
Deflection shot	Firing from a side-angle
Ditch	Force Land an a/c in water.
Dogfight	Aerial action, air to air combat
DX	RAF/8AF station code-letters for Duxford airfield.
E/A	Enemy aircraft
Element	Two a/c formation, lead and wingman, Nos., 1 & 2 or 3 & 4 men.
EM	Enlisted men/man
ETO	European Theatre of Operations
Euclid	R/T callsign, 84FS, 5-7-43
FC	Fighter Command, 8th AF FC
FG	Fighter Group
Flak	Enemy anti-aircraft fire
FLT	Flight, a formation of 8a/c made up of two sections, designated A-B-C-D Flights.
FO	Field Order
F/O	Rank of Flight Officer
Forts	B-17 Flying Fortress bombers
FS	Fighter Squadron
FW	Focke-Wulf 190
Gaggle	Loosely formatted group of flying e/a
Gaylord	R/T callsign, 84FS A-group, 1-4-44
GI	Government Issue, slang for "a soldier"
Glycol	Alcohol base liquid coolant for in-line engines
Graywall	R/T callsign, 78FG leader 7-4-43 to 4-22-44
Greyfriars	R/T callsign of m.e.w. controller, 1943
Group	48 fighter a/c, 3-16 a/c squads.
Grp	Fighter or Bomber Group
GX	RAF/8AF station code-letters for Goxhill airfield
Hardstand	Open hard-surface a/c parking spot
HDQRS	Headquarters, HQ
Hun	WW I term for German, also Jerry, Kraut, Heinie, purposely derogative
Immelman	A half-loop and roll-out at top, a course reversal height gain.
IP	The initial point, start of bomb or attack run.
Jug	Loving fond nickname for P-47 aircraft.
KIA	Killed in action
KIFA	Killed in a flying accident
Kill	Aerial or ground victory
Libs	B-24 Liberator Bomber
Little Friends	Allied fighters
Lufberry	A banking turning circle tail chase by two or more opposing a/c.
May-Day	R/T call signal for help, rescue, position fixing.
MEW	Allied microwave early warning radar
MIA	Missing in action.
NMF	Natural metal finish, aircraft unpainted, uncamouflaged.

190	FW190. Focke-Wulf German fighter, any model
109	ME109 Messerschmitt German fighter, any model
OPS	Combat operations
Overshoot	To land a/c further down runway
Phoenix	R/T callsign, 78FG leader A-group, 4-23-44 to 5-45.
POW	Prisoner of war
Prang	Aircraft crash or accident
Rack	Sharp a/c turn
RAF	Royal Air Force
RCAF	Royal Canadian Air Force
Rainbow	R/T callsign, 82FS B-group, 4-23-44 to 5-45
Ramrod	Escort of a major bomber force
Rat-race	Closely mingled aerial dog fight
Red Flight	Second flight in a squadron formation
Relvd.	Relieved of duty/assignment/command
Revetment	Walled in a/c parking pen, blast proof
Rhubarb	Low level fighter sweep by a few a/c in bad weather
Rodeo	Fighter sweeps
R/T	Aerial radio telephone/transmission, 4 channels, A-B-C-D
Rutley	R/T callsign of Duxford 8AF airfield, tower, homing beacon, 5-43 to 5-45
R/V	Rendezvous is the point at which escort joins bombers
Section	4 a/c formation, 2 elements given a color designation in 78th
Shampoo	R/T callsign. 84FS A-group, 4-23-44 to 5-45
SNAFU	Slang term for Situation Normal All Fouled Up.
Snap-roll	Fast a/c roll on a constant course
Sortie	A single a/c's flight/mission into enemy territory
Split-ess	Roll a/c inverted and dive-away aerial maneuver
Spotlight	R/T callsign, 84FS B-group, 4-23-44 to 5-45
Sqd	Squadron of 12 to 20 a/c. usually 16 a/c in combat formation
Stabilizer	Horizontal tail control surface of a/c.
Strafe	Fire guns at ground targets
Surtax	R/T callsign, 82FS A group, 4-23-44 to 5-45
10/10ths	Total cloud/overcast cover of ground, height unlimited
TRFD	Transferred, change of duty/station
Turquoise	R/T callsign, 83FS B-group, 4-23-44 to 5-45
12 o'clock	Clock hours used to indicate direction from a given point. i.e. a headon attack would come from the 12 o'clock position
U/I	Unidentified aircraft
Undershoot	To land an a/c short of the runway
WAAF	Women's Auxiliary Air Force, British
Went in	Crashed, usually fatally
WIFA	Wounded in Flying Accident
WG	Wing
White Flt.	First flight in a squadron formation
WIA	Wounded in action
Yellow Flight	Third flight in a sqd. formation

APPENDIX 1
ACES OF THE 78TH

Just as the Eighth Air Force included ground victories in their claim awards, so have I in this listing for the same valid reason. I have also included victories scored with other units as a total pilot stature view.

I am indebted to Dr. Frank J. Olynyk, 207 Chelmsford Drive, Aurora, OH 44202, for his aid with 78th victory credits and pilot encounter reports. He graciously made both available in hard copy and microfilm, his collection and his book, USAAF Credits-European Theatre Destruction of Enemy A/C in Air To Air Combat WW2. Frank offers both film and his books on AAF, USN, and USMC WW2 victories for purchase to the public. All 78th aerial victories are also in Historical Study No 85, from Albert F. Simpson Historical Research Center, Maxwell AFB, Alabama. For the above reasons I have not included the 78th kill listing in this book.

Contemporary literature has set the ace above his fellow pilots and unreasonably glorified him. I disagree with this concept. Years of study and reading hundreds of combat report have all pointed to one factor. Often, through plain simple luck, the victor was in the right place at the right time to score. There were hundreds of other pilots just as brave, skillful, and eager, but for lesser luck, they were not able to score. They took off daily at great risk with magnificent moral fortitude just like the Ace. They were the wingmen who quite often saved the ace from disaster. These men, as surely as the aces, won the skies. So, here's to the Ace and three cheers for the Wingman!

Rank-Name	Sqd	Air	Ground	Total
Col. John D. Landers	Hdqrs	14.5	20.0	34.5*
Capt. Alvin M. Juchheim	83	9	6	15
Major Quince Brown	84	12.3	2	14.3
1Lt. Francis C. Harrington	83	4	8	12
Lt.Col. Olin E. Gilbert	Hdqrs	2	9.5	11.5
1Lt. John A. Kirk	83	4	6	10
Capt. Charles M. Peal	83	2	8	10
Capt. Duncan M. McDuffie	83	4	5	9
LtCol. Eugene P. Roberts	Hdqrs	9	0	9
1Lt. Clyde E. Taylor	84	0	9	9
LtCol Joseph Myers	Hdqrs	4.5	4	8.5*
1Lt. Henry R. Slack	84	1.5	7	8.5
Major Richard A. Hewitt	82	4	4.3	8.3
Capt. John Hockery	82	7	1.1	8.1
LtCol. Richard E. Conner	Hdqrs	4.5	3.5	8
1Lt Danford E. Josey	84	0	8	8
LtCol. William H. Julian	82	5	3	8
1Lt. Richard A. Messinger	83	0	8	8
Capt. James W. Wilkinson	82	6	2	8
LtCol. Jack J.Oberhansly	Hdqrs	6	1.6	7.6

130

Rank-Name	Sqd	Air	Ground	Total
Major Norman D. Munson	82	0	7.5	7.5
1Lt. Neal Hepner	84	0	7	7
Capt. Edward R. Kulik	83	0	7	7
Capt. Peter E. Pompetti	84	5	2	7
Major Robert E. Smith	84	1	6	7
Capt. Robert T. Green	83	4.5	2	6.5
LtCol. Benjamin I. Mayo	84	4	2.5	6.5
Capt. Benjamin M. Watkins	82	2	4.5	6.5
1Lt. Robert R. Bosworth	82	1	5	6
1Lt. Gerald E. Brasher	82	1	5	6
M<ajor Gillespie Bryan	84	0	6	6
1Lt. Anthony T. Colletti	83	1	5	6
1Lt. Louis DeAnda	84	0	6	6
Capt. Donald J. DeVilliers	83	0	6	6
Capt. Herbert K. Shope	82	0	6	6
1Lt. Grant Turley	82	6	0	6
1Lt. Warren M. Wesson	82	4	2	6
1Lt. Merle R. Capp	84	2	3.5	5.5
Captain Huie H. Lamb	82	2.5	3	5.5
1Lt Eugene L. Peel	82	0.5	5	5.5
Capt. Harold T. Barnaby	83	4	1	5
Capt. Robert R. Bonebrake	83	3	2	5
Capt. Charles W. DeWitt	82	0	5	5
1Lt. Gene C. Doss	83	0	5	5
Capt. Dorian Ledington	84	2	3	5
Capt. Charles P. London	83	5	0	5
2Lt. Charles E. Parmelee	84	3	2	5
1Lt. Richard E. Phaneuf	83	0	5	5
Major Jack C. Price	84	5	0	5
1Lt. Dale S. Sweat	83	0	5	5

*Some victories were scored with other units

APPENDIX 2
COMMANDERS

78th Fighter Group Commanders

1Lt. Frank Wagner	April 6, 1942 to May 7, 1942
LtCol Arman Peterson	May 7, 1942 to July 1, 1943
Col James J. Stone, Jr.	July 1, 1943 to July 12, 1943
LtCol. Melvin F. McNickle	July 12, 1943 to July 30 1943
Col.. James J. Stone Jr.	July 31, 1943 to May 21, 1944
Col.. Frederic C. Gray, Jr.	May 21, 1944 to January 29, 1945
LtCol. Olin E. Gilbert	January 29,1945 to February 21, 1945
Col. John D. Landers	February 22,1945 to June 28, 1945
LtCol. Roy B. Caviness	June 28, 1945 to October 18, 1945

82nd Fighter Squadron Commanders

1Lt. George F. Nash	February 9, 1942 to March 20, 1942
1Lt. Frank Wagner	March 20,1942 to April 6, 1942
2Lt. Perry Leftwich	April 6, 1942 to May 5, 1942
1Lt. T.T. Crittenden	May 5, 1942 to May 11, 1942
LtCol Harry J. Dayhuff	May 11, 1942 to August 7, 1943
LtCol Jack J. Oberhansly	August 7,1943 to May 18, 1944
Maj. Norman D. Munson	May 18, 1944 to May 23, 1944
Capt. James W. Wilkinson	May 23, 1944 to June 4, 1944
Captain William A. Guilfoyle	June 4, 1944 to June 8, 1944
LtCol. Benjamin I. Mayo	June 8, 1944 to July 14, 1944
Maj. Norman D. Munson	July14, 1944 to July 20,1944
Capt. Charles R. Clark	July 20, 1944 to August 2, 1944
LtCol. Joseph Myers	August 2,1944 to August 22, 1944
LtCol Jack J. Oberhansly	August 22, 1944 to August 28, 1944
LtCol. Richard Conner	August 28, 1944 to December 2, 1944
LtCol Joseph Myers	December 2, 1944 to December 3, 1944
Maj. Harry L. Downing	December 5, 1944 to February 17, 1945
LtCol. Richard Conner	February 17, 1945 to March 4, 1945
Maj. Harry L. Downing	March 4, 1945 to March 14, 1945
LtCol. Richard Conner	March 14, 1945 to March 19, 1945
Major Richard Hewitt	March 20, 1945 to May 10, 1945
LtCol. Richard Conner	May 10, 1945 to May 12,1945
Major Richard Hewitt	May 12, 1945 to July 20, 1945

83rd Fighter Squadron Commanders

Col. James J. Stone, Jr.	May 7, 1942 to Jul 1 1943
Major Jesse C. Davis, Jr.	July 1, 1943 to January 18, 1944
LtCoL. Olin E. Gilbert	January 18, 1944 to July 13, 1944
Maj. William H. Julian	July 13, 1944 to October 9, 1944
LtCol Samuel R. Beckley	October 9,1944 to December 31,1944
Major William H. Julian	December 31, 1944 to January 6, 1945
LtCol Samuel R. Beckley	January 6, 1945 to January 12, 1945
Major William H. Julian	January 12, 1945 to March 20, 1945
LtCol Samuel R. Beckley	March 20, 1945 to October 10, 1945

84th Fighter Squadron Commanders

Capt. George M. McNeese	May 7, 1942 to August ? 1942
LtCol Eugene P. Roberts	August ? 1942 to September 28, 1943
Maj. Jack C. Price	September 28, 1943 to February 25, 1944
Major Harold E. Stump	February 25, 1944 to June 10, 1944
Captain Richard M. Holly	June 11, 1944 to July 13, 1944
LtCol Benjamin I. Mayo	July 13, 1944 to September 25, 1944
LtCol. Leonard P. Marshall	September 25, 1944 to March 14, 1945
Maj Harry L. Downing	March 14, 1945 to March 19, 1945
LtCol Richard Conner	March 19, 1945 to March 21, 1945
Capt. Dorian Ledington	March 21, 1945 to April 21, 1945
Maj. William E. May	April 21, 1945 to April 24, 1945
Maj. Bruce B. Hunt	April 24, 1945 to May 21, 1945
Maj. Gillespie Bryan	May 21, 1945 to October 10, 1945

APPENDIX 3

PILOT/STAFF ROSTERS

Information included:
1. Highest known rank attained in 78thFG
2. Name
3. Status as pilot or ground officer. Where none is given it is unknown, but probable that he was a ground officer. Also possible that he was on temporary duty, or a post VE Day transfer in during rotations.
4. Dates of tour in the 78th. To Sqd. indicates known arrival day. In Sqd indicates approximate arrival date. EOW means END OF WAR .Combat loss result is given, or next duty assignment if known.
5. In unit duty assignment with date.
6. Periods of leave between combat tours.
7. Sundry service data, remarks, etc., where relevant
8. Decorations awarded in WW2, although possibly not complete and some Korean War are included. AM signifies Air Medal
Note: Even official records assignment dates should be considered approximate.

78th Headquarters Squadron Pilots and Key Staff Officers:

Flt. Lt. Baraldi	RAF Station RAF Liason Off.
Capt. Theodore G. Barlow	Ass't Intell. Off. Grnd Off.
Capt. Henry B. Bjorkman	Ass't Intell. Off. Transferred to 353FG
Capt. Ralph C. Blair	Aerial Photo Intell. Off Grnd Off.
Capt Henry L. Bottoms	Grp Comm Off. Grnd Off
Maj. Gillespie Bryan	To Sqd 3-28—45 to 5-12-45 to 84FS. Grp. Ops Off 4-24-45
Maj. John J.B. Calderbank	To Sqd. Spring, 43 for sev wks. to 8FC, Grp. Ops. Off
Maj. Peter A. Caulfield	To Sqd, 4-9.-45 Asst Grp Ops Off
LtCol. Roy B. Caviness	To Sqd. 6-29-45 to 10-18-45 Grp CO Former 361FG CO
LtCol. Charles M. Christ	To Sqd. 9-9-44 to EOW. Asst Grp Ops Off 9-9-44. Grp Ops 2-4-45. Deputy Grp CO 4-24-25
LtCol. Richard Conner	To Sqd 5-12-45. Deputy Grp CO 5-12-45
Maj. James B. Cooper	Ass't Grp Ops Off 6-?-44
Capt. Allan B. Cowart	(23rd St. Comp. Sqd.Off) Control Tower Officer
LtCol. Thomas N. Crowley	To Sqd. 2-1-45.Grp Adjt until Summer '45
LtCol. Harry J. Dayhuff	To Sqd. 8-7-43 Deputy Grp CO 8-7-43, On DS to 8FC 9-27-43 to 11-15-43. U.S. Lve 4-19-44 to 7-11-44 to AF HQ as ass't. A-3.. 4FG CO 12-7-44. Silver Star,DFCs-AMs, Croix de Guerre, USAF Col. (Ret)
LtCol. Joseph L. Dickman	To sqd 9-?-42. Deputy Grp CO 9-?-42. WIA 4-13-43 to US hospital 7-12-43
Capt. Gray H. Doyle	To Sqd 8-?-44.Asst. Grp. Ops. Off. KIA 9-5-44
LtCol. Robert E.Eby	To Sqd 5—7-42 to 9-8-44 to Dir of Fghter Ops. 3AD.Grp Intell Off 5-7-42. Asst. Grp Ops Off 8-28-42. Grp Ops Off 3-2-44. 2 DFCs-6AMs. Col.. USAF (ret)
Maj. Charles T. Evans	To Sqd. 5-42 to EOW. Grp Supply Off. Grnd Off.
Capt. John R. Fry	To Sqd. 5-42 to 10-25-43 to 66FW.Grp Dent Off. GrndOff.
LtCol. Olin E. Gilbert	To Sqd. 7-13-44. Dep Grp CO 7-13-44. Evader 8-28-44 to 9-12-44. US leave 9-25-44 to 12-20-44. Grp CO 1-29-45 to 2-21-45. Dep.Grp. CO. To 8AF HQ 3-12-45. Silv Star,DFCs, AMs,,USAF Maj. Gen. (Ret.)

1Lt. Herbert W. Glickman	To sqd. 3-26-44. Grp. Arm&Ord. Off. Grnd. Off.
Col.. Frederic C. Gray, Jr.	To Sqd. 5-21-44 to 1-29-45 to 8AFHQ. Grp CO, 8AFDir. of Flt Ops. same dates. Silv. Star,3 Leg of Merit, DFC,5AMS,DUC,CBE.Croix de Guerre,ROK PUC.USAF Brig/Gen. deceased.
Maj. John Hannah	To sqd. 5-42 to Fall, 43. Asst. Grp Adjt. Grnd Off.
Flt.Lt. John Harrison	RAF Officer. Intell. Liason Off to 78th
Maj. Ralph F. Himes	To sqd. 8-42 to 3-2-44 to 8FC. Grp Ops Off. KIFA,1946
Maj. Robert E. Holmberg	To sqd. 5-42 to EOW.Grp Flt. Surg. Grnd Off.
Capt. Bowen I Hosford	To sqd5-42 to EOW.GrpPR,Hist. Off. Grnd. Off.
Maj. Bruce B. Hunt	To sqd. 4-23-45 to 4-24-45 to 84 FS CO.Ass.Grp Ops Off
Capt. Russell B. Hunter	To sqd. 5-42 to EOW.Grp Ord.Off.Grd. Off
Capt. Charles A. Johnson	To sqd. 5-42 to EOW.GrpSupp. Off.Grnd Off
Maj. Oliver K. Jones	To sqd 11-6-42 to Summere, 43 to 66FW.Grp Weather.Off, Grd Off. To 8AFHQ Weath Off on 12-16-44 as Lt.Col..Col.USAF (ret)
Capt. Guido G. Karrer	To sqd.5-42 to EOW Grp Personnel Off. Grd. Off.
Capt. Harden B. Kitchen	To sqd.5-42 to EOW HqSqCO Grd. Off
Walter A. Knight	Civ. pilot.Rep Av. Cor. maint.,modif.rep to 8AF,66FW,78FG
Col. John D. Landers	To sqd. 2-22-45 to 6-28-45 to US, Grp CO. 3 Silv. Strs.,4 DFC,s, 21AMs, Prp Hrt, Croix de Guerre
Capt. Morris K. Lee	To sqd 5-7-42 to 3-21-44 to US hosp. Grp Ops Off 5-7-42 to 8-28-42 Admin. pilot due to hlth &alt. restrict.
Thomas Leonard	Civ. Pilot, Pratt Whitney rep to 8FC,66FW,
Maj. John H. MacVeagh	To sqd. 11-10-42 to 12-29-44. Grp Intell Off. Grnd. Off. Former WWI AEF Off.
Lt.Col. Leonard P. Marshall	To sqd.3-14-45 to 4-21-45,KIA. Dep. Grp. CO
W/Cmdr S.L.Matthews	RAF Off .RAF Stat.CO to 6-15-43
Maj. William E. May	To sqd 9-8-44 to EOW Grp Ops Off to 12—5-44 Act. 84FS CO Grp. Tact. Insp., Asst. Grp Ops Off. two tours.
Maj. George M. McNeese	To sqd. 5-8-42 to 9-?-42 to Pac Theat.. Dep Grp CO
LtCol.. Melvin F. McNickle	To sqd. 7-12-43 to 7-30-43,POW. Grp CO same dates. AAF Liaison Off to 601 RAF sqd. at DX in Autumn, 1941. USAF Maj./Gen. (dec)
Maj Eugene R. Murphy	To sqd. 1943-1945. Grp. Supply Off. Grnd Off.
LtCol.. Joseph Myers	To sqd 12-3-44to2-21-45 to 55FG. Dep. Grp. CO 12-3-44 and later same on 2-4-45. Grp Ops Off 12-5-44.
Capt.George F. Nash	To sqd. 6-22-42 to trfd. in US in latter 1942 Grp. Adj.
LtCol. Jack J. Oberhansly	To sqd 8-28-44 to 12-3-44 to 4FG,65FW. Dep. Grp. CO
LtCol. Arman Peterson	To sqd. 5-7-42 to 7-1-43, KIA. First Grp CO. Prior 78th Serv in 77th Pursuit Sqd., Barksdale AFB 1939, to 49th Pursuit Sqd. 14th FG Moffitt/Hamilton/Mills Fld. 1939.
Lt.Col. Eugene P. Roberts	To sqd. 9-27-43 to 12-17-43 to 8FC. Grp CO same dates. DSC, Silv. Star-Amer/Brit., DFCs, AMs. Second tour as 364FG CO 1-3-45 to 11-45
Capt. Raymond E. Ruotsala	To sqd. 1943 (from 84FS) to EOW. Grp Eng. Off. Grd.Off
Maj. Robert "Rex" W. Smith	To sqd. 10-5-44. Asst. Grp. Ops Off
Capt. Reed Stayner	To sqd. 5-42 to EOW.Asst. Grp. Sup Off.Grnd. Off.
LtCol. Samuel F. Stephenson	To sqd. Hq. Det. 2-1-45 to EOOW. 79th/443rd Sev. Grp CO. Grnd Off.
Col. James J. Stone, Jr.	To sqd. 7-1-43 to 5-21-44 to 66FW as Dep. Wng CO. Grp CO same dates, except for 7-12-43 to 7-30-43 as Dep. Grp CO. On 60day US leave 5-21-44 pre 66FW duty. Silver Star, 2 DFCs,RAF DFC, 3 AMs.
Capt. Ellis R. Veatch	To sqd. 5-42 to EOW. Grp. Chaplain Grd.Off.
Maj. William C. Vincent	To sqd 12-29-44 to EOW. Grp Intell. Off. Grnd. Off.
Capt. Thomas P. Wildman	To sqd. Summer, 43 to EOW.Grp Weather Off. Grnd Off.
LtCol. Robert E. Williams	To sqd. 2-44 to 2-1-45 to 353 FG 79th Service Grp. CO. Grd. Off.
Capt. James R. Willis	To sqd 5-42 to EOW.Grp Ops offic staff Grd. Off.
Capt. William J. Zink	To sqd 5-42 to EOW.Grp Chaplain's Off. Grd. Off. Soldier's Medal 7-19-44
LtCol.. Erlath W. Zuehl	To sqd. Fall, 42 to 2-1-45 to 353FG. Grp Adj. Grd. Off.

82nd Fighter Squadron Pilots and Key Staff

2Lt. Robert B. Abernathy	Pilot, late 1944 to 1945
Capt. Robert E. Adamina	Pilot to sqd. 5-11-42 to 5-14-43, POW. Flight CO
2Lt.. James B. Allison	
2Lt.. Arthur J. Allred	Transferred from sqd. on 2-4-43
2Lt.. Bryant Y. Anderson	To sqd. 2-23-43 to 10-3-43 to 66FW
Capt. Donald E. Anderson	
2Lt.. Edwin B. Anderson	Pilot, POW on 2-24-45
1Lt. Robert H. Anderson	Pilot, A Flt. CO in March, 45
1Lt. Woodrow W. Anderson	
1Lt. Robert L. Baker	Pilot KIA on 6-10-44
2Lt. Norman W. Bandel	Transferred from sqd on 2-4-43
1Lt. Richard P. Baribault	
2Lt.Roy M. Barlow	
2Lt. Baugh	Pilot, to sqd. 5-12-42,KIFA in Summer/Fall, 42
2Lt. Homer J. Beatty	Pilot, to sqd. 2-23-43 to 7-9-43 to 12RCD
1Lt. Wayne F. Bechtelheimer	
1Lt. Harold F. Beck	Pilot to sqd. 4-6-44 to 7-15-44 to 84FS
2Lt. Rex G. Beeckman	
2Lt. Robert F. Belovich	Pilot
Maj. John R. Bertrand	Pilot To sqd 2-16-43 to 3-8-43 to 84FS
1Lt. Jack J. Bernhard	Pilot, to sqd. 2-23-43 to 6-18-44 to 8FC
Maj. Alfred A. Beuerle	
1Lt. Lucian J. Bibeau	Pilot KIA on 2-24-45
1Lt. Robert J. Blossom	Pilot, bailed out behind Allied lines on 2-20-45
Capt. Rex C. Boeckman	Pilot, D Flight CO on 11-10-44
1Lt. Ernest V. Boehner	Pilot, KIA on 3-1-45
Capt. Erwin C. Boettcher	Grd. Off. Sqd. Intell. Off.
1Lt. E.Fred Bolgert	Pilot To Sqd 6-44 to 12-44 to USA Flew 69 missions, Lt.Col. USAF ret 1981 Mech Eng.
Capt. Walker L. Boone	Pilot, B Flight CO on 7-19-43. Later USAF Col.onel and CO of McConnell AFB
1Lt.. Robert R. Bosworth	Pilot D Flight CO on 8-27-44
Capt.Henry L. Bottoms	Grnd Off. to Grp. Comm Off on 9-30-43
1Lt.. Walter E. Bourque	Pilot, In sqd. on 2-14-45
2Lt. James E. Bower	
1Lt. John J. Boyne	
1Lt. Gerald E. Brasher	Pilot, in sqd. 12-10-43
2Lt. William D. Bridges	Pilot,To sqd. April '45
2Lt.. Melvin E. Broberg	Pilot,To sqd. April '45
2Lt. Edward C. Brophy	
2Lt. Robert F. Brower	Pilot to sqd. 2-25-43 to 8-27-43, KIFA
1Lt. Jack R. Brown	
Capt. John L. Brown	Pilot, sqd Ops Off on 12-9-44
2Lt. Ora R. Brown	Pilot to sqd 2-16-443 to 6-13-43 KIA
Maj. Winfield H. Brown	Pilot, sqd Ops Off on 9-10-44 US leave inJan, 1945, returned for 2nd tour on 2-15-45. Sqd. Ops. Off till EOW
2Lt. Elroy A. Bruss	Pilot, To sqd April, 45
2Lt. George B. Burger	
1Lt. Louis R. Campi	Pilot On Ops. during April 1945
1Lt. Merle R. Capp	Pilot, to sqd. 5-44 to 7-15-44 to 84FS
2Lt. Edward J. Carroll	Pilot KIA on 4-25-45
1Lt. Lawrence R. Casey	Pilot, To sqd 4-6-44
1Lt. John E. Catlin	
2Lt. John H. Cedergren	Pilot, To sqd. April, 45
1Lt.. William P. Chattaway	Pilot, To sqd 2-16-43 to 3-10-44 to 66FW
1Lt. John C. Childs	Pilot to sqd. 8-44 to EOW
Capt. Charles R. Clark	Pilot, to sqd 2-16-43 to8-2-44 POW, sqd. CO on 7-20-44 during 2nd tour.
2lt. Guy R. Clark	Pilot, to sqd. April 45
Maj. Lloyd R. Cogswell	Grnd Off Sqd. Exec. Off.
2Lt.. James P. Col.e	
Capt Wayne L. Col.eman	Pilot, F Flt. CO on 11-10-44
1Lt. John G. Col.lins	
LtCol.. Richard E. Conner	Pilot, sqd. CO on 8-28-44. US lve 12-2-44 to 2-17-45. to 84FS on 3-19-45.Russia Evader on 3-21-45. Sqd. CO on ret. frm Russia on 5-10-45. To HQSQ 5-12-45. To sqd. on 6-2-44. 2DFCs, 11 AMs, Croix de Guerre(Fr), Bronze Lion(Neth)
Capt. Wilbur J. Coss, Jr.	Pilot, Evader on 8-26-44 to 9-16-44. B Flt. CO on 12-2-44 KIA on 2-22-45
1Lt. Sydney G. Craig	Grnd Off. Sqd Intell Off 1942 to 1944 to 9AF
1Lt. Louis D. Cross	To sqd. 2-16-43 to 3-4-44 to 551 FTG
Capt. Manford O. Croy, Jr.	Pilot, G Flt. CO on 11-10-44. KIA of 4-16-45
LtCol.. Harold J. Dayhuff	Pilot, To sqd 5-7-42 to 8-7-43 to Hdqrs Sqd. Sqd CO on 5-11-42. Flew every mission while CO.
2Lt.. August V. DeGenaro	Pilot, to sqd 5-16-43 to 7-14-43 Wounded. To US hosp. DSC, AMs.
1Lt. William F. Demme	Grnd Off. O Club Manager
Capt. Charles W. DeWitt	Pilot, wounded on 3-22-44 takeoff crash. ?Flt CO to US Fall, 1944
1Lt. Louis A. Dicks	Pilot, to sqd 4—6-44 to 8-10-44. KIA In US paprs summer, 44 for knocking stuck wingtank off fellow aircraft with his wingtip.
1Lt. John M. Dore	Transferred to 83 FS
Maj. Harry. L. Downing	Pilot. To sqd as CO on 12-5-44 to 2-17-45. Back to sqd CO on 3-4-45 to 3-14-45.
2Lt. Dregne	To sqd 5-11-42 to ?
1Lt. Richard N. Dunham	Pilot, on ops with sqd, 4-10-45. First sqd ops, Sept, '44
1Lt. Allen G. Dunken	Pilot to sqd 2-16-43 to 3-28-44 to 495 FTG
F/O Richard C. Dunlap	Pilot
2Lt. Harvey L. Eakes	Pilot, on sqd. ops. March 44 to 4-2-44 KIA.
2Lt. Troy L. Eggleston	Pilot, On sqd Ops in Sept 1 44 to 11-26-44 KIA
1Lt. George V. Elsey	Pilot to sqd11-4-44 to EOW
2Lt. Herman L. Evans	Pilot, on sqd. ops in Nov. 43 to April 1944
2Lt. Ronald S. Evans	
2Lt. Gordon Fisher	Pilot To sqd 3-28-45 On ops 4-25-45
1Lt. James T. Fitzgerald	Pilot, In sqd. 7-30-44 to 8-8—44, POW
2Lt.Andrew L. Florenz	Pilot to sqd. April. 1945
Capt. Howard R. Garabrant	Grd. Off. Sqd Eng. Off 5-42 to EOW
2Lt. William H. Genge	Pilot POW on 5-24-44
1Lt. Kal Gladstone	
1Lt. Herbert W. Glickman	Grnd Off to sqd 5-42 to 3-26-44 to Hdqrs Sqd. Sqd Arm/Chem Off.
1Lt. Claude B. Godard, Jr.	Pilot, in sqd Sept. 43 to 1-29-44, wounded. On sqd ops in May, 1944
2 Lt Warren E. Graff	Pilot, To sqd 1-21-43 to 7-30-43. POW. Escaped 11-11-43, returned 11-15-43. TO US.
Capt. William A. Guilfoyle	Pilot. To sqd 2-44 to Late Fall 44, to US. Act. sqd CO on 6-4-44 to 6-8-44. With 50FS 18 mos in Iceland pre 78th duty.
1Lt. Daniel D. Hagarty	Pilot, POW on 5-12-44. Ex bomber pilot on 2nd tour with 78th.
1Lt. Clifford B. Hahn	Pilot, KIA on 1-24-44
Capt. John H. Hanner	
2Lt. D.T. Harris	In sqd. May 44
Capt. Donald C. Hart	Pilot, To sqd. Late Summer, 1944 to EOW. E Flight CO on 11-10-44
1Lt. Phillip H. Hazelett	Pilot KIA on 5-28-44
1Lt. Roger V. Hearn	Pilot. In sqd. Nov. 43 to May 44
1Lt. William T. Hegman	Pilot to sqd. 2-25-43 to 2-9-44 to 8FC
1Lt. Frank L. Heil	Pilot To sqd. 3-28-45 to EOW

1Lt. Donald J. Henahan	Pilot, to sqd. 3-28-45 to EOW.
1Lt. Richard C. Herbst	
2Lt. John Herrick	Pilot, POW on 1-26-43
Maj. Richard A. Hewitt	Pilot, To sqd. 9-16-43 to 7-20-45 to US.US leave 5-15-44 to 8-9-44, 2nd tour. Sqd CO on 3-20-45. S.S, 4 DFCs, 13 AMs. 426 hrs. combat flying. USAF LtCol.. (ret)
Capt. Archie W. Hill	Pilot, to sqd. 2-16-43 to 11-22-43 . MTO
Capt. John J. Hockery	Pilot, In sqd. Nov 43 to 11-26-44. POW. US lve late Summr 1944. 2nd tour 9-30-44. A Flt. CO: on 10-1-44.
2Lt. Benjamin H. Hodges	Pilot. KIA on 6-20-44
F/O. Melvin F. Hoffman	Pilot
Capt. Robet B, Holmes	Pilot. To sqd. 12-18-44 to 4-16-45. KIA C Flt CO on 2-2-45
1Lt. Lynn H. Hosford, Jr.	Pilot, to sqd 4-6-44 to 9-4-44. to US A Flt CO on 7-16-44. USAF Col. (ret)
2Lt. Courtlyn W. Hotchkiss	Pilot
2Lt. ? Hubbell	Pilot. To sqd. 5-11-42 to Summer, 42 KIFA
1Lt. William E. Hydorn	Pilot, To sqd. 11-4-44 to EOW
1Lt. Donald G. Jackson	Pilot, To sqd 2-16-43 to 7-14-43. KIA. Nickname "Dixie"
2Lt. Y.V. Jones	Pilot. In sqd. Nov 43 to 2-10-44 KIA
Capt. Ivan H. Keatley	Pilot In sqd. Fall '44 to EOW. D flt. CO, 2-9-45
1Lt. Paul Keller	
2Lt. Raymond D. Kerwin	
1Lt. James E. Kinsolving	Pilot to sqd. spring, '44 to Fall '44 to US One tour plus ext. 74 missions, 274 combat hrs. A Flt. C0 9-4-44
2Lt.. Bertrand L. Kohlman	Pilot to sqd 2-16-43
2Lt. Anthony I. Kosinski	Pilot, to sqd. Spring, 44 to 5-11-44 Evader, To US
2Lt..Richard S. Kuehner	Pilot, to sqd. Spring, 1944 to 6-10-44. KIA
2Lt.. William O. Lacy	Pilot, to sqd summer 1944 to 9-10-44 KIA
Capt. Huie H. Lamb, Jr.	Pilot, to sqd. Late Summer 1944 to EOW. DFC,11AMs.
1Lt. John T. Lamb, Jr.	Pilot, In sqd. Winter 1944 to Spring 1944.
1Lt.. Paul H. Lehman	Pilot, to sqd. 2-16-43 to 2-16-44 to 495 FTG
1Lt. Kenneth E. Lepp	
F/O Harold R. Liebenrood	Pilot, to sqd. 11-4-44 to 2-28-45 POW.
2Lt. Donald E. Ludwig	Pilot, KIA on 2-10-44
Capt. George J. Lundigan	Pilot, to sqd. 5-44 to early fall, 1944. wounded, 7-1-44, D Flt. CO on 8-25-44
LtCol. Leonard P. Marshall	Pilot, To sqd. 5-11-42 to 9-8-44 to 84FS. On US leave Summer, 1944, 2nd tour. Sqd. Ops Off,8-22-44. KIA,4-21-45.
Capt. Manuel S. Martinez	Pilot, to sqd. 4-21-43 to 5-19-44 to US. Silver Star
Capt. William E. May	Pilot. To sqd. 2-25-43 to ?,44 to Hdqrs. Sqd. A Flt. CO on 7-19-43. 2 tours. Act. CO of various sqds. for short times. To US in Aug, 1945. 143 missions. 4 DFCs, 20 AMS, Purp. Hrt. P-51D Sqd. CO, Korea,1951, USAF Col. (ret)
Maj. Benjamin I. Mayo	Pilot, To sqd. 6-1-44 to 7-14-44 to 84FS.Sqd. CO on 6-8-44
2Lt. Elton E. McBrayer	
1Lt.. Emil A. Meindl	Grnd Off. To sqd Summer, 1942 to EOW. Sqd. Eng. Off comm. in field
1Lt. Austin S. Miller	Pilot, To sqd. Fall, 44 to EOW
2Lt. Richard I. Miller	Pilot, to sqd. Spring, 1944 to late Summer 1944
2Lt.. Kenneth L. Moore	Pilot, KIA on 9-9-44
F/O. George W. Morrison	Pilot, to sqd. 10-10-44 to 1-2-45. POW
1Lt.. Harold J. Morris	Pilot, KIA on 7-26-44
2Lt.. Donald R. Morsch	Pilot, KIA on 2-11-44
Maj. Norman D. Munson	Pilot, to sqd. 2-16-43 to 7-19-44. KIA C Flight CO on 7-19-43. sqd. CO on 7-14-44. USlve 5-18-44 to 7-13-44, 2nd tour. Nickname "Doug"
LtCol. Joseph Myers	Pilot, To sqd. early Aug. 44 to 12-5-44 to Hdqrs. Sqd. Sqd. Ops Off on 10-1-44. did 55FG tour prior to 78th
1Lt. William F. Neel	Pilot, To sqd. 2-16-43 to 1-24 44 KIA
2Lt. Lawrence W. Nelson, Jr.	Pilot, to sqd. Late Summr, 1944 to early 1945
Capt. Robert E. Nuernberger	Grnd Off. To sqd. 5-11-42 to EOW. Sqd. flt. Surg.
LtCol. Jack J. Oberhansly	Pilot, to sqd 5-11-42 to 8-28-44 to Hdqrs Sqd.USLve 5-18-44 to 8-22-44. Sqd. Ops Off in 5-42 Sqd CO 8—7-43 to 5-18-44 and 8-22-44 to 8-28-44.
2Lt. Ronald C. Orr	Pilot, POW on 2-29-44
2Lt. William S. Orvis	Pilot KIA on 5-28-44
1Lt. James E. Parker	Pilot, in sqd Dec 1944 to EOW
1Lt. Eugene L. Peel	Pilot, in sqd early Dec. 1944 to EOW
2Lt. Robert K. Platt	Pilot, in sqd Feb 45 to 3-5-45, KIA
1Lt. Richard I. Potter	
2Lt. Lester Price	
Capt. John C. Ramsay	Pilot. To sqd. 6-?-44 to 6-12-44. KIA
2Lt. Milton H. Ramsey	Pilot, evader,1-29-44 . retnd 6-21-44
F/O Robert J. Rauh	Pilot
1Lt. Hayden E. Richards	Pilot, To sqd. 5-44 to 9-44 to US
Capt. Arthur B. Richie	Pilot, To sqd. 2-16-43 to 2-15-44 to 12 RCD (US)
2Lt. Donald R. Roberts	Pilot, To sqd 4-6-44 to 4-13-44, POW
1Lt. Harry L. Roe	Pilot, In sqd Feb. 1944 to EOW
2Lt.. Alvin M. Rosenberg	Pilot, In sqd Dec 1944 to 4-17-45. POW
1Lt. Allen A. Rosenblum	Pilot, In sqd Sept. 44 to 4-17-45. POW
Maj. Herbert E. Ross	Pilot, To sqd. 5-11-42 to early 1943. C Flt CO in Fall, 1942. Trfd to 48 FS, MTO
2Lt. Maurice J. Ryan	Pilot, to sqd. 3-28-45 to EOW.
Capt. Raymond L. Salmon	Grnd Off. Sqd. Adj at North Island, NAS, summer 1942
2Lt. Jack S. Sandmeir	Pilot, To sqd.2-16-43 to 5-15-43 KIA
1Lt.. Joseph A. Scheibler	Pilot, In sqd Nov 43 to May 44 to US
1Lt. Edwin O. Schneider	Pilot, To sqd.10-10-44 to EOW
2Lt. Anton Schoepke	
1Lt. Howard S. Scholz	Pilot, To sqd. May 1944 to Sept 1944 to US
2Lt. Wendell Seppich	Pilot, To sqd.5-11-42 to 9-13-42 KIFA
1Lt. Fred I. Sharp	Pilot, To sqd.May 44 to Sept, 44 to US. C Flt. CO ,9-4-44

Capt. Herbert K. Shope	Pilot, To sqd.July 44 to Dec 44.C Flt. CO,11-10-44
1Lt. Harry B. Slater	Pilot, To sqd. 4-6-55 to Sept 44 wounded on 6-7-44
2Lt. Billy V. Smith	Pilot, To sqd.July 44 to 8-13-44 KIA
1Lt. Levi W. Smith	
1Lt. Robert E. Smith	Pilot, To sqd.10-144 to EOW
1Lt. Richard C. Snyder	Pilot, POW on 9-18-44
1Lt. Robert P. Spaulding	Pilot, To sqd.2-16-43 to 3-26-44 to 495th FTG 2DFCs, 3 AMs Flt CO . USAF (ret) 1964
1Lt. James B. Stallings	Pilot, To sqd.4-6-44 to 9-12-44 toUS. Flt CO in 8-44
2Lt. Richad D. Stark	Pilot, To sqd. Aug.,1944 to 9-3-44 POW
1Lt.. Paul H. Stearns	Pilot, To sqd.10-10-44 to 3-17-45 evader to Russia
2Lt. James F. Steele	Pilot, To sqd. 2-16-43 to 5-11-44 Interned in Switzerland
2Lt. Richard D. Steele	Pilot, To sqd. 4-6-44 to Sept 44 US
2Lt. John C.E. Steinwedel	Pilot, To sqd. 4-6-44 to 6-5-44. KIA
1Lt.. George W. Stillwell	Pilot, In sqd. March 45 to EOW
1Lt. Herbert A. Stinson	Pilot, In sqd. Oct 44 to 4-10-45 KIA
2Lt. Milton B. Stutzman	Pilot, In sqd March 45 to EOW
2Lt. ? Sumner	Pilot, To sqd 5-12-42 to 8-10-42, KIFA
2Lt. Delbert A. Sutherland	Grnd Off. Sqd. Adj., Nov 42 to Jan 43
1Lt. Donald H. Swankowski	Pilot, To sqd 4-6-44 to Sept. 44 US
1Lt.. William S. Swanson	Pilot, To sqd Nov. 43 to 2-11-44 KIA
2Lt. Fred R. Swauger	Pilot, To sqd early March, 45 to 4-16-45 POW
2Lt. Harry A. Thompson	Pilot, To sqd 10-10-44 to 11-21-44 POW
Lt ? Tinsley	To sqd 5-11-42 at North Island NAS
1Lt. Grant M. Turley	Pilot, To sqd Nov 43 to 3-6-44. KIA. Silver Star 2-11-44. Flew 47 Missions for 113 combat hrs.
2Lt. Estel E. Ulerick	Pilot, To sqd Feb. 44 to 3-17-45 Wounded. To US
2Lt. Vernon J. VanDrisse	
1Lt. Warren V. Van Dyk	Pilot, To sqd 4-6-44 to Sept. 44 to US
Capt. Firman B. Voorhies	Grnd Off. To sqd summer 1942 to early 1944 to 9AF P-47 Grp. Sqd Intell Off.
1Lt. Karl R. Wagner	Pilot, To sqd 6-16-43 to May 44 to US
1Lt. Willard E. Warren	Pilot, To sqd Aug 44 to 2-29-45 POW. forced down 5 times. Nickname "Skip".
Capt. Benjamin M. Watkins	Pilot, To sqd Jan 44 to Post 6-6-44 to US
2Lt. Calvin Webb	Pilot, To sqd Jan 44 to 4-1-44 KIA
Capt. Robert W.Wells	Grnd Off. Flt Sur. in May, 45
1Lt.. Warren M. Wesson	Pilot, To sqd 2-25-44 to 2-9-44 to US.Short tour at Atcham OTU
F/O. Gordon L. Weston	Pilot, To sqd 10-10-44 to 1-6-45. KIA. Arr. music for Grp Thunderbolt band
2Lt. Stephan L. White	Pilot, To sqd in 1942 in US. KIFA 1-26-43 enroute to Ireland.
F/O. Zane W. White	Pilot
Capt. James W. Wilkinson	Pilot, To sqd Nov 43 to 6-4-44 KIFA Sqd CO on 5-23-'44. DSC, Silv. Star, DFC, AMs. In 4FG prior to 78th
1 Lt Ruben E. Wilkinson	Pilot, To sqd 4-6-44 to Sept. 44 to US
1Lt. Francis R. Williams	
Capt. Robert H. Williams	
Capt. Roland L. Wolfe	Pilot, To sqd Mar 44 to 9-4-44 to US. C Flight CO in Aug 44.
Capt. Myron K. Woller	Pilot, In sqd April 44 to late summer, 44. Flt CO in sqd.
1Lt. William D. Wren	Pilot, In sqd 9-8-43 to 3-1-44 to US
1Lt. Melvin R. Wright	Pilot, In sqd 2-16-433 to 12-10-43 KIFA
Capt. Wilson G. Young	Pilot in sqd. 4-29-44 to late sumer, 44
2Lt. Dolphe C. Zboinski	Pilot, To sqd 11-4-44 to January 45.

83rd Fighter Squadron Pilots and Key Staff

2Lt. Ishmael W. Abernathy	Pilot, To sqd 4-28-43
2Lt. James B. Allison Jr.	Pilot, to sqd Sept. 44 to 3-22-45 to 5th Emergency Rescue Sqd.
1Lt. Kenneth C. Allstaedt	Pilot, To sqd April 44 to Sept 44 to US
F/O. Merrill Andrews	Pilot
2Lt. Richard A. Ariono	
Capt. Howard S. Askelson	Pilot, To sqd 2-16-43 to 3-4-44 to 557th FTG B Flt CO on 12-7-43
Capt. Harold T. Barnaby	Pilot, To sqd 2-16-43 to EOW. C Flt CO on 2-17-44. Trfd to 8FC on 2-23-44 for DS retd to 78th as sqd. Ops Off on 9-19-44, flew 106 missions. A-3 66FW 9-16-44. Silv. Star, 2 DFCs, 9 AMs EAME/6 stars.
1Lt. Donald S. Beals	Pilot KIA on 1-26-43 on ferry trip to N. Africa.
LtCol. Samuel R. Beckley	Pilot, To sqd 8-29-44 to Oct. 45 to 55 FG Germany. Sqd. Ops Off on 10-8-44. Act. Sqd. CO on 10-9-44 to 12-31-44 and Jan to 6-12-45. Full Sqd. CO 3-20-45 to Oct 45. USA LtCol.. (ret)
1Lt. Jack Beeney	Pilot,In sqd 7-4-44 and 12-29-44. F Flt CO on 11-16-44
Capt. Wallace E. Bennett	Pilot, To sqd Nov 44 to EOW. wnd. 3-14-45. Hospitalized for burns
2Lt. Marvin C. Bigelow	
2Lt. Percy Bingham	Pilot In sqd on 9-6-44. May have gone off ops after crash this date.
1Lt. Wallace G. Bland	Pilot, In sqd. Mar44 to Summer 44. B Flt. CO, 7-13-44
2Lt. Harry L. Blystone	Pilot, To sqd 2-16-43 to 3-17-44 to CBI. C Flt. CO 7-15-43. Sqd. Ops Off 12-7-43
Maj. Donald Bodenhamer	
Capt. Robert R. Bonebrake	Pilot In sqd 8-28-44 to Jan 45. B Flt. CO on 11-16-44. Sqd Ops Off on 12-30-44
2Lt. Gerald F. Boner	Pilot KIA 1-17-45
1Lt. Geroge G. Boteler	Pilot, To sqd 4-6-44 to Sept, 44 to US
F/O. William E. Bradley	Pilot, To sqd Jan 45 to 1-20-45 KIFA
2Lt. William G. Broome	
1Lt. Robert W. Brown	Grnd. Off.
1Lt. Russell L. Burgher	Pilot In sqd July 44 to March 45
1Lt. Charles L. Burman	Pilot, To sqd 4-6-44 to Nov. 44
2Lt. Ralph L. Bush	Pilot KIA 3-19-45. First Mission 3-17-45

F/O. Joseph Bzdelik	Pilot, In sqd. Aug. 44
2Lt.. Leon G. Caldwell	
2Lt.. Bruce L. Campbell	
2Lt. Thomas W. Capps	
2Lt. William J. Carey	Pilot In sqd late April 45 but still in OTU on VE Day.
2Lt. Lawrence R. Casey	Pilot, To sqd 4-29-44 to Oct 44 to US in Pacific on Iwo Jima with 414th FG, P-47 unit, USAF Col. (ret)
Capt. Peter A. Caulfield	Pilot In sqd 1-14-44 to Hdqr Sqd on 4-9-45. C Flt CO on 6-5-45. Sqd. Ops Off on 3-22-45
1Lt.. William T. Chapman	Pilot In sqd 6-25-43 to 3-2-44 to 551FTG
2Lt. Quentin Charlton	Pilot in sqd 9-8-43 to 9-22-43 KIA
Capt. Richard E. Chase	Grnd Off. Sqd Adj Trfd from sqd on 3-16-45
2Lt. Kenneth Chetwood	Pilot, To sqd. 4-22-43
Capt. Constantine S. Chioles	Pilot, Post VE-Day transferred to sqd.
1Lt.. Henry Chippindale	Pilot
1Lt. Anthony T. Col.letti	Pilot in sqd. 3-27-45 to EOW
Maj. James M. Cooper	Pilot, To sqd 42 to 7-11-44 to 356 FG. Sqd Ops Off on 7-12-43. US Lv prior to 7-11-44 transfer
1Lt. Ralph E. Cormier	Pilot KIA on 11-26-43
Capt. Sydney G. Craig	Grnd Off. to Sqd. Summer, 42 to Spring, 44 to 9 AF. Sqd Intell. Off.
F/O. Archie F. Daniels	Pilot, To sqd. 12-18-43 to 2-11-44.-KIA. RCAF pilot came into AAF in UK in Sept. 43.
1Lt. Hubert Davis	Pilot In sqd. Jan 45 to EOW
Maj. Jesse C. Davis, Jr.	Pilot, To sqd. Summer, 42 to 1-18-44 to US1st AF. Sqd. Ops Off. Sqd. CO on 7-1-43.
2Lt. Glenn K. Deatheragae	
Capt. Richard E. Decker	Pilot, To sqd. 11-10-42 to 2-13-43 to 49th FS MTO
2Lt. Lloyd K. DeMoss	
Capt. Donald J. DeVilliers	Pilot in sqd 9-23-44 to EOW
2Lt. LeRoy V. Dodd	Pilot KIFA 4-15-43
2Lt. Patrick H. Doherty	Pilot
1Lt. John M. Dore	Pilot
1Lt.. Gene C. Doss	Pilot In sqd. 12-30-44 to EOW. WIA 4-23-45
Capt. Kenneth W. Dougherty	Pilot in sqd 7-10-43 to 4-1-44 to 495 FTG B Flt CO on 2-17-44.
F/O. Edweard J. Downey	Pilot, To sqd. Dec, 43 to 3-6-44 KIA. Ex RCAF pilot.
2Lt. Kenneth P. Dunaway	Pilot, POW on 9-1-44
2Lt.. Lloyd L. Eadline	Pilot In sqd. 10-15-44 to 2-24-45 KIA
Capt. Robert E. Ealey	Pilot In sqd. 5-16-43 to 6-26-44 to 12 RCD. A Flt. CO on 12-7-43. Asst. Sqd. Ops Off on 5-29-44
F/O. James C.P. Eastwood	Pilot KIA on 12-30-43
2Lt. Raymond H. Eckert	Pilot, To Sqd. 3-13-45 to EOW. USAF LtCol.. (ret)
2Lt. Richfield Eggleston	Pilot
2Lt. Robet F. Eiermann	Pilot
1Lt. John E. Euler	Pilot To sqd. 3-27-45 to EOW Flew combat after Grp OTU.
1Lt. Frank A. Fish	Pilot in sqd 8-28-44 to Jan 45
2Lt. James F. Fisher	Pilot to sqd. 3-27-45 to EOW
1Lt. John E. Follen	Pilot
2Lt. Hugh O. Foster	Pilot in sqd. 9-23-44 to 2-14-43 to US
2Lt. Watson R. Gabriel	Pilot To sqd. 3-27-45 to EOW
1Lt. Robert H. Galstan	Pilot To sqd. 3-27-45 to EOW
1Lt. Edward H. Geary	
1Lt. Harry A. Gibson	
2Lt. Ollie E. Gibbs	Pilot In sqd 6-6-44 to 6-22-44 KIA
LtCol. Olin E. Gilbert	Pilot to sqd. Jan 44 to 7-13-44 to Hdqr Sqd. Sqd. CO on 1-18-44. Silver Star on 4-16-45
2Lt. Howard A. Gilliam	
1Lt.. William P. Gordon	Pilot to sqd. 4-22-43 to July 43 Nick-named "Flash"
1Lt.. Arthur S. Granger	Pilot In sqd 11-3-43 to 1-5-44 KIA
Capt. Robert T. Green	Pilot In sqd 8-28-44 to EOW D Flt CO on 11-16-44.
2Lt. Ralph E. Hamilton	Pilot POW on 2-22-45
1Lt.. Willard D. Hamilton	To sqd. 4-21-43
1Lt. Maynard A.Hanson	Grnd Off. Sqd Arm Off.
1 Lt. Francis E. Harrington	Pilot In sqd 9-23-44 to EOW. D Flt. CO
1Lt. Dunstan D. Hartley	Pilot In sqd 8-28-44 to 9-23-44 KIA
1Lt. Randal B. Hathway	Pilot In sqd 4-29-44 B Flt CO on 6-5-44
Maj. Charles W. Havens	
Capt. Foy C. Higginbottom	Pilot To sqd. 4-6-44 to EOW. Sqd Ops Off on 4-9-45
F/O. Marquis D. Hilbert	Pilot To sqd.Late Fall 44 to 3-22-45
2Lt. Kenneth Hindersinn	Pilot In sqd 11-30-43 to 1-5-44 POW
1Lt. Eldridge M. Hobbie	Pilot In sqd 12-15-44 to EOW
1Lt. Jack D. Hodge	Pilot In sqd 11-30-44 to 3-11-45 KIA
1Lt. Paul C. Holden	Pilot In sqd 4-29-44
1Lt. Richard L. Holloway	Pilot In sqd 3-27-45 to EOW. To 55 FG in Germany in Oct. 45.
2Lt. Walter J. Hopton	Pilot In sqd April, 1945
2Lt. Courtlyn W. Hotchkiss	Pilot In sqd 1-14-44 to 3-17-44 POW
Maj. Bruce E. Hunt	Pilot To sqd. 5-12-45 from 84FS as Sqd. Ops Off
Capt. Kent N. Hunt	Grnd Off Sqd Flt Surg in May 45
Capt. Carl P. Hurst	Pilot In sqd 11-30-43 to Summer 44. A Flt CO, 6-5-44
2Lt. Andrew R. Innocenzi	Pilot In sqd 11-30-44 to 2-14-45 to evader to Russia. Did not return to 78th after Russia.
2Lt. Joseph W. Jackson	Pilot In sqd July 44
2Lt. Alan R. Jacobson	Pilot In sqd 7-4-44 to 11-9-44 KIA
1Lt. Dean C. Johnson	Pilot In sqd 11-30-44 to 3-12-45. Evader toSweden Ret'd to DX in March, 45. Sent to US
2Lt. John H. Johnson	Pilot In sqd 1-14-44 to 2-22-44, POW
2Lt. Robert N. Jones	Pilot In sqd 7-4-44 to 9-1-44 KIA
Capt. Alvin M. Juchheim	Pilot In sqd 3-5-28-44. POW. A Flt CO on 3-23-44. Asst Ops Off on 4-19-44. 76 missions. 237 combat hrs.
Maj. William H. Julian	Pilot In sqd 5-16-43 to 3-20-45 to 339FG on US lve after first tour 10-9-44 to 12-31-44. C Flt. CO on 12-7-43. Sqd. Ops. Off on 3-23-44. Sqd. CO on 7-13-44.
1Lt. John A. Kirk	Pilot in sqd 11-30-44 to EOW Flight CO In sqd.
1Lt. Edward T. Kitley	Pilot In sqd 3-6-44 to 7-1-44 KIA
1Lt. Peter W. Klassen	Pilot In sqd 9-5-44 to EOW
1Lt. Robert H. Knapp	Pilot To sqd 2-16-44 to 2-23-44 to 8FC. 119 missions
2Lt. Francis J. Kochanek	Pilot In sqd 5-27-44 WIA 6-10-44, did not return to group after hospital
2Lt. Bertrand L. Kohlman	Pilot In sqd 5-16-43 to 6-4-44 to 12RCD
1Lt. John K. Kolb	Pilot In sqd 11-30-43 to Spring 44
2Lt. Williard J. Korsmeyer	POW on 7-31-44
2Lt. Richard I. Kuehl	Pilot In sqd 3-1-45 to 4-10=45. POW. Back to DX on 4-15-45.
Capt. Edward R. Kulik	Pilot In sqd 8-28-44 to EOW
2Lt. Charles E. Kuykendall	Pilot MIA on 9-5-44, evaded until Allies reached Holland
1Lt. Jack LaGrange, Jr.	Pilot In sqd 8-28-44 to 10-15-44 POW
Capt. Douglas A, Lawhead	Pilot To sqd. Feb 44 to 8-7-44 to US A Flt CO on 6-27-44. In Iceland 18 mos. with 50 FS prior to 78th.
1Lt. Major C. Leach	Pilot KIA 1-5-44
Capt. Vernon A. Leatherman	
1Lt. John R. Loegering	Pilot POW on 9-18-44
Capt. Charles P. London	Pilot to Sqd. 5-11-43 to 11-1-43 to US. A Flt CO on 7-15-43, First 8AF Ace on 7-30-43. DSC, 2DFC, RAF DFC, 4 Ams.
1Lt. Russell C. MacDuffee	Pilot In sqd 8-28-44 to 9-18-44 POW
Capt. John C. Mackall	Grnd Off. Sqd. Intell. Off.
1Lt. William H. Madole	Pilot In sqd 5-16-43 to 11-22-43 to MTO. BFlt CO,7-15-43
2Lt. George C. Maitland	Pilot, KIA 3-8-44
F/O. Samuel R. Martinek	Pilot, POW 5-14-43
1Lt. Vincent J. Massa	Pilot In sqd 3-6-44 to 6-10-44 KIA
1Lt. William M. McDermott	Pilot In sqd 3-6-44 to 6-10-44 KIA D Flt CO on 6-5-44.
Capt. Duncan M. McDuffie	Pilot In sqd 11-3—44 to EOW. Sqd Ops Off, Mar 45.
Maj. Donald W. McLeod	Pilot, Evader on 6-10-44, rets 9-1-44. To US 9-4-44. Sqd Ops Off, June 44.
Capt. Elmer E.McTaggart	Pilot, Evader, 5-14-43. ret'd 6-21-43 via Spain. US,
1Lt. Harry B. Meredith	
1Lt. Richard A. Messinger	Pilot, In sqd. March,45 to EOW.
Capt. Joel L. Meyer	Grnd Off In sqd Feb, 43 to EOW. Sqd Eng. Off.
1Lt. Edwin H. Miller	Pilot, In sqd. 7-4-44 to 3-31-45 to US A Flt CO in sqd.
1Lt. Jack B. Miller	Pilot, In sqd. 7-4-44 to 8-18-44 KIA
2Lt. Edwin Milliron	Pilot, In sqd. Fall, 44 to Jan, 45
1Lt. Royce H. Mintener	
1 Lt Donald R. Monteith	Pilot, In sqd. Dec 44 to EOW
1Lt. Jmaes M. Montfort	Pilot,To sqd. 4-28-43 to June, 1944
1Lt. James A. Moothart	Pilot, In sqd. 7-4-44 to Jan-Feb 45.
1Lt. John D. Motsenbocker	Pilot, In sqd. 1-14-44 to 5-8-44 POW
1Lt. Robert E. Mullins	Pilot, In sqd. 5-27-44 to 7-6-44 KIA
1Lt. Elmer K. Nieland	Pilot, In sqd. 10-15-44 to 3-19-45 POW
Capt. Ettry J. Oates	
F/O. Charles R. O'Brien	Pilot, In sqd. 12-29—44 to 2-26-45 KIA
2Lt. Martin G. O'Connell, Jr.	Pilot, To Sqd. 6-4-44 to 4-15-44 KIFA
1Lt. Leonard S. Olson	Pilot, In sqd. 12-15-44 to 2-26-45 POW
1Lt. Richard W. Oxley	Pilot, In sqd. 4-29-44
1Lt. Anthony A. Palopoli	Pilot, 12-15-44 to EOW
Capt. Charles M. Peal	Pilot, To Sqd 4-28-43 to 8-14-44 KIA. A Flt CO on 7-13-44. On 2nd tour, had 40 missions total.
1Lt. Henry L. Perry	Pilot, To Sqd 42 to 1-26-43 KIFA
1Lt. James S. Peterson	Pilot, In sqd 12-15-44 to EOW. Evader to Russia on 2-14-45 to 3-22-45. Resumed combat tour on return.
1Lt. Richard E. Phaneuf	Pilot to Sqd.11-13-44 to EOW Flew 49 Missions.
Capt. Donald G. Pickrell	
F/O. Robert E. Poole	Pilot, In sqd11-3-43
1Lt. Everett W. Powell	Pilot, In sqd 6-25-43 to 3-4-44 POW Nicknamed "Jake"
1Lt. Harley N. Powell	
1Lt.. Franklin R. Pursell	Pilot, In sqd 4-29-44
1Lt. Melvin D. Putnam	Pilot, In sqd 5-16-43 to 1 5-44 KIA
2Lt. Cleon W. Raese,Jr.	Pilot, In sqd KIA on 7-1- 44
Capt. Julian Reems	Pilot, In sqd 5-27-44 to 11-16-44. D Flt CO on 11-15-44.
1Lt. William H. Reese	Pilot, In sqd 1-14-44 to 4-11-44 KIA
2Lt. Frederick J. Regner	Pilot, To sqd 3-27-45 to EOW.
2Lt. Gennaro Riccardo	Pilot, In sqd 4-13-44 to after 7-5-44 when he was KIFA
2Lt. George Rich III	Pilot, POW on 9-6-44
Maj. Gilman C. Ritter	Grnd Off. In sqd. 1942 to 3-16-45.Ttrf'd Sqd Adj.
2Lt. Thomas F. Roche, Jr.	
1Lt. Harry C. Roff	Pilot, In sqd 5-16-43 to 3-4-44 to 551 FTG
1Lt. Robert F. Rohm	Pilot, In sqd 2-14-45 to EOW.
F/O. Robert I. Ronning	Pilot To sqd. 2-11-43 to 3-1-43. KIFA ex-RCAF pilot.
1Lt. Elwood E. Rugh	
1Lt. Henry Scharoff	Grnd Off In sqd. on VE-Day. Asst. Sqd. Intell Off
Capt. Philip A. Schifalacqua	
1Lt. Howard L. Seeley	Pilot, In sqd 8-28-44 to 4-2-45
1Lt. William B. Senarens	Pilot, In sqd 8-28-44 to 2-3-45 POW
1Lt. Thomas W. Shepard	Pilot, To sqd. 4-28-43 to April, 44. D Flt CO on 3-23-44. C Flt CO on 4-7-44, B Flt CO on 4-19-44
Capt. Montimore C. Shwayder	Grnd Off To sqd. summer, 42 to EOW. Sqd Flt Surg.,Thunderbolt band leader. Nickname "Monty".
2Lt. Jayson M. Smith	Pilot, To sqd 4-21-43 to 8-15-43 KIA Flew 20 missions
Maj. Robert "Rex" W. Smith	Pilot, In Sqd 4-29-44 to 12-27—44 to 3AD. USleve, Oct, 44 to 12-3-44. Sqd. Ops Off on 7-13-44
1Lt. Warrn B. Sommer	Pilot, In Sqd 10-15-44 and 11-16-44
1Lt. Boyd W.Sorenson	Pilot, In Sqd 4-29-44 to Fall 44. C Flt CO on 7-13-44. 89 missions. Ex-RCAF 1941-43. Flew 72 missions in Korea in an L-19. Nickname "Swede".
1Lt.. William B,Spengler	Pilot To sqd. Feb 45 to EOW
2Lt. Hanry M. Staub	Pilot, In sqd 2-14-45 to 3-2-45 POW
1Lt. James E. Stokes	Pilot, In Sqd 6-25-43 to 2-23-44 to 8FC. BFlt CO on 2-10-44
Col. James J. Stone, Jr.	Pilot to Sqd 5-11-42 to 7-1-43 to Hdqrs Sqd.Sqd.CO 5-11-42

1Lt. Earle W. Strobel | Pilot, In Sqd 3-45 to EOW
1Lt. Ford L. Sturdivant
1Lt. Dale S. Sweat | Pilot to sqd. 3-27-45 to EOW USAF Lt Gen (ret)
2Lt. Robert H. Talbot | Pilot, In Sqd 3-1-45 to 4-7-45 POW
2Lt. William Thomas
1Lt. Robert L. Thorkelsen
1Lt. Jerome R. Toffler
1Lt. Walter Tonkin | Pilot, In Sqd 11-30-43-to 3-16-44 KIA
F/O. John D. Tucker | Pilot
2Lt. John B. Wade | Pilot, In Sqd 12-29-44 to 2-23-45 POW
1Lt. William H. Waldheim | Pilot, In Sqd 4-22-43 and Jan, 44
Capt. Stuart B. Warwick | Grnd Off. to sqd. Summer 1942 to EOW. Sqd Intell Off. Thunderbolt Orch musician

2Lt. Albert B. Werde | Pilot KIA 3-30-44
1Lt. Frederick White | Pilot, In Sqd 4-29-44 D Flt CO on 7-13-44
2Lt. Donald Whitright
Capt. Dwight E. Wilkes | Pilot, In Sqd 6-25-43 to Sept 44. A Flt. CO on 4-19-44. Ex-RAF pilot. 3 DFCs, 3 AMs. KIFA on 11-30-50 at Nellis AFB.

Capt. Robert E. Wise | Pilot, In Sqd 1-14-44 to 3-31 45 to 7ORCD. CO of Sqd Flts.
1Lt. Harding R. Zumwalt | Pilot, To Sqd 2-11-43 to 4-20-44 to 495 FTG. C Flt. CO on 3-23-44. 2 DFCs, 3 AMs. Ex-RAF. Thunderbolt Orch. 71 missions, 200 combat hrs. in WW2. Qualified in 45 a/c types USAF Brig. Gen (ret)

84th Fighter Squadron Pilots and Key Staff

1Lt. Luther J. Abel | Pilot, In Sqd 3-6-44 to approx 7-6-44
F/O. Paul Ankney | Pilot, In Sqd April 45. No combat pre VE Day
Capt. Leon J. Armalavage | Grnd Off.
1Lt. Arthur N. Arpin | Pilot, In Sqd May 42 to Feb 43 to N. Africa DS to ferry P-38s. 51st FG, CBI, USAF Maj. (ret)
Capt. Noel H. Assink | Grnd Off. To Sqd. Oct 42 to Hdqrs Sqd. in 1943. Sqd. Personnel/Finance Off.
1Lt. Andrew M. Barba | Pilot, To Sqd. 2-16-43 to 5-17-44 to 495 FTG
1Lt. Richard L. Baron | Pilot, To Sqd.6-26-44 to 11-8-44 to US C. Flt CO,9-25-44
2Lt. Donald A. Bath | Pilot In Sqd. 11-10-44 to 3-7-45 KIFA
1Lt. Harold F. Beck | Pilot, To Sqd. 7-15-44 to 9-19-44 to 7ORCD. D Flt CO on 8-29-44. Previously in 82FS.
1Lt. Willard P. Behm | Pilot, In Sqd. 4-5-45 to EO:W
Capt. Robert E. Belliveau | Pilot, To Sqd. 4-22-43 to 4-18-44 to US
2Lt. Dwight G. Belt | Pilot, To Sqd. 7-24-44 to 10-1-44 KIFA
1Lt. Cyril Thomas Bendorf | Pilot, To Sqd. 11-10-44 to EOW
Maj. John R. Bertrand | Pilot, To Sqd. 2-16-43 to 5-24-44 to 495FTG. Sqd. Ops Off on 3-22-44.
1Lt. Warren S. Blodgett | Pilot, In Sqd. 11-11-44 to EOW
1Lt. Frederick G. Blumenthal
2Lt. James A Bolen | Pilot, To Sqd. 2-16-45 to 3-19-45 KIA
1Lt. John S. Bond | Pilot, To Sqd. 2-16-45 to EOW
2Lt. Lonnie E. Bowman | Pilot, In Sqd. April 45. No combat preVE Day
1Lt. Herbert L. Boyle | Pilot, In Sqd. Mid-Jan 44 to 7-27-44 to US. B Flt. CO on 7-15-44. Flew 86 missions, had 3 assigned P-47s in tour.
1Lt. Merle V. Brendle | Pilot, To Sqd. 12-16-44 to 2-20-45 KIA
2Lt. Richard Bretherton | Pilot, To Sqd. 12-16-44 to EOW
F/O. Charles R. Brown | Pilot POW on 5-16-43
2Lt. Charley W. Brown
Maj. Quince L. Brown | Pilot, To Sqd. 4-21-43 to 9-6-44 KIA. Sqd. Ops Off on 5-26-44. US lve after 1st tour.Back for 2nd tour on 8-28-44. First 8AF strafer on 7-3-43
Maj. Gillespie Bryan | Pilot, To Sqd. 5-12-44 as Sqd. CO from Hdqrs. Sqd.
Capt. Gerald E. Budd | Grd. Off in Sqd 1943 to EOW/Sqd. Eng. Off.
1Lt. James F. Byers | Pilot, In Sqd 4-17-43 to 7-30-43 KIA
1Lt. Severino B. Calderon | Pilot, To Sqd. 6-26-44 to 1-3-45 to Station 590 ASC
Capt. Carl E. Calloway | Pilot, To Sqd.7-29-44 to 3-28-45 to US D Flt DO, 1-18-45
1Lt. John D. Calvin | Pilot, To Sqd.2-16-45 to EOW
1Lt. Merle R. Capp | Pilot, To Sqd.7-15-44 from 82FS, 9-19-44 to 70th RCD. B Flt CO, 8-29-44. See also 82FS.
1Lt. James F. Casey | Pilot In Sqd 9-8-43 to 6-10-44. POW A Flt CO,5-26-44
1Lt. Martin J. Chaves | Grnd Off.Sqd. Eng. Off.
2Lt. Wayne M. Chavis
LtCol.. Charles M. Christ | Pilot, To Sqd. 7-24-44 to 9-9-44 to Hdqrs Sqd.
1Lt. Robert E. Clague | Pilot, In Sqd. 11-26-43 to 9-10-44 POW
Capt. Frank C. Clark
2Lt. Lawton E. Clark | Pilot, To Sqd. 6-26-44 TO 9-10-44 KIA
1LClark W. Clemons | Pilot, To Sqd. 2-16-45 To EOW
1Lt. Louis E. Coburn | Grnd Off
1Lt. Charles F. Coffee | Pilot, To Sqd. 2-16-45 To EOW
2Lt. John H. Coit | Pilot, To Sqd. April, 45 to EOW No combat pre-VE Day
1Lt. William M. Col.lins | Pilot, To Sqd.April, 45. No combat pre VE Day
2Lt. Rueben S. Connelly | Pilot, To Sqd.3-19-45 to 3-21-45. Evader to Russia.
LtCol.. Richard E. Conner | Sqd. CO on 3-19-45.
Maj. James M. Cooper | Pilot, To Sqd.6-20-44 from Hdqrs Sqd., trfd 7-13-44 to 356 FG
1Lt. Richard K. Corbett | Pilot, To Sqd. 12-16-44 to EOW
Capt. Lloyd K. Covelle | Pilot In Sqd. 8-23-43 to 6-24-44 to US.A flt. CO on 6-11-44. Nicknamed "Curly"
2Lt. Robert W. Cox
2Lt. Carl E. Cross | Pilot, InSqd 9-8-43 to 10-24-43
F/O. Gene T. Cummings | Pilot, To Sqd.7-29-44 to 8-6-44 POW
1Lt. William K. Dacci | Pilot In Sqd 1-24-44 to 6-21-44 to US. sqd Flt CO. Name changed to Dacy.
1Lt. Louis DeAnda | Pilot, To Sqd.10-8-44 to EOW
1Lt. William J. DeGain | Pilot In Sqd. 11-11-44 to EOW
2Lt. Kenneth J. DeMaagd | Pilot, To Sqd. 12-16-44 to 1-20-45, POW

F/O. Louis C. Dion | Pilot
2Lt. Dean W. Ditlevson
2Lt. Wayne M. Dougherty | Pilot, To Sqd.4-21-43 to 11-26-43 POW
1Lt. Andrew H. Downing | Pilot To Sqd. 4-22-43 to 12-9-43 to 495 FTG
Maj. Harry L. Downing | Pilot, To Sqd.10-9-44 to 12-54-44 to 82FS. Sqd. Ops Off on 10-9-44. To Sqd 3-14-45 to 3-19-45 POW. Sqd. CO on 3-14-45
Capt. Gray H. Doyle | Pilot, To Sqd.4-28-43 to Feb 44 to Hdqrs Sqd. Sqd. Ops Off on Feb 44.
Capt. Alfred F. Eaton | Pilot, In Sqd. 6-11-44 to 11-21-44 to US
1Lt. Herbert W. Elin | Pilot, To Sqd.7-29-44 to 1-13-45 KIA
Capt. James M. Farmer | Pilot, To Sqd. 9-22-44 to KIFA on a post VE Day trng flt.
1Lt. John R. Fee | Pilot, To Sqd. 12-24-43 to 9-18-44 POW
1Lt. Walter R. Fisher
Capt. Edward F. Fleming | Pilot, To Sqd. 2-16-43to 4-5-44 to 496 FTG C Flt CO, 3-4-44
2Lt. Lester E. Ford | Pilot, To Sqd. 6-26-44 to 7-11-44 POW
1Lt. George E. Gallant | Pilot, To Sqd. 3-28-45 to EOW
1Lt. Alfred A. Garback | Pilot, To Sqd. 9-2-44 to EOW Flt CO in Sqd.
1Lt.. Lake Giles | Pilot, To Sqd. 4-6-44 to 9-1-44 to US
Lt. Goldsworthy | Pilot In Sqd 3-3-45 to 4-6-45 Flew 10 missions.
2Lt. Robert N. Gore | Pilot, To Sqd. 2-16-43 to 11-10-43 to 310th Ferry Sqd.
Capt. Wilbur K. Grimes | Pilot, To Sqd. 6-26-44 to 1—16-45 to 7ORCD D Flt CO on 9-25-44 USAF Col.onel (ret)
1Lt. Leon M Grisham | Pilot, To Sqd. 9-22-44 to 2-3-45 POW
2Lt. Wallace R. Hailey | Pilot, In Sqd. 5-27-44 to 6-18-44 to transferred.
1Lt. Allen P. Haning | Pilot In Sqd. 6-11-44 to 11-26-44 to US.B Flt CO, 9-25-44
1Lt. William J. Hardin | Pilot In Sqd. 12-24-443 to 6-22-44 to US
1Lt. George T. Hartman | Pilot, To Sqd. 2-16-43 to 1-5-44 KIA
2Lt. D.D.Haskins | Pilot, To Sqd.3-28-45 to EOW
Capt. George J. Hays | Pilot, In Sqd.4-29-43 to 5-17-44 to 495 FTG
1Lt. John S. Hemphill | Pilot, To Sqd. 3-28-to EOW Flew combat pre VE Day
2Lt. Paul R. Henderson | Pilot, To Sqd. 3-28-45 to EOW
Capt. Carroll D. Henry
1Lt. Neal Hepner | Pilot, To Sqd.3-28-45 to EOW
2Lt. Louis R. Hereford | Pilot, To Sqd. 12-16-44 to 3-4-45 KIA
1Lt. Roy D. Higgins | Pilot, To Sqd. 7-24-44 to 3-1-45 KIA A Flt CO, 1-18-45
Capt. Richard M. Holly | Pilot, To Sqd. Feb,44 to 8-5-44 to 12RCD. Sqd CO on 6-11-44. Silver Star, 2DFCs, 7AMs. Ex-14FG/50FS P-'38 pilot in Iceland for 18 mos prior to 78th.
Maj. Bruce B. Hunt | Pilot, To Sqd. 4-24-45 to 5-12-45 to 83FS Sqd CO, 4-24-45
Capt. William F. Hunt | Pilot, To Sqd. 4-28-43 to 6-10-44 KIA. Sqd. Ops Off, 5-26-44
F/O. Franklin E. Hupe | Pilot, Transferred 4-15-43 to 6FW and later 4FG
Maj. John D. Irvin | Pilot, In Sqd. summer 42 to 3-17-44 to 8FC. Sqd. Ops Off in late 1943 /early 1944
1Lt. Danford E. Josey | Pilot, To Sqd. April 45 to EOW
1Lt. Harry H. Just, Jr. | Pilot, In Sqd.3-2-44 to 6-7-44 KIA
Capt. Peter T. Keillor | Pilot, To Sqd. 9-2-44 to EOW B Flt CO 12-2-44. Tour in Pacific prior to 78th. Sqd. Ops Off, 1945
2Lt. Walter Keller | Grnd Off to Sqd. 10-8-44
1Lt. William G. Kelly | Pilot, In Sqd. Oct/Nov 44 to 11-9-4 KIFA
1Lt. Charles N. Keppler | Pilot, To Sqd.4-21-43 to 2-6-44 to US
Capt. Glenn H. Koontz | Pilot, To Sqd.4-28-43 to 6-20-44 to US. C Flt CO on 5-26-44.
1Lt. Harold W. Kramer | Pilot In sqd 5-1-44 to 9-1-44 to US. Nicknamed "Pop"
2Lt.. John F. Lacey | Pilot, To Sqd. 4—6-44 to 8-28-44 POW
1Lt. Robert O. Laho | Pilot, To Sqd. 6-26-44 to 11-29-44 to US
1Lt. Ernest S. Lang | Pilot, In Sqd. 10-20-43 to 4-26-44 to US
Capt. Philip R. Larson | Pilot, To Sqd. 4-21-43 to 1-11-45 to 70th RCD.US Lve 4-12-44 to 7-14-44,ret'd for 2nd tour. Ass't Sqd Ops Off on 8-29—44.Nickname "Swede"
Capt. Harry T. Lay | Pilot, To Sqd. 6-26-44 to 7-17-44 KIA Ex-B-17 pilot on 2nd tour
Capt. Vernon A. Leatherman
Capt. Dorian Ledington | Pilot, In Sqd. 1-11-44 to 4-21-45 KIA on US lve. 6-24-4 to 10-2-44. Sqd CO on 3-21-45. Flew tour in RCAF prior to 78th
1Lt. Norbert G. Lentz | Pilot, To Sqd. 2-16-43 to 6-26-44 to 27 ATG.
1Lt.. Wilburn D. Lockwood | Grnd. Off.
2Lt. Daniel T. Loyd | Pilot, To Sqd. 6—6-44 to 6-10-44 KIA
Capt. William J. Luckey | Pilot, In Sqd. 5-1-44 to 9-24-44 to 7ORCD A Flt CO on 7-31-44
1Lt. Willis H. Lutz | Pilot, To Sqd.10-8-44 to EOW
Capt. Charles L. Lyle | Pilot, In Sqd. 10-15-44 to 2-20-45 KIA
Capt. William G. MacDonald | Grnd Off Sqd Flt Surg. May 1945
1Lt. Macie V. Marlow | Pilot, In Sqd. 10-20-43 to 4-26-44 to US
2Lt. Donald M. Marshall | Pilot InSqd. 4-17-43 to 6-13-43 POW
LtCol. Leonard P. Marshall | Pilot, To Sqd. 9-8-44 to 3-14-45 to Hdqrs Sqd. Sqd CO, 9-25-44.
1Lt. Lloyd Q. Marshall | Pilot, To Sqd. 6-26-44 to 11-21-44 to US
Capt. Julius P. Maxwell | Pilot, To Sqd. 4-28-43 to 1-4-45 to 7ORCD. On US lv 5-15-44 to 8-9-44. 2nd tour. B Flt CO 3-5-44. A Flt CO 8-29-44. 133 missions, 432 combat hours. Nickname "Max" DFCs and AMs.
Maj. William E. May | Pilot, To Sqd. 4-23-45 to 4-24-45 to hdqrs sqd. Acting Sqd CO on 4-23-45 Back to Grp Tact. Insp. on next day.
LtCol.. Benjamin I Mayo | Pilot, To Sqd. 4-15-44 to 6-8-44 to 82FS. ret'd to sqd on 7-13-44 to 9-25-44 to US on detached service. Trf'd to US on 2-5-45. Sqd. CO on 7-13-44, 2DFCs, 13 AMs, 2 Bronze Stars, 2 Croix de Guerre,USAF Col.(ret) Deceased 1-23-83
1Lt. William F. McCarthy | Grnd Off. to Sqd. Summer, 42 to EOW. Sqd Personal Equipm Off. Sqd Adj on 8-29-44
1Lt. William M McClellan | Pilot, To Sqd. 10-8-44 to EOW

1Lt. Allen G. McGuire	Pilot, To Sqd. 6-26-44 to 11-27-44 to US
1Lt. Robert J. McIntosh	Pilot, In Sqd. 5-1-44 to 6-10-44 POW
2Lt. Paul H. McKenney	Pilot, To Sqd. 6-26-44 to 9-10-44 POW
2Lt. William H. Miller	Pilot In Sqd. 6-23-44 to 9-1-44 to US
1Lt. James E. Moores	Pilot In Sqd. 11-11-44 to EOW
Capt. Jesse B. Morrison	Grnd Off. to sqd. Summer, 42 to EOW Sqd. Intell Off. nicknamed "Duke"
2Lt. Lonnie L. Mosely	Pilot, To Sqd. 6-26-44 to 7-4-44 POW
F/O Joseph W. Mundy	Pilot, In Sqd.1—28-44 to 4-15-44 KIA
1Lt. John L. Murphy	Pilot, To Sqd. 12-16-44 to EOW
2Lt. Richard A. Murray	Pilot In Sqd. 4-29-43 to 5-20-43 KIA
1Lt. Louis R. Musgrave	Pilot In Sqd. 10-8-44 to 2-24-45 KIA
2Lt. John J. Myler	Pilot, To Sqd. 7-24-44 to 8-5-44 KIA
2Lt.. Burton J. Newmark	Pilot, To Sqd.10-8-44 to 2-21-45 POW
1Lt. William Newton III	Pilot, In Sqd. 5-27-44 to 7-5-44 KIA
1Lt. James A. Nunley	Pilot, In Sqd.March 45 to EOW
1Lt. Frank E. Oiler	Pilot, To Sqd. 6-26-44 to 3-28-45 to US. F Flt CO, 2-22-45
1Lt. Charles S. Oldfield	Pilot, To Sqd. 11-13-44 to 2-25-45 Evader.Ret'd from working with Dutch Underground on 4-21-45.
1Lt. Paul S. Ostrander	Pilot, To Sqd.9-22-44 to 3-31-45 E Flt CO on 2-22-45.
1Lt. Ross Orr	Pilot, In Sqd.1-28-44 to 7-1-44 POW
1Lt. Allen R. Packer	Pilot, To Sqd. 9-22 -44 to 1-17-45 POW
2Lt. William R. Palmer	Pilot, To Sqd. 6-26-44 to 9-10-44 KIA
2Lt. Charles E. Parmelee	
1Lt. James O. Patton	Pilot In Sqd. 2-4-44 to 9-1-44 to US. D Flt CO Aug,44.
1Lt.Donald K. Pearson	Pilot, To Sqd.4-28-43 to 4-27-44 to US Nickname "Deacon".
1Lt. Earl M. Peterson	Pilot, In Sqd.11-26-43 to 4-26-44 to US
1Lt.Peter E. Pompetti	Pilot, To Sqd.2-16-43 to 3-17-44 to POW
Maj. Jack C. Price	Pilot, To Sqd. 5-10-42 to 2-25-44 to US. On US lv 2-25-44 to 10-14-44. ret'd for 2nd tour with 20FG in 67FW. Sqd CO, 9-28-43.104 mission, 290 combat hrs.
1Lt. John B. Putnam, Jr.	Pilot, To Sqd 4-26-44 to 7-19-44 KIFA
2Lt. Thomas N. Reeves	Pilot, In Sqd. 11-13-44 to 3-19-45 POW
1Lt. Franklin B. Resseguie	Pilot, In Sqd. Oct 43 to 10-18-43 POW
1Lt. Harold Hamilton Rice	Pilot In Sqd. 1-4-44 to 6-7-44 POW (used name 'Hamilton' only)
1Lt. George G. Rickett	Pilot, In Sqd. 5-27-44 and flew missions in June, 44 Trf'd to 5th Emergency Rescue Squad on 2-19-45
LtCol.. Eugene P. Roberts	Pilot, To Sqd. 5-10-42 to 9-3-44 to Hdqrs Sqd. Sqd CO in Aug 42. 190 combat hours on first tour.
1Lt. Anton A. Rosengreen	Pilot In Sqd. 1-15-45 to E OW
Capt. Raymond E. Ruotsala	Grnd Off. To Sqd. Summer, 42 to 8-29-44. Sqd. Adjt. prior to 8-29-44.
1Lt. Ernest E. Russell	Pilot, In Sqd.10-24-43 to 5-1-44 to US
F/O. Frank A. Ryan	Pilot, In Sqd.1-30-45 top EOW
Capt. Paul W. Saffold, Jr	Pilot, To Sqd. 2-16-43 to May,44 to US. B Flt CO on 3-22-44 Flew 96 combat missions.
2Lt. Warren J. Sawall	Pilot, To Sqd. 11-13-4 to 2-3-45 POW
1Lt. Carl H. Schneider	Pilot, To Sqd.4-26-44 to 9-19-44 to 70th RCD
1Lt. Edwin H. Schneider	
2Lt. George R. Schoenfeldt	Pilot, To Sqd. 3-28-45 to EOW
F/O. Lawrence B. Sheppard	Pilot
Capt. Charles W. Silsby	Pilot, In Sqd.5-4-43 to 4-15-44 KIA A Flt. CO on 3-22-44
1Lt. Henry R. Slack	Pilot To sqd. 11-13-44 to EOW
1Lt. Eugene F. Smith	Pilot, To Sqd. 1-30-45 to EOW
1Lt. Martin H. Smith Jr	Pilot In Sqd 1-14-44 to 7-19-44 KIFA A Flt CO,7-15-44
Maj. Raymond E. Smith	Pilot, To Sqd. Mar,43 to 3-28-45 to 70th RCD. U.S. lve 5-15-44 to 8-9-44, back for 2nd tour. Sqd Ops Off 9-25-44. Two Silver Stars, DFCs,AMs
2Lt. Robert D. Smith	Pilot In Sqd 9-26-44 to 10-7-44 KIA
Maj Verne W. Smith	Grnd Off to Sqd. Summer, 42 to EOW Sqd Exec.
2Lt. John R. Sole	Pilot, To Sqd. 1-30-45 to 4-21-45. KIA
2Lt. Roger A. Spaulding	Pilot, To Sqd. 1-30-45 to 4-10-45 POW
1Lt. Richard H. Spooner	Pilot, To Sqd. 9-2-44 to 1-15-45 POW
Capt. Earl L. Stier	Pilot, To Sqd. 9-22-44 to EOW Co of Flt, Spring, 45
Capt. Warren G. Straley	Pilot, To Sqd. March 43 to 3-17-44 to CBI Theatre Sqd. Ops Off, 2-28-44
Maj. Harold E. Stump	Pilot, To Sqd. 5-10-42 to 6-10-44 KIA on US lv May, 44 to 6-8-44 Sqd CO 2-25-44
2Lt. Raymond Symons	Grnd Off. to Sqd 12-16-44 to EOW
1Lt. Clyde E. Taylor	Pilot, To Sqd. 1-30-45 to EOW
1Lt. Howard M. Taylor	Grnd Off Sqd. Armament Off. Nicknamed "Buck"
2Lt. Richard W. Taylor	Pilot, In Sqd. 1-15-45 to EOW
1Lt. Thomas V. Thain	Pilot, To Sqd. 1-30-45 to EOW
1Lt. William D. Townsend	Pilot, In Sqd. 11-16-44 to 3-1-45, KIA.
F/O. William H. Vallee	Pilot
1Lt. Stephen Wasylyk	
2Lt. Roy E. Wendell	Pilot, In Sqd. 2-6-44 to 3-13-44 KIFA
1Lt. Charles D. Whitefield	Pilot, In Sqd.7-6-44 to 11-25-44 to US
1Lt. Harold T. Wilheim	
1Lt. George W. Willingham	Grnd Off.
1Lt. Donald R. Wilson	Pilot, In Sqd. 2—6-44 to 7-28-44 to US D Flt CO, 7-15-44
1Lt. Mark T. Wilson	Pilot,To Sqd.9-2-44 to 2-25-44. Evader. Ret'd 4-21-45
1Lt. Hugh V. Wingfield	Pilot In Sqd.March 45 to EOW
2Lt. Eugene W. Wood	Pilot,To Sqd.9-2-44 to 9-18-44 KIA

APPENDIX 4

PERSONNEL LOSSES

Legend for Loss Listing

1. Date of the loss given in U.S.Civil Style month/date/year. Losses are listed chronologically
2. Casualty's name, with the last name first.
3. Rank of the casualty at time of loss.
4. Unit to which casualty was assigned at time of loss.
5. Casualty's fate i.e. KIA, KIFA,WIA,POW or Evader
6. Location
7. Brief details of the loss
8. Type, serial number and code letters of the a/c lost with the casualty where known.

Summer, 1942	**Hubbell** 2Lt. 82FS KIFA North Island NAS, CA.
8-10-42	**Sumner** 2Lt. 82 FS KIFA P-38.
Summer/Fall	**Baugh** 2Lt. 82FS KIFA P-38.
9-13-42	**Seppich, Wendell** 2 Lt. 82FS KIFA Pacific Ocean off LaJolla,CA P-38.
1-26-43	**Beals, Donald S.** 1 Lt 83FS Missing on a ferry flight to North Africa P-38 41-7576.
1-26-43	**Perry, Henry L.** 1Lt. 83FS KIFA Enroute to Langford Lodge, Ireland. He had a midair Col.lision with Lt. White. P-38F 42-12905.
1-26-43	**White, Stephan L.** 2 Lt. 82FS KIFA See perry above. P-38F 42-12928.
3-1-43	**Ronning, Robert I** F/O 83FS KIFA Goxhill A/F UK. Had a mid-air Col.lision with another landing P-47. He crashed and exploded on the base parade ground. P-47C.
4-15-43	**Dodd, LeRoy V** 2Lt. KIFA North of RAF station Tensford, near Bedford P-47 41-6241 HL-W.
5-14-43	**Adamina Robert E** Capt. 82FS POW In the North Sea off Belgium. He ditched in the sea due to B/D in a dogfight near Antwerp. P-47C 41-6198 MX-D.
5-14-43	**Martinek, Samuel R.** F/O 83FS POW in the North Sea. He called MayDay and bailed out 10 mi northwest of Knocke, Belgium. P-47C 41-6208 HL-T.
5-14-43	**McTaggart, Elmer E.** Capt. 83FS Evader in Belgium. Returned through France and Spain on 6-21-43 P-47C 41-6382 HL-C.
5-14-43	**Sandmeier, Jack S** 2Lt. 82FS KIA In the North Sea enroute to Rotterdam. Bailed out due to engine trouble and was last ssen in his dinghy. ASR did not find him. P-47.
5-16-43	**Brown, Charles R.** F/O 82FS POW In the Maldegen /Eccloo, Belgium area . Shot down in combat P-47 41-6318 MX-K.
5-20-43	**Murray, Richard A.** 2Lt. 84FS KIA Forty miles off the UK coast in the North Sea. Bailed out but was not seen to get into his dinghy. ASR was unsuccessful. P-47 41-6383 WZ-S..
6-13-43	**Brown, Ora R** 2Lt. 82FS KIA Loss data unknown P-47.
6-13-43	**Marshall, Donald M.** 2Lt. 84FS POW Lumbres, Belg. area. Shot down in an airfight P-47 41-6353 WZ-D.
6-28-43	**Feril Rudolfo H.** Cpl 82FS Killed in England. Whittlesford, Cambs, UK. Was hitchhiking to Grimsby, Lancs. when a British tank broke a track and pinned him against a wall.
7-1-43	**Peterson, Arman** LtCol. Hdq. Sqd. KIA 40 miles fromthe UK coast toward Ouddorp, Belgium. Last seen at 29,000 feet engaging enemy aircraft P-47 42-7948 MX-P.
7-14-43	**Jackson, Donald G.** 1 Lt. 82FS KIA Believed hit and killed by fire from B-17 gunners. P-47 41-6222 MX-J.
7-30-43	**Byers, James F.** 1 Lt. 84 FS KIA Winterswijk, Netherlands. Col.lided in mid-air withLtCol. McNickle at 28,000 feet just as enemy aircraft were engaged. P-47 42-7935 WZ-I.
7-30-43	**Graff, Warren E.** 2 Lt. 82FS Evader Bailed out over Holland. Returned to UK 11-15-43 and was sent home. P-47 41-6391 MX-Y.
7-30-43	**McNickle, Melvin F.** LtCol. Hdq. Sqd POW Winterswijk, Netherlands. His aircraft oxygen failed and he passed out, coming to in the crashed wreckage of his plane. P-47 42-7961 WZ-M.
8-15-43	**Smith, Jayson M** 2Lt. 3FSA KIFA Lost control of the aircraft and crashed fatally 2 and one half miles west of the base. P-47 42-7952 HL-Y.
8-27—43	**Brower, Robert F.** 2Lt. 82FS KIFA Near Henlow Airfield. UK Spun out of cloud an crashed during the flight to a coastal airfield for show staging. P-47.
9-22-43	**Charlton, Quentin** 2Lt. 83FS KIA In the North Sea. Bailed out due to a fuel leak. While seen in the sea, he did not get into his dinghy. ASR was unsuccessful. P-47 41-6411 HL-N.
10-18-43	**Resseguie, Franklin B.** 2 Lt.84 FS POW Near Lens & St. Omer, France. Had engine trouble and was last seen 10,000 feet below the Goup gliding inland. P-47 41-6240 WZ-E.
10-24-43	**Cross Carl E.** 2Lt. 84 FS KIFA Killed during a routine training flight in the UK. P-47 unk.
11-26-43	**Cormier Ralph E.** F/O 83 FS KIA Paris, France area. Shot down in aerial combat. P-47 42-8681 HL-E.
11-26-43	**Dougherty, Wayne M** 2Lt. 84FS POW. North of Paris, France. Hit by an ME 109 and seen to split-ess under control, but smoking and he was not seen again. P-47 42-8573 WZ-L.
11-26-43	**Herrick, John** 2 Lt. 82FS POW 10 miles northeast of Beauvais, France. He was shot down in the big air battle. P-47 41-6188 MX-U.
12-10-43	**Wright, Melvin R.** 1 Lt 82FS KIFA On a practice flight near Duxford he split-essed from 8,000 feet and went straight in. P-47 unk.
12-30-43	**Eastwood, James C.P.** F/O 83FS KIA In the English Channel 50 miles south of Beachy Head, UK. Bailed out and was seen to get into his dinghy, but ASR did not find him. P-47 41-6540 HL-A.
1-5-44	**Granger, Arthur S** 2Lt. 83FS KIA In France on mission return. One of five pilots low on gas when enemy aircraft jumped them. P-47 42-8622 HL-N.
1-5-44	**Hartman, George T.** 1 Lt 84 FS KIA North of LaRochelle, France. Jumped by enemy aircraft last seen with P-47 42-8538 WZE smoking.

136

1-5-44	**Hindersinn, Kenneth** 2Lt. 83FS POW Probably in the same area as Lt. Hartman, one of five pilots shot down on mission return. P-47 42-74652 HL-K.
1-5-44	**Leach, Major C.** 1Lt. 83 FS KIA Same as above P-47 41-6331 HL-L
1-5-44	**Putnam, Melvin D.** 1Lt. 83 FS KIA same area as above P-47 41-6581 HL-Q.
1-24-44	**Hahn Clifford B.** 1 Lt. 82 FS KIA Missed England, UK radar tracked them 30 degrees off course out into the Atlantic Ocean from Dieppe, France. Was with Lt. Neel on show return and neither had working radios. P-47 42-7923 MX-I.
1-24-44	**Neel, William F** 1Lt. 82FS KIA With Lt. Hahn, same as above. P-47 42-22467 MX-J.
1-29-44	**Ramsey, Milton H.** 2Lt. 82FS Evader. Bailed out over France after a dogfight with 25 enemy aircraft near Coblenz, Germany. Returned to sqd. on 6-21-44. P-47 42-22463 MX-J.
2-10-44	**Jones, Y.V.** 2Lt. 82FS KIA Lost in arial combat P-47 42-7883 MX-X
2-10-44	**Ludwig, Donald E.** 2 Lt. 82 FS KIA In the North Sea. He was hit by flak and his engine quit. Last seen coming out over the Dutch Coast. P-47 41-6249 MX-H.
2-11-44	**Daniels, Archie F.** F/O 83FS KIFA Near Nuthampstead, UK Crashed in a forced landing due to a runaway prop. P-47 42-7963. HL-T .
2-11-44	**Morsch, Donald R.** 2Lt. 82 FS KIA Crashed 12 km southwest of Arras, France. Last seen with Lt. Swanson near Luxembourg. They were bouncing an ME109 into clouds at 6-7,000 feet. Buried in British Soldier's Cematery at FiCheux, France P-47 42-22755 MX-D.
2-11-44	**Swanson, William S.** 1 Lt. 82FS KIA He was with Lt. Morsch when last seenand was lost about the same time. P-47 42-74733 MX-P.
2-22-44	**Johnson, John H.** 2 Lt 83FS POW Over Holland. He was shot down by FW 190s on the mission return. P-47 41-6335 HL-A.
2-29-44	**Orr, Ronald C.** 2 Lt. 82FS POW Amiens/Lille, France area. He bailed out when his engine caught fire. P-47 42-7916 MX-O.
3-4-44	**Powell, Everett W.** 1 Lt 83 FS POW Between Antwerp and Brussels, Belgium. He bailed out due to mechanical failure. P-47 41-6374 HL-U.
3-6-44	**Downey, Edward J.** F/O 83FS KIA Near Haselvenne, Germany between Dummer and Steinhuder Lakes was last seen being attacked by an FW190D P-47 42-7983 HL-W.
3-6-44	**Turley, Grant M.** 1 Lt. 82FS KIA Near Haselvenne, Germany He was shot down during an airfight. P-47 42-7998 MX-N.
3-8-44	**Maitland, George C.** 2 Lt. 83FS KIFA At Barking, near Needham Market, Suffolk, UK. Returning from mission in bad clouds and crashed. P-47 41-6229 HL-J.
3-13-44	**Wedell, Roy E.** 2 Lt. 83 FS KIFA Details unknown.
3-16-44	**Tonkin, Walter** 1 Lt 83FS KIA In France attacking an enemy aircraft on the deck, his wing hit the ground. P-47 42-8543 HL-U.
3-17-44	**Hotchkiss, Courtlyn W.** 2 Lt. 83FS POW Rheims, France area.He was strafing an airdrome and was hit by flak. P-47 42-8688 HL-B.
3-17-44	**Pompetti, Peter E.** 1 Lt 84FS POW Pierrefitte, France. He was hit by flak strafing Beauvais Airdrome. P-47 42-74641 WZ-Z.
3-17-44	**Ulerick, Estel E.** 2 Lt. 82 FS WIFA on an English bomber base. During a P-47 test hop. He was badly burned about his face and neck. P-47 42-8476 MX -? "Little Demon".
3-30-44	**Werder, Albert B.** 2Lt. 83FS KIA Venlo Airdrome, Netherlands. Hit by small arms fire while strafing and bailed out. P-47 42-7906 HL-R.
4-1-44	**Webb, Calvin** 2Lt. 82FS KIA Details unknown P-47 41-6535 MX-I.
4-5-44	**Eakes, Harvey L.** 2 Lt. 82FS KIA Hit by flak while strafing. P-47 42-75602 MX-E..
4-11-44	**Reese, William H.** 1 Lt 83FS KIA In the Lingen Germany area. Hit by flak as he pulled up from strafing a locomotive. P-47 41-6210 HL-M.
4-13-44	**Roberts, Donald R.** 2Lt. 82FS POW Attacked from the rear by an FW190. Last seen going into clouds with his plane smoking. P-47 42-76074 MX-H.
4-15-44	**Mundy, Joseph W.** F/O 84FS KIA In the North Sea. He stuck with his leader, Captain Silsby, who dove out of a climb at 21,000 feet through overcast. Neither answered R/T calls or were seen again. ASR impossible due to bad weather. P-47 42-76412 WZ-V.
4-15-44	**Silsby, Charles W.** Capt. 84FS KIA In the North Sea. See Mundy for details. P-47 42-25537 WZ-A.
4-15-44	**O'Connell, Martin G. Jr.** 2Lt. 83FS KIFA On a local flight and crashed in sight of the base P-47 42-76474 HL-O.
5-8-44	**Motsenbocker, John D.** 1Lt. 83FS POW Near Verden, Germany Shot down in air battle by ME109s. P-47 42-76227 HL-P.
5-11-44	**Kosinski, Anthony L.** 2Lt. 82FS Evader Dijon, France. Engine shot up by the airdrome flak and he bailed out near the field. MX-O.
5-11-44	**Steele, James F.** 2Lt. 82FS Interned in Switzerland. Flak hit in his engine while strafing Dijon Airdrome, France and bailed out. P-47 42-25994 MX-Q.
5-12-44	**Hagarty, Daniel D.** 1 Lt. 82FS POW Trier, Germany area. He was shot down in a giant dogfight with 100 plus enemy aircraft after destroying 2-0-1 FW190s P-47 42-26025 MX-R.
5-24-44	**Genge, William H.** 2Lt. 82FS POW South of Alkamaar, Netherlands. Was seen bailing out due to engine trouble. P-47 42-76585 MX-F.
5-27-44	**Hartman, John P.** Sgt. 82FS Killed on Duty. A squadron armorer, bicycling 6 miles east of DX. A P-51 buzzing the 409 BG's Little Walden base Col.lided with an A-20 taking of. John ran to the crash and rescued a gunner, helped by a passing nurse. Both he and the nurse were blown 40 feet when the plane's bombs went off. He died 7 hours later in hospital.
5-28-44	**Hazelett, Phillip H.** 1Lt. 82FS KIA Osnabruck, Germany area. Was hit by flak strafing an airdrome and he bailed out. P-47 unk. MX-Y.
5-28-44	**Juchheim, Alvin M.** Capt. 83FS POW Gardelegen, Germany. Was at 22,000 feet maneuvering to attack enemy aircraft when he

	Col.lided head on with a 363FG P-51 . The P-51 blew up killing its pilot. Alvin parachuted. P-47 42-26016 HL-A.
5-28-44	**Orvis, William S., Jr.** 2Lt. 82FS KIA Osnabruck, Germany area. Believed to have bailed out, but not seen to go down. P-47 unk MX-W.
6-4-44	**Wilkinson, James W.** Capt. 82FS KIFA Near Llandovery, Carmarthenshire, South Wales, UK, P-47 unk. MX-G.
6-5-44	**Steinwedel, John C.E.** 2Lt. 82FS KIA Last seen near Amiens Fr. His flight was climbing through severe icing at 16,000 feet when he dropped out of it with 6-8" icicles protruding into the slipstream from his guns. P-47 unk MX-Y.
6-7-44	**Just, Harry H ,Jr.,** 1 Lt. 84FS KIA Montdidier, France. He ran into 20 plus ME109s jumping him from below the overcast and he was shot down. P-47 42-25712 WZ-T.
6-7-44	**Rice, H. Hamilton** 1Lt. 84FS POW Montdidier France. Was in the dogfight with 20 plus bouncing ME109s below overcast and he was shot down. P-47 42-76184 WZ-K.
6-10-44	**Baker, Robert L.** 82FS KIA During low-level strafing. Flak possibly hitting his two underwing bombs. P-47 42-8471 MX-X.
6-10-44	**Casey, James F.** 1Lt. 84FS POW Near Argentan, France. Shot down by 20 plus bouncing enemy aircraft as the 78th was doing bomb runs. P-47 42-26149 WZ-M.
6-10-44	**Hunt, William F.** Capt. 84FS KIA Near Argentan Fr. Killed in the fight with 20 plus Germans catching the Group in their bomb runs. P-47 42-26031.WZ-W.
6-10-44	**Kuehner, Richard S.** 2Lt. 82FS KIA Beaumont LeRoger, Fr. Hit a tree or pole on a bomb run and crashed with his bombs exploding. P-47 42-26317 MX-X.
6-10-44	**Loyd, Daniel T.** 2Lt. 84FS KIA Presumed killed in the fight with 20 plus enemy aircraft jumping the Group. P-47 42-25981 WZ-Z
6-10-44	**Massa, Vincent J.** 1 Lt. 83 FS KIA Near Argentan, FR same as above. P-47 43-25319 IIL-S.
6-10-44	**McDermott, William M.** 1Lt. 83FS KIA South of London, UK While climbing through the overcast outbound, he had a mid-air Col.lision with Lt. Kochanek and crashed. P-47 42-26053 HL-E.
6-10-44	**McIntosh, Robert J.** 1 Lt 84FS .POW near Argento, FR. Same battle as Loyd. P-47 42-76506 WZ-O.
6-10-44	**McLeod, Donald W.** Major 83FS Evader. Same battle as Loyd. On the ground he counted P-47 and ME109 wreckage, Returned to Allied Lines on DX on 9-1-44. P-47 42-76505 HL-V.
6-10-44	**Stump, Harold E.** Major 84 FS KIA Same battle as Loyd. Was on his first mission after US leave. P-47 42-25736 WZ-X.
6-12-44	**Ramsey, John C.** Capt. 82FS KIA His aircraft got a direct hit by heavy flak, while fighter bombing a rail yard. Crashed in flames. First mission. P-47 42-75591 MX-C.
6-20-44	**Hodges, Benjamin H.** 2Lt. 82FS KIA Shot down by ME109s. P-47 42-26446 MX-I.
6-22-44	**Gibbs, Ollie, E.** 2Lt. 83FS KIA His plane developed prop trouble on takeoff. Tried to land with full load of belly tank and two bombs and crashed. P-47 42-26623 HL-E.
June, 1944	**Riddick, Montell** T/Sgt 83FS WIA A Crew chief, he fell off his bicycle directing a taxiing P-47 and was clipped by its prop on his left arm and leg. Two months in hospital, discharged in Jan. 1945.
7-1-44	**Kitley, Edward T.** 1 Lt 83FS KIFA During takeoff with 2-250 lb. bombs and a full belly tank, had a mid-air Col.lision with his wingman, Lt. Raese, about 300 yds west of the field at 150 ft. altitude. Both pilots died instantly in the crash and fire. P-47 43-25513 HL-R.
7-1-44	**Orr, Ross** 1 Lt. 84FS POW St. Quentin, FR. Was bounced by 30 plus ME109s at 16,000 feet with a full bomb load. Last seen at 14,000 feet, diving straight down with cockpit in flames. P-47 42-26640 WZ-X.
7-1-44	**Raese, Cleon W., Jr.** 2 Lt 83FS KIFA See Kitley loss for details. P-47 43-25588 HL-F.
7-4-44	**Moseley, Lonnie L.** 2 Lt 84FS POW Near Routot, Fr. Engine froze due to oil loss over Paris. Bailed out. Chute opened at 100 ft. P-47 43-25529 WZ-L.
7-5-44	**Newton, William, III** 1 Lt. 84 FS KIA Details unknown P-47 42-26583 WZ-T.
7-6-44	**Mullins, Robert E.** 1 Lt. 83FS KIA Rambouille, Fr. area. Believed shot down by FW190s. P-47 42-26536 HL-M.
7-11-44	**Ford, Lester E.** 2Lt. 84FS POW Picked off when 10 plus ME109s attacked. P-47 43-25313 WZ-N.
7-17-44	**Lay, Harry T.** Capt. 84FS KIA Liffel-LeGrand, Fr. Hit by flak while strafing troop train. Bailed out, landing in field. Last seen runing into woods to the east. P-47 42-26652 WZ-Z.
7-19-44	**Munson, Norman D.** Major, 82FS KIA Freundenstadt Airdrome, Germany. Plane hit by flak and crashed and burned on the edge of the field P-47 42-26671 MX-X.
7-19-44	**Putnam, John B., Jr.** 1 Lt. 84FS KIFA His friend, a co-pilot in the 401 BG at Deenethorpe, took him and others for a joy ride in his B-17 which clipped a beacon on the 84FS hangar while buzzing the field.
7-19-44	**Smith, Martin H. Jr.** KIFA He was a passenger with Lt. Putnam in the B-17 which clipped the beacon on base.
7-19-44	**Taylor, Ernest** Sgt. 83FS KIFA He was in the 83FS barracks when the B-17 with a full load of fuel crashed ino the building.
7-26-44	**Morris, Harold J.** 1Lt. 83FS KIA West of Laval, Fr. While strafing trucks, he hit the tree tops and crashed into a small forest. P-47 42-26461 MX-V.
7-31-44	**Korsmeyer, Willard J.** 2Lt. 83FS POW Neustad Airdrome, Germany. Engine got a direct hit on the deck and he pulled up and bailed out. P-47 42-26672 HL-V.
8-2-44	**Clark, Charles R.** Capt. 82FS POW His engine was hit while strafing; bailed out. P-47 42-26314 MX-F.

8-5-44	**Myler, John J.** 2 Lt. 84FS KIA 20 miles east of Bremen, Ger. He crashed in a vertical diving attack at an A/D. P-47 42-74723 WZ-P.
8-6-44	**Cummings, Gene T.** F/O 84 FS POW Bailed out over enemy territory when his prop ran away. P-47 42-76584 WZ-H.
8-8-44	**Fitzgerald, James T.** 1 Lt. 82FS POW East of Brias, Fr. on St.Pol/ Lille Road. Shot down by a flak battery P-47 43-25536 MX-J.
8-10-44	**Dicks, Louis A.** 1 Lt. 82FS KIA North of Epernay, Fr. Hit by flak while strafing a m/y and crashed in flames. P-47 42-26333 MX-Q.
8-13-44	**Smith, Billy V.** 2Lt. 82FS KIA 3 miles from DX on return. His last control wire broke as he peeled off to land and he went straight into the ground. P-47 42-26512 MX-?.
8-14-44	**Peal, Charles M.** Capt. 83FS KIA Near Noyon, Fr. Last seen in heavy flak after his bomb run on a train. P-47 42-26449 HL-X.
8-18-44	**Miller, Jack B.** 1 Lt. 83FS KIA Near Bottisham, Cambs, UK Returning from a show and Col.lided in mid-air with a 361 FG P-51. P-47 42-26458 HL-S.
8-26-44	**Coss, Wilbur J.** Capt. 82FS Evader Last hard on the R/T that he was climbing for altitude to bail out. Returned to DX on 9-16-44. P-47 42-26685 MX-K.
8-28-44	**Gilbert, Olin E.** LtCol. Hdq. Sqd. Evader Charleroi A/D, Belgium. His aircraft was hit by flak and he bellied in safely. He evaded back to the UK in a fortnight. P-47 42-28408 HL-X.
8-28-44	**Lacy, John F.** 2Lt. 84FS POW Beaumont, Belgium area. Strafing a train when ordnance explosion damaged his aircraft and he bellied in. P-47 42-8650 WZ- O.
9-1-44	**Dunaway, Kenneth P.** 2Lt. 83FS POW Gilze Rijen Airdrome, Neth. Hit by light flak an bailed out near Brussels, Belg. P-47 42-22776 HL-U.
9-1-44	**Jones, Robert N.** 2 Lt. 83FS KIA Hit by an exploding locomotive and he bailed out. P-47 42-26543 HL-K.
9-3-44	**Stark, Richard D.** 2Lt. 82FS POW Near Maastricht, Neth area. Hit by flak and crashlanded. P-47 42-27607 MX-G.
9-3-44	**Marsh, Wayne T.** Sgt. 989th M.P. Co. Killed on Duty. At Pampisford, Sawston. Went to the crash site of an RAF Halifax bomber to assist in rescue. Was killed when its bombload detonated.
9-3-44	**Shoemaker,William M.** 1Lt. 2027th. Engineering Fire-Fighting Platoon. Killed on duty. Pampisford, Sawston, Cambs., UK See above.
9-3-44	**Streb, Louis F.** 1 Lt. 989th MP Co. Killed on duty, 78FG Provost Marshall. See above.
9-5-44	**Doyle, Gray H.** Capt. Hdq. Sqd. KIA In the Metelen Bel. area. Was seen to spin into the ground after strafing a train. P-47 44-19573 HL-P.
9-5-44	**Kuykendall, Charles E.** 2Lt. 83FS Evader After being hit by light flak while strafing a train, he belly landed and was seen walking away from his aircraft. Hid out for 3 months with a Dutch family. P-47 42-76563 HL-B.
9-6-44	**Brown, Quince L.** Maj. 84FS KIA Near Schleiden, Germany. Scouting Vogelsang A/D near Weirmuehle, Ger. when he was hit by flak. Bailed out. Shortly after he landed, a German civilian shot him dead. P-47 44-19569 WZ-Z.
9-6-44	**Rich, George III** 2 Lt. 83FS POW Near Heuzer, Ger. Flak damage to his a/c and he bailed out. P-47 76486 HL-I.
9-9-44	**Moore, Kenneth L.** 2Lt. 82FS KIA At Dellhofen 2 km south of Oberwesel, Ger. His unit was split by attacking FW190s and he was last heard of crossing the Rhine River. P-47 42-76351 MX-O.
9-10-44	**Clague,Robert E.** 1 Lt 84FS POW Hit by flak at an A/D and he bellied in. P-47 42-25698 WZ-F.
9-10-44	**Clark, Lawton** 2Lt. 84FS KIA At Heilbronn, Ger. Strafing a M/Y and flew into target. P-47 42-26590 WZ-E.
9-10-44	**Lacy, Wiliam O.** 2Lt. 82FS KIA At Mainbullan A/D, Ger. Hit by intense flak, a/c rolled over on its back and crashed. P-47 42-75243 MX-B.
9-10-44	**McKenny, Paul H.** 2Lt. 84FS POW at Aschaffenburg aux. A/D, Ger. After being hit by flak, he pulled away from the A/D apparently to belly in and was not seen after that. P-47 43-25303 WZ-I.
9-10-44	**Parmelee, Charles E.** 2Lt. 84FS KIA Near Wiesbaden, Ger. His a/ c was hit by flak. He was belly landing and ran into a stone wall. P-47 43-25593 WZ-L.
9-18-44	**Fee, John R.** 1 Lt 84FS POW At Nijmegen, Neth. Hit by flak at the north end of the Nijmegen bridge and seen to spin into a lake fro 2-3,000 feet. P-47 42-25985 WZ-C..
9-18-44	**Loegering, John R.** 1Lt. 83FS POW 5 miles southwest of Goch, Neth. Hit by flak and belly landed his a/c. P-47 42-76587 HL-Q.
9-18-44	**MacDuffee, Russell C.** 1Lt. 83FS POW 5 miles north of Turnnout, Neth. Hit by heavy flak and bailed out. P-47 42-26020 HL-M.
9-18-44	**Snyder, William C.** 1Lt. 82FS POW Southwest of Rotterdam, Neth. He belly landed after a flak hit. P-47 42-75551 MX-M.
9-18-44	**Wood, Eugene W.** 2Lt. 84FS KIA Near Arnhem/Nijmegen, Neth. He was afire by Light flak while strafing and seen to crash. P-47 43-25297 WZ-D.
9-23-44	**Hartley, Dunstan D.** 2Lt. 83FS KIA Heteren, Neth. Went into the ground west of the town after being hit by light flak. P-47 42-28635 HL-X.
10-1-44	**Belt, Dwight G.** 2Lt. 84FS KIFA Details of his death in the UK are unknown.
10-7-77	**Smith, Robert D.** 2Lt. 84FS. KIA 6 miles northwest of Neustadt, Ger. After his 2nd pass at a locomotive, he was seen to mush into a woods. P-47 43-25305 WZ-I.
10-15-44	**LaGrange, Jack, Jr.** 1 Lt. 83FS POW Was not seen after a strafing pass at Fassberg A/D near Munster, Ger. Later he radioed that his engine was hit and he didn't know if he could get home. P-47 42-28544 HL-K.

11-9-44	**Jacobson, Alan R.** 2 Lt. 83FS KIA At Eisenberg, Ger. After being hit by flak, he was seen to bail out at 1,200 feet. His chute came out of its pack, but he was too low for it to deploy properly. P-47 44-19932 HL-B.
11-9-44	**Kelly, William G.** 1Lt. 84FS KIFA Details of his death in the UK are unknown.
11-21-44	**Thompson, Harry A.** 2 Lt. 82FS POW At Gutersloh A/D Ger. After flak got him, he bellied in and set his a/c on fire, and ran from the site. Evaded for a time but tired of wandering and surrendered in Warensdorf, Ger. P-47 44-19908 MX-B.
11-26-44	**Eggleston, Troy L.** 2Lt. 82 FS KIA In the Dummer Lake/Rheine, Ger. area. Last seen during an air battle in this vicinity. P-47 42-27297 MX-V.
11-26-44	**Hockery, John J.** Capt. 82FS POW The Rheine, Ger. area. Dogfighting three FW 190s and lost part of his wing to gunfire and crashlanded. He got 2-1-0 in the fight. P-47 44-19950 MX-L.
1-2-45	**Morrison, George W.** F/O 82FS POW 25 miles north of Saarbrucken, Ger. His engine quit and he bailed out. P-51 44-11657 MX-D.
1-6-45	**Grimes, Wilbur K** Capt. 84FS Evader One half mile north of Marche, Belg. Hit by flak at Speyer, Ger. and developed oil leak. Engine froze at 1,200 ft and he bailed out. The Underground helped him to evade. P-51 44-11691 WZ-F.
1-6-45	**Weston, Gordon L.** F/O 82FS KIA 20 miles from DX on the return. Flying in fog when he hit a smokestack and exploded in mid-air. P-51 44-11672 MX-L.
1-13-45	**Elin, Herbert W.** 1Lt. 84FS KIFA Near Royston, UK. He had instrument failure in heavy clouds and crashed near Bassingbourn. P-51 44-63181 WZ-C.
1-15-45	**Spooner, Richard H.** 1Lt. 84FS POW East of Bruchstat, Ger. Strafing locomotives, he was struck by flak and his aircraft crashed P-51 44-15720 WZ-I.
1-17-45	**Boner, Gerald F.** 2Lt. 83FS KIA In the North Sea 55 miles east of Great Yarmouth, UK. Engine quit, turned back for England and bailed out at 5,000 ft. He was seen to hit the water and his yellow raft popped out. ASR arrived 15 minutes later, but couldn't find him. P-51 44-15506 HL-G.
1-17-45	**Packer, Allen R.** 1Lt. 84FS POW. 4 miles east of Elmshorn, Ger northwest of Hamburg. Hit by flak at the target, and bailed out. P-51 44-63188 WZ-J.
1-20-45	**Bradley, William E.** F/O 83FS KIFA In the English Channel near the Isle of Grange, UK On a training flight flying Lt. McDuffie's wing. He spun out of a turn and into the sea from 25,000 ft. An ASR boat saw his crash but he was killed on impact. P-51 unk.
1-20-45	**DeMaagd, Kenneth J.** 2Lt. 84FS POW West of the Rhine River and Wessel, Ger. His engine quit and he crashlanded in a field. P-51 44-11682 WZ-I.
2-3-45	**Grisham, Leon M.** 1Lt. 84 FS POW Luneburg Heath A/D Ger. Hit by flak on 4th strafing pass. Last R/T call asked that he get credit for his 3 ground kills. P-51 44-63182 WZ-M.
2-3-45	**Sawall, Warren J.** 2Lt. 84FS POW Luneburg Heath A/D. Shot down by A/D flak. P-51 44-15746 WZ-N.
2-3-45	**Senarens, William B.** 1Lt. 83FS POW Wilhelmshaven, Ger. Hit by flak over the city on the way in and is believed to have bailed out. P-51 44-15729 HL-T.
2-9-45	**Warren, Willard E.** 1 Lt 82FS POW Frankfurt, Ger. Engine failed and he bailed out. P-51 44-63185 MX-Q.
2-14-45	**Innocenzi, Andrew R.** 2 Lt 83FS Evader Inowroclaw, Pol. Had generator trouble and his radio failed. Left the formation, dropped his tanks, and headed 60 degrees from Chemnitz, Ger. to Poland, escorted by Lt. J.S. Peterson. P-51 44-14852 HL-F.
2-14-45	**Peterson, James S.** 1Lt. 83FS Evader Inowroclaw, Pol. See above. Returned to DX on 3-22-45. P-51 44-11695 HL-N.
2-20-45	**Brendle, Merle V.** 1Lt. 84FS KIA Near Valenciennes, Fr Hit by light flak while strafing locomotives near Stuttgart, Get. P-51 44-63207 WZ-G.
2-20-45	**Lyle, Charles L.** Capt. 84FS KIA Hit by flak near Stuttgart, Ger. Attempted to bail out near Haussy, Fr. P-51 44-11694 WZ-D.
2-21-45	**Newmark, Burton J.** 2 Lt. 84FS POW Southwest of Coblenz, Ger. Hit by flak and was presumed to have bailed out 60 miles from the Allied Lines. P-51 44-63171 WZ-K.
2-22-45	**Coss, Wilbur R.** Capt. 82FS KIA Near Valenciennes, Fr. Had a mid-air Col.lision with Lt. R.E.Smith of 82FS and was unable to gain control of his aircraft before crashing to his death. P-51 44-11663 MX-D.
2-22-45	**Hamilton, Ralph E.** 2Lt. 83FS POW Northwest of Wurtzburg, Ger. Hit by flak while strafing troop trains at Crailsheim, Ger and bailed out. P-51 44-15650 HL-J.
2-23-45	**Wade, John B.** 2Lt. 83FS POW Near Donauworth, Ger. Suffered a flak hit near Ingolstadt, Ger. and bailed out. P-51 44-11364 HL-H
2-24-45	**Anderson, Edwin B.** 2Lt. 82FS POW Near Dummer Lake, Ger. Hit by flak and was not seen afterward. P-51 44-63177 MX-C.
2-24-45	**Bibeau, Lucian J.** 1 Lt 82 FS KIA Near Dummer Lake, Ger. Hit by flak and went straight into the ground. P-51 44-11688 MX-U.
2-24-45	**Eadline, Lloyd L.** 2Lt. 83FS KIA In the Zuider Zee, Neth. Flak from barges in the Quackenbruck, Ger. area hit him. He bailed out into the sea after a 4FG pilot heard his MayDay call. P-51 44-63248 HL-Y.
2-24-45	**Musgrave, Louis R.** 1Lt. 84FS KIA Near Einbeck/Hanover, Ger. After being hit by flak, he bailed out at 5,000 feet. P-51 44-15359 WZ-F.
2-25-45	**Oldfield, Charles S.** 1Lt. 84FS Evader Near Crailshem A/D and Speyer, Ger. He was downed while strafing He returned to DX on 4-21-45 from the Dutch Underground. P-51 44-63555 WZ-C.
2-25-45	**Wilson, Mark T.** 1 Lt 84FS Evader He went down in the same

<table>
<tr><td>2-26-45</td><td>locality and time as Lt. Oldfield and both worked with theDutch Underground until their return to DX on 4-21-45. P-51 44-15740 WZ-N.</td></tr>
</table>

locality and time as Lt. Oldfield and both worked with theDutch Underground until their return to DX on 4-21-45. P-51 44-15740 WZ-N.

2-26-45 **O'Brien, Charles R.** F/O 83FS KIA He had electrical trouble at the target and started home escorted by Lt. L. Olson. A forced belly landing behind enemy lines ensued and he was taken POW to gain medical help. Later, shot to death while attempting escape. P-51 44-11627 HL-J.

2-26-45 **Olson, Leonard S.** 1 Lt. 83FS POW Started hom from the target escortingF/O O'Brien. When O'Brien belly landed in enemy territory, Olson tried to land for rescue but crashed in the attempt and became a POW. P-51 44-11655 HL-A.

2-28-45 **Liebenrood, Harold R.** F/O 82FS POW Twenty mile east south east of Col.ogne, Ger. Had engine failure and bailed out P-51 44-63203 MX-G.

3-1-45 **Boehner, Ernest V.** 1 Lt 82FS KIA West of Kassel at Korbach, Ger. Hit by flak while strafing and his aircraft was seen to hit the ground. P-51 44-11652 MX-F.

3-1-45 **Higgins, Roy D.** 1Lt. 84FS KIA At Boblingen A/D, Ger. Making his second pass when flak hit him. He bailed out, but his chute did not open. P-51 44-72178 WZ-N.

3-1-45 **Townsend, William L.** 1Lt. 84FS KIA Near Heimsheim, Ger. While strafing autobahn, he caught his wingtip on a truck and crashed. P-51 44-72190 WZ-E.

3-2-45 **Staub, Henry M.** 2Lt. 83FS POW Near Magdeburg, Ger. After the sqd. engaged 24 ME109s he asked his element leader what his position was but was not heard from again. P-51 44-63285 HL-R.

3-4-45 **Hereford, Louis R.** 2Lt. 84FS KIA Southeast of Nordlingen, Ger. He was last heard on the R/T flying in solid cloud just before the target. P-51 44-63209 WZ-S.

3-5-45 **Platt, Robert K.** 2Lt. 82FS KIFA Killed in crash on takeoff at DX . P-51 44-63238 MX-K.

3-7-45 **Bath, Donald A.** 2Lt. irFS KIFA While practice dogfighting at low level near DX he stalled out and crashed. P-51 44-63799 WZ-G.

3-11-45 **Hodge, Jack D.** 1Lt. 84FS KIA In the North Sea near Vesjle, Den. His engine coolant popped at 20,000 feet and he headed into low clouds for Sweden, trying to restart his engine. He bailed out and was not seen again. P-51 44-15627 HL-Q.

3-12-45 **Johnson, Dean C.** 1 Lt 83FS Evader Near Laaland /Sjaelland Island, Den. Bailed out from a coolant leak and evaded to Sweden. P-51 44-72214 HL-A.

3-17-45 **Stearns, Paul H.** 1 Lt 82FS Evader Near Ruhland, Ger. He aborted and headed for Russia, landing at Poltava, USSR. P-51 44-63183 MX-Y.

3-19-45 **Bolen, James A.** 2Lt. 84FS KIA In the Hesepe/Vorden/Achmer, Ger. area. He is believed to have spun into the ground during major air battle. P-51 44-72386 WZ-D.

3-19-45 **Bush, Ralph L.** 2Lt. 83FS KIA In the Hesepe/Vorden/Achmer, Ger area. Killed in air battle P-51 44-72351 HL-T.

3-19-45 **Downing, Harry L.** Maj. 84FS POW See detail above. P-51 44-72407 WZ-E.

3-19-45 **Nieland, Elmer K.** 1Lt. 83FS POW See detail above P-51 44-15721 HL-C.

3-19-45 **Reeves, Thomas N.** 2Lt. 84FS POW See detail above P-51 44-15675 WZ-W.

3-21-45 **Conner, Richard E.** LtCol. 82FS Evader. Alt Lonnewitz A/D, Ger. Hit by flak and smoke filled his cockpit. Headed for Poltava, USSR but crashed on the east side of the Oder River. Ended up in Moscow and returned to DX on 5-10-45. P-51 44-72233 MX-D.

3-31-45 **Ostrander, Paul S.** 1Lt. 84FS KIA In North Sea 50 miles off the Hague, Neth. Light flak hit on the way home near Rheine, Ger. Bailed out over sea, . His sqd. mates circled him until an ASR Warwick arrived but couldn't locate him. P-51 44-63215 WZ-A.

4-7-45 **Talbot, Robert H.** 2Lt. 83FS POW Near Dummer Lake, Ger. He said he had been fired on by another P-51 and that he would have to bail out. P-51 44-72217 HL-H.

4-10-45 **Kuehl, Richard I.** 2Lt. 83FS POW At Brandenburg/Briest A/D, Ger. Flak got him wile strafing and he bailed out over woods near Helmstadt, Ger. Captured walking west and 36 hours later was freed by the 84th Division overrunning the area. He was back at DX on 4-15-45. P-51 44-15702. HL-X.

4-10-45 **Spaulding, Roger A.** 2Lt. 84FS POW At Brandenburg, Ger. He was hit by flak at Werder A/D. Said on the R/T that his engine was rough and that he was bailing out. P-51 44-64156 WZ-O.

4-10-45 **Stinson, Herbert A.** 1Lt. 82FS KIA At Werder A/D Ger. Last seen strafing the drome. P-51 44-15556 MX-Z.

4-16-45 **Croy, Manford O.** Capt. 82FS KIA At Straubling A/D near Platting, Ger. Hit by flak and bailed out too low for his chute to open P-51 44-72165 MX-G.

4-16-45 **Holmes, Robert B.** Capt. 82FS KIA At Ganacker A/D, Ger. Last seen going down for a pass at the A/D. P-51 44-63214 MX-R.

4-16-45 **Swauger, Fred R.** 2Lt. 82FS POW At Marienbad A/D, Hit by small arms fire while strafing and crashed. P-51 44-15495 MX-E.

4-17-45 **Rosenberg, Alvin M.** 2Lt. 82FS POW West of Adorf, Ger. Bailed out and was captured. P-51 44-72357 MX-D.

4-17-45 **Rosenblum, Allen A.** 1 Lt. 82FS POW at Kralupy A/D Czech. hit by flak while chasing a landing jet and had to belly land just off the runway. P-51 44-72367 MX-C.

4-21-45 **Ledington, Dorian** Capt. 84FS KIA West of Coblenz, Ger. His flight was tree top level trying to find an airfield for his wingman, Lt. Sole, who was low on gas. Visibility turned to zero and he apparently crashed. P-51 44-72772 WZ-A.

4-21-45 **Sole, John R.** 2 Lt. 84FS KIA West of Coblenz, Ger. Was Capt. Ledington's wingman and only had ten minutes of gas left. On the deck looking for an airfield when the weather closed down to zero. His left wing hit a tree and he climbed calling for aid. Lt. Stier told him to climb and bail out, but he was only at 300 feet and his chute failed to open. P-51 44-63712 WZ-B.

4-21-45 **Marshall, Leonard P.** LtCol. Hqd. Sqd KIA Twenty miles north of Strasbourg, Fr. Last seen flying upside down in an overcast at 28,000 feet in the Mannheim, Ger. area. Possibly a victim of oxygen or instrument failure. His body and unopened parachute were found north of Strasbourg, FR. P-51 44 63212 WZ-Z.

4-25-45 **Carroll, Edward J.** 2Lt. 82FS KIA Near Sawston, UK Returning from a mission in very dense fog. He crashed several miles from DX. P-51 44-15382 MX-W.

APPENDIX 5
RECORD OF DESTRUCTION

Enemy Aircraft	Destroyed	Probably Destroyed	Damaged
Air to Air Claims	326	25	123
Ground Claims	362	2	256
Total	688	27	379

Locomotives	530
Boxcars	836
Rail tankcars	268
Motor transport	397

Index to Narrative and Captions